UNDERSTANDING
SOCIAL SECURITY

Other titles in the series

Understanding the finance of welfare
What welfare costs and how to pay for it

Howard Glennerster, Professor Emeritus of Social Policy, London School of Economics and Political Science

"... a brilliant and lively textbook that students will enjoy. It makes the complex subject of financing welfare accessible to all those studying and working in the field." **Ian Shaw, School of Sociology and Social Policy, University of Nottingham**

PB £17.99 (US$26.95) **ISBN** 1 86134 405 8

HB £50.00 (US$59.95) **ISBN** 1 86134 406 6

240 x 172mm 256 pages May 2003

Forthcoming

Understanding social citizenship
Themes and perspectives for policy and practice
Peter Dwyer
PB ISBN 1 86134 415 5
HB ISBN 1 86134 416 3
May 2004

Understanding research for social policy and practice
Themes, methods and approaches
Edited by Saul Becker and Alan Bryman
PB ISBN 1 86134 403 1
HB ISBN 1 86134 404 X
June 2004

Understanding work–life balance
Policies for a family-friendly Britain
Margaret May and Edward Brunsdon
PB ISBN 1 86134 413 9
HB ISBN 1 86134 414 7
May 2004

Understanding the policy process
Theory and practice of policy analysis
John Hudson and Stuart Lowe
PB ISBN 1 86134 540 2
HB ISBN 1 86134 539 9
May 2004 tbc

INSPECTION COPIES AND ORDERS AVAILABLE FROM

Marston Book Services
PO Box 269
Abingdon
Oxon OX14 4YN
UK

INSPECTION COPIES
Tel: +44 (0) 1235 465538
Fax: +44 (0) 1235 465556
Email: inspections@marston.co.uk

ORDERS
Tel: +44 (0) 1235 465500
Fax: +44 (0) 1235 465556
Email: direct.orders@marston.co.uk

UNDERSTANDING SOCIAL SECURITY

Issues for policy and practice

Edited by Jane Millar

The POLICY

P P

PRESS

First published in Great Britain in May 2003 by

The Policy Press
University of Bristol
Fourth Floor, Beacon House
Queen's Road
Bristol BS8 1QU
UK

Tel +44 (0)117 331 4054
Fax +44 (0)117 331 4093
e-mail tpp-info@bristol.ac.uk
www.policypress.org.uk

British Library Cataloguing in Publication Data

A catalogue record for this book is available from the British Library

ISBN 1 86134 419 8 paperback

A hardcover version of this book is also available

Jane Millar is Professor of Social Policy at the University of Bath and Director of the Centre for Analysis of Social Policy.

Cover design by Qube Design Associates, Bristol.
Printed and bound in Great Britain by Hobbs the Printers Ltd, Southampton.

Contents

Detailed contents

About the contributors

Saul Becker is Professor of Social Policy and Social Care at Loughborough University. He has researched and published extensively on issues concerned with poverty, social services, community care and informal family care, and in particular the relationship between these policy fields. He was a tutor at the Department of Social Security (DSS)/Department for Work and Pensions (DWP) Summer Schools for eight years (1995-2002). See www.lboro.ac.uk/departments/ss/depstaff/staff/bio/becker.html

Alex Bryson is a Principal Research Fellow at the Policy Studies Institute. He evaluates welfare-to-work programmes for government departments. He has recently been involved in the evaluations of ONE, the New Deal for Young People, and Working Families Tax Credits. His earlier research included evaluations of Project Work, Family Credit, Jobclubs, Work Trials, the Job Interview Guarantee and the Enterprise Allowance Scheme. He has been a tutor at the DSS/DWP Summer Schools since 1998. See www.psi.org.uk/

Tania Burchardt is a Research Fellow at the ESRC Centre for Analysis of Social Exclusion at the London School of Economics and Political Science. She is currently working on assessing the impact of the National Minimum Wage on disabled workers. More broadly, her research interests include definitions and measurement of social exclusion, and changing patterns of public and private welfare provision. She has been a tutor at the DSS/DWP Summer Schools since 1998. See http://sticerd.lse.ac.uk/case/

Emma Carmel is a Lecturer in Social Policy at the University of Bath and Assistant Editor of the *Journal of European Social Policy*. Her research interests include the politics and governance of social policy; comparative European politics and social policy; and the changing roles and practices of social democratic parties in Europe. She is currently working on a project concerned with discourse and governance of social policy in the European Union. See http://staff.bath.ac.uk/sssekc/

Karen Kellard is a Research Fellow in the Centre for Research in Social Policy (CRSP) at Loughborough University. Karen's current and recent research includes the evaluation of the New Deal for Disabled People programme, and a qualitative evaluation of the new Jobcentre Plus service. Other research interests include the administration and delivery of social security services, disability and employment, and job retention and advancement. Karen has been a tutor at the DSS/DWP Summer Schools since 2000. See www.crsp.ac.uk

Theodoros Papadopoulos is a Lecturer in Social Policy at the University of Bath and Visiting Professor of Social Policy at the University of Turku, Finland. His research interests include the theory and politics of social policy making in Britain; methodology of comparative social policy research; unemployment compensation schemes and family policies in OECD countries; and the Nordic welfare state model. He has been a tutor at the DSS/DWP Summer Schools since 1999. See http://staff.bath.ac.uk/hsstp/

Lucinda Platt is Lecturer in the Department of Sociology at the University of Essex. Her research interests are in ethnic minorities, poverty and social security, child poverty and welfare state history. She has recently published *Parallel lives? Poverty among ethnic minority groups in Britain* (CPAG). She was a tutor on the DSS/DWP Summer School in 2000 and 2003. See www.essex.ac.uk/sociology/people/staff/platt.shtm

Stephen McKay is Deputy Director of the Personal Finance Research Centre, University of Bristol. He has conducted research on the living standards of families with children, on the effects of the social security (and tax credit) system, and on pensions. He is currently evaluating the pilot Saving Gateway project, aimed at encouraging low-income people to save, and analysing the effects of tax credits. He has been a tutor at the DSS/DWP Summer Schools on six occasions (1995-99, and 2002). See www.ggy.bris.ac.uk/research/pfrc/

Jane Millar is Professor of Social Policy at the University of Bath, and Director of the Centre for the Analysis of Social Policy. Her research interests include family support; unemployment and incentives; benefits and other support for lone parents; and gender and social security policy. She has recently been working on the evaluation of the New Deal for Lone Parents, on cross-national comparisons of policies to increase lone-parent employment, and the implementation of tax credits. She was tutor at the DSS/DWP Summer Schools for seven years (1989-95) and director for seven years (1996-2002). See www.bath.ac.uk/~hssjim/

Tess Ridge is a Research Fellow at the University of Bath. Her research interests include childhood poverty and social exclusion, and policies for children and their families. In particular, her research examines how children fare within the policy process, and how best to formulate policies which truly benefit them, including social security policies and Child Support. At present, she is the recipient of an ESRC Fellowship Award and her recent publications include *Childhood poverty and social exclusion: From a child's perspective* (The Policy Press, 2002). She has been a tutor at the DSS/DWP Summer School since 2000. See http://staff.bath.ac.uk/ssstmr/

Karen Rowlingson is a Lecturer in Social Research at the University of Bath. Her research interests cover three areas: social security policy; the financial circumstances of individuals, families and households; and changing family forms, particularly in relation to lone parenthood. She has been a tutor at the DSS/DWP Summer School on three occasions from 1997-2002. She is co-author, with Stephen McKay, of *Social security in Britain* (Macmillan, 1999). Find out more on her web page at: http://staff.bath.ac.uk/ssskr/

Roy Sainsbury is a Senior Research Fellow in the Social Policy Research Unit at the University of York, and has a long-standing research interest in benefit fraud. He has conducted work on Housing Benefit fraud, the link between fraud and changes in circumstances, and fraudulent overpayments. He has worked with the Benefit Fraud Inspectorate on fraud measurement, and was a member of the Steering Group for the Scampion review of organised fraud. He has been a tutor at the DSS/DWP Summer School since 1996. See http://www1.york.ac.uk/inst/spru/

Bruce Stafford is a Director of the Centre for Research in Social Policy at Loughborough University. He has undertaken extensive research on social security, including the New Deal for Disabled People, the contributory principle, Housing Benefit administration and the delivery of benefits. His research interests are policy evaluation; the administration and delivery of welfare services; welfare-to-work; and the links between social security and specific client groups, notably older people and disabled people. He has been a tutor at the DSS/DWP Summer School between 1996 and 2002, and was Director of the School in 2003. See www.crsp.ac.uk

Sharon Wright is Lecturer in Social Policy at the University of Stirling. Her research interests are in social policy making and implementation, social security, unemployment, welfare-to-work and poverty. Her most recent research has been an in-depth case study of the implementation of unemployment policy in one case study Jobcentre office. She has also contributed to a cross-national review of the role of employment offices. She has been a tutor at the DSS/DWP Summer School since 2001. See www.stir.ac.uk/appsocsci

Nicola Yeates lectures in social policy at Queen's University, Belfast where she teaches social security, gender and international issues in social policy. She has researched and published extensively on Irish social policy and on 'globalisation' and social policy. Nicola has been a tutor at the DSS/DWP Summer School since 1998 and the Director of Academic Studies for the Irish Social Welfare Summer School since 2000. See www.qub.ac.uk/ssp/nicola.htm

List of tables, figures and boxes

Tables

Figures

Boxes

Foreword

Social security is at the heart of government social policy. It is the largest single area of state expenditure, costing over £100 billion per year. We will all come into contact with it at some stage in our lives. The living standards and opportunities of millions of citizens are heavily influenced by this one area of policy making and delivery. How the system (and the people who work in it) treat the 'users' of social security – and particularly the most vulnerable and powerless in society – is the real test of a 'decent' and responsible society.

But social security is changing. Welfare reform has washed away some of the traditional policy objectives and administrative arrangements for delivering benefits, and new agendas and structures have emerged. Policy and delivery have been brought closer to employment priorities, with 'work for those who can, and security for those who cannot' becoming defining principles for policy and practice.

Jane Millar and the team of contributors who have written this book cut through the policy rhetoric to offer us insights into how and why policy is made, how it is implemented, and what its outcomes are for those at the receiving end. We need to understand how social security works, in theory and in practice, so that we can assess whether it is operating effectively and fairly, and to identify where and how it might be improved. The contributors to this book are well placed to provide this assessment, drawing on rigorous research evidence and evaluation of the system actually in operation. It is critical that any analysis of the social security system, of the mechanisms for delivering benefits, and of welfare reform more generally, is based on the best and most trustworthy evidence available – evidence which also reports and gives voice to the experiences of those directly involved, either as 'users' or as 'providers'.

The contributors to this volume are renowned for their research, writing and expertise in social security issues. All of them are employed in academic departments or research centres that have a respected track record for social security research and evaluation. They have also worked together for many years as tutors to the Department of Social Security (now Department for Work and Pensions) annual summer schools. Their 'expertise' is based on their authority and skills as researchers, and from their active engagement with policy makers, practitioners and users of social security.

Understanding social security will be essential reading for undergraduate and postgraduate students in Social Policy, Social Work, Sociology and Politics. It also needs to be read by policy makers and social welfare practitioners – those people who come into daily contact – or whose clients come into daily contact – with the social security system and who need to understand how it works.

Understanding welfare series

This emphasis on policy making and delivery is a key feature of all the books in the *Understanding welfare: Social issues, policy and practice* series. The series was commissioned by the Social Policy Association (SPA) and is published in partnership with The Policy Press. It is the first book series that the SPA has initiated and it has clear aims and objectives, not least of which is to provide over time a library of key texts that are central to understanding major social issues, such as income security, the finance of welfare, and the policy process, to name but a few.

The subject matter and orientation of the books have also been informed by the requirements of various subject benchmark statements produced for the Quality Assurance Agency for Higher Education (2000). These benchmark statements provide a means for the academic community (and others) to describe the nature and characteristics of programmes in particular subject areas, including Social Policy and Administration, Social Work, Sociology, and so on. Books in the *Understanding welfare* series have been especially mindful of the Social Policy and Administration and Social Work subject benchmark statements produced in 2000 by a group chaired by Professor Pete Alcock. *Understanding social security*, and the other books commissioned for the series, are the first which could be termed 'benchmark compliant'; that is, their content (and the knowledge and skills which they hope to foster) are central to the subject areas of Social Policy, Social Work and other applied social sciences. In particular, *Understanding social security* covers topics including "the provision, finance and regulation of social security" (para 3.2.2), and "knowledge of human and social needs in the UK and other countries and of social policies and welfare institutions which exist to meet them" (para 4.2.5). The book also addresses some of the key skills, including "to assess the outcomes of these interventions, and their impact on users" (para 4.2) and "to separate the technical, normative, moral and political differences that affect policies and their consequences" (para 4.3.4).

Useful website resources

The Social Policy and Administration and Social Work subject benchmark statement can be found at: www.qaa.ac.uk/crntwork/benchmark/social_work.pdf

The SPA website can be found at: www.social-policy.com

Saul Becker, Series Editor

Acknowledgements

We are grateful to the staff and students at the Department of Social Security/ Department for Work and Pensions Summer School who have, over the years, helped us to think about the issues involved in the design and delivery of social security support in the UK. The debates and discussions at the School have always been stimulating and thought-provoking, as well as enjoyable and interesting. Thanks to you all. We hope that the School will continue to flourish into the 21st century.

Thanks to Faith Howard at the University of Bath for her work in putting this typescript together. Thanks to all at The Policy Press – Helen Bolton, Karen Bowler, Laura Greaves, Julia Mortimer, Dawn Rushen and Alison Shaw – for their encouraging support and efficient work.

Jane Millar
University of Bath

List of abbreviations

ABR	Area benefit review
ACT	Automated Credit Transfer
ASEAN	Association of South-East Nations
AVCs	Additional Voluntary Contributions
CAP	Common Agricultural Policy
CCG	Community care grant
CSA	Child Support Agency
CSJ	Commission on Social Justice
CSR	Comprehensive Spending Review
CPAG	Child Poverty Action Group
DfEE	Department for Education and Employment
DPTC	Disabled Person's Tax Credit
DSS	Department of Social Security
DWP	Department for Work and Pensions
EITC	Earned Income Tax Credit
EU	European Union
FSA	Financial Services Authority
GDP	Gross Domestic Product
ICT	Information and communication technology
IGO	International governmental organisation
ILO	International Labour Organization
IMF	International Monetary Fund
IOP	Instrument of payment (fraud)
ISA	Individual Savings Account
ISSA	International Social Security Association
LMS	Labour Market System
MERCOSUR	Southern Core Common Market
MIG	Minimum Income Guarantee
NASS	National Asylum Support Service
NDDP	New Deal for Disabled People
NDLP	New Deal for Lone Parents
NDYP	New Deal for Young People
NMW	National Minimum Wage
OECD	Organisation for Economic Co-operation and Development
ONS	Office for National Statistics
OPRA	Occupational Pensions Regulatory Authority
PAYE	Pay-As-You-Earn
PAYG	Pay-As-You-Go

SADC	Southern African Development Community
SEN	Special educational needs
SENDA	1997 Special Educational Needs and Disability Act
SERPS	State Earnings-Related Pension
SOC	Standard Occupational Classification
S2P	State Second Pension
TNCs	Transnational corporations
UN	United Nations
WFTC	Working Families Tax Credit
WTC	Working Tax Credit
WTO	World Trade Organization

one

Social security:
means and ends

Jane Millar

Reform of the social security and tax systems is at the heart of the Labour government's aspirations to combat social exclusion, to eradicate child poverty, to increase employment rates among all people of working age, and to modernise the welfare state. Since the May 1997 General Election, there have been major developments in **social security policy** and **administration**. These include policy reforms outlined in various Green and White Papers (including principles, disability, child support, pensions, and fraud); new labour market programmes for specific groups of claimants (the New Deal schemes); significant institutional change (the creation of the Department for Work and Pensions, the merger of the Benefits Agency and the Employment Service, the growing involvement of the Inland Revenue in assessment and delivery); and the introduction of tax credits to replace some social security benefits.

Social security policy is changing both in respect of key goals and the means to achieve these. But radical changes can be difficult to achieve, and the outcomes difficult to foresee. Social security policy and provision have a long history and are embedded in our society in many ways. Millions of people are reliant upon social security benefits for all or part of their incomes and any changes to social security policy have a very direct effect on their incomes and living standards. Social security forms the largest single component of government expenditure, providing a mechanism for the pursuit of both economic and social goals. The UK is a very unequal society, with high levels of poverty, and the social security system is one of the most important instruments for income redistribution. This redistribution can take different forms, including vertical redistribution (from richer to poorer) and horizontal redistribution (across people in different circumstances, from childless people to those with children, for example). Social security also plays an important role in helping to smooth incomes over the lifecourse, with people making contributions or withdrawals depending on circumstances and need. And social security provisions may have an impact on how people live their lives, in their decisions about jobs, about savings, about retirement, about family formation and about family dissolution.

There are a number of different goals that can be identified for social security policy, both immediate (for example, to replace earnings lost because of unemployment, to meet the additional costs arising from disability, to contribute to the costs of raising children) and ultimate (for example, to eliminate poverty, to create a more equal society, to create a more socially just society). Views about goals, and specifically the normative question of what policy goals should be, rest in turn upon different ideologies of welfare, upon different views about the state and citizenship, and upon different views about human nature and motivation (Dwyer, 2000; Hewitt, 2000; Deacon, 2002). These are issues that are currently under intense debate, with the Labour government seeking to create a social security system that actively promotes paid employment for as many people as possible, and which attaches more conditions to the receipt of state support[1].

The aim of this book is to provide a *critical examination of current social security policy and practice* at this time of change.

Types of benefits/income transfers

Table 1.1 summarises the main features of the UK income transfer system. This shows three main types of benefits, differentiated by the method of funding and the main conditions for receipt[2]. *Categorical*, or *universal*, *benefits* are funded by general taxation, they take no account of income and are paid to those who fit the designated category (for example, Child Benefit for all children). *Social insurance*, or *contributory*, *benefits* are funded by contributions from workers, employers and the government, and cover interruptions or loss of earnings for specified reasons (retirement, unemployment, sickness, and for women, widowhood). *Social assistance*, or *means-tested, benefits* are funded by general taxation and are paid to people with low incomes, taking account of their particular circumstances and family situation. These include benefits for people with no other sources of income as well as various other benefits intended to meet particular needs (for example, housing costs) or circumstances (for example, low wages, large families). In addition to these three main types of benefit, there are also *tax-based* and *occupational* income transfers. The former

---

[1] For overviews of the Labour government's approach and record since 1997, see Bennett (2002); Brewer et al (2002); Hewitt (2002).

[2] For general introductions to social security provisions in the UK, see Barr (1998); Ditch (1999); McKay and Rowlingson (1999); Dean (2002).

Table 1.1: Income maintenance in the UK: types of provision

Social security				Tax system	Occupational system			
'Universal'/contingent or categorical benefits (non-means-tested/non-contributory)	Social insurance benefits (contributory)	Social assistance benefits (selective/means-tested)		Tax credits	Fiscal benefits (tax allowances/exemptions)	Employment-related benefits		
		Regulated schemes	Discretionary schemes			Statutory	Non-statutory	Private (contracted out)
Child Benefit	Retirement Pension and Second State Pension	Income Support/Disability and Pensioners' Minimum Income Guarantee/Pension Credit		Working Tax Credit	Personal Allowance	Statutory sick pay	Occupational sick pay/maternity or paternity pay/health insurance benefits	Personal pension plans
Disability Living Allowance/Attendance Allowance	Jobseeker's Allowance				Exemptions on pension contributions	Statutory maternity/paternity pay	Occupational pensions	Stakeholder pensions
Carer's Allowance (currently Invalid Care Allowance)	Incapacity Benefit		Social Fund	Child Tax Credit				
Industrial injuries and war pensions schemes	Bereavement Benefits	Housing Benefit	Discretionary housing payments					

Source: Adapted from Dean (2002, Table 5.1)

3

use the tax, rather than the benefits, system as the vehicle for making the income transfer. These have become an increasingly important part of the income transfer system in the UK under the Labour government, and this has given the Inland Revenue a more central role in delivering financial support. Occupational benefits are paid by employers, for example occupational pension schemes, but regulated by government. They also include some schemes that employers are obliged to provide, such as statutory sick pay and statutory maternity pay. The *private market* also plays a role, particularly in respect of pensions, with membership of private pensions schemes encouraged by state subsidies and regulated by government.

Finally, it should also be noted that the *family* plays a major role in income transfers and defining family obligations – who should be required to support whom – is an important aspect of social security policy. The assumption that married women would be financially dependent upon their husbands was, for example, central to the post-war national insurance benefit system. Married women were largely excluded from these benefits on the grounds that they could rely on their husbands for financial support. Married men received allowances for their wives as dependants. This established a particular structure that had wide-reaching and long-term implications (Millar, 1996). Family means tests, as for Income Support and for Working Tax Credit, are based on the assumption that families are single economic units, sharing income and needs in common.

In 2002/03 annual expenditure on social security benefits (not including tax transfers and occupational provision) was in the region of £105 billion for Great Britain (£110 billion for the UK as a whole). This is about one third of total expenditure, and equivalent to about 11% of GDP (DWP, 2002). **Table 1.2** shows how this is allocated across different age groups and different types of benefit[3]. Just under half (48%) of the total is spent on social insurance/contributory benefits, with about 29% on means-tested benefits and about 22% on universal categorical benefits. Different age groups tend to be in receipt of different types of benefits. For children it is categorical benefits, specifically Child Benefit; for those over retirement age it is contributory benefits, specifically Retirement Pensions. For people of working-age, means-tested benefits make up just over half of the total. For this group, tax credits will increasingly play an important role and by 2005/06 expenditure on tax credits is planned to reach about £14,500 million.

---

[3] For an analysis of trends in expenditure and receipt over time, see Walker with Howard (2000).

Table 1.2: Social security expenditure, by type of benefit and age group (2001/02)

	Children	Working age	Over working age	Total
	£m	£m	£m	£m
Contributory	221	9,016	43,175	51,076
Means-tested	4,184	16,896	10,266	30,581
Categorical	9,715	6,272	7,995	23,455
Total	14,120	32,183	61,436	105,111
(row %)	(13%)	(30%)	(57%)	(100%)
	%	%	%	%
Contributory	1	28	70	48
Means-tested	30	53	17	29
Categorical	69	19	13	22
Total	100	100	100	100

Source: DWP (2002, Tables 1 and 4), estimated out-turn for 2001/02, Great Britain

Reading this book

The various chapters in this book examine key issues in current policy and, in different ways, cover issues of policy goals, programme design and implementation, outcomes and impacts. This is a book about the 'how' of administration as much as it is about the 'why' of policy, not least because elegantly designed policies, tackling important goals, are of no value if they cannot be put into practice. Each chapter is organised in the same way, starting with a brief summary of the contents, and including an overview at the end with revision questions and a full list of references for further reading.

The authors are well placed to subject the social security system to this sort of detailed scrutiny of both means and ends. All are, or have been, members of the tutorial team of the Department for Work and Pensions' annual Summer School. The Summer School was established in 1955 as the 'National Assistance Board Summer School' and so has been running throughout most of the post-war welfare state[4]. Over the years it has survived different political leaders and different institutional arrangements, and has maintained the original goal of giving the people who are responsible for delivering policy – the frontline staff – the opportunity to reflect on the wider policy context of their work. It

---

[4] The programme for the first school in 1955 included lectures on 'The development of social sciences in the twentieth century', 'rehabilitation', 'the economics of social security', and 'the relationship between national insurance and national assistance'.

also gives the tutorial team, who are engaged in various aspects of social security research and teaching, the unique opportunity to explore a wide range of social security issues with people whose day-to-day work directly involves them in policy making and implementation.

The book is divided into three main parts. **Part 1** explores the *changing context for current policy issues and debates.* **Karen Rowlingson** analyses the impact of changing lifecourse and employment patterns on the demand for social security. **Emma Carmel** and **Theodoros Papadopoulos** discuss the changing governance of social security policy and issues of policy formulation and delivery. **Nicola Yeates** discusses the nature and impact of transnational and supranational policy developments on the UK.

Part 2 focuses on the *key groups and issues targeted for reform,* in each case considering both policy objectives and implementation. The first two chapters analyse the meaning and impact of two of the government's key policy goals – **Alex Bryson** examines policies in respect of 'work for those who can' and **Saul Becker** considers 'security for those who cannot'. The next chapter, by **Jane Millar**, looks at the increasing importance of social security provision as a supplement to wages, rather than as a wage replacement, and discusses how and why tax credits have come to play this role. **Tania Burchardt** discusses how disabled people have been affected by the new policy agenda. The final two chapters in this section examine policy developments in relation to the two main groups of people outside the 'working age' policy agenda. **Tess Ridge** analyses changing policy in respect of children, in particular the pledge to end child poverty; and **Stephen McKay** analyses the pensions debate and the recent pensions reforms.

Part 3 focuses in more detail on *delivery issues* and *the new challenges these present.* **Bruce Stafford** takes an overview of the changing modes of delivery and the impact of these on both claimants and staff. **Sharon Wright** examines the nature of 'street-level' practice, and hence policy, in the delivery of unemployment-related benefits. **Lucinda Platt** explores equity in delivery in the context of a multi-racial society and examines variations in benefit take-up rates across different ethnic groups, and the reasons for these. **Roy Sainsbury** discusses the way in which fraud is defined and measured, and the policy measures intended to combat fraud. In the final chapter **Karen Kellard** looks at the impact of developments in information technology on the delivery of financial support to individuals and families.

Social security?

In our discussions about this book we debated the title many times, and in particular the use of the words 'social security'. Now that we no longer have a government department with this name, and now that the tax system is increasingly part of delivery, it could be argued that the phrase 'social security' is no longer a good way to encapsulate the institutional arrangements for policy making about, and the delivery of, income transfers. But the phrase 'social security' does capture other important things, apart from institutional arrangements. The word 'social' indicates that this is a shared system. We are all part of it – as contributors, as recipients, as taxpayers, as citizens – and social security provisions involve various forms of redistribution that are an expression of our values as a society and our commitment to social and economic justice. The word 'security' highlights one of the key goals, which is to ensure that people are not simply at the mercy of the market, but can meet needs now and plan for the future. The conditions that create the need for income security, for some assurance that our lives will be protected from the vagaries of economic and social change, take different forms today compared with the 1940s (when Beveridge devised his plan for 'national insurance and allied services'), or with the early 20th century (when the first insurance-based old age and widows pensions were being introduced), or with the 1830s (when the new Poor Law workhouses started), or with the 1600s (when the Elizabethan Poor Law identified different provisions for different types of 'paupers'). But the need for such security is as strong, if not stronger, than ever.

References

Barr, N. (1998) *The economics of the welfare state*, Oxford: Oxford University Press.

Bennett, F. (2002) 'Gender implications of current social security reforms', *Fiscal Studies*, vol 23, no 4, pp 559-84.

Brewer, M., Clark, T. and Wakefield, M. (2002) 'Social security in the UK under New Labour: what did the third way mean for welfare reforms?', *Fiscal Studies*, vol 23, no 4, pp 505-37.

Deacon, A. (2002) *Perspectives on welfare: Ideas, ideologies and policy debates*, Buckingham: Open University Press.

Dean, H. (2002) *Welfare rights and social policy*, London: Pearson Education.

Ditch, J. (1999) *Introduction to social security: Policies, benefits and poverty*, London: Routledge.

DWP (Department for Work and Pensions) (2002) 'Benefit expenditure tables 2002', www.dwp.gov.uk

Dwyer, P. (2000) *Welfare rights and responsibilities: Contesting social citizenship*, Bristol: The Policy Press.

Hewitt, M. (2000) *Welfare and human nature: The welfare subject in twentieth century social politics*, Basingstoke: Macmillan.

Hewitt, M. (2002) 'New Labour and the redefinition of social security', in M. Powell (ed) *Evaluating New Labour's welfare reforms*, Bristol: The Policy Press, pp 189-210.

McKay, S. and Rowlingson, K. (1999) *Social security in Britain*, Basingstoke: Macmillan.

Millar, J. (1996) 'Women, poverty and social security', in C. Hallett (ed) *Women and social policy*, Brighton: Harvester/Wheatsheaf, pp 52-64.

Walker, R. with Howard, M. (2000) *The making of a welfare class?: Benefit receipt in Britain*, Bristol: The Policy Press.

Part 1: Changing contexts

Source: © Dave Brown, *The Independent*, 19 March 1999, supplied by the Centre for the Study of Cartoons, University of Kent, http://library.kent.ac.uk/cartoons

two

'From cradle to grave': social security over the life cycle

Karen Rowlingson

Summary

There have been major changes in British employment and demographic structures since the 1950s. The fundamental assumptions on which the Beveridge social security system was based have subsequently become increasingly invalid, and the ability of the system to provide support 'from cradle to grave' increasingly challenged. This chapter:

- reviews the changes in employment structures, characterising them as a change from the full male employment of the 1950s to a more flexible labour market at the beginning of the 21st century;

- reviews the changes in demographic structures, arguing that there has been a breakdown in the 1950s male breadwinner/housewife model towards more diverse family forms;

- explores the extent to which the social security system caused these changes;

- examines whether the social security system is (still) able to support people from cradle to grave, given these substantial changes;

- considers possible reforms of the social security system to reflect better the current employment and demographic structures.

Introduction: changing family and employment structures

William Beveridge set down the main foundations of today's social security system in the 1940s. The **Beveridge Plan** aimed to provide state support from cradle to grave and thereby eliminate the 'five giants' of Want, Disease, Ignorance, Squalor and Idleness. Within the social security system this was to be achieved by placing insurance (contributory) benefits at the centre of the social security system. National assistance (means-tested) benefits were expected to be a safety net to which few people would have to resort. This system was based on certain assumptions about family and employment patterns. Central to this was the idea of the *male breadwinner*, working full-time throughout the course of his life and married to a *housewife*, looking after home and family. The 1950s and 1960s were relatively unusual in British history in that this breadwinner/housewife model was the norm, even if it was never universal. But the 1970s saw the beginnings of fundamental change in this model and by the 1980s and 1990s family and employment patterns had changed considerably. This chapter aims to consider the *relationship between the social security system* and these *changes in family and employment structures*.

From full male employment to the flexible labour market

The 1950s and 1960s were unusual in British history in terms of their low unemployment rates, averaging about 2.5% (Nickell, 1999). This was an era of 'full employment', when most men at least could be guaranteed to have full-time employment from leaving school to reaching state retirement age. The mid-1970s onwards, however, saw a dramatic upsurge in unemployment – to 9.6% in 1981 (Nickell, 1999). Unemployment varies with the economic cycle and so fell back in the late 1980s but then rose again in the early 1990s before falling back once more in the late 1990s. Nevertheless unemployment in 2002, at 5.2%, was still twice the level experienced in the 1950s and 1960s (*Labour Market Trends*, July 2002). And particular groups of men, such as those with no qualifications, have particularly high rates of unemployment – around 15% in the late 1990s (Nickell, 1999). **Table 2.1** summarises changes in unemployment rates by gender from 1975 to 1998.

The 1980s and 1990s therefore saw considerable increases in unemployment, and mass unemployment became a key feature of the British labour market. These decades also witnessed a new phenomenon: *male economic inactivity* on a massive scale. *Economic inactivity* is a term used to describe people who are not in paid work but who are also not unemployed, that is, they are not actively seeking work and nor are they available for work. The term can include

Table 2.1: **Labour market trends, by gender (1975-98) (%)**

| | Unemployment | | Economic inactivity | |
	Men	Women	Men	Women
1975	5.1	4.1	2.6	36.5
1979	4.4	3.9	4.7	34.6
1983	10.7	6.6	8.2	34.4
1987	10.0	6.8	9.6	29.8
1990	6.7	5.0	8.9	26.9
1993	10.7	5.5	11.3	27.9
1998	5.8	3.8	13.2	26.9

Source: Gregg and Wadsworth (1999)

people looking after the home/family, sick and disabled people who are out of work and those who are 'early retired' but not yet receiving the state pension.

Table 2.1 shows that a relatively high percentage of women are defined as 'economically inactive' but this declined from 36.5% in 1975 to 26.9% in 1998. As far as men are concerned, only 2.6% of men were 'economically inactive' in 1975, rising to 13.2% in 1998. In terms of numbers rather than percentages, 'only' 400,000 men of working age were 'economically inactive' in 1975, rising to 2.3 million in the late 1990s (Gregg and Wadsworth, 1999). The inactivity rate was highest in the 1990s among men aged 50 and over and among the least skilled. It was concentrated in areas of high unemployment. But, whereas unemployment is cyclical and fell in the late 1990s, the rate of male inactivity has, more or less, been on a constant increase. As mentioned earlier, however, women's economic inactivity has actually declined.

So, increases in unemployment and, in particular, inactivity, have largely affected men, whereas women, by contrast, substantially increased their employment rates in the latter half of the 20th century. This trend was particularly striking in respect of mothers of young children. In 1975, more than 92% of working-age men had a job compared with only 59% of working-age women. By 1998 the figures were 81% and 69% respectively (Desai et al, 1999). Table 2.2 shows women's employment rates by the age of their youngest child and their relationship status. It shows that there was a substantial increase in the employment of women with their youngest children under the age of 5. The increase is most pronounced among women with working partners. In 1981, only 19% of women in a couple with a working partner and youngest child aged 0-1 years were employed. By 1998 this figure had increased to 56%. For women with working partners and youngest children aged 2-4 years, the employment rates increased from 33% to 64%.

The gender employment gap has closed considerably and so too has the gap between the earnings of men and women: one in five women now earn more than their working partners compared with only one in fourteen in the 1970s.

Table 2.2: **Women's employment rates, by age of youngest child and relationship status (1981-98) (%)**

	Youngest child (0-1 year)			Youngest child (2-4 years)			Youngest child (5-10 years)		
	LP	NWP	WP	LP	NWP	WP	LP	NWP	WP
1981	18	13	19	27	18	33	51	40	61
1986	13	11	30	24	15	45	43	31	65
1990	18	15	42	28	30	55	50	41	74
1993	17	20	52	27	29	59	44	37	75
1998	20	26	56	32	28	64	49	34	78

Note: LP = lone parent, NWP = woman in a couple with a non-working partner, WP = woman in a couple with a working partner.

Source: Desai et al (1999)

But this still leaves four out of five men earning more than their female partners. Much of this difference in earnings is due to the fact that women are much more likely than men to work in part-time jobs. About 40% of employed women in 2000 were working part time compared with only about 7% of employed men. But the difference in hours worked cannot completely account for differences in earnings as data shows that, per hour worked, women's earnings are only 82% of men's (all figures above from ONS, 2001).

Another important change in the labour market in the 1980s was a *general increase in wage inequality*. In other words, the gap between the highest paid and lowest paid increased. In particular, those with better education and qualifications saw their pay rise considerably while those with fewer qualifications lost out. All of these changes contributed to Britain becoming near the top of the international low-pay league of the countries in the Organisation for Economic Co-operation and Development (OECD, 1996). Casual workers, those in small firms, those in non-union firms, workers from minority ethnic groups and less-skilled manual workers were all more likely to be low paid (Stewart, 1999). One in every six male workers over the age of 24 was low paid at the end of the 1990s compared with one in thirty in 1968 (Stewart, 1999). And there was strong evidence of a cycle of low pay and no pay, with those on low pay more likely to lose their jobs than increase their wages, and those out of work more likely to get low-paid jobs when they rejoined the labour market.

The introduction of a National Minimum Wage (NMW) in 1999 seems to have reduced wage/income inequality to some extent. In the spring of 1999, when the NMW came into effect, 1.5 million jobs (6.5%) were paid less than the level of the NMW (£3.60 an hour). One year later, only 300,000 jobs (1.2%) were paid less than the NMW and yet the distribution of hourly earnings above the £3.60 mark has been largely unaffected (Stuttard and Jenkins, 2001).

But Toynbee's (2003) experiences highlight the continuing grim reality of life in low-paid jobs: the insecurity of the work; the near-certainty of debt; and the hard, dirty and/or boring work itself.

Another fairly new phenomenon in the 1980s and 1990s was the *workless household*. Work has polarised across households as there has been a rise in the number of dual-earner households and the number of no-earner households. Table 2.3 shows that only 4% of households in 1968 were workless, rising to 16.7% in 1995. During this period lone-parent families have been most at risk of worklessness, followed by single adults. But there has also been a substantial increase in worklessness among couples over the last 30 years. So the old model of a male breadwinner with a housewife at home has greatly declined. According to Gregg et al (1999), about one third of the rise in the number of workless households was due to changes in family structures (such as the growth of lone parenthood). But most – two thirds – of the change was caused by variations in access to employment for different types of household. In other words (as indicated in Table 2.2 above), in better-off households, women were joining their partners in the labour market whereas in worse-off households, men were joining their partners in the home.

The growth of part-time employment and self-employment in the 1980s, alongside the strengthening of employers' powers to 'hire and fire', has been characterised by some commentators as the development of a 'flexible labour market'. But the extent of this flexibility has been questioned; so, too, has the issue of whether the flexibility is more to the advantage of employers or the employed (Meadows, 1999). However, the term 'flexibility' generally reflects a much more diverse and fluid labour market than the fairly rigid system that predominated in the 1950s.

Table 2.3: **Trends in workless households (1968-95) (%)**

	Total	Single adults	Lone parents	Couples, no children	Couples, with children
1968	4.0	11.3	23.4	2.7	1.6
1975	6.2	13.2	36.5	3.4	3.0
1981	10.6	17.5	40.7	5.8	7.3
1985	15.7	22.1	30.2	11.0	10.5
1990	13.3	19.2	48.8	7.9	6.1
1995	16.7	26.5	50.4	9.3	7.3

Source: Gregg et al (1999)

Key changes in structures of employment

- The mid-1970s saw a dramatic upsurge in (mostly male) unemployment. It fell back again in the late 1980s before rising again in the early 1990s and then declining once more. By the end of the 1990s, the unemployment rate was 5.2%.
- The 1980s and 1990s witnessed a new phenomenon: male economic inactivity on a massive scale – to 2.3 million (13.2%) of men in 1998.
- Women's employment rates increased, especially among mothers with working partners and young children. Women are much more likely than men to work part time and there is still a significant gender pay gap.
- Wage inequality increased in the 1980s. Britain is classified as a low-pay country but the NMW, introduced in 1999, has increased the pay rates of some previously low-paid jobs.
- There has been a polarisation of employment, with a growth of both dual-earner households and workless households.

From the male breadwinner/housewife model to diversity in family life

The previous section outlined the major changes in employment patterns that occurred in the second half of the 20th century. This period also saw considerable *changes in demographic patterns*. There was relative uniformity in terms of family life from the late 1940s to early 1960s – most children grew up in married couple families, most young adults got married without cohabiting (or 'living in sin' as it was considered at the time) first. Most people had children after getting married and divorce was relatively unusual. Much of this changed from the 1970s onwards as patterns of family life became increasingly diverse.

One of the first changes, occurring in the early 1960s, was a considerable *growth in the number of divorces* (see **Table 2.4**). This increase continued throughout the 1970s before tailing off in the 1980s and actually declining in

Table 2.4: **Trends in marriage in the UK (1961-99) (000s)**

	First marriages for both partners	Divorces	Remarriages for one or both partners
1961	339.5	27.2	57.1
1971	368.6	79.3	90.8
1981	263.2	157.0	134.6
1991	222.4	173.5	127.4
1999	178.8	158.7	122.3

Source: ONS; General Register Office for Scotland; Northern Ireland Statistics and Research Agency

the 1990s. Nevertheless, there were almost six times as many divorces in 1999 compared with 1961. At the same time, the number of first marriages declined by half between 1961 and 1999 (ONS, 2001). There has been considerable research into the factors relating to divorce and the picture is complex, but it is generally the case that women from poorer economic groups are more likely to divorce and women that do divorce are more likely to become poor(er). These trends might lead us to conclude that marriage became increasingly unpopular over this period but, in fact, there was a considerable increase in the number of remarriages for one or both partners (more than doubling between 1961 and 1999). So marriage as an institution was not being rejected wholesale over this period.

Another potential challenge to the institution of marriage is *cohabitation*. It has now become the norm for couples to live together before they get married. Haskey (1996) found that, in the mid-1960s, fewer than 5% of never-married women cohabited prior to marriage; in the early 1990s 70% cohabited. Cohabitation is not necessarily seen as an alternative to marriage as most couples cohabit as a precursor to marriage, but some couples cohabit between marriages and sometimes they make a conscious decision never to marry. Many cohabiting couples decide to marry before having children, but it is increasingly common for couples to have children while still cohabiting, and one fifth of all families with dependent children were cohabiting in the early 1980s (Haskey, 1996). Cohabiting couples with dependent children are more likely to be on Income Support, to live in council housing, in deprived inner-city areas, and are in the lower socioeconomic groups (Kiernan and Estaugh, 1993; McRae, 1993; Haskey, 1996).

Along with conceptions and births within cohabitation there has also been an increase in the number of conceptions and births to single women. Putting these two phenomena together we are able to estimate the number of extra-marital conceptions. In the 1950s and 1960s, the existence of an extra-marital conception was a source of shame, perhaps leading to a 'shotgun wedding'. However, the 1967 Abortion Act provided another route for single women to take if they fell pregnant, and by the late 1990s about one in five of extra-marital conceptions ended in a termination. **Figure 2.1** shows that just under 40% of all births in 1999 were outside marriage (compared with under 10% in 1975). Most of this increase is in births that are registered to two parents living at the same address.

As a consequence of declining rates of marriage, increasing rates of extra-marital births and rising divorce rates, there has been a substantial rise in lone parenthood since the 1970s. The percentage of dependent children living in lone-parent families more than tripled between 1972 and 2000 to almost one in five (ONS, 2001). Divorced lone mothers were the most common type of lone mother in the 1970s and 1980s but in the 1990s, never-married lone mothers became increasingly common. This was largely due to the breakdown

Figure 2.1: Births outside marriage as a proportion of all live births in Great Britain (1975-99) (%)

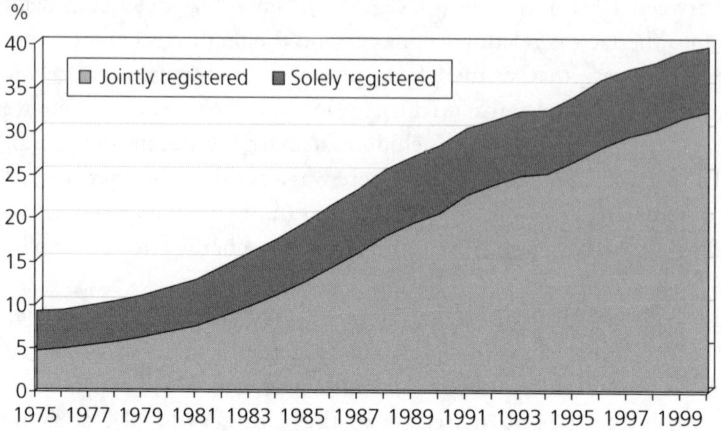

Source: ONS (2002); General Register Office for Scotland

of cohabiting relationships, but was also due to the growth in the number of births to single women (Rowlingson and McKay, 2002).

As a further consequence of declining marriage, rising divorce and rising cohabitation, there has also been an *increase in the number of stepfamilies*. By 1998/99, 6% of families with children (where the head of the family was under the age of 60) were stepparent families (ONS, 2001).

Another major change in family forms has been the *growth in people living alone*. In 1950, fewer than one in twenty people in Britain lived alone. By 1970, 18% of households in Britain were single-person households. By 1991, this figure had risen to 27% (Hall et al, 1999). Older age groups, particularly widows and widowers, dominate this group, but the largest increase has been among those under retirement age. Younger people are choosing to set up their own independent households and those in middle age are also doing so, perhaps following a partnership breakdown.

Immigration is another important demographic phenomenon which occurred after the Second World War. African and Asian people have lived and been born in Britain since at least the turn of the 16th century (Fryer, 1987), but the arrival of 492 Jamaicans on the Empire Windrush on 22 June 1948 heralded a new era in terms of immigration from the New Commonwealth and from Pakistan. The British government and British industry were keen to have more workers to help with post-war recovery and in particular to staff public services such as the National Health Service. But these workers soon faced racial discrimination and higher levels of poverty than the White British population. Over the next 50 years, patterns of ethnic disadvantage have become fairly complex, with some groups, such as Pakistanis and Bangladeshis, suffering the most severe economic disadvantage (Berthoud, 1997; see also

Chapter Thirteen in this volume). People from minority ethnic groups currently form a small, though significant, proportion of the overall population.

In the 1990s, attention has turned from immigration to *asylum*. During the late 1980s around 4,000 people a year were seeking asylum in Britain and this figure rose to around 71,000 in 1999 (ONS, 2001). Most asylum-seekers in 1999 came from the Federal Republic of Yugoslavia, Somalia, Sri Lanka and Afghanistan, areas that have all seen recent escalations of conflict.

The final, major change in family forms has sometimes been referred to as the *demographic time-bomb* (see Chapter Ten in this volume). Over the 1920s and 1930s, male life expectancy at birth increased slowly to a figure of 59.4 in 1940. This was roughly the point at which Beveridge was formulating his Plan. By 1951 male life expectancy had increased dramatically to 66.2. From then on, life expectancy increased steadily to 73.2 in 1991. The figures for women were 63.9 in 1940, 71.2 in 1951 and 78.9 in 1991 (Laslett, 1996). Thus the number of years that people spend in retirement (receiving state Retirement Pension) has increased substantially. At the same time, people today often aspire to retire early.

Box 2.2: Key changes in demographic structures

- Cohabitation is now commonplace and is no longer regarded as 'living in sin'.
- There has been an increase in births to single women and cohabiting couples.
- Divorce rates rose substantially between 1960 and 1990, and then levelled out.
- From the 1970s onwards, there has been an increase in the number of lone-parent families and stepfamilies.
- More and more people are living alone – both younger people and older people.
- Immigration from the 1950s onwards has led to much greater diversity in culture and ethnicity. The late 1990s saw an increase in applications for asylum.
- Life expectancies have increased and people now spend much greater amounts of time in retirement.

Has the social security system been a key cause of these trends?

So far in this chapter we have seen that there have been substantial changes in economic and social life since the 1950s. This section reviews the extent to which social security provision has caused such changes. For example, has the social security system led to increases in unemployment and inactivity by reducing people's willingness to work? Has it caused a breakdown in the male breadwinner/housewife model? And has it affected the types of families that people form – in particular, whether they are more likely to become lone parents, or to have more children?

Disincentives to work?

The early 1970s were perhaps the halcyon days of the social security system. Benefits had been expanded in an attempt to reduce the poverty that had been 'rediscovered' in the 1960s, but a storm was approaching that was to lead to major problems for the system. From the mid-1970s onwards, as mentioned earlier, unemployment grew dramatically. This economic change was largely caused by changes in the global economy that were heralded by the hike in oil prices in 1974. Manufacturing and heavy industry declined in Britain as the country moved towards a post-industrial economic base. There is no evidence, however, that the social security system played any role in the growth of unemployment. It is sometimes claimed that high levels of social security will encourage people to leave work or discourage those out of work from moving into jobs (see Bryson and McKay, 1994 and Millar and Ridge, 2001 for further discussion). But, over the period we are looking at, social security payments were not significantly increased and so did not pose an increasing disincentive to work. The growth of unemployment was due to fundamental economic change and the social security system acted as a safety net to prevent the most severe hardship that would otherwise have been experienced by many.

A similar story can be told of the growth of economic inactivity as a whole, which also reflected changing economic and social conditions. However, it is sometimes claimed that the growth in the number claiming **Sickness and Disability/Incapacity Benefits** in the 1980s happened at least in part because benefit officers (with the government's implicit approval) encouraged 'unemployed' people to sign on as sick or disabled so that the unemployment figures did not rise too much. In addition, Incapacity Benefits are more generous than Unemployment Benefits, which may also have encouraged people to try and claim these. This relative generosity had existed prior to the 1970s but the introduction of new Disability Benefits in the 1970s probably made economic inactivity a more financially rewarding position to be in compared with unemployment. Berthoud (1998), however, contends that there is no strong evidence to suggest that those on Sickness and Disability Benefits in the 1990s were not actually sick or disabled.

While there is no strong evidence that the social security system has played a major role in causing unemployment or economic inactivity, certain groups of people may face greater disincentives to work than others. By the late 1960s it was clear that families with children faced particular disincentives to work as the benefit system took into account family size whereas wages did not. **Family Income Supplement** was introduced in 1971 to reduce any disincentives to work. Since then, governments have continued in this vein, first with the introduction of **Family Credit** and then with **Working Families Tax Credit** (WFTC), replaced by **Working Tax Credit** in April 2003. So governments do believe that benefit systems have an effect on people's work-related behaviour.

In couples without children, partners of unemployed people are another group for whom there appear to be particular disincentives to work (Cooke, 1987; McKay et al, 1999). Means-tested benefits can certainly make it not worthwhile for only one person in such couples to work part-time. The **New Deal for Partners of the Unemployed** has been one recent attempt to confront this issue and the new **Working Tax Credit** should also provide better incentives to work for people without children. However, once again, there is relatively little evidence to suggest that it is the benefit system that is responsible for the lower rates of employment of partners of unemployed people. Other factors might be more important. For example, both members of the couple might be living in an area with poor job opportunities. And another factor might be that people tend to have partners with similar characteristics (for example, low educational qualifications, and so on). And finally, traditional norms about gender relations might discourage women from working if their partners are out of work. Research suggests that the main reason why partners of unemployed people have low employment rates is that they share similar characteristics with their partners (for example, low level of education and skill, limited work experience and so on) (for a review, see McKay and Rowlingson, 1999). The social security system does have effects on behaviour among this group, but other factors are more important.

A similar picture can be drawn in relation to lone-parent employment rates. In an attempt to counteract any disincentives to work, governments have continually improved in-work benefits for lone parents. And indeed, employment rates of lone parents have risen as a result of these social security reforms. But there are a number of other factors that explain why most lone parents do not engage in paid work. For example, various studies have found that lone mothers already had lower rates of employment prior to becoming lone mothers (Holtermann et al, 1999; Marsh et al, 2001). Also, difficulties with finding suitable and affordable childcare provides another barrier, as does the simple desire to stay at home and care for their children personally (Ford, 1996; see also Millar and Ridge, 2001).

The barriers to work are therefore not mainly due to the level of social security payments. Another example of this is that people sometimes prefer to remain on a low but secure benefit income rather than risk moving to a potentially more insecure income from earnings (McLaughlin et al, 1989). One of the chief causes of insecurity is entitlement to Housing Benefit. When on Income Support, all rent is paid but when people take a job, they often lose some, if not all, of their Housing Benefit. The uncertainty around this can create a disincentive to take a job. Once again, governments have tried to deal with this issue by providing benefit run-ons so that people do not have to switch immediately from one source of income (benefits) to another (wages).

A challenge to the male breadwinner/housewife model?

The 1940s welfare state never intended to challenge the male breadwinner/ housewife model. Indeed, this model was the very basis of the social security system's insurance principle. Women would gain coverage through their husband's entitlement to contributory benefits. However, women have entered and remained in the labour market for increasingly long periods and their own independent access to insurance benefits has increased, but they still do not have the same level of entitlement as men because they do not remain in the labour market for the same length of time and their wages are lower. Also, just as women's labour market participation has increased, governments have reduced the role of insurance benefits so that the *main benefits in the social security system are means-tested rather than contributory*.

Means-tested benefits pose particular problems for women as they are based on the assumption that couples pool their income in an equitable manner. This has been shown to be a flawed assumption. McLaughlin et al (2002) argue that the assumptions surrounding the 'traditional' family unit should be abandoned in favour of a more individualised system. They make this argument on a number of grounds, including:

- gender equality and justice in the welfare state and within the family;
- work–life balance;
- labour supply;
- anti-poverty alleviation;
- the value that should be attributed to care and caring, by government on behalf of society as a whole.

Recent policy reforms in Australia have moved towards individualisation, with a partial disregard of partners' earnings for unemployed couples receiving jobseekers' benefits. Australia has also introduced a **Parenting Allowance** to reward the caring of children in the home (McLaughlin et al, 2002). Such a reform can be seen in different ways: as recognising the value of paid work carried out in the home, or as reinforcing the male breadwinner/housewife model by providing support to parents to stay in the home. Until there are major changes in gender identities and relations it is inevitable, however, that it will be mothers rather than fathers who will be the main recipients of such benefits for parents.

As mentioned earlier, in-work benefits in the UK have helped lone parents to gain employment and therefore encouraged these women to leave the home and enter the labour market (McKay, 2003). But these benefits have the opposite potential effect on mothers in couples. As Rake (2001) argues, benefits such as the WFTC, with its couple-based assessment, provide a disincentive for both partners in a couple to work. This disincentive is reinforced by the credit given if one partner works 30 hours or more – such credits cannot be split between two earners and so it reinforces the idea of a full-time male breadwinner and a female housewife model. Having said this, the figures given in Table 2.2 about the rise in the employment rates of women with working partners suggest that such disincentives for both members of a couple to work are not quite as strong as they might appear. So there is little evidence to suggest that the social security system has caused or contributed to the breakdown of the male breadwinner/housewife model.

Disincentives to marry or cohabit? Have children?

There has long been concern that the existence of the social security system (and the availability of council housing) has created incentives for women to become lone parents. There is, however, no strong evidence to support such concern (for a review, see Rowlingson and McKay, 2002). Research suggests that the welfare state provides support for women who become lone parents but does not positively encourage them to do so. The reasons for this are similar to those given in relation to people's decisions around work. Many factors are involved in causing people to behave in particular ways. Financial issues are one factor but not always the most important one. Cultural norms are important in relation to decisions about family life and so are broader economic and social conditions. People generally do not make narrow financial cost–benefit analyses before deciding what to do in their personal lives. Much broader factors are taken into account and people often act on impulse rather than with the benefit of cold calculation.

However, there is some belief within governments, particularly in the US, that the *welfare system does affect behaviour in relation to family life*. In some states, the welfare system is being deliberately used as a form of social engineering to discourage lone parents from having more children while on benefit. A *family cap* is placed on families such that they will receive no more money for any extra children. The effects of these specific reforms are not yet known although there is some evidence that employment rates of lone parents have increased. So, too, however, have poverty rates (Waldfogel et al, 2002). Current debate in the US is focusing upon whether, and if so how, welfare systems can be used to encourage and support marriage (*The American Prospect*, 2002).

Cradle to grave: now and the future?

Beveridge's Plan for 'cradle to grave' support through a system of universal national insurance has not been realised. There were always gaps in coverage among people with less than full employment records, for example young people who had never worked, many disabled people, some women with gaps in their employment or with part-time jobs (Baldwin and Falkingham, 1994). But government policies over the decades have been significant. In the 1970s, the commitment of the Conservative government to reduce public expenditure and 'roll back the frontiers of the state' led to a significant reduction in the scope of national insurance benefits. New time limits were applied to Unemployment Benefit (now Jobseeker's Allowance) and Invalidity Benefit (now Incapacity Benefit). Invalidity Benefit was also made subject to tax. And the level of the state Retirement Pension was linked to inflation rather than average earnings. These changes meant that increasing numbers of people both above and below working age had to resort to Income Support to bring their income to a bare minimum.

As a result of many of the trends (social, economic and political) discussed in this chapter, poverty and inequality grew dramatically in the 1980s and early 1990s. In 1995/96, about one in five people in Britain were living in poverty compared with fewer than one in ten in 1979 (Burgess and Propper, 1999). Economic growth in the 1980s was not shared across households – most of it went to the wealthiest households while poorer households failed to benefit. Children have been one of the main groups to suffer from these trends – in 1979, one in twelve children lived in a poor household. By 1995/96, this had increased to about one in three. The system had failed to keep pace with the new and increasing demands placed upon it.

Looking to the future, can the social security system be reformed to adapt to these changing family and employment patterns? A number of reforms to the system are possible. For example, one approach would be to *return to the basic principles of the Beveridge system* and to increase the role of insurance benefits in the social security system (see CSJ, 1994). The Labour government is keen to promote paid work, and if most people were in employment we could perhaps afford more generous insurance benefits. But this may still mean that some people are not covered. For example, despite increasing numbers of women working, women still do much less paid work than men over the course of their lives, and they get paid less for it (Dench et al, 2002). Lone parents in particular are much less likely to work (full-time in particular) than other people. The government is aiming to increase lone-parent employment (to 70% by 2010), but even if this ambitious target were met it is likely that women (and therefore children) will be entitled to less than men under most types of insurance-based systems.

One way around this problem could be to credit women during the periods in which they are providing care in the home. We could also credit people doing voluntary work or other forms of 'productive work'. However, if we extend such credits to a large number of people outside the labour force, the cost of the system increases and the principle of insurance is blurred. We may as well introduce universal benefits instead. Another problem with the current insurance system is that it is geared towards insuring the kinds of risks that mostly affect men, such as unemployment. There are no insurance benefits to protect against the risk of caring for children or separating from a partner.

Another option is to try to *target benefits more effectively*. This approach has been popular with both Conservative and Labour governments from the mid-1980s onwards. 'Targeting' rather than 'means testing' has been the preferred terminology although in practice the main way of targeting benefits is in the form of relating entitlement to levels of income and savings (in other words, means-testing). Any form of means testing is likely to suffer from problems of take-up, stigma, disincentives to work and/or save, incentives to commit fraud and administrative expense. Another issue is that the test is usually at the household level and so can reinforce the idea of dependence within relationships. Until recently, means-tested benefits (mainly Income Support) have been set at a very low level and poverty could only be avoided if levels were increased. This would then increase the scope of such benefits and therefore increase the number of people subjected to work disincentives. Having said all this, WFTC is available to families on relatively high levels of income and so the question is: do we target the very poor or include those on more middling incomes? The higher we go up the income distribution, the closer we get to a more universal system of benefits.

So what would a system look like if it were based on the principle of universality? Basic income schemes (sometimes called **Citizen's Income**) are based on the simple idea that *every individual should have a basic level of income paid by the state* (Fitzpatrick, 1999; McKay and Van Every, 2000; van Parijs, 2000). The most universal of these schemes includes paying a basic income to people no matter what their circumstances. Other variations of the scheme link payment of the basic income to some form of 'participation' such as looking after children, actively seeking work and so on. However, the 'purer' form of the scheme has the advantage of requiring no administrative checking on people. Administrative costs are therefore very low. Take-up and stigma would not be problems as all would be given the money without any need to apply for it. It would be a socially inclusive scheme in which all individuals would be treated equally. There would be no direct disincentives to work and/or save, as individuals would keep the basic income even if they earned or saved large sums of money.

However, it is argued that if basic income payments were set at a level to cover people's needs, there may be no incentive for people to work at all. This would then lead to a problem of very high tax rates on those in employment to pay for the scheme, and hence declining incentives to work. The purer forms of basic income schemes would be a radical departure from the current social security system, and few governments seem keen to propose such a departure, but another way of achieving a similar end might be to increase levels of Child Benefit as this benefit is universal and so has similar advantages to aspects of a basic income scheme.

Another radical measure might be to *dismantle social security altogether.* It could be argued that people should be left to insure themselves and to provide for their own financial security. Such an approach is the very opposite of the basic income idea. Rather than having a universal and socially inclusive approach, private welfare systems are based on a much more individualistic ethos. It is unlikely that the social security system would ever be completely dismantled, as even in the 19th century the Poor Law existed to provide some relief for people who fell on hard times. A return to private welfare would no doubt be accompanied by a return to public squalor and the very evils that Beveridge hoped to eradicate in the 1940s. None of the main parties is considering such radical reform but both Conservative and Labour governments at the end of the 20th century were keen to encourage greater provision of private welfare, particularly in the field of pensions.

The current direction of government policy appears to suggest that radical reform is not on the agenda. Policy seems to hinge on the primacy of *work as the best form of welfare* and, linked to this, the idea of moving towards tax credits and away from social security benefits. Such a move reflects the growing interest and power of the **Treasury** in relation to this field of policy. Many in government see social security benefits as hand-outs encouraging dependence, whereas tax credits are seen as much more closely related to work and therefore independence from the state. Tax credits are seen as the new panacea for all ills but it is impossible to tell at present whether they will provide the much-needed solution; one scenario is that they will add yet another layer of complexity to an already confusing system.

Overview

- There were dramatic changes in employment and demographic structures in the second half of the 20th century. Family life has become more diverse, with increases in cohabitation, divorce, lone parenthood, and so on. Male employment/economic activity has declined while female employment/economic activity has increased.

- The basis of the Beveridge social security system (namely full male employment and the male breadwinner/housewife model) was fundamentally challenged from the mid-1970s onwards. The social security system itself has not caused the breakdown of the male breadwinner/housewife model.

- Governments responded to these changes by cutting back on entitlement to national insurance benefits. The expansion of means-tested benefits, alongside all the other social and economic changes from the 1970s onwards, led to a massive increase in poverty, particularly among children.

- The current social security system does not sit well with contemporary employment and demographic structures but there are as yet no radical plans for reform on the government's agenda. Current policy approaches include tax credits, the promotion of work as the best form of welfare (for example, through the New Deals), targeting more help on children, and encouraging more private pension provision.

Questions for discussion

1. Why did the Beveridge Plan fail to provide 'cradle to grave' support?

2. What is the relationship between the social security system and social and economic behaviour?

3. What aspects of the current social security system are most at odds with contemporary patterns of employment and family life? How could the system be reformed to better meet these needs?

References

Baldwin, S. and Falkingham, J. (1994) *Social security and social change: New challenges to the Beveridge model*, Hemel Hempstead: Harvester Wheatsheaf.

Berthoud, R. (1997) 'Income and standards of living', in T. Modood, R. Berthoud, J. Lakey, J. Nazroo, P. Smith, S. Virdee and S. Beishon, *Ethnic minorities: Diversity and disadvantage*, London: Policy Studies Institute.

Berthoud, R. (1998) *Disability benefits: Reviews of the issues and options for reform*, York: Joseph Rowntree Foundation.

Bryson, A. and McKay, S. (1994) 'Is it worth working? An introduction to some of the issues', in A. Bryson and S. McKay (eds) *Is it worth working? Factors affecting labour supply*, London: Policy Studies Institute, pp 1-18.

Burgess, S. and Propper, C. (1999) 'Poverty in Britain', in P. Gregg and J. Wadsworth (eds) *The state of working Britain*, Manchester: Manchester University Press, pp 259-75.

Cooke, K. (1987) 'The withdrawal from paid work of the wives of unemployed men', *Journal of Social Policy*, vol 20, no 4, pp 537-65.

CSJ (Commission on Social Justice) (1994) *Social justice: Strategies for national renewal* (chair: Sir Gordon Borrie), London: Vintage.

Dench, S., Aston, J., Evans, C. and Meager, N. (2002) *Key indicators of women's position in Britain*, London: Women and Equality Unit.

Desai, T., Gregg, P., Steer, J. and Wadsworth, J. (1999) 'Gender and the labour market', in P. Gregg and J. Wadsworth (eds) *The state of working Britain*, Manchester: Manchester University Press, pp 168-84.

Fitzpatrick, T. (1999) *Freedom and security: An introduction to the basic income debate*, London: Macmillan.

Ford, R. (1996) *Childcare in the balance*, London: Policy Studies Institute.

Fryer, P. (1987) *Staying power: The history of black people in Britain*, London: Pluto Press Ltd.

Gregg, P. and Wadsworth, J. (1999) 'Economic inactivity', in P. Gregg and J. Wadsworth (eds) *The state of working Britain*, Manchester: Manchester University Press, pp 47-57.

Gregg, P., Hansen, K. and Wadsworth, J. (1999) 'The rise of the workless household', in P. Gregg and J. Wadsworth (eds) *The state of working Britain*, Manchester: Manchester University Press, pp 75-89.

Hall, R., Ogden, P. and Hill, C. (1999) 'Living alone: evidence from England and Wales and France for the last two decades', in S. McRae (ed) *Changing Britain: Families and households in the 1990s*, Oxford: Oxford University Press, pp 265-96.

Haskey, J. (1996) 'Population review (6): families and households in Great Britain', *Population Trends*, vol 85, pp 7-24.

Holtermann, S., Brannen, J., Moss, P. and Owen, C. (1999) *Lone parents and the labour market: Results from the 1997 Labour Force Survey and Review of Research*, London: Employment Service Report 23.

Kiernan, K. and Estaugh, V. (1993) *Cohabitation, extra-marital childbearing and social policy*, London: Family Policy Studies Centre.

Laslett, P. (1996) *A fresh map of life* (2nd edn), Basingstoke: Macmillan.

McKay, A. and Van Every, J. (2000) 'Gender, family and income maintenance: a feminist case for Citizens Basic Income', *Social Politics*, vol 7, no 2, pp 266-84.

McKay, S. (2003) *Working Families' Tax Credit in 2001*, Leeds: Corporate Document Services.

McKay, S. and Rowlingson, K. (1999) *Social security in Britain*, Basingstoke: Macmillan.

McKay, S., Smith, A., Youngs, R. and Walker, R. (1999) *Unemployment and jobseeking after the introduction of Jobseeker's Allowance*, DSS Research Report No 99, Leeds: Corporate Document Services.

McLaughlin, E., Millar, J. and Cooke, K. (1989) *Work and welfare benefits*, Aldershot: Gower.

McLaughlin, E., Yeates, N. and Kelly, G. (2002) *Social protection and units of assessment: Issues and reforms: A comparative study*, TUC Welfare Reform Series No 44, London: TUC.

McRae, S. (1993) *Cohabiting mothers: Changing marriage and motherhood?*, London: Policy Studies Institute

Marsh, A., McKay, S., Smith, A. and Stephenson, A. (2001) *Low-income families in Britain: Work, welfare and social security in 1999*, DSS Research Report No 138, Leeds: Corporate Document Services.

Meadows, P. (1999) *The flexible labour market: Implications for pension provision*, London: National Association of Pension Funds.

Millar, J. and Ridge, T. (2001) *Families, poverty, work and care: A review of the literature on lone parents and low-income couple families with children*, DWP Research Report No 153, Leeds: Corporate Document Services.

Nickell, S. (1999) 'Unemployment in Britain', in P. Gregg and J. Wadsworth (eds) *The state of working Britain*, Manchester: Manchester University Press, pp 7-28.

OECD (Organisation for Economic Co-operation and Development) (1996) 'Earnings inequality, low-paid employment and earnings mobility', *Employment Outlook*, Paris: OECD, pp 59-108 (www.oecd.org/pdf/m00028000/m00028000.pdf).

ONS (Office for National Statistics) (2001) *Social Trends*, vol 31, London: The Stationery Office.

ONS (2002) *Social Trends*, vol 32 (www.national-statistics.gov.uk).

Rake, K. (2001) 'Gender and New Labour's social policy', *Journal of Social Policy*, vol 30, no 2, pp 209-31.

Rowlingson, K. and McKay, S. (2002) *Lone parent families: Gender, class and state*, Harlow: Pearson Education.

Stewart, M. (1999) 'Low pay in Britain', in P. Gregg and J. Wadsworth (eds) *The state of working Britain*, Manchester: Manchester University Press, pp 7-28.

Stuttard, N. and Jenkins, J. (2001) 'Measuring low pay using the New Earnings Survey and the LFS', *Labour Market Trends*, The Stationery Office, vol 109, no 1, pp 55-66.

The American Prospect (2002) *The politics of family*, special edition at www.prospect.org/issue_pages/children/

Toynbee, P. (2003) *Hard work*, London: Bloomsbury.

van Parijs, P. (2000) 'Basic income and the two dilemmas of the welfare state', in C. Pierson and F. Castles (eds) *The welfare state reader*, Cambridge: Polity Press, pp 355-9.

Waldfogel, J., Danziger, S.K., Danziger, S. and Seefeldt, K. (2002) 'Welfare reform and lone mothers' employment in the US', in J. Millar and K. Rowlingson (eds) *Lone parents, employment and social policy: Cross-national comparisons*, Bristol: The Policy Press, pp 37-60.

Website resources

Child Poverty Action Group	www.cpag.org.uk
Citizen's Income Online	www.citizensincome.org
Department for Education and Skills	www.dfes.gov.uk
Department for Work and Pensions	www.dwp.gov.uk
DWP statistics on pensioners	www.dwp.gov.uk/asd/pensioners.html

Gingerbread	www.gingerbread.org.uk
Jobcentre Plus	www.jobcentreplus.gov.uk
Low Pay Commission	www.lowpay.gov.uk
National Council for One Parent Families	www.ncopf.org.uk
National Statistics	www.national-statistics.gov.uk
Organisation for Economic Co-operation and Development	www.oecd.org
Pension Service	www.thepensionservice.gov.uk
Pensions Policy Institute	www.pensionspolicyinstitute.org.uk

three

The new governance of social security in Britain

*Emma Carmel and
Theodoros Papadopoulos*

Summary

The objectives and organisation of social security policy under the Labour government have changed considerably since 1997. Using the concept of 'governance' as a framework, this chapter explores:

- the government's policy goals, and the key principles underpinning them, such as the redefinition of social security as mere support rather than protection, the conflation of security with work, the reconfiguration of rights and responsibilities, the emphasis on contractualisation and monitoring behaviour, and the pursuit of 'selective universalism';

- the operational side of social security policy and particularly the ways in which the organisation and management of policy delivery has altered, such as the creation of the new Department for Work and Pensions and various agencies; the ways in which the Treasury increasingly exerts control of these through the use of 'quasi-contracts', operational targets and performance management; and the dominance of the business model in the government's discourse.

Introduction: explaining governance

On 8 June 2001, the day of 'New' Labour's second general election victory, the Department 'of Social Security (DSS) was 'transformed' into the **Department for Work and Pensions** (DWP). Replacing the DSS, a department that existed in one form or another for almost a generation, the new DWP comprises parts of the former DSS, parts of the Department for Education and Employment (DfEE), and two new agencies, the **Jobcentre Plus** and the **Pension Service**. Other parts of the former DSS are now under the competence of the Treasury and the Ministry of Defence. This extensive institutional reorganisation and its symbolic manifestation in the removal of the words 'social security' from the title of the new department are the starting points for this chapter's reflections on the *changing governance of social security* in Britain. It is argued that these changes were neither merely administrative nor procedural, but that they symbolically marked key shifts in the objectives, logic and organisation of social security policy making. As such this chapter offers both a *general introduction* to what these changes have been, and also an *initial evaluation* of their significance.

In order to do this, we apply the concept of governance to the case of social security policy in Britain. The term *governance* is used here to describe a form of political regulation of social subjects – that is, individuals, social groups or institutions – initiated, organised and partially controlled by an actor or actors vested with the political authority to act in an area of public policy. Governance involves the 'steering' of the subjects' behavioural practices towards particular social and politico-economic goals via a set of institutions and processes that aim to maintain or change the status quo.

The concept of governance thus enables us to focus on a crucial feature of government policy making: that government is not only about legislation and rule creation, but is also about "how government is to be done" (Culpitt, 1999, p 44). It thus facilitates an analysis of policy making in two distinct but clearly related domains:

- the first concerns the content of policy, the legislation and regulations that embody policy principles, objectives and intended outputs, which we will refer to as *formal* policy;
- the second concerns the *mode of doing policy*: the organisational arrangements and procedures for policy delivery, referred to here as *operational* policy.

The analytical power of the concept of governance is that it allows enough flexibility to separately analyse both formal and operational policy while simultaneously highlighting their unity. This unity concerns policy means and ends. The means (operational policy) are inexorably connected to the ends (formal policy); the *how* of doing policy affects the *what* of formal policy and vice versa.

Furthermore, both the how and the what of social security policy involve the regulation of categories of welfare subjects. Indeed, the latter are inseparable from, and are reproduced by, the very institutions, regulations and procedures of which they are the focus. The formation of these categories is also inseparable from the discourse that produces them. Thus, for example, the constitution of a person through public policy as a citizen or as a consumer, as a 'jobseeker' or as unemployed, depends on the discourse through which formal policy is expressed and made sense of, a discourse that encapsulates a particular vision of how the social world is and should be. In our view, governance is immersed in discourse; forms of governance involve the institutional crystallisation of particular discourses. For this reason, our analysis of social security governance in Britain includes an examination of the ways in which categories such as the above are formed through official discourse.

Governance in the *formal* policy domain of social security

This section analyses the key principles guiding the Labour government's social security policies as well as the socioeconomic goals that underpin them. Our aim here is not to provide a definitive analysis examining the detail of policy developments; other chapters in this book offer these. Rather, we provide a general overview of the normative aspects of social security governance so that its logic as a new form of political regulation can be clearly identified.

Social security as support

The term 'social security' as applied to state income maintenance programmes first appeared in the US in 1934 to describe the instigation of the Roosevelt administration's 'New Deal'. Originally entitled the Economic Security Act, Roosevelt's Social Security Act was justified as a 'safeguard' against the 'man [sic]-made' contingencies of market failures, evident in the mass unemployment of the Depression years (Box 3.1). In this original vision of social security – which after the Second World War found an even bolder expression in the constitution of the UN's International Labour Organization (see Box 3.1) – society was understood to require protection by the state in response to circumstances explicitly considered to be socioeconomic. Thus, underlying this form of social security governance was the principle that the state should provide *protection* – not merely *support* – to individuals. This was protection from socioeconomic situations for which they were not individually to blame and which were perceived to be amenable to state action.

A similar vision underpinned Beveridge's position. He viewed the contributory principle – benefits paid out in return for previous contributions – as an essential part of a system in which social security was predominantly to be provided as of right, rather than according to need. This was *a right to protection against the contingencies that affect labour market participation* (McKay and Rowlingson, 1999, pp 60-3). Although it was not meant to "guarantee a standard of life beyond subsistence level, [for] men whose powers of earning diminish must adjust themselves to that change", this right nevertheless was to be accompanied by "full use of powers of the state to maintain employment and to reduce unemployment" (Beveridge, 1941, quoted in Fraser, 1984, p 288).

When those original visions for social security are compared to the ones held by British governments at the end of the 20th century, also summarised in **Box 3.1**, a number of differences emerge. One of them concerns the role of benefits. The new consensus is that they should not provide protection but, rather, *support*. The crucial difference between these two conceptualisations of security – protection versus support – can be illustrated by considering an

---

Box 3.1: Visions of social security

1 **Franklin D. Roosevelt**
Message to Congress, June 1934, prior to the passing of the 1935 Social Security Act
(cited in Digby, 1989, p 16)
Among our objectives I place the security of the men, women and children of the nation first.[...] People [...] want some safeguard against those misfortunes which cannot be wholly eliminated in this man-made world of ours.

2 **William Beveridge**
December 1942, radio interview, the day his report was published
(cited in Fraser, 1984, p 216)
The Plan for Britain is based on the contributory principle of giving not free allowances to all from the State, but giving benefits as of right in virtue of contributions made by the insured persons themselves.

3 **International Labour Organization**
The 1944 Declaration of Philadelphia. Principles of the International Labour Organization
(a) Labour is not a commodity; (b) Freedom of expression and of association are essential to sustained progress; (c) Poverty anywhere constitutes a danger to prosperity everywhere; (d) All human beings, irrespective of race, creed, or sex, have the right to pursue both their material well-being and their spiritual development in conditions of freedom and dignity, of economic security, and of equal opportunity [...] peace can be established only if it is based on social justice.

Box 3.1 continued

3 **John Moore, Secretary of State for Social Services**
   Interview in the Sunday Times, *28 September 1987*
   A welfare state worthy of the name aims at the real welfare of its citizens. It works to widen the understanding that dependency can be debilitating and that the best kind of help is that which gives people the will and ability to help themselves.

4 **Department of Social Security**
   New ambitions for our country: A new contract for welfare, *Green Paper on Welfare Reform, March 1998*
   The Government is determined to build an active welfare system which helps people to help themselves and ensures a proper level of support in times of need. (p 16)

   The new welfare state should help and encourage people of working age to work where they are capable of doing so. The government's aim is to rebuild the welfare state around work. (p 23)

example of how the term is used in other contexts. For instance, when a private company offers security to a person whose life is threatened, this is clearly meant to be protection from harm, not support once the harm is done. Social security-as-support is a 'hollowed out' security; its essence – protection – has been changed. In this vision, social security is not primarily about protection from failures of socioeconomic conditions and processes that state action can alter. Rather, it is a 'helping hand' so that an individual can alter his/her own behaviour to match the demands arising from these conditions and processes. Indeed, in this paternalistic vision of 'hollowed-out security', the emphasis on 'help for self-help' implies that benefit recipients are themselves to a large degree responsible for their status; with some (conditional) help, they will be able to end their status as benefit claimants.

For the Labour government, the Beveridge-inspired post-war settlement in social security policy, with its subsequent modifications and its curtailments during the years of conservative rule, has run its historical course (DSS, 1998; and Chapter One, this volume). There were at least two clear objectives that the first Labour government elected in 1997 had in respect of the social security system. The first was to make *(re)employment the central feature of provision for people of working age.* The second was to *'modernise' social security* to meet this goal, although the means to deliver it was the focal point of competing visions and discourses. Framed in this way, the normative assumptions of Labour's social security governance represented a clear departure from traditional Labour Party principles of "extensive and progressive redistribution [...] without recourse to means-testing" (Brewer et al, 2002, p 3). In 'thinking the unthinkable' – to use the catchphrase of this period – some policies were clearly crossed off the list of 'unthinkable' options.

Two competing visions of the principles on the basis of which social security was to be 'modernised' can be found in the debates at that time (Timmins, 2001, pp 559ff; Brewer et al, 2002, pp 3-5, 14-15). One vision, expressed by Frank Field, the then Minister for Welfare Reform in the DSS, emphasised the need to provide benefits through social insurance, that is, on the basis of the contributory principle. This was necessary in order to overcome the morally debilitating and economic disincentive effects of means-tested benefits, which had increased in importance over the post-war period, and which discouraged people from taking responsibility for securing their own income. For Field, linking benefits to contributions was the means to promote individuals' engagement in paid work as well as independence. It would also, particularly for pensioners, maintain the idea that access to social security was a right.

The alternative vision, favoured by the Treasury, questioned Field's emphasis on social insurance, and emphasised outcomes. As Alistair Darling (who became Secretary of State at the DSS from the Treasury in 1998 after the post of Minister for Welfare Reform was abolished and Frank Field left the Department) argued: "the important difference in social security is not whether [benefits] are insurance based or means-tested but whether or not they provide enough help to get people back to work and improve their lives" (quoted in Brewer et al, 2002, p 4; see also DSS, 2000b, paras 6, 25, and introduction, para 2). This vision was eventually adopted as the government's policy.

A new configuration of rights and responsibilities

Despite the above claim and the government's assurance that the abolition of contributory benefits is not yet on the agenda (DSS, 2000b, para 8), there has been a further erosion of contributory benefits and an expansion in means testing. A **contributory system** is a 'something-for-something' deal between the state and the individual, where (to use 'New' Labour speak) *the right to protection is gained through the previous exercise of responsibility*. As the Labour government is supposedly committed to end the 'something-for-nothing' welfare culture then, logically, one should have expected that it would have strengthened not weakened the contributory principle. This, however, is contrary to the observed trend of expanding means-tested benefits. How can this paradox be explained?

One way to make sense of these developments is to view them as indicative of a reconfiguration of the contract between the state and the citizen. In a contributory system, establishing the right to protection is the end result of a process during which the claimants, via their contributions, demonstrate their responsible behaviour. Conditions are mainly attached *before* the claim is made and the right of the state to steer and monitor the claimant's behaviour after the claim is made is rather weak. Having fulfilled their obligations vis-à-vis contributions, the right of the claimant to protection is strengthened. Conversely, in the new arrangements, the claim for support marks the beginning of a different process whereby conditions are attached *after* the claim is made. What is strengthened here is the right of the state to steer and monitor a claimant's behaviour after the claim is made. In this context, the Labour government's social security policy *marks a new distribution of rights and responsibilities* between the state and the individual, where *security is seen as support* and not a right, whereby the state establishes its right to demand behavioural changes from the claimant in return for providing them with support. The *New contract for welfare*, as the government's Green Paper on welfare reform was called, was precisely that.

Work as security

Very different from the original visions of social security, and probably the most significant normative aspect in Labour's vision, is the apparent equivalence drawn between work and security. For a working-age person there is no clear or explicit right to security. Instead, paid work is seen as replacing security. However, this paid work is itself not secure. It is neither guaranteed by the state, nor is it significantly 'protected' when one is in work, notwithstanding the introduction of the **National Minimum Wage** (NMW). Also, its narrow definition as paid work in a labour market underlines an exclusionary vision. Important welfare-creating activities that are not part of the cash/market nexus and thus are not 'registered' as productive are absent from such definition (Levitas, 1998; Lund, 2000, pp 202-3), two obvious examples here being care work or voluntary work (see Chapter Six, this volume). Further, work seen in this way potentially enhances the social differences between able-bodied and disabled people of working age, and echoes a rather narrow vision of social life – *we do not work to live but rather live to work*.

Alongside this, there has been a retreat from the principle that the state should ensure full employment; that is, from the idea that security should primarily be created through the provision of jobs (for men). As indicated in the 1944 White Paper on Employment, full employment meant that the state had a responsibility "to maintain a high and stable level of employment" (Digby, 1989, p 58). This approach is markedly different from the 'New' Labour approach of 'work for those who can'. Under the recent redefinition of full employment as 'full employability' (for example, DWP and HM Treasury, 2001), the reason for unemployment is now firmly anchored to an individual's capacities and capabilities, implying that they themselves are responsible for their employment status. The state's responsibilities are to provide only opportunities for training and skills development, which the risk-taking individual is required to take up. Thus the entire construct of opportunity and employability evident in the government's discourse involves a "privatisation of risk management" (Rose, 1996, p 58) and the 'management of insecurity' (Dean and Shah, 2002). The individual of working age is made responsible for their employment status, and for the provision of their own security, including in old age.

Thus Labour's vision of 'security' for people of working age is the further expansion of individual labour supply in a 'flexible' and insecure labour market. Social security policies are no longer a means to protect society from potential failures of a market economy, nor a means to steer the economy to respond and meet social needs. Rather, they are to become a means to steer the behaviour of individuals to make them adaptable to what are perceived by the government as the demands of this market economy (Grover and Stewart, 1999). If this trend continues, social security runs the risk of becoming nothing more than an "obligation to endlessly manufacture a future where one is not a drain on the entrepreneurial activities of others" (Fitzpatrick, 2002, p 15).

Contractualisation and behavioural monitoring

Although the previous Conservative governments introduced some compulsory interviews for unemployed claimants, under the Labour government this process has gone much further (see Chapter Five, this volume). The **New Deal**, established in Labour's first term of office, either required or encouraged different groups of working-age claimants to attend interviews, training or to take up employment. The separate New Deals for young people, lone parents, long-term unemployed people, older unemployed people, the partners of long-term unemployed people and for people with disabilities each had different conditions in respect of benefit entitlement. Thus only the New Deals for young people and long-term unemployed people aged between 25 and 50 were made compulsory, with sanctions for non-compliance with the scheme. This variety of conditions implied that although ideally all people of working age should take up employment, there are some people for whom this could be made into requirement.

This process appears to have accelerated in 2002. There have been extensions to the group characterised as required to consider employment, heralded in the introduction of a restructured New Deal for the over-25s, and the requirement from April 2003 for all lone parents to attend work-focused interviews, irrespective of the age of their children. All new claimants for benefits are, in the Jobcentre Plus organisation, required to attend such an interview at the time of their first claim (DWP, 2001b, pp 3-4)[1], adopting the approach taken with the ONE gateway that acted as the pilot scheme to the introduction of Jobcentre Plus (Osgood et al, 2002).

This could indicate a reconstitution of welfare subjects even more explicitly through their age/labour market status, in which claimants are dealt with in a similar 'work-focused way' regardless of the reason for their benefit claim.

---

[1] There are two exceptions to this regulation: Maternity Allowance and Industrial Injuries Benefit.

The underlying principle is clear. A contract is to be established between these groups of working-age people and the state, whereby the state has the right to insist on particular kinds of labour market behaviour in exchange for providing benefits (Heron and Dwyer, 1999)[2].

Selective universalism

The key way in which welfare subjects are constituted in Labour's social security policies is through their relationship to potential labour market status. Thus, the population is divided into children (below working age), working-age people, and pensioners. The distribution of rights, responsibilities and risks in social security varies according to this age/labour market status categorisation. "The welfare system should support a number of objectives: delivering work for those who can, helping those who need it most – families with children and the poorest pensioners" (DSS, 2000b, para 9). In clarifying the phrase 'security for those who cannot', (poor) pensioners and families with children are treated as special cases because they are perceived as "unable to affect their own incomes through work.(...) By contrast work could still be viewed as the best form of welfare for most working-age adults" (Brewer et al, 2002, p 7). Future pensioners are expected and are being encouraged to save and invest for their retirement (DSS, 1998; DWP, 2002), a development towards what Hewitt (2002) calls *assets-based welfare*.

This strategy of *selective universalism* (see Timmins, 2001, p 574) indicates that the government is not committed to poverty alleviation in general nor to income redistribution across the board. Rather, its commitment is to poverty alleviation for particular sociodemographic groups, while its agenda for redistribution is more "about the distance between the bottom of the income distribution and the middle, but not between the middle and the top" (Brewer et al, 2002).

To conclude this section, in the normative vision of Labour's social security governance, *security is redefined as support*, and *work as employability*. At the same time, contractualisation and monitoring of claimants' behaviour enforces a new distribution of rights, responsibilities and risks. This approach is anchored in a productivist logic, in which the main task of government is to create the conditions for economic competitiveness in an internationalised market economy (Grover and Stewart, 1999; Jessop, 1999). Subordinate to this goal, this type of social security policy shares many normative attributes of a neo-liberal conception of security. Notably, that it is "an individual, an autonomous, private 'security', gained by self-responsibility through the market: which, by

---

[2] It is important to note, however, that this contract is not contracted between equal parties, as the terms of the contract are liable to change by one party (that is, the state) at its leisure. The other 'contractee' has nowhere else to go to make an alternative contract.

definition, is part of the hazard of the ever-changing dynamism of the world"
(Culpitt, 1999, p 48).

Governance in the *operational* policy domain of social security

In the context of these changes in the formal policy domain, the logic and
goal of the associated departmental reorganisation and renaming becomes clear.
Taken together, the changes represent a new distribution of rights and
responsibilities in the operational policy domain of governance, which enhance
the characteristics of governance in the formal policy domain. This new
distribution is evident in three ways:

- First, the move of parts of the former DfEE – notably the Employment
  Service – into the newly named Department for Work and Pensions reflects
  the government's constitution of welfare subjects by age and labour market
  status. It also enhances the productivist logic that underpins the changes in
  the formal policy arena.
- Second, the role of the Treasury has changed to become that of a quasi-
  contractor and monitor of services provided through the DWP and its sub-
  contracting agencies.
- Third, through the continuing use of business models and metaphors, and
  the emphasis on particular kinds of performance measurements and targets
  as a means to steer the activities of frontline DWP staff.

New departmental structures

Regarding the first change, the renaming of the Department of Social Security
into the Department for Work and Pensions and its reorganisation can be
clearly connected to the constitution of welfare subjects in the formal policy
domain. Thus pensioners are dealt with in the new Pension Service; people of
working age are dealt with in the new Jobcentre Plus; and benefits for children
are now primarily delivered through the Inland Revenue. There are some
anomalies in this formulation, so that the new Pension Credit will also be
delivered through the Inland Revenue, while a range of benefits will continue
to be provided in Jobcentre Plus (Invalid Care Allowance, Maternity Allowance,
Social Fund payments) which do not, or do not yet, have work-focused
'responsibilities' attached to them. In addition, the Child Support Agency
(CSA) continues under the DWP. Nonetheless, the departmental renaming,
the creation of Jobcentre Plus, and the justifications provided for these, make
the links to formal policy objectives explicit.

In the summer of 2000, the then Secretaries of State for the DfEE and DSS

(David Blunkett and Alistair Darling respectively) appeared together before the relevant House of Commons Select Committees to explain the proposed reorganisation. Darling argued that "we need to change the whole culture of the organisation just as we are changing the whole culture of the benefits system", while Blunkett referred to the need to overcome the invalid distinction between working-age benefit claimants who were looking for work and those who were not, given that the new aim of the agency was to expand the pool of employable people (SSSC, 2000). The process of "building a new culture of work first" (DWP and HM Treasury, 2001, para 1.21) required action to steer the behaviour of DWP staff in order to change the culture of the DSS/DWP itself. Thus the new agency, Jobcentre Plus, "will have a new culture, based on helping people to become independent, and will help further to embed a culture of responsibilities and rights within the welfare system" (DWP, 2002, p 16).

However, the move of the Employment Service into the DWP, to be integrated in Jobcentre Plus as the latter is extended nationally in 2003, strikingly reveals the productivist vision in the new social security governance. The Employment Service had two sets of clients – 'jobseekers' and employers. As employers are integrated into the DWP's set of clients, a different emphasis is introduced into the DWP's services for people of working age. The goals of Jobcentre Plus (see **Box 3.2**) embrace a particular set of rights and responsibilities, different from those of the DSS. In consequence to the integration of the former Employment Service into the Benefits Agency, the agency must now explicitly meet the needs of employers (see also Chapter Eleven in this volume).

Jobcentre Plus aims to meet employers' needs more effectively so that "planning, provision and delivery are geared towards employers' recruitment needs" (DWP, 2002, p 53; also pp 12, 15). This sentence offers an interesting light on the role of the new agency: provision and delivery require a product

---

Box 3.2: The goals of Jobcentre Plus

- A work focus to the benefits system
- A dedicated service to enable employers to fill their vacancies quickly and successfully
- Swift, secure and professional access to benefits
- A much better service for everyone who needs help
- Active help from personal advisors
- A safer and more professional working environment for staff
- Greatly improved IT accommodation and support services.

Source: DWP (2002, pp 15-16)

to be provided and delivered. It seems in this case that the 'product' is work-ready, employable benefit claimants. Hence these operational policy changes, and the logics of behaviour that they induce, suggest that even greater emphasis is placed on the creation of employability among claimants than might be assessed from analysing formal policy. The DWP has gained a new responsibility in respect of maintaining the economy. "It will be important that everyone, employers, individuals and the Government, take seriously their responsibility to deliver a high skill, high productivity economy" (DWP and HM Treasury, 2001, para 4.47, also para 4.40).

The role of the Treasury

The second set of changes in the operational policy domain concern the role of the Treasury. The Treasury has famously been the most powerful single department in British policy making for many years (for example, Hennessy, 1989). However, in the past, its power over other departments and ministers has primarily been exercised through annual budget negotiations, about how much money a department might need or get in order to implement its agenda and meet government commitments. At first sight, then, the decision of Chancellor Gordon Brown early in the Labour government's first term to initiate a **Comprehensive Spending Review** (CSR), which would establish spending requirements and budgets over a three-year period, rather than annually, might suggest that departments would gain greater control over their spending across this three-year period. Certainly as departments are granted under this regime greater leeway to 'carry over' unspent money to the next period, this appeared to offer departments greater flexibility and predictability in financing policy initiatives. This was certainly the case made by the Treasury itself (HM Treasury, 2000).

However, as part of the CSR, departments were required to draw up, in conjunction with the Treasury, a **Public Service Agreement**. The Public Service Agreements set out individual departments' policy objectives for the following three years (DWP, 2001a). At the time of writing, the most recent Public Service Agreements were published in 2000, for the years 2001-04, although a new set were to be agreed by the autumn of 2002. Public Service Agreements were also supplemented by **Service Delivery Agreements**, a second set of agreements, in which departments were required to specify how their policy objectives would be met. These were then also supplemented, in the 2000 round of agreements, by 'technical notes', which further specified the indicators against which departmental performance would be measured (for example, DSS, 2000a)[3], and on which the department would have to report annually.

---

[3] The technical note for the DWP's 2001-04 Public Service Agreement is available, as indicated in this chapter's references, on the Department's website, as is the Public Service Agreement itself.

This series of *quasi-contracts* is of profound importance, not only for social security governance, but also more widely. Thus Rouse and Smith (2002, p 49) are correct to argue that Public Service Agreements "have centralised the importance of performance (…) by requiring accountable contracts from public service providers". However, at the same time, Rouse and Smith suggest that these developments permit departments and agencies greater freedom than under the previous managerialist regime to shape their own approach to problems or issues (Rouse and Smith, 2002, p 48). Certainly it seems possible that institutions may be able to shape some aspects of governance in this framework, and may, consciously or otherwise, subvert the objectives established in Public Service Agreements and Service Delivery Agreements, as has occurred in previous managerialist regimes (Clarke and Newman, 1997). However, the claim of greater freedom for agencies under Labour than under the Conservative regime appears to miss the key consequence of these new arrangements, and does not account for the context in which the new governance regime has developed. The new agreements substantially change the degree to which the Treasury is able to set not only the constraints for departments' policy making, as in the past, but also what policies are to be made. The *policy objectives themselves, how policies are delivered*, and *how that delivery is to be measured* are all now subject to Treasury approval and monitoring.

This involves a micro-level scrutiny of departmental actions and institutions, and intrusion into departmental autonomy unprecedented in Britain. It is also perhaps worth remembering that in these 'quasi-contractual' negotiations, the terms and conditions of this contract can largely be established by the Treasury, as it still guards access to funds, which departments need[4]. Indeed, the Treasury in these negotiations still places emphasis on what in the *Modernising government* White Paper was called 'earned autonomy' (Cabinet Office, 1999). That is, that departments, agencies, local authorities, schools and hospital trusts which met the government's objectives would be subject to fewer constraints, while sanctions and threats would be exerted on the unsuccessful – as measured by performance targets (Cutler and Waine, 2000, pp 55-6; Newman, 2001, pp

---

Note 3 continued However, the technical note seems not to have been updated to reflect the Department's change of name, and so is listed as Department of Social Security (2000a). The Public Service Agreement itself, however, has had its reference and Internet links updated, and so is listed under Department for Work and Pensions, and rather confusingly, as 2001, not 2000. The two documents refer to the same agreement, applying to the same three-year period of 2001-04.

[4] It is possible to imagine cases where departments have a stronger hand, for example in pursuing a policy initiative with the express patronage of the Prime Minister, or where a minister has powerful political support for their personal agenda which the Chancellor is unable to threaten. And of course, the Prime Minister has the technical capacity to remove the Chancellor, which might act as a threat. At the moment, however, such a radical step seems politically unfeasible, and, as practised in the DWP, the Public Service Agreements and Service Delivery Agreements appear to confirm a remarkable congruence between the Treasury's agenda and that of the successive Secretaries of State.

91-3). A key moment in the governance of social security then is the establishment of these criteria – the performance targets – and it is in this process that the Treasury has gained unprecedented powers over social security governance.

Contractualism within government: performance management

So, the changing role of the Treasury demonstrates a shift of responsibilities and rights in the operational policy domain, between it and the DWP. However, contractualisation extends far beyond that of Public Service Agreements and Service Delivery Agreements. Ever since the introduction of the Benefits and Child Support Agency, and indeed agencies in other government departments from the late 1980s onwards, mechanisms have been required in order to exert control of this process of *agencification* (Rhodes, 1997). This was done through framework agreements with the agencies delivering policy, an audit of the services provided, and the use of performance management imported from the private sector (Rose, 1996b; Clarke and Newman, 1997). In addition to these arrangements – for what might be called departmental subcontractors for policy delivery – contracts and framework agreements are also developed for the private and voluntary sector organisations that now run some Jobcentre Plus offices. Furthermore, additional 'partnership working' between the Pension Service and other organisations dealing with the over-65s is planned (DWP, 2001c), for which we can perhaps expect more 'service-level agreements' to establish the responsibilities of relevant parties, similar to those already established with local authorities (for example, Benefits Agency, 2002, p 20).

Given the extent of this contractualisation, the emphasis on performance management in meeting policy objectives in Labour governance generally has been described as "a liberal dose of accountability through accountancy" (Massey, 2001, p 31). That is, audits are used as a means of *comptrol* – that is, financial control – to assess service delivery and organisational responsibilities. To view the maintenance and creation of accountability as solely through accountancy is, however, too narrow. Indeed the Labour government can be distinguished from its predecessors precisely on this point. If the previous governments were concerned with cost, efficiency and value for money (Newman, 2001, p 91), the first two terms of the Blair government have ushered in a performative managerialism, characterised by a 'developmental approach'. In contrast to previous Conservative governments, this approach is outcome- and objective-oriented, primarily concerned with achieving particular outcomes with the money that is spent (Rouse and Smith, 2002, p 47). This approach was articulated in both the 1999 *Modernising government* White Paper (Cabinet Office, 1999) and the review of the Paper's impact and implementation (CMPS, 2001). In **Box 3.3**, what was described by the government as "the nine features of modern policymaking" (CMPS, 2001, p 14) are shown. The characteristics of this outcome-oriented, performative management are demonstrated in the importance of objectives and outcomes in points 1, 3 and 6. In addition, under points 6-9, it is clear that implementation, and control of implementation directed towards the achievement of objectives, is central to Labour's operational policy strategy.

A wide array of government, as opposed to parliamentary, performance measurement and review mechanisms has been adopted to identify and assess the achievement of these objectives. These range from the Audit Office to no fewer than 10 different processes or review groups and institutions operating under the umbrellas of the Cabinet Office and Treasury (see **Table 3.1**). Furthermore, these mechanisms are additional to those instituted by the DWP to evaluate agency and service performance, such as annual reports and oversight bodies. In turn, these have been supplemented by micro-level performance management such as **Performance Improvement Teams** which investigated and publicised best practice in the Benefits Agency; the encouragement of customer service managers to engage in performance evaluation procedures; and the creation of dedicated absentee managers to monitor staff attendance (Benefits Agency, 2002, pp 18, 32-3, 44).

Yet, as Cutler and Waine (2000, pp 52-3) point out, the close specification of targets and indicators are likely to stifle innovation and interfere with the development of 'joined-up government'. Staff at all levels can become oriented

---

Box 3.3: The nine features of modern policy making

1 *Forward looking:* identification of outcomes; accounting for long-term government strategy
2 *Outward looking:* looks to other countries and policy mechanisms; presentation strategy prepared
3 *Innovative, flexible and creative:* defines success in terms of outcomes already identified; manages risk; team working; involvement of outsiders on 'policy team'
4 *Evidence-based:* commissions research; reviews existing research; consults experts
5 *Inclusive:* consults service implementers; consults those affected by policy; seeks feedback; conducts impact assessment
6 *Joined-up:* cross-cutting objectives identified at the outset; definitions of joint working arrangements; implementation is part of policy making process
7 *Review:* ongoing review programme; meaningful performance indicators; redundant or failing policies abandoned
8 *Evaluation:* defined purpose for evaluation at the outset; success criteria defined; evaluation process built in from the outset; use of pilots
9 *Learns lessons:* dissemination of good practice; account of what was done in response to lessons learned; distinction between failure to implement and failures of implementation

Source: CMPS (2001, p 14)

Table 3.1: Government performance measurement and improvement strategy mechanisms

Department or office	Institution or group	Role
Audit Office		Value-for-money; lesson learning
Treasury	Spending reviews	Review and evaluation of policy aims and budgetary needs/constraints
	Public Service Agreements	Identification of targets for final policy outcomes
	Service Delivery Agreements	Clarification of how resources are to be managed to reach targets
	Service Delivery Agreements regulations	Specification of performance indicators for each policy objective
	Public Services Productivity Panel	Review of policy for 'customer focus' throughout policy making; 'self-analysis' tools for policy makers to improve performance
Cabinet Office	Prime Minister's Delivery Unit	Monitoring to ensure government meets objectives in priority policy areas. Includes private sector staff
	Office of Public Services Reform	Review of public and civil services reform
	Performance and Innovation Unit	'Big issues' work on forecasting and strategic thinking
	Centre for Management and Policy Studies	Training and development; best practice dissemination; promotion of evidence-based policy and excellent policy research
	Public sector benchmarking project	Transfer of 'Business Excellence Model' of benchmarking for comparing public/public and public/private sector performance

towards completing, or seeming as if they are completing, such targets; or they focus on complying with procedures at the expense of programme aims (Newman, 2001, p 93). Indeed, meeting these multiple targets can involve contradictory tendencies which are not easily reconcilable for frontline staff, especially when they involve both sets of Jobcentre Plus 'customers' – employers and claimants/jobseekers (as discussed in Chapter Twelve).

The dominance of the 'business model'

One further feature of policy making from **Box 3.3** deserves attention, in terms of what it reveals about the dominance of 'business'-style models and metaphors in social security governance. Point 5 concerns the inclusion of non-governmental actors – both frontline staff, and those on whom services impact – in the development of policies. The DWP, however, does not appear to have engaged in this process; as Lister (2001, p 106) points out, there is little or no evidence of service user involvement in deciding how services are delivered (see also Chapter Eleven in this volume). It is certainly the case that numerous reviews and evaluations of social security policies have been conducted under this plan, but such evaluations often treat service users as customers, in which the sociopolitical character of state-provided services is glossed over. After all, one adage of customer service in the private sector is that the customer is king or queen: this seems a perverse reading of the highly conditional 'new contract' analysed in the previous section of this chapter. Yet this contradictory construction of benefit claimants as customers, and of agencies and even the department, as businesses, is inescapable in documents discussing service delivery (for example, Alistair Darling, in Social Security Select Committee, 2000; Benefits Agency, 2002; DWP, 2002). Thus, the intention in Jobcentre Plus is to ensure that "the service is customer-focused and tailored to individual needs" (DWP, 2001c, p 7), and that teams of staff in the Pension Service "manage and support the entire customer experience ... delivering the best customer experience" (DWP, 2001/02, p 3).

Many of the measures introduced under such claims certainly seem likely to improve the experience of claiming benefit: unscreened offices; the ability to initiate a claim over the telephone; avoiding the need to go to more than one office when claiming different benefits. Others seem more spuriously related to claimants' needs, so that the provision of Internet and e-mail-based services for precisely those people least likely to have access to such facilities does not seem to offer a particularly improved 'customer experience' (Selwyn, 2002; see Chapter Fourteen, this volume).

From a governance perspective, however, a more significant point can be raised with regard to these measures. We do not need to describe claimants as 'customers' to justify such operational policy changes. Such changes could be easily be justified as a means to meet claimants' needs. In this case, then, the choice to describe claimants as customers is concerned with steering the behaviour of staff to perform their work 'as if' claimants were customers and as if they were part of an entrepreneurial and profit-seeking 'business'. The importation of business models of performance management is made to make sense by considering the role of everyone in the department to be oriented towards the business-style goals of customer service, and, of course, product delivery.

The new governance of social security

This chapter has explored the policy principles, objectives and intended outputs of the Labour government, and the organisational arrangements and procedures for policy delivery. In both domains we can observe a 'quasi-contractualisation' of social security: between the DWP's policy makers and the Treasury, between service providers and the DWP and, last but by no means least, between the individual benefit recipient and the DWP. Furthermore, we argue that under this new form of governance, individuals and social groups are steered to act as 'risk and opportunity takers' and as entrepreneurs.

In terms of its formal content, social security policy for all people of working age has been transformed to *serve labour market policy objectives*; that is, to be a means with which to manage labour market behaviour. It is only with regard to policies for children that we can see a commitment to socioeconomic security, although this is now primarily delivered through the Treasury. In terms of operational policy, these role changes are reflected in the departmental renaming/reorganisation, as well as in the DWP's stated vision and policy objectives. Further, the official use of the term 'social security' policy has become less of a descriptor of policies providing socioeconomic security underwritten by the state, but rather a descriptor of policies that 'encourage' particular kinds of individual behaviour in the face of insecurity.

Thus, the new governance of social security in Britain can be characterised as a *new form of political regulation* in which the DWP and the Treasury construct and steer social subjects towards a set of socioeconomic goals, which are clearly anchored in a productivist vision of the role of social security in an internationalised market economy. A new distribution of rights, responsibilities and risks for individuals and institutions is established through increasing contractualisation of their relationships and extensive monitoring of their behaviour and performance. As such, this is a new chapter in the history of social security in Britain; a new kind of social security, that is not very social and even less secure.

Overview

- This chapter analyses social security policy using the concept of 'governance'. Governance is used to describe how the behaviour of individuals, institutions and social groups is politically regulated, and steered, to meet socioeconomic goals. Analysing a form of governance in a policy domain involves the examination of both the 'formal' and operational aspects of policy making.

- Regarding formal policy, the key principles and goals of social security under the Labour government involve a redefinition of the policy content of security from protection based on rights, to support based on obligations; a reconstitution of welfare subjects predominantly in relation to their labour market status and age; the conflation of security with (paid) work; and an increase in contractualisation and monitoring of claimants' behaviour accompanied by selective universalism.

- Regarding operational policy, the renaming and reorganisation of the DSS into the DWP confirmed the productivist logic associated with formal policy changes, with a clear emphasis on labour market integration for all working-age benefit claimants; an explicit institutional commitment to meet the demands of employers; the introduction and extension of 'business' discourse and performance management in all areas of the DWP; and, an unprecedented increase of the Treasury's capacity to control policy making in the DWP.

Questions for discussion

1. Explain the distinction between formal and operational policy. How are they related in the case of social security?

2. In what ways do conceptualisations of 'social security' differ between the Beveridgean ideal and that expressed by the Labour government?

3. Identify and explain the main changes in social security operational policy since 1997. Which of these changes is the most significant, and why?

4. Is it appropriate to talk about benefit claimants and recipients as 'customers'?

References

Benefits Agency (2002) *Annual Reports and Accounts 2001-2*, London: The Stationery Office.

Brewer, M., Clark, T. and Wakefield, M. (2002) 'Social security in the UK under New Labour: what did the third way mean for welfare reform?', *Fiscal Studies*, vol 23, no 4, pp 359-84.

Cabinet Office (1999) *Modernising government*, Cm 4310, London: The Stationery Office.

Clarke, J. and Newman, J. (1997) *The managerial state: Power, politics and ideology in the re-making of social welfare*, London: Sage Publications.

CMPS (Centre for Management and Policy Studies) (2001) *Better policy-making*, London: Cabinet Office.

Culpitt, I. (1999) *Risk and social policy*, London: Sage Publications.

Cutler, T. and Waine, B. (2000) 'Managerialism reformed? New Labour and public sector management', *Social Policy and Administration*, vol 34, issue 3, pp 318-32.

Dean, H. and Shah, A. (2002) 'Insecure families and low-paying labour markets: comments on the British experience', *Journal of Social Policy*, vol 31, no 1, pp 64-80.

Digby, A. (1989) *British welfare policy: Workhouse to workfare*, London: Faber and Faber.

DSS (Department of Social Security) (1998) *New ambitions for our country: A new contract for welfare*, Cm 3805, London: The Stationery Office.

DSS (2000a) 'Public Service Agreement 2001-4: technical note', www.dwp.gov.uk/publications/dss/2000/psa_tech/psatech.pdf

DSS (2000b) *Report on the Contributory Principle. Reply by the Government to the Fifth Report of the Select Committee on Social Security*, London: HMSO.

DWP (Department for Work and Pensions) (2001a) 'Public Service Agreement for Department for Work and Pensions 2001-4', www.dwp.gov.uk/publications/dss/2001/dwp_psa/psa.pdf

DWP (2001b) *Touchbase* newsletter, issue 24.

DWP (2001c) *Touchbase* newsletter, issue 25.

DWP (2001/02) *Touchbase* newsletter, issue 26.

DWP (2002) 'Departmental Report on Government's Expenditure Plans 2002-3', London: The Stationery Office, www.dwp.gov.uk/publications/dwp/2002/dwpreport/.

DWP and HM Treasury (2001) 'The changing welfare state: employment opportunity for all', London: The Stationery Office, www.dwp.gov.uk/publications/dwp/2001/emp-opp/employment.pdf

Fitzpatrick, T. (2002) 'In search of a welfare democracy', *Social Policy and Society*, vol 1, issue 1, pp 11-20.

Fraser, D. (1984) *The evolution of the British welfare state*, London: Macmillan.

Grover, C. and Stewart, J. (1999) '"Market workfare": social security, social regulation and competitiveness in the 1990s', *Journal of Social Policy*, vol 28, issue 1, pp 73-96.

Hennessy, P. (1989) *Whitehall*, New York, NY: Free Press.

Heron, E. and Dwyer, P. (1999) 'Doing the right thing: New Labour's attempt to forge a New Deal between the individual and the state', *Social Policy and Administration*, vol 33, issue 1, pp 91-104.

Hewitt, M. (2002) 'New Labour and the redefinition of social security', in M. Powell (ed) *Evaluating New Labour's welfare reforms*, Bristol: The Policy Press, pp 189-210.

HM Treasury (2000) *Prudent for a purpose: Building opportunity and security for all. Public Spending Plans 2001-4*, Cm 4808, London: The Stationery Office (www.hm-treasury.gov.uk/Spending_Review_2000/Spending_Review_Report/).

Jessop, B. (1999) 'Narrating the future of the national economy and the national state? Remarks on remapping regulation and reinventing governance', in G. Steinmetz (ed) *STATE/CULTURE: State formation after the cultural turn*, Ithaca, NY: Cornell University Press, pp 378-405.

Levitas, R. (1998) *Social inclusion and new Labour*, London: Macmillan.

Lister, R. (2001) '"Work for those who can, security for those who cannot": a third way in social security reform or fractured social citizenship?', in R. Edwards and T. Glover (eds) *Risk and citizenship: Key issues in welfare*, London: Routledge, pp 96-110.

Lund, B. (2000) *Understanding state welfare: Social justice or social exclusion?*, London: Sage Publications.

McKay, S. and Rowlingson, K. (1999) *Social security in Britain*, Basingstoke: Macmillan.

Massey, A. (2001) 'Policy management and implementation', in S.P. Savage and R. Atkinson (eds) *Public policy under Blair*, London: Palgrave, pp 16-33.

Newman, J. (2001) *Modernising governance: New Labour, policy and society*, London: Sage Publications.

Osgood, J., Stone, V. and Thomas, A. (2002) *Delivering a work-focused service: Views and experiences of clients*, DWP Research Report No 167, Leeds: Corporate Document Services.

Rhodes, R.A.W. (1997) *Understanding governance: Policy networks, governance, reflexivity and accountability*, Buckingham: Open University Press.

Rose, N. (1996) 'Governing the advanced "liberal" democracies', in A. Barry, T. Osborne and N. Rose (eds) *Foucault and political reason: Liberalism, neo-liberalism and rationalities of government*, Chicago, IL: Chicago University Press, pp 37-64.

Rouse, J. and Smith, G. (2002) 'Evaluating New Labour's accountability reforms', in M. Powell (ed) *Evaluating New Labour's welfare reforms*, Bristol: The Policy Press, pp 39-60.

Selwyn, N. (2002) 'E-stablishing an inclusive society? Technology, social exclusion and UK government policy making', *Journal of Social Policy*, vol 31, no 1, pp 1-20.

SSSC (Social Security Select Committee) (2000a) *Report on the Contributory Principle. Fifth Report on Social Security*, HC 56-I, London: The Stationery Office.

SSSC (2000b) Minutes of Evidence, 3 July, www.parliament.the-stationery-office.co.uk/pa/cm199900/cmselect/cmsocsec/662/0070301.htm

Timmins, N. (2001) *The five giants: A biography of the welfare state* (revised edn), London: Harper Collins.

Website resources

Department for Work and Pensions	www.dwp.gov.uk
International Labour Organization	www.ilo.org/public/english
International Social Security Association	www.issa.int/engl.homef.htm
Jobcentre Plus	www.jobcentreplus.gov.uk
Public Service targets	www.hm-treasury.gov.uk/performance
Social Policy Virtual Library	www.social-policy.org
Social Security Advisory Committee	www.ssac.org.uk
Work and Pensions Select Committee (UK)	www.parliament.uk/commons/selcom/workpenhome.htm

four

Social security in a global context

Nicola Yeates

Summary

There is growing recognition of the importance of the transnational, supranational and global contexts in which social policy is formulated and implemented. Relating the global context to social security policy and administration in the UK, this chapter:

- reviews the global applicability of the term 'social security', and uses this to explore how statutory social security systems operate within broader welfare systems;

- contextualises the UK social security system in relation to the variety of systems globally, both in 'developed' and 'developing' countries;

- examines the transnational nature of social security;

- reflects on current policy approaches of international institutions to the issues of social justice, equity and security.

Introduction: social security and social protection

In the UK 'social security' predominantly refers to the system of cash benefits administered mainly by central government. This equation of social security with state-administered cash benefits is not, however, the international norm. As the International Labour Organization (ILO) notes, "in many countries a sharp distinction is commonly drawn between social security on the one hand, and poverty alleviation measures on the other" (2000, p 29). Thus, in the US social security refers only to social insurance retirement, survivors' and disability benefits; social assistance payments are referred to as 'welfare'. In France and many Latin American countries social security refers to social insurance benefits, including healthcare benefits and excludes some social assistance benefits delivered at local level[1]. In the Republic of Ireland, the term 'social welfare' is used in preference to 'social security', and while these terms are broadly synonymous, social welfare benefits do not include some disability, sickness and maternity benefits that are referred to as 'health-related' payments and administered by regional health boards.

The strict identification of social security with government activity and, more specifically with a particular department is, of course, becoming less applicable to the UK due to the relocation of responsibility for the collection of national insurance contributions to the Inland Revenue and the Revenue's growing role in the administration of tax credits (see Chapter One in this volume). More generally, however, the focus on public arrangements neglects the importance of market-based arrangements and non-statutory providers, such as employers (occupational pensions, sick and maternity pay) and commercial agencies (personal pensions, private savings, private unemployment and care insurance). An exclusive emphasis on public arrangements also neglects informal arrangements. The recognition of informal arrangements is relevant to both 'developed' and 'developing' countries alike, although it is of particular significance in countries that do not have comprehensive statutory social security systems. These arrangements include culturally determined obligations and practices emanating from kinship, neighbourhood and community ties, and in many countries family members are expected to support one another (Midgley and Kaseke, 1996; Millar and Warman, 1997). Such arrangements also include charitable donations arising from religious norms such as *alms-giving* in Christianity and *zakât* in Islam[2], and cooperative associations or mutual

---

[1] This integration of healthcare within social security is why the ILO includes public spending on healthcare in addition to benefits in cash and in kind in its social security expenditure data.

[2] *Zakât* is an obligatory form of alms-giving for Muslims, who are required to give a minimum of 2.5% of their wealth for the benefit of the poor in the Muslim community. These funds are collected and distributed by *zakât* agencies (see www.submission.org/zakat.html; www.zpub.com/aaa/zakat.html).

benefit societies, such as funeral, credit and informal savings societies providing assistance in cash and in kind (Midgley, 1997). Informal or 'traditional' systems often operate at local level without any state recognition or support, although in some countries statutory and informal systems have been integrated as a means of supporting informal systems and/or extending statutory coverage (Midgley and Kaseke, 1996).

This recognition that income security derives from market and informal arrangements as well as from public arrangements is captured by the term *social protection*. The advantage of this term is to draw attention to the broad range of non-statutory welfare arrangements and institutions that individuals and households turn to to meet their income need. The distinction between 'social security' and 'social protection' is shown in **Box 4.1**. In addition, social protection could also include agricultural schemes aiming to maintain farmers' and peasants' incomes, such as micro-credit and crop insurance schemes, farm subsidies and food security programmes (Gough, 2000). Arguably, the EU's Common Agricultural Policy (CAP) could be regarded as a type of income maintenance system for farmers insofar as it aims to "ensure a fair standard of living for the agricultural community, in particular by increasing the individual earnings of persons engaged in agriculture" (Treaty of Rome, 1957, Article 39(b); Kleinman and Piachaud, 1993).

Box 4.1: Social security versus social protection

Social security is "the protection which society provides for its members through ... public measures:

- to offset the absence or substantial reduction of income from work resulting from various contingencies (notably sickness, maternity, employment injury, unemployment, invalidity, old age and death of the breadwinner;
- to provide people with healthcare; and
- to provide benefits for families with children".

This definition includes social insurance, social assistance, extra costs and universal benefits.

Social protection includes "not only public social security schemes but also private or non-statutory schemes with a similar objective ... provided that the contributions to the schemes are not wholly determined by market forces".

This definition includes, for example, mutual benefit societies and occupational pension schemes, in addition to social security benefits.

Source: Adapted from ILO (2000, pp 29-30)

The provision of cash benefits to individual claimants is only one way in which governments pursue the goal of income maintenance. Other ways of doing so include subsidising the prices of welfare goods and services, such as housing, food and energy. This provides a safety net of substantial indirect wage subsidies which may complement limited cash benefits systems or substitute for them entirely. Some countries subsidise specific food and other costs incurred by certain benefit recipients. Finally, we should not discount the importance of employment as a social security system. Where lifetime employment is guaranteed there is no need for the state to provide unemployment benefits. This has been the case for many public sector workers and civil servants around the world, although the introduction of employment flexibility pursuant to public sector reforms has led to the extension of coverage of unemployment benefits to these groups. In addition, state subsidies to employers and other forms of corporate welfare are sometimes presented as a form of social protection for employees.

Social security around the world

The *establishment of global social security principles* can be considered one of the foremost achievements of international politics in the 20th century. Dixon (1999, p 1) notes that "as a mechanism for meeting human needs social security has achieved nearly universal acceptance", while Hoskins (2001, p 3) argues that social security is "one of the most successful social and economic innovations of the [20th] century".

Access to social security was accepted as a human right under the 1948 Universal Declaration of Human Rights (**Box 4.2**), and was reiterated in Article 9 of the 1966 International Covenant on Economic, Social and Cultural Rights, which "recognises the right of everyone to social security, including social insurance". This right was reaffirmed more recently by the Copenhagen Declaration on Social Development, adopted at the World Summit for Social Development in 1995, which committed signatory countries to "ensure that all people have adequate economic and social protection during unemployment, ill health, maternity, child-rearing, widowhood, disability and old age" (Commitment 2(d): www.visionoffice.com/socdev/wssdco-0.htm). At the European level, the European Social Charter (1961) of the Council of Europe and the Charter of the Fundamental Social Rights of Workers (1989) of the EU similarly emphasise basic rights to adequate social security benefits.

Coverage

Social security is now an established feature of the advanced industrialised countries where statutory coverage has reached almost 100%. However, outside of these countries coverage is much more restricted; indeed, from a global

> **Box 4.2: Social security and the 1948 Universal Declaration of Human Rights**
>
> Everyone, as a member of society, has the right to social security and is entitled to realization ... of the economic, social and cultural rights indispensable for his dignity and the free development of his personality. (Article 22)
>
> Everyone who works has the right to just and favourable remuneration ensuring for himself and his family an existence worthy of human dignity, and supplemented, if necessary by other means of social protection. (Article 23.3)
>
> Everyone has the right to a standard of living adequate for the health and well-being of himself and of his family, including ... the right to security in the event of unemployment, sickness, disability, widowhood, old age or other lack of livelihood in circumstances beyond his control. (Article 25.1)
>
> Motherhood and childhood are entitled to special care and assistance. All children, whether born in or out of wedlock, shall enjoy the same social protection. (Article 25.2)

perspective, the level of provision in countries like the UK is an exception rather than the rule. As van Ginneken notes, "more than half of the world's population (workers and their dependants) are excluded from any type of statutory social security protection" (1999, p 1). Social security coverage of the working population ranges from 5-10% in sub-Saharan Africa and South Asia, 50-80% in Central and Eastern Europe, 10-80% in Latin America, and 10-100% in South East and East Asia (the exact percentage depends on the risk or group in question) (van Ginneken, 1999, p 1). At the end of 1998, only one in four underemployed and unemployed people around the world received some kind of unemployment benefit, and most of these lived in the 'developed' countries (ILO, 2000, p 147).

There are a number of reasons why so many people are excluded from social security benefits. The first reason is the absence of statutory schemes. The number of countries with such schemes grew from 57 countries in 1940 to 172 countries by 1995, but 49 countries and territories around the world affecting 66 million people still do not have any known statutory social security scheme (Dixon, 1999, p 2). Many of these are low-income countries, but there are notable exceptions. The United Arab Emirates (UAE), one of the richest countries in the world, does not have a statutory social security system. The second reason for exclusion from social security benefits is due to the fact that statutory schemes may not be comprehensive in the coverage of all social risks or groups. Programmes in respect of old age, disability, death, sickness and maternity are most widespread, while programmes in respect of unemployment, family and children are less common (Dixon, 1999). Fewer than one in ten (8%) of the 172 countries and territories in Dixon's study had programmes for all of the following contingencies: old age, disability, death (including survivors' benefits), sickness, maternity, unemployment, family and children. Most likely to be excluded from statutory schemes are workers in cottage and small-scale industries, small shops, urban informal workers, agricultural workers, domestic workers and home workers[3]. Third, even people formally covered by schemes may not receive benefit, either because they have not made enough contributions or because they have exhausted their benefit entitlement. In some parts of the world, particularly Central and Eastern Europe and parts of Africa, people do not receive benefits because statutory schemes have collapsed or rendered inoperative due to war, natural disasters or severe economic dislocation (Dixon, 1999).

The absence of comprehensive statutory social security for millions of workers raises a number of issues about the design of social security systems and the state capacity necessary to operate them. An effective social security system requires a strong participatory basis, and social insurance schemes require a large proportion of the workforce to have a regular job whose earnings can be monitored and from which mandatory contributions can be collected. This condition does not apply to a growing proportion of workers worldwide experiencing irregular employment and earnings (van Ginneken, 1999; Beattie, 2000). Moreover, participation in social security schemes is often incomplete because of weaknesses in law enforcement; compliance may be further reduced because people are focused on immediate survival and cannot spare the resources necessary for saving for unemployment or old age. More generally, effective statutory schemes require a strong public infrastructure and sophisticated managerial and administrative capacities in order for taxes to be collected, entitlements to be calculated and benefits to be delivered (van Ginneken, 1999). The absence of such an infrastructure is a key impediment to the development of an adequate social security system, particularly in 'developing' countries:

> [Social assistance schemes] require sophisticated administration to determine who is really deserving and to ensure that the benefits reach the target population effectively. Thus the costs of delivering the benefits are high and, without an efficient and accountable control and monitoring system, leakages or corruption are likely.... [Moreover] many social security administrations in developing countries find it difficult to cope with the volume of administrative tasks associated with the operation of a social insurance scheme, which requires the maintenance of accurate lifetime records for insured persons. (van Ginneken, 1999, pp 9, 13)

---

[3] See www.ilo.org/public/english/protection/condtrav/unprotected

Expenditure

Social security worldwide is characterised not only by inequality of coverage but also variance in expenditure levels. Globally, public social security expenditure[4] amounted to on average 9.6% of GDP in 1990, but there are sharp regional disparities. Social security expenditure accounted for 18.5% of GDP in Europe, 11.2% of GDP in Oceania (Australia, New Zealand and Fiji) and 9.1% of GDP in North America. Trailing well behind the expenditure 'leaders' are Latin America and the Caribbean at 6.0% of GDP, Asia at 3.7% of GDP and, finally, Africa at 2.6% of GDP (ILO, 2000, table 14, p 312). There are strong intraregional differences too. Thus, in Western European countries (EU member states plus Norway, Switzerland and Iceland), social security spending accounted for on average 19.1% of their GDP, while in Central and Eastern European countries social security spending accounted for 12.6% of GDP (1996) (ILO, 2000, table 14, p 312). The UK spends less than the Western European average and more closely approximates the so-called 'Latin Rim' countries in this respect.

Design features

Of course, social security expenditure in itself tells us little about the effectiveness or efficiency of the social security system in achieving its various goals or the quality of social rights. One way of judging the quality of social security systems is by looking at their design features. Dixon's study (1999) is a good illustration of this way of evaluating social security systems. He ranked 172 countries according to how well they met ILO minimum social security standard benchmarks. His methodology articulated a comprehensive set of 860 design and administration features for basic and supplementary social security services. These features incorporated financing, administration, coverage, eligibility and provision (for example, periodicity of payment; benefit generosity relative to prevailing living standards). Scores were assigned for each feature (see Dixon, 1999, pp 199-205 for a full account of methodology). Countries were then ranked into four 'league tables' or tiers (**Box 4.3** lists the first 10 countries in each tier). Second-tier countries are those with a design score between 10 and 20% below that of the best-designed (first-tier) systems, third-tier countries have design scores between 20 and 30% below first-tier systems, while fourth-tier countries have design scores of more than 30% below that of the best designed system (Dixon, 1999, pp 217-20) . The UK was ranked 37th (jointly with Brazil) and is classed as a second-tier system. It

---

[4] Social security expenditure here covers expenditure on pensions, employment injury, sickness, family, housing and social assistance benefits in cash and in kind, including administrative expenditure.

Box 4.3: Global social security design rankings: first 10 countries in each tier (1995)

First tier 20 countries	Second tier 38 countries	Third tier 49 countries	Fourth tier 66 countries
1 Australia	21 Iceland	58 Malta	106 St Vincent/Grenadines
2 Sweden	22 Poland	59 Cape Verde	107 Côte d'Ivoire
3 France	23 Ireland	59 Trinidad/Tobago	108 India
4 Denmark	23 Italy	59 Turkey	109 Sri Lanka
5 New Zealand	25 Estonia	62 Ecuador	110 Jamaica
6 Russia	26 Slovakia	62 US	111 Dominican Republic
7 Finland	27 Bolivia	64 South Africa	112 Mauritania
8 Austria	28 Albania	65 Barbados	113 Burkina Faso
9 Spain	28 Kyrgyzstan	66 Colombia	114 Kenya
10 Germany	30 Tunisia	67 Burundi	115 Kazakhstan

Source: Adapted from Dixon (1999, appendix 10.1, pp 223-31)

should be emphasised that this evaluation methodology measures statutory intent, rather than actual delivery.

The ranking of Australia as having the best-designed social security system in the world may come as a surprise to many, as Dixon notes, since it has pursued a social assistance strategy which in the UK has negative cultural and institutional connotations with the Poor Law. The main difference between the UK and Australian systems is that the former targets income need through a means test which requires claimants to prove their poverty in order to receive benefits, while the latter does so through an 'affluence test' which includes all but the highest income groups[5]. Thus, in the Australian system "the net is broad and the means testing innocuous", while it also provides additional provision for particular categories (for example, disabled people) and for those in greatest need (Dixon, 1999, pp 217-18). In principle then, "Australia's social assistance system provides a social security safety–net that provides modest benefits to many, with additional support provided to those deemed to be in most need, and that is financed, without imposing significant contribution burdens on employees or employers, from taxation revenue" (Dixon, 1999, p 218). After Australia, it is notable that in none of the next five 'best' social security systems has means testing been integral to the extent that has been and still is the case in the UK; instead, they are built on contributory and universal principles with a much more residual role assigned to means testing.

---

[5] The UK's tax credits go further up the income scale than traditional means-tested benefits in this country and the income testing is intended to be simple and unobtrusive (see Chapter One in this volume).

The presence of four Central and Eastern European countries in the first tier is attributed to the socialist origins of their social security systems, although all are beset by financial crises that inhibit their ability to actually deliver their statutory obligations (Dixon, 1999).

Advanced social security systems are sometimes believed to be associated with a high level of economic development. Thus it is argued that only the richer, more economically 'advanced' countries are able to afford 'better', more comprehensive social security systems. However, Dixon's ranking places most of the Central and Eastern European countries, which are otherwise classified by the World Bank as low- to middle-income countries, in the first-tier rank, while the US and Kuwait, which are among the richest high-income countries, only achieve a ranking of 62nd and 163rd respectively, and the UAE does not have a statutory social security system at all. As Dixon comments, the US is "the only developed Western country with a third-tier social security system", which he attributes to its preference "to leave employers and individuals to take responsibility for meeting social security needs" (1999, p 221). The level of economic development alone is therefore insufficient to explain why some countries have better designed systems than others. In order to understand this we also need to consider national social, cultural, religious and political traditions, arrangements and institutions, as well as the national balance of political power between the state, labour, capital and civil society (Yeates, 2001).

Welfare regimes

The above cross-national comparisons are based on levels of expenditure and on the design features of social security systems. In addition there is a large and growing literature that explores the similarities and differences in *welfare regimes*, and analyses the ways in which different types of regime respond to the challenges of economic, social and demographic change. The concept of the *welfare state regime* was used by Esping-Andersen (1990, p 2) "to denote the fact that in the relation between state and economy a complex of legal and organisational features are systematically interwoven". He used the term to distinguish between two approaches to the study of the welfare states. The first (and prevailing) approach is an association of the welfare state with social amelioration policies and programmes. The second approach embraces these policies and programmes, but also links them to their influence on the employment and general social structure (Esping-Andersen, 1990, p 2). Thus, an interest in social security from a welfare regimes perspective would not only be concerned with the characteristics of the various benefits or how much was spent on them; it would also attempt to understand how countries arrive at particular public–private sector mixes, the extent to which people are dependent on selling their labour and on market income to maintain an adequate standard of living, the wider impact of provision on employment, and the extent to which different social security systems enhance or diminish status and class differences.

A key feature of the welfare regimes approach is the grouping of countries into clusters or groups. This grouping is undertaken either by using a complex quantitative scoring methodology using a wide range of variables and countries to determine the wider impact of welfare provision, or by using a qualitative approach and a smaller number of variables to reveal assumptions underpinning that provision as well as the effects of these assumptions on access to provision. Esping-Andersen (1990) is an exemplar of the former approach, while Lewis (1992, 1997) is an exemplar of the latter approach. The welfare regimes literature has been preoccupied with questions such as how many different clusters or regimes exist, and which countries belong to which regime (see Abrahamson, 1999, for a review of these debates). For the purposes of this chapter, suffice it to say that Esping-Andersen's methodology and typology have been criticised on many fronts. Feminists argue that in focusing on the interplay of state and market and on the public realm of employment Esping-Andersen sidelines gender as a structuring principle of welfare regimes since he ignores the informal, familial sphere and unpaid work (see Lewis, 1992, 1997; Sainsbury, 1994, for an overview of feminist critiques). Esping-Andersen's work has also been criticised for excluding or misunderstanding the welfare regimes of the 'peripheral' countries of Italy, Greece, Spain, Portugal and Ireland, and for denying the existence of a specific 'southern' model (see Ferrera, 1996; Cousins, 1997). The criticism that Esping-Andersen's work is 'core-centric' is one that can in fact be made of many analyses of the welfare state and social security, be they cross-national comparative or focused on a single country. As Cousins (1997, p 225) rightly points out, the majority of such analyses focus on 'core' Western capitalist states and either exclude 'non-core' countries (be they from the Third World or the European periphery) or include them on the assumption that they would eventually develop along the lines of 'core' Western welfare systems.

The transnational dimension

Globalisation has prompted more widespread recognition of the importance of attending to the transnational dimension of social policy in addition to the national one. Globalisation has been variously defined and used (see Yeates, 2001, pp 14-17, for further discussion), but it basically refers to an *extensive network of economic, social, cultural and political interconnections and processes* which routinely transcend national boundaries (Yeates, 2001, p 4). Of course, transnational interactions are by no means recent phenomena, but social, environmental and economic issues are increasingly being perceived as global in scope and as requiring global solutions, often coordinated at the level of supranational and international governmental institutions (Bretherton, 1996; Deacon, with Hulse and Stubbs, 1997).

International collaboration in social security

The principal international institutions currently concerned with social security matters are the **World Bank**, the **International Monetary Fund** (IMF), and the **United Nations** (UN) and its various 'satellite' agencies, notably the ILO. Social security matters are also central to the work of the **Organisation for Economic Co-operation and Development** (OECD), a transnational policy forum of the world's 29 richest countries. Most recently the **World Trade Organization** (WTO) has demonstrated an interest in social security and pensions issues. Regional formations have also shown an interest in social security issues. Most prominent among these is the EU. Other regional formations such as the Southern African Development Community (SADC), the Association of South-East Nations (ASEAN) and the Southern Core Common Market (MERCOSUR) have, or are considering developing, social and labour regulation, although to date only MERCOSUR countries have gone as far as a supranational law on the mutual recognition of social security rights in the region (Deacon, 2001). More recently, regional development banks, such as the Asian Development Bank and the Inter-American Development Bank, have become involved in social security and protection debates (Lustig, 2001; Ortiz, 2001). These institutions are not only a debating forum on social security matters; they attempt to intervene in domestic policy processes in a range of ways, such as sponsoring research, reports and conferences, providing information, auditing compliance with international standards, and adding authority to critics when domestic policies are judged to fall short of international standards (Burden, 1998).

Social security is one of the longest established areas of international collaboration. The **International Social Security Association** (ISSA) was founded in 1927 as a research, training and advisory resource to members, typically managers, administrators, policy makers and researchers in the field of social security. The ILO, founded in 1945, has acquired particular expertise in social security due to its focus on labour issues. Advocating guaranteed minimum standards it has adopted over 30 Conventions and 20 Recommendations that deal exclusively with social security (Otting, 1994). Policy implementation and enforcement is a weak area for international institutions because they depend on the cooperation of national and local officials and politicians. Indeed, the ILO has no powers to enforce national compliance and relies on moral persuasion to achieve its objectives.

Social security is one of the more important social policy areas of interest to these institutions because of its relationship to labour supply, labour mobility, production and competitiveness. As regards the EU, for example, although the Treaty of Rome (1957) was vague about the relationship between economic and social matters and social policy largely remained outside the competence of the Community (Majone, 1993), social security was considered central to the objective of economic integration so it was identified as one of the fields where member states should cooperate closely (Article 118)[6]. The EU's interest in social security has primarily been with the removal of obstacles to labour mobility between member states and it is in relation to the social security rights of trans-frontier migrant workers (salaried and self-employed) that the EU has been most active and its powers the strongest (one of the first Directives concerned the social security rights of such workers). Another major interest of the EU in social security is in matters of gender equality, owing to the inclusion of Article 119 on equal pay for men and women in the Treaty of Rome. The involvement of the EU in gender equality stemmed less from concerns about social justice than from concerns that the absence of equal pay obligations in all member states would undermine the economic competitiveness of countries where equal pay was a statutory obligation. Notwithstanding the motive behind this commitment to gender equality, various Directives since the late 1970s have prohibited direct and indirect sex discrimination in employment matters and statutory social security. More recently, the EU has also emphasised the right to an adequate income, although currently it can only make recommendations in this area (for further reading on EU social policy see Cram, 1998 and Geyer, 2000; for an overview of EU social security policy see Ditch, 1999).

For much of the 20th century the ILO was the dominant international institution in social security matters. It emphasised that the primary goals of social security should be to *ensure access to a minimum standard of living* and raise living standards, and its concerns have been with the gradual extension of statutory social security coverage, particularly to informal sector workers. The ILO's social security and labour Conventions and Recommendations gained international acceptance and influenced legislation used by 'developed' and 'developing' countries alike (Kay, 2000). However, by the mid-1990s other international institutions had partially displaced the ILO as the dominant international governmental organisation (IGO) in social security matters. The entry of the IMF and World Bank and most recently the WTO into social security debates, particularly in the area of pensions, sparked a vigorous global debate about the aims of social security, the desirable 'welfare mix' in the financing and provision of social security, and the role of the state and public expenditure in promoting socioeconomic development more broadly. More generally, governments, transnational corporations (TNCs), social movements, trades unions, professional associations and trade associations are also increasingly

---

[6] The other areas were employment, labour law and working conditions; vocational training; occupational health and safety; collective bargaining; and the right of association.

directing political action towards these global arenas in an attempt to influence how global capitalism and national territories are governed. Accordingly, the international arena has become a battleground over which political struggles about desirable models of social security, and the appropriate role of each of the public, commercial, voluntary and informal sectors, are fought out (Deacon, with Hulse and Stubbs, 1997; Yeates, 2001).

The global debate in social security

One of the key axes of this global debate concerns the goals of social security, namely, *should social security only aim to alleviate poverty or should it also aim to prevent poverty?* This debate ties into policy discussions about the role of public policy more generally in underwriting the social costs of economic and political reform. Prompted by the most recent international financial crisis – that which took place in Asia in 1997 and which made its effects felt globally (that is, in the West) – the policy question now being addressed is not *whether* but *how* globalisation can be harnessed in support of social standards. It is now accepted that globalisation increasingly exposes people to global economic risks and that this strengthens rather than lessens the need for better social security systems (for further reading on the implications of economic globalisation for social security see Hoskins, 2001, and Sigg and Behrendt, 2002). But what constitutes a 'better' system? And should social (security) policy only play 'handmaiden' to economic growth, or should it be conceived of as a means of promoting social justice and equity?

The World Bank is a prominent advocate of the argument that the aim of social security policy should be to *enable poor groups to better manage the financial effects of the various social risks they face*. Its *social risk management* approach regards social security as primarily a safety net for the critically poor, but also a springboard out of poverty insofar as social security systems should, at the very least, not discourage risk-taking among the poor (Holzmann and Jørgensen, 2000, p 3; World Bank, 2001). The World Bank regards informal and market-based social protection as best suited to what it calls 'idiosyncratic' risks of a health (illness, injury, disability), life cycle (birth, old age, death), social (crime, domestic violence) and economic (unemployment, harvest failure and business failure) nature. A limited amount of public subsidies for low-income groups is justifiable because the poor cannot secure their livelihoods through informal means or commercial schemes alone. However, non-poor groups are expected to make their own private 'risk management' arrangements by, for example, drawing on their own savings and resources or purchasing commercial social security protection. Thus, the primary objective of social risk management is to support the 'critically poor'; commercial provision and the family are social security systems of the 'first resort', bolstered by philanthropic and voluntary efforts to compensate for withdrawn or pared down 'last resort' public provision. The social risk management approach does not consider as a legitimate goal the promotion of a more egalitarian income distribution, be it achieved through tax-transfer mechanisms or comprehensive public goods provision (Holzmann and Jørgensen, 2000, p 21). This policy orientation reflects neo-liberals' preference for individual responsibility that enhances 'choice', self-interest and enforceable contractual rights over collective responsibility that enhances social cohesion, integration and equity (Dixon, 1999).

The World Bank's approach contrasts with that of the ILO. As noted earlier, the ILO has long advocated the idea of an entitlement to basic social protection as a human right, and it has been concerned with defining minimum standards and extending social security coverage. In recent years, it has been rethinking its traditional labourist strategy in the light of current economic and political conditions, and is attempting to devise new forms of universal social protection systems (Deacon, 2002; Standing, 2002). In this context, the ILO's concept of *decent work* (ILO, 1999, 2001) and its associated *decent work strategy* aims to achieve universal social security coverage which protects living standards rather than just alleviating poverty once it occurs. More generally, the strategy aspires to the creation of "decent and productive work in conditions of freedom, equity, security and human dignity" (ILO, 1999; Standing, 2002). The essential idea here is that, in return for participation in the social and economic progress of the country or community, there should be a positive duty to promote equality, inclusion and empowerment and an entitlement to a fair share of that country's or community's resources. The ILO accordingly advocates the need for universal social security schemes for the working-age population, but also recognises that these schemes have to be adapted to maximise inclusion within them. Among the social security reform ideas being considered are those that support extended family forms of care; extend benefit entitlements to informal sector workers and to the risks attached to the means of liveliehood other than formal work, such as agricultural work; and develop new forms of mutuality and social insurance among self-employed workers (Deacon, 2002). The infusion of collectivist values in the design of social security and protection systems positively embraces the policy goals of equity and the redistribution of resources, both on an intra-country and a transnational basis. The issue of transnational redistribution is of crucial importance since not all countries are able to afford the same level of social security. Transnationally redistributive mechanisms include a Global Social Trust Fund, the fulfilment of existing development aid commitments and the provision of more concessional financing (Euzéby, 2002; Sigg and Behrendt, 2002; Townsend and Gordon, 2002).

The case of pensions

Pensions is a key terrain over which these debates about the appropriate goals of social security and the respective roles of the public, commercial, voluntary and informal sectors have been waged. Minns (2001) characterises this global struggle as a 'new Cold War' between Anglo-American models of pension provision on the one hand, and European, Asian-Pacific and Eurasian models on the other. Both the World Bank (1994, 2000; Holzmann and Jørgensen, 2000) and the IMF (1996) have been at the forefront of attempts to encourage the global diffusion of the Anglo-American model, already in place in the US, UK, the Netherlands, Ireland, Switzerland, Chile, Australia and Canada. This has entailed dismantling comprehensive publicly managed and provided pensions, on the one hand, and building up private pensions systems, on the other. This has been undertaken with a view to *encouraging private savings, stimulating pensions markets*, and *maximising the role of private financial institutions* in income maintenance provisions for pensioners. Thus, the World Bank regards the legitimate role of the state as essentially limited to the regulation of the (private) pensions industry and the provision of a low-level, means-tested, non-contributory state pension for the poorest of the population. It recommends for people who wish to make additional provision a second pillar of mandatory personal pensions and a third pillar of voluntary supplementary schemes. The World Bank envisages a greater role for the second and third pillars than for the first pillar[7].

Such endorsements have effectively transformed pension privatisation "from a radical idea to a mainstream, global policy prescription" (Kay, 2000, p 192), and provided legitimacy and support for new 'policy templates' (Kahler, 1992). The World Bank has advised governments in Central and Eastern Europe (Deacon, with Hulse and Stubbs, 1997; Deacon, 2000), Latin America (Cruz-Saco and Mesa-Lago, 1998) and in China (World Bank, 1997), trying to persuade them to adopt its preferred pension model. This advice has in many cases been backed up by the provision of institutional, human and financial resources to assist governments – many of which are dependent on the World Bank for development finance – to reform their pensions along the preferred lines. But how successful has the World Bank been in persuading governments to follow its policy prescriptions? Much has been made of the dominance of the Anglo-American model and the Washington Consensus in international policy circles, but far less attention has been paid to how these prescriptions are still dependent on the national context in determining how far and in what form the model is actually implemented. Thus, in Latin America, only Chile's pension system comes closest to the World Bank paradigm; Bolivia, El Salvador and Mexico fit the World Bank paradigm partially; the remaining

---

[7] See Chapter Nine in this volume, for a discussion of the main pillars of the UK pension system.

countries enacted reforms closer to the ILO paradigm than to the World Bank one (Cruz-Saco and Mesa-Lago, 1998). Similarly, Fultz and Ruck (2001) show that most Central and Eastern European countries are reforming their public schemes without establishing a mandatory private pillar. Of course, the influence of the World Bank's policy paradigm should not be dismissed because even if the policy prescriptions are not followed to the letter, the paradigm has legitimised the World Bank's active partnership with a range of institutions in individual countries, the individualisation and marketisation of provision, and governments' retreat from the goal of income redistribution (Deacon, 2000; Dixon and Hyde, 2001; Cruz-Saco, 2002).

The World Bank's approach has also had an impact on the ILO's pensions policy prescriptions, which traditionally stressed the importance of a compulsory universal flat-rate public pension within a tripartite system (the other pillars being public earnings-related schemes and private voluntary schemes) (Otting, 1994). For 'developed' countries the ILO now recommends a four-pillar model consisting of:

- a means-tested tier, financed from general revenue;
- a Pay-As-You-Go (PAYG), defined-benefit pension worth 40-50% of lifetime average earnings;
- a compulsory, capitalised, defined-contribution pension; and
- an upper tier of voluntary retirement savings and non-pension sources of income.

For 'developing' countries, the ILO recommends prioritising the expansion of coverage to workers in the informal sector, and/or a national programme that excludes higher-income workers who would be required to participate in a more expensive (probably private) programme. In addition, it argues that the basic state programme could be limited to disability and survivors' benefits or provide retirement benefits that start at a relatively high age, such as 65 or 70 (Gillion, 2000, p 20; Gillion et al, 2000). As the ILO itself acknowledges, this model represents an important shift in its thinking, justified as "allowing for greater diversification of retirement income risks" (2000, p 20). The retreat of the ILO from universal pension provision and its acceptance of a larger role for private pension provision is for some indicative that "the social security department of the ILO can no longer be regarded as a bulwark against Bretton Woods policies" (Deacon, 2000, pp 11-12).

Although the UK is not dependent on the World Bank and IMF for development finance, the pervasiveness of these institutions' policy paradigms can be measured by their infiltration into British social security discourse and policy. The British government's marketisation and privatisation agenda has involved both the transfer of responsibility for benefits provision and administration to the private sector and the incorporation of private sector values into public sector provision (Walker, 2001). Examples of the former can be found in the area of pensions, sickness benefits and long-term care benefits, and in the privatisation of Housing Benefit, Sickness Benefit and family benefits administration. Examples of the latter are seen in the corporatisation of social security administration which is "increasingly being run on business principles with an emphasis on efficiency and targets, but with less attention to effectiveness in meeting individual need" (Walker, 2001, p 139). Overall, although the state continues to play a major role in social security provision and administration, Walker (2001, p 139) concludes that the marketisation agenda means in the long term "a less adequate public social security system" in which "poverty is privatised with its cost falling to the individual and his or her family".

Bilateralism and policy shopping

Other notable forms of transnationalism in social security are bilateralism and 'policy shopping'. **Bilateral aid** has traditionally been a key form of international development assistance provided by 'rich' countries to 'poor' ones. In addition to providing finance, governments regularly send civil servants abroad to provide technical or policy advice to other governments setting up, expanding or restructuring their social security systems. The recommendations of these experts reflect the political and policy orientations of the donor government or agency (de la Porte and Deacon, 2002). More generally, the mobility of people and the transnational diffusion of culture and ideas have given rise to greater interest in, and opportunity to compare, how other countries 'do' social policy and to the emergence of social policy 'communities' "through which policies are developed, refined and borrowed" (Manning and Shaw, 1999, pp 120-1). Governments and policy makers now routinely examine what appears to work elsewhere and to consider how it might be applied in their own territories. This **policy shopping** is evident in the UK system of pensions, child support, welfare-to-work and tax credits. Of course, transnational policy diffusion and mobility is nothing new in the history of welfare states. Lenin's programme for a socialist social security system and the UK's early social security provisions were modelled on the German Bismarckian system, while the social security systems of former British colonies still bear the imprint of that country's colonial rule. However, now the possibilities of such diffusion have been enhanced by supranational and international institutions actively encouraging transnational policy cooperation, comparison and learning either by disseminating their preferred policy templates and trying to ensure that national governments follow them as discussed above, or by encouraging national experts to compare their systems and approaches to those of other model countries. The OECD, for example, encourages policy debate and dialogue between countries in Europe, North America and the major Pacific economies, particularly around issues such as the social (security) implications of labour market changes and population ageing. The EU and Council of Europe do similarly among their member states. Of course, the existence of such 'policy shopping' does not mean that policies which (seem to) work abroad are brought home and implemented in their original form; indeed, this could not be the case because each country operates in a different social, political, economic and cultural context. Ultimately, whether other countries' policies and programmes are ignored as irrelevant or unworkable or whether they are chosen for import depends on the politics of those doing the 'shopping' as well as the national context in which the policies are to be implemented. The example of the transnational diffusion of the Bismarckian scheme cited above demonstrates that both socialist and liberal social security regimes were able to accommodate its principles, although for different reasons and ultimately in very different forms.

Overview

- Social security is something UK citizens take for granted, but despite the international establishment of a right to social security more than half a century ago, this right remains an abstract one for the majority of the world's population.

- A concern with minimum standards and extending statutory social security coverage has been the priority of the ILO and this model has influenced the development of diverse national systems throughout the 20th century.

- Debates about the appropriate balance between statutory, commercial and informal arrangements for social security, and about the goals of prevention versus alleviation of poverty are currently also of global significance.

- The most recent phase of the globalisation of social security has entailed the entry of the World Bank and the IMF into global social security debates. As 'carriers' of neo-liberal, conservative welfare ideologies, they have been less concerned with issues of redistribution and equity, and have instead advocated selectivist public social security systems operating within a predominantly marketised and informalised set of provisions.

- Ultimately, any reform proposal must be evaluated in the light of whether it makes the right to adequate income security a meaningful one for everyone rather than for just a privileged minority.

Questions for discussion

1. What are the issues involved in defining social security from a global perspective?

2. How important is the statutory benefits system in ensuring an adequate income for individuals and households? What other sources of income may also be available? What are the advantages and disadvantages of statutory and non-statutory sources?

3. To what extent is the global right to social security actually realised in practice?

4. How does the UK system compare with other countries in terms of expenditure, design, coverage and outcomes?

5. Consider the range of different ways in which 'globalisation' impacts, directly and indirectly, on social security.

6. Compare the approaches of the World Bank and the ILO to (i) the role of social security generally and (ii) the future of pensions specifically. What are the merits and demerits of each approach?

References

Abrahamson, P. (1999) 'The welfare modelling business', *Social Policy and Administration*, vol 33, no 4, pp 394-415.

Beattie, R. (2000) 'Social protection for all: but how?', *International Labour Review*, vol 139, no 2, pp 129-48.

Bretherton, C. (1996) 'Introduction: global politics in the 1990s', in C. Bretherton and G. Ponton (eds) *Global politics: An introduction*, Oxford: Blackwell, pp 1-19.

Burden, T. (1998) *Social policy and welfare: A clear guide*, London: Pluto.

Cousins, M. (1997) 'Ireland's place in the worlds of welfare', *Journal of European Social Policy*, vol 7, no 3, pp 223-35.

Cram, L. (1998) 'UK social policy in European Union context', in N. Ellison and C. Pierson (eds) *Developments in British social policy*, Basingstoke: Macmillan, pp 260-75.

Cruz-Saco, M.A. (2002) *Labour markets and social security coverage: The Latin American experience*, Extension of Social Security paper no 2, Geneva: Social Security Policy and Development Branch, ILO.

Cruz-Saco, M.A. and Mesa-Lago, C. (eds) (1998) *The reform of pension and health care systems in Latin America: Do options exist?*, Pittsburgh, PA: University of Pittsburgh.

de la Porte, C. and Deacon, B. (2002) 'Contracting companies and consultants: the EU and the social policy of accession countries', Globalisation Social Policy Programme Occasional Paper No 9/2002, Helsinki, Finland: STAKES.

Deacon, B. (2000) *Globalisation and social policy: The threat to equitable welfare*, Occasional Paper 5, Geneva: UNRISD.

Deacon, B. (2001) *The social dimension of regionalism: A constructive alternative to neo-liberal globalisation?*, Globalism and Social Policy Programme Occasional Paper no 8/2001, Helsinki, Finland: GASPP/STAKES.

Deacon, B. (2002) 'Globalization and the challenge for social security', in R. Sigg and C. Behrendt (eds) *Social security in the global village*, New Brunswick, NJ: Transaction, pp 17-30.

Deacon, B., with Hulse, M. and Stubbs, P. (1997) *Global social policy: International organisations and the future of welfare*, London: Sage Publications.

Ditch, J. (1999) 'Poverty and social security in the European Union', in J. Ditch (ed) *Introduction to social security: Policies, benefits and poverty*, London: Routledge, pp 227-38.

Dixon, J. (1999) *Social security in global perspective*, Westport, CT: Praeger.

Dixon, J. and Hyde, M. (eds) (2001) *The marketization of social security*, Westport, CT: Quorum Books.

Esping-Andersen, G. (1990) *The Three worlds of welfare capitalism*, Cambridge: Polity.

Euzéby, A. (2002) 'The financing of social protection in the context of economic globalization', in R. Sigg and C. Behrendt (eds) *Social security in the global village*, New Brunswick, NJ: Transaction, pp 31-46.

Ferrera, M. (1996) 'The "southern" model of welfare in Europe', *Journal of European Social Policy*, vol 6, no 1, pp 17-38.

Fultz, E. and Ruck, M. (2001) 'Pension reform in central and eastern Europe: emerging issues and patterns', *International Labour Review*, vol 140, no 1, pp 19-43.

Geyer, R. (2000) *Exploring European social policy*, Cambridge: Polity.

Gillion, C. (2000) *The development and reform of social security pensions: The approach of the International Labour Office*, Geneva: ILO, www.ilo.org/public/english/protection/socsec/publ/exec.htm.

Gillion, C., Turner, J., Bailey, J. and Latulippe, D. (eds) (2000) *Social security pensions: Development and reform*, Geneva: ILO.

Gough, I. (2000) 'Welfare regimes: on adapting the framework to developing countries', Global Social Policy Programme, Institute for International Policy Analysis, University of Bath.

Holzmann, R. and Jørgensen, S. (2000) *Social risk management: A new conceptual framework for social protection, and beyond*, Social Protection Discussion Paper no 6, Washington DC: World Bank.

Hoskins, D.D. (2001) 'The redesign of social security', in D.D. Hoskins, D. Dobbernack and C. Kuptsch (eds) *Social security at the dawn of the 21st century*, New Brunswick, NJ: Transaction, pp 3-14.

ILO (International Labour Organization) (1999) *Decent work*, Report of the Director-General of the ILO to the 87th Session of the International Labour Conference, Geneva: ILO.

ILO (2000) *World Labour Report 2000: Income security and social protection in a changing world*, Geneva: ILO.

ILO (2001) *Social security: A new consensus*, Geneva: ILO.

IMF (International Monetary Fund) (1996) *Aging populations and public pension schemes*, Washington, DC: IMF.

Kahler, M. (1992) 'External influence, conditionality, and the politics of adjustment', in S. Haggard and R.R. Kaufman (eds) *The politics of economic adjustment*, Princeton, NJ: Princeton University Press, pp 89-136.

Kay, S. (2000) 'Recent changes in Latin American welfare states: is there social dumping?', *Journal of European Social Policy*, vol 10, no 2, pp 185-203.

Kleinman, M. and Piachaud, D. (1993) 'European social policy: conceptions and choices', *Journal of European Social Policy*, vol 3, no 1, pp 1-19.

Lewis, J. (1992) 'Gender and development of welfare regimes', *Journal of European Social Policy*, vol 2, no 3, pp 159-73.

Lewis, J. (1997) 'Gender and welfare regimes: further thoughts', *Social Politics*, vol 4, no 2, pp 160-77.

Lustig, I. (ed) (2001) *Shielding the poor: Social protection in the developing world*, Washington, DC: Inter-American Development Bank.

Majone, G. (1993) 'The European Community between social policy and social regulation', *Journal of Common Market Studies*, vol 31, no 2, pp 154-70.

Manning, N. and Shaw, I. (1999) 'The transferability of welfare models: a comparison of the Scandinavian and state socialist models in relation to Finland and Estonia', in C. Jones Finer (ed) *Transnational social policy*, Oxford: Blackwell, pp 120-38.

Midgley, J. (1997) *Social welfare in global context*, London: Sage Publications.

Midgley, J. and Kaseke, E. (1996) 'Challenges to social security in developing countries', in J. Midgley and M.B. Tracy (eds) *Challenges to social security: An international exploration*, Westport, CT: Auburn House, pp 103-22.

Millar, J. and Warman, A. (1997) 'Family-state boundaries in Europe', in M. May, E. Brunsdon and G. Craig (eds) *Social Policy Review 9*, London Guildhall University/Social Policy Association, pp 276-89.

Minns, R. (2001) *The Cold War in welfare: Stock markets versus pensions*, London: Verso.

Ortiz, I. (ed) (2001) *Social protection in Asia and the Pacific*, Manila: Asian Development Bank.

Otting, A. (1994) 'The International Labour Organization and its standard-setting activity in the area of social security', *Journal of European Social Policy*, vol 4, no 1, pp 51-7.

Sainsbury, D. (ed) (1994) *Gendering welfare states*, London: Sage Publications.

Sigg, R. and Behrendt, C. (2002) 'Social security in the global village: mapping the issues', in R. Sigg and C. Behrendt (eds) *Social security in the global village*, New Brunswick, NJ: Transaction, pp 1-13.

Standing, G. (2002) *Beyond the new paternalism: Basic security as equality*, London: Verso.

Townsend, P. and Gordon, D. (2002) 'Conclusion: constructing an anti-poverty strategy', in P. Townsend and D. Gordon (eds) *World poverty: New policies to defeat an old enemy*, Bristol: The Policy Press, pp 413-31.

van Ginneken, W. (1999) *Social security for the excluded majority: Case studies of developing countries*, Geneva: ILO.

Walker, C. (2001) 'The forms of privatization of social security in Britain', in J. Dixon and M. Hyde (eds) *The marketization of social security*, Westport, CT: Quorum Books, pp 123-42.

World Bank (1994) *Averting the old age crisis: Policies to protect the old and promote growth*, New York, NY: Oxford University Press.

World Bank (1997) *Old age security: Pension reform in China*, Washington, DC: World Bank.

World Bank (2000) *World Development Report 1999/2000: Entering the 21st century*, Oxford: Oxford University Press.

World Bank (2001) *Social protection sector strategy: From safety net to springboard*, Washington, DC: World Bank.

Yeates, N. (2001) *Globalization and social policy*, London: Sage Publications.

Website resources

Council of Europe	www.coe.int
International Council on Social Welfare	www.icsw.org
International Labour Organization	www.ilo.org/public/english
International Monetary Fund	ww.imf.org/external
International Social Security Association	www.issa.int/engl.homef.htm
Organisation for Economic Co-operation and Development	www.oecd.org
Social Protection Advisory Service	www.worldbank.org/sp
World Bank	www.worldbank.org
World Trade Organization	www.wto.org

Part 2: Changing goals

five

From welfare to workfare
Alex Bryson[1]

Summary

- A new welfare-to-work regime is emerging in Britain, one that expects most working-age benefit claimants to be work-focused.

- The regime uses a range of welfare-to-work tools reflecting the complex underlying causes of unemployment. Many date back some years, but developments such as the introduction of a National Minimum Wage, the New Deals and tax credits mark a new departure.

- Tackling unemployment through welfare-to-work programmes can have positive and negative economic and social consequences for the claimant, their family, other jobseekers, the Exchequer and the economy. Which effects prevail is an empirical question.

- Many criteria can be used to judge the success or otherwise of welfare-to-work initiatives. Using the criterion of improving individual claimants' job prospects, early evidence indicates that some initiatives have proved successful, either by improving the incentives to take work, reducing employers' labour costs, or intervening to help jobseekers and claimants manage the risks they face when making a job match.

[1] I would like to thank the Regent Street Polytechnic Trust for financial support.

Introduction: welfare-to-work

"Work is the best form of welfare" (DWP, 2002a, p 2). It pays better than welfare. A string of psychological studies testify to the fact that *workers are psychologically better off than non-workers* (Warr, 1987), and it is the chief means by which families can break out of poverty (Bryson et al, 1997; Dickens and Ellwood, 2003: forthcoming). It follows that increasing the proportion of the adult population in work should be a central tenet of government policy. This is easier said than done. What do you actually do to get people into work – and make sure they stay there? Who do you prioritise for this assistance, and who should you leave out? What should we expect from recipients in return for assistance? Anyway, is it really the case that work is better for all? We know, for example, that there is some evidence suggesting that children's education can suffer if their mothers work (Ermisch and Francesconi, 2000); some people have caring roles in the home that limit their job opportunities (see Chapter Six in this volume); and, while some disabled people may benefit from working, others clearly do not (see Chapter Eight in this volume).

Answering questions like those posed above involves ethical, moral, political, and economic judgements which are central to policy making, and which have faced all governments, here and elsewhere, when devising programmes designed to help people off welfare and into work. This chapter explores some of the questions that need to be addressed to appraise the value of welfare-to-work policies:

- the problems welfare-to-work seeks to address;
- the policy options;
- Labour's policy approach
- the ways in which the success or otherwise of the measures can be judged;
- what we know about what works.

The problems that welfare-to-work policies seek to tackle

Welfare-to-work refers to those programmes and measures that are intended to move those reliant on the state for financial support (on welfare) into a position of relative financial independence through paid work (into work). They are directed towards two main groups of benefit claimants. First, those who are classified as *unemployed 'jobseekers'*, that is, people who are not employed but who are required to be available for, and seeking, employment as a condition of benefit receipt. This group has traditionally been the focus of these sorts of programmes. Second, they include the much wider group of *non-working claimants receiving other benefits* (Income Support, some Invalidity Benefits) who are not required to be available for, or seek work, as a condition of benefit receipt. These are a relatively new target group for these labour market focused programmes. As we shall see below, these two groups are treated in somewhat different ways in current policy, but overall the goal of welfare-to-work is to reduce not just unemployment, but the wider problem of worklessness.

Broadly speaking, three views of the causes of unemployment and worklessness have influenced the development of welfare-to-work policies in Britain: economic, behavioural and institutional views.

Economic theories identify deficiencies in the demand for labour, on the one hand, and the supply of labour available to employers, on the other, as key factors generating unemployment. More people may be desirous of jobs than there are jobs in the economy, resulting in unemployment. There may be an absolute dearth of jobs in the economy as a whole or differential rates of growth across regions that can produce a mismatch between jobs generated and locally available labour. Deficiencies in demand can be cyclical, arising during downturns in economic activity, as occurred in the early 1980s and the early 1990s. Even when the economy picks up, recession can leave its mark on individuals who become unemployed because employers prefer to recruit those with no unemployment history. This results in periods of extended unemployment for some, producing rising long-term unemployment, as experienced in the mid-1980s. There are also secular trends in economic development that have resulted in a gradual decline in employers' demand for unskilled labour and manual labour more generally. This, coupled with pressures from international competition to shed labour in efforts to raise productivity, has led to the disappearance of many jobs traditionally undertaken by those leaving unemployment.

Since the 1970s, it has become unfashionable for governments to respond to these problems by seeking to manage industrial development or to influence the demand for labour by injecting money into the economy to generate job-creating growth. Even if a government was minded to do this, it is by no means certain that employers would welcome demand-management by government, and governments' room for manoeuvre would be severely limited by the dictates of European monetary union and responses from investors and the stock market. Direct subsidies to declining industries are usually prohibited under EU rules.

Instead, governments have adopted a **supply-side** approach, developing means by which governments can assist individuals and employers overcome some of the shortfalls in the economy. These include:

* *subsidies* to reduce the cost of recruiting unemployed people – including direct wage subsidies, grants to meet (re)training costs, and reduced payroll taxes;

- *training* unemployed people in the skills employers require;
- *'make work' schemes* giving unemployed people work experience which they might not otherwise receive in the open market;
- efforts geared to *improving the number of job offers* received by unemployed people, including job search assistance and employer placements.

It is not only the dearth of jobs that economists point to as a cause of unemployment. A second issue is the nature of jobs created since the demise of the fabled 'male breadwinner job' that permitted families to prosper as single-earner households (see Chapter Two in this volume). The rise of the service economy and increased international competition in the trading sector has resulted in more flexible labour practices since the 1970s, with an increased proportion of jobs being low paid, often offering part-time or temporary contracts with limited career prospects and poor non-wage benefits. At the beginning of the 1980s, earnings-related supplements to benefits and benefits which rose with earnings meant these deficiencies in the labour market created real incentives problems since, for many, work did not pay. Consequently, unemployed people did not enter employment as quickly as they might otherwise have done. The problem of financial incentives has spawned a number of policies since then, including:

- *widening the gap* between out-of-work benefits and in-work income through more generous in-work wage supplementation and reductions in the real value of out-of-work benefits;
- *lowering hours thresholds* governing entitlement to wage supplements;
- *alterations in rules* governing how much workers can earn before their benefits are affected ('earnings disregard' rules) which help workers smooth their incomes during dips in earnings;
- *assistance with expenses* incurred on entering work, such as single payments for work-related expenditures, help with travel and childcare costs, and delays in the withdrawal of out-of-work benefits covering housing costs.

Moving from economic to **behavioural** theories regarding the roots of unemployment, these come in two varieties. First, there are those that hold that unemployment is a reflection on the character of unemployed people. It is not that jobs are unavailable: rather, unemployed people are unprepared to take those jobs that are available. The problem becomes the unemployed people themselves who hold unrealistic expectations about their job prospects. Their moral fibre is called into question. In the language of the 19th century they were regarded as 'feckless'. In the late 20th century they were described as an 'underclass' (Smith, 1992), dependent on the state for their survival. Mead (1986, 1997) contends that unemployed people are 'incompetent' in the sense that they wilfully refuse to do what is in their best interests, namely participate constructively in society by taking work[2].

The policy implications of this behavioural diagnosis of the unemployment problem are clear-cut and have informed the design and implementation of policy in respect of unemployment for centuries. To discourage dependency, one must ensure that any assistance offered to the unemployed individual must fall short of the benefits derived from work. In the language of the New Poor Law of 1832, the recipient's condition must be 'less eligible' than that of the poorest labourer. In addition, unemployed people should be required to perform certain activities in return for assistance. In its more liberal form, compulsion is confined to activities that are intended to improve the claimant's job prospects, such as attendance at work-focused interviews, job search, training, or supported employment. In its less liberal form, these activities encompass character forming activity which may not directly improve the claimant's job prospects but, by building the moral fibre of the individual, will help the individual into a position of independence. The *objective is to change the character and behaviour of unemployed people.*

The second type of behavioural theory points to the demotivating effect of longer-term unemployment on the individual arising from the debilitating effect it has on the individual's morale, material resources and social contacts. This *motivational problem* emanates directly from long-term unemployment, rather than the character of unemployed people. However, the policy prescriptions required to tackle the problem are similar to those stemming from other behavioural diagnoses, with the onus on the state coaxing individuals back to work using sticks as well as carrots if necessary.

The **institutional** view points to the role of welfare state institutions in creating and sustaining unemployment and worklessness. Some argue that the emphasis on entitlement, rather than conditionality, creates perverse incentives for benefit claimants who are "responsible for the loss of key civic values of work, honesty and thrift" (Field, 1997, p 61). Again, this leads to consideration of increased conditionality of benefit payment and improved work testing. More fundamentally, some maintain that the welfare system is beyond reform and should be abolished (Murray, 1984). Others blame the system for spending too much time on work testing and too little time on servicing employers: these analysts argue that the primary purpose of a job placement service should be to serve employers efficiently by focusing attention on offering suitable candidates to employers on terms which increase claimants' chances of job entry. Policies congruent with this analysis include *active engagement with*

---

[2] Unemployment may also be seen as part of a breakdown in social mores more generally, so that the causes of unemployment are akin to those causing crime and family breakdown, namely a general deterioration in societal mores.

employers – along similar lines to those adopted by private employment agencies – offering 'sweeteners' to employers in the form of wage subsidies, training grants, and tax or national insurance contribution breaks, and policies allowing employers to *'sample' claimants' suitability* without making a long-term commitment (for instance, through work trials). Seen in this way, work testing may be counterproductive, since it signals to the employer that candidates from the public job placement service are unwilling applicants.

These different definitions of the problem of unemployment and worklessness thus lead to different sorts of policy prescriptions. However, these are not necessarily *alternatives* for policy. Unemployment may arise from any or all of these causes in combination and so policies may seek to address a number of these different factors. There may also be a wider policy agenda including concerns about poverty and social exclusion, equal opportunities in employment, and concern for the most disadvantaged groups in the labour market. And there will often be tensions in policy, whereby the achievement of one aim can make it difficult to achieve another. For instance, benefit sanctions designed to ensure claimants attend job interviews may increase claimants' job search activity but will do nothing to improve their job prospects if employers believe that they are 'work-shy' and not attending of their own volition. Or, more broadly, policies may succeed in getting individuals into work but not in ensuring that they have adequate incomes to keep themselves and their families out of poverty.

Labour and welfare-to-work policies

On coming to power in 1997, Prime Minister Tony Blair proclaimed: "This will be the welfare-to-work-government" (Blair, 1997) and **Box 5.1** summarises the key measures that have been introduced. Labour's analysis of the problem linked *economic, behavioural and institutional factors*. For example, the first welfare reform Green Paper (DSS, 1998) argued that the existing system of support was 'too passive', offering cash payments and expecting little in return. Thus behavioural outcomes (unemployed people lacking the motivation to seek work) were linked to institutional structures (the system failing to create the conditions for active engagement with the labour market).

The government wanted to devise a system that was more 'active', offering claimants 'a hand up, not a hand out' (Harman, 1997). In practice, this meant making benefit payments more conditional on undertaking activities geared to labour market (re-)entry. In recent times, this approach can be traced back to 1986 when periodic work-focused interviews were introduced for the longer-term unemployed. These interviews, known as **Restart** interviews, were compulsory in the sense that individuals' benefits could be reduced or withdrawn if they continually refused to attend without good cause. Attendance at work-focused training courses such as **Employment Training** also became

Box 5.1: Welfare-to-work in Britain: key measures since 1997

Year	Development
1997	• New Deal for Lone Parents introduced as a voluntary programme offering advice on jobs, benefits, training, and childcare through personal advisers. Target group is lone parents with children of school age
1998	• Labour's Welfare Reform Green Paper offered "a new welfare contract between the citizen and the state with rights matched by responsibilities. We will rebuild the welfare state around the work ethic: work for those who can; security for those who cannot.... It is the responsibility of government to provide positive help; it is the responsibility of the claimant to take it up"
	• New Deal for Young People introduced as a compulsory programme for those aged under 25 after six months unemployed – flagship for New Deal programmes: initial intensive job search assistance followed by one of four options (subsidised employment, Environment Task Force, work in voluntary sector, or full-time education/training)
	• New Deal for Long-term Unemployed introduced – compulsory for those aged 25 plus and unemployed for 12 or 18 or 24 months (depending on the area)
	• New Deal for Disabled People introduced – voluntary programme offering advice and information
	• Prototype Employment Zones set up providing more intensive support for the most disadvantaged jobseekers in high unemployment areas
	• Work-Based Training for Young People available to 16- to 18-year-olds not in full-time education or a job
	• National Childcare Strategy aims to provide quality and affordable care for all children aged 0-14
1999	• Introduction of the statutory National Minimum Wage
	• Replacement of Family Credit and Disability Working Allowance by Working Families Tax Credit and Disabled Person's Tax Credit respectively: more generous and usually paid direct from employer
	• New Deal for Partners of the Unemployed extends job search assistance and training opportunities to partners of unemployed people, on a voluntary basis
	• New Deal 50 Plus, on a voluntary basis, offers information and advice, and in-work tax credits and training grants to those aged 50+ on benefits
	• Work-Based Learning for Adults provides vocational and pre-vocational training to adults after six months' unemployment
2000	• 1999 Welfare Reform and Pensions Act comes into force requiring attendance at work-focused interviews; full family benefit sanction
	• The ONE pilot integrates benefit claiming and institutes work-focused case-loading for all claimants of working age
	• Target set that 70% of lone parents should be in employment by end of the decade

Box 5.1 continued

2001	•	Introduction of joint claims for childless couples requiring both satisfy benefit receipt conditions
	•	Learning and Skills Councils replace Training and Enterprise Councils as bodies responsible for post-16 training
2002	•	Jobcentre Plus created: "will provide a single point of delivery for jobs, benefits advice and support and help, using a personal adviser system" (DWP, 2002b)
	•	Compulsory work-focused interviews required for new claimants to Income Support
	•	New Deal 25+ replaces the New Deal for Long-Term Unemployed, conforming more to the New Deal for Young People model
	•	Extension of joint claims to childless couples aged under 45
2003	•	Child Tax Credit and Working Tax Credit introduced

Note: for more comprehensive information see House of Commons (2000).

a condition of entitlement. Labour chose to emphasise these elements of the Conservative legacy, with organisations such as the Organisation for Economic Co-operation and Development (OECD) also identifying active labour market policies as a key ingredient for non-inflationary economic growth (OECD, 1994).

Under compulsory **New Deal** programmes, greater powers of sanction (including the 'full family sanction' in which all benefit can be reduced) were introduced. Claimants such as lone parents, disabled people and partners of unemployed people are now required to attend work-focused interviews and can also be sanctioned for non-attendance at these.

There has also been an increase in the intensity with which review interviews are used: continual review is the hallmark of case-loading, a method for dealing with claimants which seeks to create a personal relationship between the state official (often referred to as a *personal adviser*) and the claimant (the *client*).

Underpinning this approach was a shift in the way government perceived the relationship between the state and the claimant. Labour described this as a *change in the contract between the state and the individual*: a new settlement would involve new rights for the claimant in return for an acceptance of new responsibilities (DSS, 1998; King, 1999). Those rights included the right to expect government to guarantee the availability of good quality training places for those required to take these up. In effect, the government was underwriting a guarantee to be the 'employer of last resort' for some groups of claimants, which represents a break with previous Conservative policy. Claimants could also expect access to good quality job search advice and training provision offered directly by the state, or by private providers under contract to the state.

The government also sought to guarantee a minimum rate of pay in the marketplace through the statutory **National Minimum Wage** (NMW). The minimum wage is the only far-reaching welfare-to-work policy Labour has adopted which tackles deficiencies in labour demand, and is motivated by a belief in *making work pay* because benefit claimants would only take work if there was sufficient financial incentive to do so. This consideration also explains the enhanced system of wage supplementation introduced with tax credits. Tax credits sought to strengthen financial incentives to enter work by increasing the generosity of payments, offering substantial assistance for those with childcare costs, reducing the rate at which the credit was removed with higher earnings, and paying the credit direct through the employer to emphasise the link with working.

The **New Deal for Young People**, the government's flagship welfare-to-work programme, exemplifies the new approach. It targets young people in the belief that early intervention in individuals' careers can enhance long-term job prospects by eliminating the early scarring effects of long-term unemployment. After an initial intensive period of job search and assistance with overcoming immediate barriers to employment, it offers some choice to claimants in the form of four options (subsidised employment, environmental work, voluntary work, and full-time education or training) guaranteeing minimum quality standards. There is 'no fifth option' (Brown, 2000) of non-participation. Those who do not leave the programme after their option return to the intensive job search and assistance element of the programme and may enter new options. The programme effectively abolishes long-term unemployment for young claimants outside the programme by requiring continued participation until leaving benefit.

The different measures and provisions used to achieve the policy goal of helping people move from welfare to work are very diverse and include a wide range of different types of support targeted on different groups. Box 5.2 identifies nine areas of welfare-to-work provision, each tackling the perceived causes of unemployment, but from different angles. All these policies coexist, reflecting government recognition of the complex causes of unemployment. Some (the NMW, tax credits, work-focused interviews for lone parents and sick and disabled people) mark new departures, while others build on past experience[3].

Judging the success of welfare-to-work policies

By what criteria should the success of welfare-to-work policies be judged? This is a more complex matter than it appears at first sight since, although these policies appear to have a relatively narrow focus – getting claimants into

---

[3] They also reflect *lesson learning* from other countries (Dolowitz, 1998; King, 1999; Dolowitz and Marsh, 2000).

Box 5.2: UK welfare-to-work measures and programmes

Job search assistance
New Deals; Jobplan Workshops; Jobfinder Plus; Programme centres (previously Jobcentres); Job interview guarantee scheme; Jobfinder Grant; Travel to Interview scheme

Training provision
New Deals; Work-Based Training for Young People; Advanced and Foundation Modern Apprenticeships; Work-Based Learning for Adults; Career Development Loans; In-work Training Grants

Job sampling
New Deal employer option; New Deal voluntary sector option; Work trials

'Make work' schemes
Environment Task Force under New Deal for Young People; New Deal for Long-Term Unemployed; StepUp

Review/case-loading
ONE pilots; New Deals

Employer assistance
Work Trials; Wage and training subsidies under New Deals for Young People and Long-Term Unemployed

'Making Work Pay'
Working Families Tax Credit; Disabled Person's Tax Credit; Childcare payments; Statutory National Minimum Wage; In-Work Training Grant for Lone Parents; Earnings disregard

Community-based initiatives
Employment Zones; New Deal for Communities; Action Teams for Jobs

Assistance with caring responsibilities
National Childcare Strategy; in-work credits covering childcare costs; improved maternity rights, introduction of paid parental leave

work – in reality they perform a number of functions for government, claimants and the economy. These are grouped under six headings below.

The most obvious criterion by which welfare-to-work programmes might be judged is **economic outcomes for individual participants**. These outcomes can be measured in terms of:

- the number of claimants leaving benefit, or the speed with which they leave benefit;
- the number of claimants moving into work (as opposed to simply leaving for economic inactivity);

- the time claimants spend in work on leaving benefit;
- the extent to which claimants are better off, either financially or in terms of skills, qualifications, or job readiness.

On entering government, Labour signalled its concern that welfare-to-work programmes ought to be judged by their ability to get claimants into work, rather than simply moving them off benefit. Policy initiatives can only reduce benefit rolls if they increase the rate at which claimants leave benefit without increasing the rate of inflow to benefit. This is why Labour was concerned about *churning*, whereby those leaving benefits reclaim shortly afterwards. This has led to a concern about the sustainability of employment, which is why attention has recently focused on *efforts to keep ex-claimants in work*, thus reducing the rate of inflow to benefit claiming. There are other ways to reduce the number of new claims, such as *diversion tactics* – common in the US – that make it harder for people to make a claim for benefit, and narrowing eligibility for benefits, but it is questionable whether these approaches would improve the economic well-being of the individuals concerned.

A second criterion by which welfare-to-work programmes may be judged is their effect on **economic outcomes for households**. This raises the issue of income distribution within and across households. Welfare-to-work policies may tackle widening income inequality by redistributing income from 'job rich' to 'job poor' households – for example, by using the tax system to provide large financial incentives for lone parents to enter work. Such policies can also redistribute jobs from dual-earner to no-earner households by tackling the work disincentives facing unemployed couples and single parents. Measures of success could include reducing the income gap between rich and poor families and halting the growth in no-earner households. Policies that redistribute income across individuals within the home can also be effective welfare-to-work tools. For instance, Child Benefit, which is typically paid to the mother and spent on the needs of children, can encourage job entry because it is retained on entering work, providing some income guarantee during the period in which benefits stop and the first pay packet has yet to arrive. Since it does not count as 'income' for the purposes of estimating tax credit entitlements, it can also hold people in work by 'making work pay' without blunting financial incentives. (This is also the case with maintenance payments that, since 2001, have been discounted in estimating tax credit entitlements.) By focusing resources on both partners in an unemployed couple, the New Deal for Partners and the joint claims initiative has the potential to raise economic activity rates among those who, traditionally, did not claim.

A third criterion is **economic outcomes for the economy**. The ultimate goal of welfare-to-work policies is to increase the proportion of the working-age population in work. They can do this by one of two means. First, they can increase the effective supply of labour available to employers. They can do this by increasing the number of potential workers available to employers by 'reconnecting' economically inactive people to the labour market through encouragement to search for and accept available jobs. They can also do it by improving the quality of available labour, ensuring that jobseekers have the requisite skills to take available jobs. Second, they can increase the rate at which the economy generates jobs without generating inflation (Layard et al, 1991). This will occur if policies reduce the costs of labour – by lowering jobseekers' wage expectations, offering wage subsidies to employers, or by improving the efficiency with which potential workers are matched to jobs. The cost of labour is also reduced by policies that make workers more productive, thus increasing workers' output for a given wage. Policies that help claimants to become 'better' workers are those that improve what economists term 'human capital' and include training and work habituation programmes. All of this is to no avail if participants in welfare-to-work policies are assisted to the detriment of others competing for the same jobs. If this occurs, welfare-to-work substitutes one set of workers for another, simply shifting the burden of unemployment from participants to non-participants. This is largely avoided where policies target the most disadvantaged in the labour market since these people can be helped with minimal effects on the rest of the labour market.

A fourth criterion is **gains for the Exchequer** from improved tax revenues and lower benefit spending. A programme which gets claimants into jobs but at a high cost per claimant may still be cost-effective if benefit savings are made and taxes generated through sustained employment. Even if unit costs are low a programme offers poor value-for-money if it simply places claimants in work who would have entered work without the programme (a problem known as *deadweight*).

A fifth criterion used to judge the success of welfare-to-work policies is **programme popularity**. Popularity among claimants can be measured in terms of the proportion of eligible claimants taking up a programme, or participant satisfaction with a policy. Of course, policies may prove effective according to the other criteria identified above even if claimant satisfaction with them is low, but it is hard to imagine a successful policy that has very low take-up among those it is targeted at. Popularity with the electorate is also important since, if the electorate does not like a government's welfare-to-work policies it may vote them out at the next election, regardless of how well the policies are operating for claimants.

Finally, policies may be regarded as successful where they encourage claimants to take a more positive attitude to work and making a contribution to society. This might be termed **the moral or ethical dimension**. Such changes may be visible in terms of changing behaviour, or measured by attitude surveys. This criterion is valid if policy makers are content to get people 'closer to work' by increasing their employability, even if they do not actually take work.

There have been efforts to measure such effects (Bryson et al, 2000) but it is notable that studies often find that unemployed people have higher employment commitment than those in work (Jackson, 1994).

What works?

When do we know that a programme or policy change has been successful? It is not enough simply to show that a policy has helped claimants into work: to identify the causal impact of the policy, we need to know what would have happened to them in the absence of the policy. This involves isolating the effect of the policy from other factors which influence claimants' work prospects, such as the claimant's attributes (character, skills, motivation), family and local conditions, the state of the labour market, and the effects of other policies (Purdon et al, 2001, and Purdon, 2002 describe these problems and some of the solutions). We also need to know what the impact of the policy is on others in the labour market to establish whether the policy has had a net economic benefit. This means trying to understand what the labour market would have looked like in the absence of the programme or policy. Even when evaluations are carefully conducted, however, caution must be used when drawing policy inferences from results, not least because conditions prevailing at the time of the study may subsequently shift in ways that influence the effectiveness of a policy. So, for example, although evidence on the economic effects of welfare-to-work programmes in the US is broadly encouraging, almost without exception they have been conducted against a backdrop of sustained economic growth. It is difficult to deduce from these studies what the impact of these policies might be in a period of economic downturn.

Careful evaluation of policy initiatives is a relatively new phenomenon (King, 1995; Walker, 2000). Although evaluation methods are advancing rapidly they remain controversial, and so few results can be regarded as definitive. Furthermore, evaluations have to date focused almost exclusively on the effectiveness of policies in getting claimants off benefits and into employment. This has begun to change with evaluations of the wider labour market impacts of the New Deal for Young People (White and Riley, 2002), and the evaluation of community-level interventions. The section below is confined to British evidence regarding the success of some policies currently in vogue in getting claimants off benefits and into work[4].

Regular review interviews

The essence of case-loading is the periodic work-focused interview, first introduced under **Restart** in 1986. Restart increased the rate at which

---

[4] For other reviews of the literature see Gardiner (1997) and Blundell (2001a).

unemployed claimants left benefit and lowered the time they spent unemployed on leaving benefit (White and Lakey, 1992). Claimants tended to leave benefit around the time they had the interview or received the letter requesting attendance, a finding analysts suggest is consistent with Restart scaring people into signing off (Dolton and O'Neill, 1996). However, Restart also increased the rate at which claimants entered jobs, suggesting that Restart increased the rate at which claimants received job offers, "either through initiation of contact with employers or through improvements in the search behaviour of the unemployed" (Dolton and O'Neill, 1995). Restart therefore indicates that regular review interviews may have benefited claimants through a 'threat' effect and by improving job search behaviour.

Compulsion

There were indications from the Restart evaluation that making benefit receipt conditional on active programme participation could assist in speeding claimants' exit from unemployment. However, the value of compulsion depends on the nature of the intervention, the target group, labour market conditions, and the way in which the programme is delivered. For instance, recent evidence on the effects of regular review interviews suggests the positive effects are most apparent when the interviews are a condition of benefit receipt. Voluntary reviews under ONE (Green et al, 2001) had little impact, but, since ONE interviews became a condition of benefit receipt, the programme has had a small effect in increasing the rate at which lone parents leave benefit (Kirby and Riley, 2001). However, there was no effect on Jobseeker's Allowance claimants or sick or disabled people. Furthermore, the effect for lone parents is confined to delivery through Jobcentres, and is not apparent where ONE is delivered through call centres and the private sector.

There is other evidence that 'threat' effects can encourage claimants to sign off. Long-term unemployed claimants participating in the **Project Work** programme (which informed the design of the New Deal for the Long-Term Unemployed) signed off benefits at a much faster rate than a comparator group of non-participants as they approached a 'make work' scheme after an intensive period of job search. However, they were no more likely to move into jobs than non-participants (Bryson et al, 1998). A threat effect was also discernible in the evaluation of **Joint Claims**, with some couples in the stock of claimants ending their Jobseeker's Allowance spells to avoid converting to a Joint Claim which would have extended job search and availability requirements to both in the claimant couple. However, there was no effect on job entry (Bonjour et al, 2002).

Compulsion is counterproductive when employers believe claimants have been compelled to make job applications or attend interviews, and when it results in employers being flooded by unsuitable candidates simply wishing to satisfy benefit eligibility requirements (Bryson and Jacobs, 1992). It proves ineffectual when administrators view requirements as unfair or unethical: in these cases, administrators refuse to enforce them, so they become a 'dead letter' (that is, something that has no effect in practice) (Bryson and Jacobs, 1992).

Job search assistance

Up until the mid-1990s, efforts to improve claimants' job search did little to improve their job chances because, even if claimants increased the intensity with which they sought work, or became more flexible about the jobs they were prepared to take, changes in job search behaviour did little to increase the rate at which they received job offers (Bryson and White, 1996). Although Dolton and O'Neill (1995, 1996) thought that the positive effects of Restart may have been attributable to changes in job search behaviour, the survey evidence does not support this contention (White and Lakey, 1992). Jobclubs had a positive impact on women's job chances, but they had no effect on men's, despite a negative effect on their wages once they entered work (White et al, 1997). However, evidence from the New Deals suggests that job search assistance during the first four months of New Deal for Young People does benefit young participants (see below for details).

Bringing claimants into closer contact with employers

One of the reasons that employers give for not offering jobs to claimants is concerns about the suitability of claimants for their particular vacancies (Bryson and Jacobs, 1992). Policies which bring claimants into close proximity with the employer help overcome that uncertainty and have proved successful in helping claimants into work. **Work trials**, which allow employers to 'sample' claimants before taking them on, has the largest effect of any programme to date (White et al, 1997). Employers' concerns about taking on unemployed people are also allayed by advisers' efforts to screen claimants to ensure that they find suitable matches for the employer's vacancy. This tailored service for the employer, embodied in the **Job Interview Guarantee** programme, has raised, in particular, female participants' job chances although not men's (White et al, 1997).

Proximity to an employer is also the hallmark of more successful training and work experience programmes. For example, **Training for Work**, a large training programme targeted at long-term unemployed adults and the forerunner to Work-Based Learning for Adults, had a positive effect on participants' job chances. However, this effect was largest for those who had employer placements, as opposed to off-the-job training or project placements (Payne, 2000). Similar evidence emerges from the evaluation of its predecessors

Employment Training and **Employment Action** (Payne et al, 1996). In addition, these evaluations showed that training leading to a qualification was better at helping claimants off benefit than training that did not lead to a qualification.

The level and duration of benefit payments

Benefit payment can have ambiguous effects on claimants' likelihood of work: they can reduce the incentives to take a job, but can also facilitate job search. The evidence suggests that, at the benefit levels paid in Britain, out-of-work benefit payments generally have no detrimental effect on claimants' incentives to enter work, although they do reduce the rate at which young people enter work (Narendranathan et al, 1985; Arulampalam and Stewart, 1995). Nor do they influence job search activity (Schmitt and Wadsworth, 1993a). Indeed, some have expressed concern that benefit levels may have a detrimental impact on claimants' job chances by "plunging families into poverty the instant they become unemployed" (Nickell, 1999, p 28). This research may have made it easier for the government to boost child-related out-of-work benefits in the belief that they would have little detrimental impact on work incentives. Even so, the focus remains firmly on making work pay (see below).

In countries such as the US, time limits to benefit receipt and 'step' reductions in benefits paid with the lengthening of unemployment have been used with some success to increase the rate at which claimants leave benefit, although it is not always clear whether those claimants enter sustainable employment (Evans, 2001). As yet, no British government has sought to time-limit means-tested assistance. Perhaps one reason for this reticence is the evidence showing how valuable being 'in the system' can be in terms of ensuring that claimants retain a positive attachment to the labour market; this is indicated by a reduced likelihood of becoming economically inactive compared with 'like' non-claimant counterparts (Wadsworth, 1992). Consistent with this is the finding that the reduction in the proportion of unemployed people qualifying for Unemployment Benefit as a result of changes to the benefit system in the 1980s reduced the effective supply of labour in the economy, reducing aggregate job search (Schmitt and Wadsworth, 1993b).

The way that out-of-work benefits are paid and the conditions attached to receipt does appear to matter. An international comparative study (Dex et al, 1995) concluded that the low work rates among women married to unemployed men is due to the disincentives for those women to enter or remain in work once their partners become unemployed. This may be due to the limits placed on an individual's ability to earn while in receipt of means-tested benefits, the difficulties faced by low-paid workers in commanding a wage which takes them well above benefit levels, and the uncertainties associated with managing the transitions between benefit receipt and earnings

(McLaughlin, 1991, 1994). Although others argue that the relationship between partners' labour market transitions is due to other factors (Irwin and Morris, 1993; Pudney and Thomas, 1993), the research has resulted in new policy initiatives such as Joint Claims and the New Deal for Partners.

Claimants often prefer the certainty of (albeit low) income from Unemployment Benefit compared with the uncertainty of making the transition into a job which may be short term and pay little (McLaughlin, 1991). In response to this research efforts have been made to facilitate claimants' transition into work by extending the period in which Housing Benefit payments remains unaffected, and reintroducing some assistance to meet work-related costs, notably costs of childcare.

Making work pay

Low pay is invariably cited as the main reason for claimants refusing job offers, so 'making work pay' policies would seem to be important in easing claimants' entry to work. Certainly, the expansion of wage supplementation policies since the early 1990s has coincided with a modest increase in lone parents' likelihood of working (Blundell, 2001a). **Family Credit** made recipients financially much better off in work than they would have been on out-of-work benefits (Marsh and McKay, 1993), but its incentive effect was blunted somewhat by uncertainty surrounding eligibility for it and its interaction with other income sources (Kempson et al, 1994). However, it encouraged lone parents to take part-time work, matching their earnings from work with Family Credit income (Marsh and McKay, 1993). And early evidence on the operation of the Working Families Tax Credit (WFTC) confirms a positive incentive effect for lone parents (Blundell, 2001a).

In-work benefits can also increase employment levels by helping workers stay in work during a dip in earnings, thus extending the time that people stay in work and reducing the likelihood of them re-entering unemployment in the future (Bryson and Marsh, 1996). However, there are two negative aspects to wage supplementation through in-work benefits or tax credits. First, *wage supplementation can limit earnings progression in the medium term*, trapping employees in a long-term reliance on state assistance while in work (Bryson et al, 1998): withdrawing the wage supplement as earnings rise can create disincentives to train, seek promotion or work longer hours. Second, the evaluations of both Family Credit (Marsh and McKay, 1993) and WFTC (Blundell, 2001a) show that *wage supplements are a disincentive to two-earner status among couples*, and discourage work by the non-recipient.

The statutory **National Minimum Wage** (NMW) also helps make work pay. There have been no adverse employment effects on those whose wages would have needed to be raised to comply with the minimum (Stewart, 2002), and the availability of higher wages has drawn previously economically inactive people into the labour market.

The New Deals

The New Deals mark something of a departure from previous welfare-to-work programmes. First, they are multifaceted, offering different things to participants as they move through the programme. Second, claimants have some – albeit constrained – *choice* as to which option to take up if they are still out of work after initial intensive jobsearch assistance. Third, benefit receipt is conditional on *participation* for those claimants within the eligible group. So, has the approach been successful in getting claimants into work? Evaluations of most of the New Deals are yet to be published, so we focus on the New Deals for Young People and the Long-term Unemployed[5]. The answer appears to be 'yes' as far as the New Deal for Young People is concerned. The programme appears to have increased the rate at which young men leave unemployment for jobs (Blundell, 2001a). Some of this effect is due to intensive job search assistance at the beginning of the programme (Blundell, 2001a; Blundell et al, 2001). It is not obvious why this has worked when previous job search programmes have not. One possibility is that case-loading clients results in better quality advice and increased trust between adviser and claimant. Another is the prospect of the Options phase of the programme looming after four months on the programme: if claimants do not like the look of any of the options, this may increase their desire to leave the programme. The remainder of the effect is accounted for by the job subsidy element of the programme (Blundell, 2001a; Dorsett, 2001; Bonjour et al, 2001)[6]. There are some parts of the programme which appear to have worked less well, notably the full-time education and training option. This was least effective in getting claimants into work, but it was effective in ensuring people continued in education or training on leaving the programme.

Evidence on the impact of the New Deal for the Long-Term Unemployed is more mixed, perhaps because the target group is more difficult to place in jobs. However, the subsidised employment component has improved participants' job entry rates (Winterbotham et al, 2001).

---

[5] The quantitative evaluation of the New Deal for Lone Parents will be available in Summer 2003. For a synthesis of the evaluation material to date see Evans et al (2002) and Millar (2002).

[6] Bell et al (1999) review the impact of wage subsidy schemes in Britain and elsewhere and suggest that the New Deal wage subsidy may enhance young people's employability by improving their productivity.

There are policies and then there's implementation

It is not simply *what* welfare-to-work policies are used, but *how they are implemented*, which determines how successful they are. **Box 5.3** identifies some of the implementation issues influencing success and failure. Studies

---

Box 5.3: Choices to be made in implementing welfare-to-work policies

Who gets what?
- Claimants versus non-claimants
- Sub-groups within the claimant population (unemployed, lone parents, sick and disabled)

When to intervene?
- Short-term versus long-term unemployed
- Younger versus older workers
- Conducive economic conditions
- Pilot before national roll-out versus pilot to test whether viable at all

Where to intervene?
- National versus local schemes
- Rural versus urban

Who will deliver the programme?
- Agency collaboration
- Who will lead?
- Public versus private provision
- Local discretion versus central control
- Getting employers on-side

Programme design
- Carrot versus stick (compulsion for eligible group or selective use of sanctions)
- Sequencing of elements in the programme
- Components to be delivered (job search, training, 'make work' schemes, subsidies)

Financing of the policy
- How to pay (windfall tax, spending review, matching funds from elsewhere)
- Incentives to succeed (output-related funding)

Staffing
- Case-loading
- Training
- Discretion
- Support (information systems, management)
- Benefit payment, job placement or both?
- Budget holders or administrators?

---

show wide variation in the success of a single policy across areas (for example, Evans et al, 2002), and there is clear evidence in the US that the quality of provision and the nature of delivery are critical (Evans, 2001).

Overview

Many of the problems identified by Labour on entering government in 1997 persist today – work rates among lone parents and women with unemployed partners remain low (Blundell, 2001b), the quality of labour available to employers is not sufficient to meet the demands of available jobs, and low pay is endemic in low-skilled occupations. Other government policies can help, not least the compulsory education system and higher education. Nevertheless, a lot is riding on the success of welfare-to-work policies. The New Deals are having a positive, if small, effect on groups such as young people and tax credits have led to a substantial transfer of income to poorer working families. However, some big policy departures have yet to be fully evaluated, while the fact that the programmes are relatively recently established means that it is difficult to appraise what the longer-term effects of these policies might be. The real test will come when the economy faces a downturn.

Questions for discussion

1. Is work testing unemployed people compatible with the creation of a job placement service which satisfies the needs of employers?

2. Is compulsion to work justified?

3. How can welfare-to-work policies 'work'?

4. What evidence is there that welfare-to-work policies actually work/don't work?

References

Arulampalam, W. and Stewart, M.B. (1995) 'The determinants of individual unemployment durations in an era of high unemployment', *The Economic Journal*, vol 105, pp 321-32.

Bell, B., Blundell, R. and Van Reenen, J. (1999) *Getting the unemployed back to work: The role of targeted wage subsidies*, Working Paper W99/12, London: Institute for Fiscal Studies.

Blair, T. (1997) 'The will to win', Speech as Prime Minister, Aylesbury Estate, Southwark, 2 June.

Blundell, R. (2001a) 'Welfare-to-work: which policies work and Why?', Keynes Lecture in Economics, London: University College London and Institute for Fiscal Studies.

Blundell, R. (2001b) 'Welfare reform for low income workers', Hicks Lecture 1999, *Oxford Economic Papers*, vol 53, pp 18-214.

Blundell, R., Costa Dias, M., Meghir, C. and Van Reenen, J. (2001) *Evaluating the employment impact of a mandatory job search assistance program*, Working Paper 01/20, London: Institute for Fiscal Studies.

Bonjour, D., Dorsett, R., Knight, G. and Lissenburgh, S. (2002) *Joint Claims for JSA – Quantitative evaluation of labour market effects*, Report to the Working Age Evaluation Division of the DWP, London: DWP.

Bonjour, D., Dorsett, R., Knight, G., Lissenburgh, S., Mukherjee, A., Payne, J., Range, M., Urwin, P. and White, M. (2001) *New Deal for Young People: National survey of participants: stage 2*, Employment Service Report ESR67, London: DWP.

Brown, G. (2000) 'Chancellor of the Exchequer's Budget Statement', 21 March.

Bryson, A. (1998) 'Lone mothers' earnings', in R. Ford and J. Millar (eds) *Private lives, public responses: Lone parenthood and future policy in the UK*, London: Policy Studies Institute, pp 167-92.

Bryson, A. and Jacobs, J. (1992) *Policing the workshy: Benefit control, labour markets and the unemployed*, Aldershot: Avebury.

Bryson, A. and Marsh, A. (1996) *Leaving Family Credit*, DSS Research Report No 48, London: The Stationery Office.

Bryson, A. and White, M. (1996) *Benefits and effective job search*, Mimeo, London: Policy Studies Institute.

Bryson, A., Ford, R. and White, M. (1997) *Making work pay: Lone mothers' employment and wellbeing*, York: Joseph Rowntree Foundation.

Bryson, A., Knight, G. and White, M. (2000) *New Deal for Young People: National survey of participants: stage 1*, Employment Service Research and Development Report ESR44, Sheffield: Employment Service.

Bryson, A., Lissenburgh, S. and Payne, J. (1998) 'The First Project Work Pilots: a quantitative evaluation', Report to the Employment Service and DfEE, Report ESR10.

Dex, S., Gustafsson, S., Smith, N. and Callan, T. (1995) 'Cross-national comparisons of the labour force participation of women married to unemployed men', *Oxford Economic Papers*, vol 47, pp 611-35.

Dickens, R. and Ellwood, D.T. (2003: forthcoming) 'Whither poverty in Britain and the US? The determinants of changing poverty and whether work will work', in R. Blundell, D. Card and R. Freeman (eds) *Seeking a premier league economy*, Chicago, IL: University of Chicago Press, www.nber.org/books/tcf/

Dolowitz, D. (1998) *Learning from America: Policy transfer and the development of the British workfare state*, Brighton: Sussex Academic Press.

Dolowitz, D. and Marsh, D. (2000) 'Learning from abroad: the role of policy transfer in contemporary policy making', *Governance: An International Journal of Policy and Administration*, vol 13, no 1, pp 5-32.

Dolton, P. and O'Neill, D. (1995) 'The impact of Restart on reservation wages and long-term unemployment', *Oxford Bulletin of Economics and Statistics*, vol 57, no 4, pp 451-70.

Dolton, P. and O'Neill, D. (1996) 'Unemployment duration and the Restart effect: some experimental evidence', *The Economic Journal*, vol 106, pp 387-400.

Dorsett, R. (2001) *The New Deal for Young People: Relative effectiveness of options in reducing male unemployment*, PSI Discussion Paper No 7, London: Policy Studies Institute.

DSS (Department of Social Security) (1998) *New ambitions for our country: A new contract for welfare*, Cm 3805, London: The Stationery Office.

DWP (Department for Work and Pensions) (2002a) 'Department for Work and Pensions Service Agreement', www.dwp.gov.uk/publications/dss/2001/dwp-psa/psa.pdf

DWP (2002b) 'Budget help for lone parents', Press release EMP1704-BLP, 17 April, London: DWP press office.

Ermisch, J. and Francesconi, M. (2000) *The effect of parents' employment on children's education*, ISER Working Paper, 2000-31, www.iser.ac.uk/pubs/workpaps/pdf/w000-31.pdf

Evans, M. (2001) *Welfare to work and the organisation of opportunity: Lessons from abroad*, CASE Report 15, London: Centre for Analysis of Social Exclusion, London School of Economics and Political Science.

Evans, M., McKnight, A. and Namazie, C. (2002) *The New Deal for Lone Parents: First synthesis report of the national evaluation*, DWP Report No 116, www.dwp.gov.uk/waed/esr116rep.pdf

Field, F. (1997) 'Re-inventing welfare: a response to Lawrence Mead', in L. Mead (ed) *From welfare to work: Lessons from America*, London: Institute of Economic Affairs.

Gardiner, K. (1997) *Bridges from benefit to work: A review*, York: Joseph Rowntree Foundation.

Green, H., Connolly, H., Marsh, A. and Bryson, A. (2001) *The medium-term effects of voluntary participation in ONE*, DWP Research Report No 149, London: DWP.

Harman, H. (1997) 'New Deal for Lone Parents is welfare reform in action', DSS press release, 23 October.

House of Commons (2000) *Employment and training programmes for the unemployed*, House of Commons Research Paper 00/81, www.parliament.uk/commons/lib/research

Irwin, S. and Morris, L. (1993) 'Social security or economic insecurity? The concentration of unemployment (and research) within households', *Journal of Social Policy*, vol 22, no 3, pp 349-72.

Jackson, P.R. (1994) 'Influences on commitment to employment and commitment to work', in A. Bryson and S. McKay (eds) *Is it worth working?*, London: Policy Studies Institute, pp 110-21.

Kempson, E., Bryson, A. and Rowlingson, R. (1994) *Hard times: How poor families make ends meet*, London: Policy Studies Institute.

King, D. (1995) *Actively seeking work? The politics of unemployment and welfare policy in the United States and Great Britain*, Chicago, IL and London: University of Chicago Press.

King, D. (1999) *In the name of liberalism: Illiberal social policy in the United States and Britain*, Oxford: Oxford University Press.

Kirby, S. and Riley, R. (2001) *The employment effects of ONE: Interim findings from the full participation phase*, Report for the DWP, London: DWP.

Layard, R., Nickell, S. and Jackman, R. (1991) *Unemployment: Macroeconomic performance and the labour market*, Oxford: Oxford University Press.

McLaughlin, E. (1991) 'Work and welfare benefits: social security, employment and unemployment in the 1990s', *Journal of Social Policy*, vol 20, no 4, pp 485-508.

McLaughlin, E. (1994) 'Flexibility in work and benefits', Paper for the Commission on Social Justice, London: IPPR.

Marsh, A. and McKay, S. (1993) *Families, work and benefits*, London: Policy Studies Institute.

Mead, L. (1986) *Beyond entitlement*, New York, NY: Free Press.

Mead, L. (1997) *From welfare to work: Lessons from America*, London: Institute for Economic Affairs Health and Welfare Unit.

Millar, J. (2002) 'The art of persuasion? The British New Deal for Lone Parents', in R. Walker and M. Wiseman (eds) *The welfare we want? The British challenge for American reform*, Bristol: The Policy Press.

Murray, C. (1984) *Losing ground: American social policy, 1950-1980*, New York, NY: Basic Books.

Narendranathan, W., Nickell, S. and Stern, J. (1985) 'Unemployment benefits revisited', *The Economic Journal*, vol 95, pp 307-29.

Nickell, S. (1999) 'Unemployment in Britain', in P. Gregg and J. Wadsworth (eds) *The state of working Britain*, Manchester: Manchester University Press, pp 7-28.

OECD (Organisation for Economic Co-operation and Development) (1994) *The OECD jobs study: Evidence and explanations*, Paris: OECD.

Payne, J. (2000) *Evaluating training programmes for the long-term unemployed*, PSI Research Discussion Paper No 1, London: Policy Studies Institute.

Payne, J., Lissenburgh, S., White, M. and Payne, C. (1996) *Employment training and employment action: An evaluation by the matched comparison method*, DfEE Research Series No 74, London: DfEE.

Pudney, S. and Thomas, J. (1993) 'Unemployment benefit, incentives and the labour supply of wives of unemployed men: econometric estimates', Mimeo, Cambridge: Department of Applied Economics, Cambridge University.

Purdon, S. (2002) *Estimating the impact of labour market programmes*, DWP Working Paper No 3, www.dwp.gov.uk/asd/asd5/WP3.pdf

Purdon, S., Lessof, C., Woodfield, K. and Bryson, C. (2001) *Research methods for policy evaluation*, DWP Working Paper No 2, www.dwp.gov.uk/asd/asd5/WP2.pdf

Schmitt, J. and Wadsworth, J. (1993a) 'Unemployment benefit levels and search activity', *Oxford Bulletin of Economics and Statistics*, vol 55, no 1, pp 1-24.

Schmitt, J. and Wadsworth, J. (1993b) *Job search activity and changing Unemployment Benefit entitlement: Pseudo-panel estimates for Britain*, CEP Discussion Paper No 148, London: London School of Economics and Political Science.

Smith, D. (1992) *Understanding the underclass*, London: Policy Studies Institute.

Stewart, M.B. (2002) 'The impact of the introduction of the UK minimum wage on the employment probabilities of low wage workers', Conference paper presented at the European Association of Labour Economists, Paris, 19-22 September, London School of Economics and Political Science.

Wadsworth, J. (1992) *Unemployment benefits and labour market transitions in Britain*, CEP Discussion Paper No 73, London: London School of Economics and Political Science.

Walker, R. (2000) 'Welfare policy: tendering for evidence', in H.T.O. Davies, S.M. Nutley and P.C. Smith (eds) *What works?: Evidence-based policy and practice in public services*, Bristol: The Policy Press.

Warr, P.B. (1987) *Work, unemployment and mental health*, Oxford: Oxford University Press.

White, M. and Lakey, J. (1992) *The Restart effect: Does active labour market policy reduce unemployment?*, London: Policy Studies Institute.

White, M. and Riley, R. (2002) *Findings from the macro evaluation of the New Deal for Young People*, DWP Research Report 168, London: DWP.

White, M., Lissenburgh, S. and Bryson, A. (1997) *The impact of public job placing programmes*, London: Policy Studies Institute.

Winterbotham, M., Adams, L. and Hasluck, C. (2001) *Evaluation of New Deal for Long-term Unemployed People: Enhanced national programme*, Employment Service Research Series, Sheffield: Employment Service.

Website resources

Benefits Now	www.benefitsnow.co.uk
Child Poverty Action Group	www.cpag.org.uk
Department for Education and Skills	www.dfes.gov.uk
Department for Work and Pensions	www.dwp.gov.uk
HM Treasury	www.hm-treasury.gov.uk
House of Commons library	www.parliament.uk/commons/lib/research
Inland Revenue	www.inlandrevenue.gov.uk

Institute for Fiscal Studies (Pensions and Savings section)
www.ifs.org.uk/pensionsindex.shtml

International Labour Organization
www.ilo.org/public/english

Jobcentre Plus
www.jobcentreplus.gov.uk

Low Pay Commission
www.lowpay.gov.uk

Organisation for Economic Co-operation and Development
www.oecd.org

Policy Studies Institute
www.psi.org.uk

Social Exclusion Unit, Cabinet Office
www.socialexclusionunit.gov.uk

Social Security Advisory Committee
www.ssac.org.uk

Trade Unions Council: welfare-to-work, etc
www.tuc.org.uk/welfare

Unemployment Unit and Youthaid (now the Centre for Economic and Social Inclusion)
www.cesi.org.uk

Work and Pensions Committee (UK)
www.parliament.uk/commons/selcom/workpenhome.htm

Worktrain (the national jobs and earning site)
www.worktrain.gov.uk

www.worldbank.org
World Bank

six

'Security for those who cannot': Labour's neglected welfare principle

Saul Becker

Summary

'Work for those who can, security for those who cannot': this is the basis for Labour's welfare reforms, but welfare policies and delivery have to date concentrated heavily on the first half of the equation, and neglected the 'security for those who cannot' – there is no standard or measure as to what 'security' actually means in practice. This chapter:

- assesses whether the benefits system under Labour provides 'security' to those who cannot by examining evidence from a range of living standard proxy indicators, and the Social Fund;

- explores the meaning of 'security';

- examines the new phrase being used to guide delivery, 'the work you want, the help you need', and what this means in practice;

- explores the adequacy of cash payments in providing security for those who cannot work;

- considers how the policy focus on 'work for those who can' has undermined the promotion of *real* security for those who cannot.

Introduction: welfare, work and independence

Labour committed itself to modernising the welfare state and to attacking the so-called problem of 'benefit dependency'. It has also set itself distinct and ambitious targets and performance indicators for tackling poverty and social exclusion, and for the promotion of opportunity and social inclusion 'for all' (DSS, 1999, 2000; DWP, 2001a).

During its first and second terms, Labour has gradually and determinedly redefined the relationship between benefits ('welfare') and work, not least through its New Deals and welfare-to-work programmes, but also by 'making work pay' through the introduction of an array of tax credits and tax changes, adjustments in national insurance, and the introduction of a National Minimum Wage (NMW) (Oppenheim, 1999; Lister 2001a). Labour has reformed some benefits (for lone parents and disabled people, for example) and transformed the systems for the delivery of payments. It has cast away old bureaucracies and replaced them with modern departments and agencies, including the Department for Work and Pensions, Jobcentre Plus and the Pension Service. These reforms have dovetailed in with other social policy developments, in an effort to 'join-up' policy making and delivery.

Prime Minister Tony Blair had always made it clear that "there is no greater challenge than reform of the welfare state", but that this "must be done with care and compassion" (Blair, 1998, p iii). To a large extent, Labour achieved in its first term the type and scale of welfare reform that was talked about by the Conservatives under Margaret Thatcher and John Major, but which managed to evade them during 18 years in government.

The principles for this reform agenda were set out in Labour's Green Paper, *New ambitions for our country* (DSS, 1998a) and in *A new contract for welfare: Principles into practice* (DSS, 1998b). This also established the duties of government and individuals – what Labour defines as a *new welfare contract*. Essentially, the duty of government is to make work pay and to provide people with the assistance they need to find jobs; the duty of individuals is to seek training or work and to take up the opportunity to be independent where they are able to do so (see Chapter Five in this volume). But what of those people who cannot work, either because of old age, illness, disability, mental disorder, frailty or caring/family responsibilities? There is a well established association between many of these circumstances and conditions, and worklessness – which is itself strongly associated with low income and hardship. Many people in these groups face particular barriers to accessing the labour market and keeping paid employment. For example, in families with children the biggest constraints on taking paid work are illness, disability and caring responsibilities (Marsh et al, 2001). Many family carers – people who provide unpaid care to other family members – find it hard to access or retain paid employment because of the demands of caring responsibilities, especially those who are full-time carers providing more than 50 hours of care per week (Becker and Silburn, 1999). Full-time carers invariably live in families reliant on social security. Many experience poverty and social exclusion (Howard, 2001). Over two thirds of those receiving care from family members also live in households whose main source of income is social security benefits (Becker, 2000).

This raises two key questions. First, how can we draw the line between those who can and those who cannot work? Second, how should those individuals and groups who cannot work be treated by the state? This chapter focuses on this second question[1] and reviews the evidence about the level of security offered by benefits, in particular by Income Support (the basic safety net of the social security system) and by the Social Fund (which is intended to meet additional or one-off needs of Income Support and other recipients). The chapter also examines the support offered by local authorities through social services and the relationship of this to social security support.

'Security for those who cannot'

Traditionally, the British social security system has not been overly generous in the amount of money it provides through benefit payments, not least because of a belief, inherited from Poor Law days, that generous benefits will undermine paid work and low-paid work in particular. Today, the level of Income Support paid to unemployed adults is still just 20% of average earnings – and this is down from 30% in 1983 (Rahman et al, 2001). Labour's mantra, 'work for those who can, security for those who cannot' (DSS, 1998a) suggests, however, a rejection of this principle of 'less eligibility'. Rhetorically at least, the implication is that those who cannot work should be provided with 'security'. As a society we have an accepted notion of what security means in principle, even if the concept is more problematic to operationalise in practice. Security is very much about the *condition* of being secure, having freedom from worry and uncertainty, and of being protected from danger, anxiety or apprehension. It is associated with a feeling of confidence, certainty and safety (**Box 6.1**).

Box 6.1: The meaning of 'security'

I. The condition of being secure. 1. The condition of being protected from or not exposed to danger; safety. 2. Freedom from doubt. Now chiefly, well-founded confidence, certainty. 3. Freedom from care, anxiety or apprehension; a feeling of safety.

Source: Oxford English Dictionary (1973, p 1927)

---

[1] The first question is addressed in a paper by the SSAC (2002) and we also return to it in the conclusions to this chapter.

Within the work-focused contract of duties and obligations, Labour confirms that: "Those people for whom work is not an option are entitled to an income which allows for *a decent life*" (DSS, 1998a, p 63; emphasis added). Labour also identifies a responsibility of government to "Support those unable to work so that they can lead *a life of dignity and security*" (DSS, 1998a, p 80; emphasis added). Here we have further insights into what 'security' might comprise, particularly how it can be applied *in practice*. Security is closely linked with 'a decent life' and with 'a life of dignity'. **Dignity** is defined in the *Oxford English Dictionary* as "The *quality* of being worthy or honourable; worth, excellence" (*Oxford English Dictionary*, 1973, p 548; emphasis added).

Thus, *security is a type of human condition*, and *dignity is a quality of human worth*. When linked together in policy discourse, security and dignity are concerned with valuing people unconditionally for what they are, and providing them with a standard of living which provides them with protection, safety and certainty in their living arrangements and quality of life. These principles are articulated further, for example, in Labour's pledge to give disabled people "the support they need to lead a fulfilling life with dignity" (DSS, 1998a, p 51).

We need to note in these phrases not just what is said but also what is not. The references throughout are to security and dignity – not *some* security and *some* dignity – and not for *some* disabled people or for *some* of those who cannot work – but presumably 'for all'. Labour seems to be saying that there is some *absolute standard* that could be defined as 'a decent life', 'a life of dignity and security' and 'a fulfilling life with dignity' and that this outcome should be available unconditionally to all those who cannot work.

In practice, however, Labour has never revealed or articulated what that standard of security and dignity might be. Despite outlining some general 'success measures' relating to its welfare principles (DSS, 1998a), Labour has no specific performance indicators or measures to operationalise 'security' for those who cannot work. This is an unfortunate neglect, especially given all the other useful and less useful indicators that it has developed during its first term. And because there are no specific indicators or targets for 'security', there is no official research being conducted within the Department for Work and Pensions research programme to assess whether or not 'security' has been achieved for those who cannot work. This research programme is dominated by projects associated with the *work* side of the mantra, not the *security* side.

Despite the lack of an official 'security' standard, it is still possible to assess whether or not those who cannot work are living a life of dignity and security. To do this we need to turn to 'proxy' indicators of security, or more accurately, indicators of a *lack of security and dignity*.

Triangulating the evidence on security

There is an abundance of evidence on the circumstances, lifestyles and well-being afforded to people who cannot work and who rely on social security benefits for some or most of their income. Various sources are available, including pressure groups, academics, poor people and government itself. An advantage of drawing on different sources and forms of evidence is that it enables *triangulation of data* to take place and helps us determine more fully, and from different perspectives, whether or not 'security' has been achieved. At the same time, we need to be aware that "Quite often the same researchers and research organisations appear in different guises conducting research for government and research trusts, and writing for pressure groups and think-tanks" (Walker, 2000, pp 141-2). So, for example, the **Child Poverty Action Group** (CPAG) has chronicled this evidence for over 30 years and uses data from academics, official sources and more recently from poor people themselves.

Pressure group evidence

CPAG's *Poverty: The facts* (Howard et al, 2001) contains much contemporary data on the experiences and living standards of people living on benefits, drawing on many different sources. It shows the long-term effects of living on a low income, how people must manage to get by from day-to-day, and the sacrifices they make in their daily lives, opportunities and aspirations. People living on means-tested benefits often go without basic household items and amenities which many of us expect as part of ordinary modern living; many people do not have enough food and cannot afford a nutritious diet; they do not have enough money for fuel or to meet their clothing needs; many experience considerable or severe hardship and debt. "For some, very serious consequences such as ill-health, homelessness or premature death can follow" (Howard et al, 2001, p 9).

Academic research

This picture is confirmed by evidence from academic sources. **Budget standard** work conducted with lone-parent and two-parent families, and among other groups, provides scientific data which show that benefit levels are not adequate to provide modest or even basic standards of living or to cover the costs associated with varying circumstances and conditions, including illness, disability and old age (Dobson and Middleton, 1998; Parker, 1998, 2000). Budget standards are specified baskets of goods and services which, when priced, represent predefined living standards. The methodology can be used to measure the living standards below which good health, social integration and satisfactory standards of living are at risk for different groups of people.

For example, Family Budget Unit data for families with children show that, when Labour came to power, Income Support in 1998 was paid at a rate below the level of a **Low Cost but Acceptable** living standard for lone-parent and two-parent families, with a shortfall of £32 per week for two-parent families and £24 per week for lone-parent families with two children under the age of 11 (Parker, 1998). In other words, at the start of Labour's first term, Income Support for families out of work was too low to enable them to achieve even a Low Cost but Acceptable standard of living. Other evidence from that time shows that parents spent far more on their children, including on food, than was allowed in the Income Support allowances for children (Middleton et al, 1997). And evidence from qualitative, in-depth studies on how people on low income manage shows the difficulties of making ends meet with limited resources (as summarised by Kempson, 1996).

Poor people's evidence

Findings on the hardship and poverty experienced by people who cannot work are also triangulated by other sources of evidence and 'knowledge', including the statements and voices of poor people themselves, who have been empowered through participatory research and 'user-led' organisations to speak out about their experiences. Living on benefits is often experienced in punitive and exclusionary ways. Low benefit levels reinforce poverty and social exclusion rather than enabling people to live a life of security and dignity; they also make it hard if not impossible to gain or maintain independence (Beresford et al, 1999; ATD FourthWorld, 2000; Turner, 2000; UK Coalition Against Poverty, 2000; Mumford and Power, 2003). It is rare for the voices and accounts of poor people to be regarded as 'evidence' in the policy-making process, despite their first-hand experience and position of being able to make informed judgements about the success or otherwise of benefits policy and delivery (Lister, 2002).

Official data

Another source of contemporary evidence is the government's own data. Detailed interviews with around 5,000 low-income families in 1999 conducted for the then Department of Social Security show that many lone-parent and two-parent families outside the labour market and living on Income Support are not sustaining a standard of living consistent with good health and family well-being (Marsh et al, 2001); in other words, their security and dignity are severely compromised. Focusing on three main dimensions of living standards, including material well-being (the ability to afford key items of food, clothing, leisure and entertainment and consumer durables), the quality of housing (type and condition of housing, adequacy of heating, incidence of overcrowding), and money management (the use of financial services, savings and debt and perceived financial well-being), researchers asked respondents about 34 items on which families indicated whether they possessed the item (or took part in the activity), and if not, whether this was because they did not want/need the item or because they could not afford it.

The findings show that living standards are particularly low for many non-working groups. Substantial numbers of non-working lone parents and couples reported difficulties affording even the most basic food and clothing items. Few made use of basic financial services such as bank accounts and more than half had accumulated debts. Forty per cent of non-working families were in severe hardship, and this affected lone parents disproportionately since fewer were working. Overall, more than eight in ten children in all non-working households were living in hardship (Marsh et al, 2001).

Not all the differences between families in hardship and those who were not can be accounted for in cash terms (their average difference in incomes was £34 a week). Greater hardship was independently associated with ill-health and disability, caring responsibilities and having larger families. Illness and disability are common among non-working families and are typically the biggest constraints on working. It is the presence of *illness, disability and caring responsibilities* that is most likely to increase the hardship that non-working families experience.

Improving security and dignity?

How far have the government's policies since 1997 been able to meet their promise of 'security for those who cannot work'? Increasing the level of benefit for families and others who are not in work should, in theory, make a real difference in *lifting* their standards of living. By the start of Labour's second term, following a series of increases in Income Support/income-related Jobseeker's Allowance rates for children, the shortfall between Income Support levels and a Low Cost but Acceptable standard for families had been reduced significantly. The shortfall in Income Support for a couple with two children was £11 per week, and for a lone-parent family with two children just £6 per week (Bradshaw, 2001). By October 2001, the position had changed dramatically. The weekly shortfall for a couple with two children was now just under £2. For a lone-parent family with two children the shortfall had been replaced by a surplus of over £2 per week (J. Bradshaw, personal correspondence). It seems, therefore, that following a series of benefit increases some families had moved closer to a position of security and dignity – expressed as a Low Cost but Acceptable standard of living. Lister (2001b, p 436) has observed that Labour has "kept remarkably quiet" about the "progressive improvement" in the rates for children, not only because it remains fearful of adverse reaction by some media and sections of the public, and it does not want to appear as "soft", but also because it is "redistributing with a purpose" (Lister, 2001a, p 107) – to promote responsibility, inclusion and opportunity for families with children.

There have also been structural changes intended, at least in part, to provide better support to those who cannot work. The introduction of **Jobcentre Plus** and the **Pension Service** in 2001/02, to replace the Benefits Agency and Employment Service, have been described by the then Secretary of State for Work and Pensions, Alistair Darling, as "the most comprehensive shake-up of welfare delivery for a generation with a clear focus on individual need" (DWP, 2002b). While 'work for those who can, security for those who cannot' remains the defining principle for welfare reform, along with the introduction of Jobcentre Plus came a new phrase to guide delivery: *the work you want, the help you need*. In future, 'security for those who cannot' will be supplemented by 'the help you need'. Jobcentre Plus personal advisers will be the first port of call, and could, for example, direct those unable to work to other sources of help, assistance and support – such as social services departments and health professionals. Jobcentre Plus personal advisers, and those working for the new Pension Service, will have a clear 'help-oriented' focus to their work; their concern is not solely to get the right benefits to the right clients at the right time, but to ensure that they also receive any other help that they might need (Box 6.2). This is an important development, in that it recognises that many people who cannot work have multiple needs, and while an adequate income

---

Box 6.2: 'Help' available from Jobcentre Plus and the Pension Service

Jobcentre Plus, rolled out nationally between 2001 and 2006, was introduced to "improve the way support is provided to people of working age who are claiming benefits. In line with a welfare system that provides active support to help people become more independent, based on work for those who can and security for those who cannot" (DWP, 2001b, p 3). Jobcentre Plus will provide a single point of delivery for jobs, benefits advice and support and help, using a personal adviser system, and childcare coordinators and a mentoring service for lone parents wanting to return to work (DWP, 2002c).

The **Pension Service**, established in 2002, offers a national service to 11 million pensioners, delivered locally by local-based teams, and includes outreach activity such as home visiting, private interviews in locations that suit pensioners and drop-in services. The Pension Service also provides 'partnership services', building on existing structures and developing new links with local authorities and voluntary sector organisations, to help achieve a joined-up service for meeting individual pensioners' needs for cash and care-related services.

is central to this, so too might be the need for health and social care support, particularly for those who have illness, disability or caring responsibilities (Becker, 1997).

Thus benefit levels have been increased and the system reformed to offer more 'joined-up' support. However, levels of poverty and social exclusion remain high, for some particular groups. For example, the annual monitoring of social exclusion conducted by the New Policy Institute and Joseph Rowntree Foundation (Rahman et al, 2001) showed that, for the first time since the series was launched in 1998, the number of indicators of social exclusion that have improved (between 2000-01) exceeded the number that got worse (by 24 to 8). The number of people living in households with less than 60% of the median income (one of the preferred thresholds of income poverty used by both the EU and UK government) was 13.3 million in 1999-2000, compared with 13.4 million a year earlier, only a small decrease (Rahman et al, 2001). This picture, of around *one fifth to one quarter of the population living in income poverty*, is confirmed by other academic sources, including a national Poverty and Social Exclusion Survey which measured poverty by reference to the enforced lack of socially perceived necessities (Gordon et al, 2000). At the end of 1999, 14.5 million people (26%) were living in poverty – defined as lacking two or more socially perceived necessities. And it is also confirmed by the government's own statistics – the **Households Below Average Income** series – which show that there has been significant income growth in real terms at the lower end of the income distribution since 1997, and a fall of 4 million in the numbers living below low-income thresholds that are fixed in real terms (the *absolute* poverty threshold). However, using *relative* indicators the improvement is not so dramatic. While there has been a drop of 1 million people living in relative poverty since Labour was first elected, 12.9 million people (23% of the population) continue to live in households with below 60% of median income after housing costs (the relative low-income indicator). Certain groups are clearly identified as having above-average risk of low income, including workless families, families with children, pensioners, people from minority ethnic groups, disabled people, local authority or housing association tenants, and those with no educational qualifications (DWP, 2002a).

These sources of data show that while there has been a considerable improvement in the benefit levels for children, and some improvement in tackling social exclusion for the population as a whole, there are still millions of people in Britain today living on very low disposable incomes and experiencing considerable hardship and an enforced lack of necessities. The groups most likely to be in these situations are largely predictable – those who for one reason or another cannot work or are unable to find work.

The Social Fund

In considering 'security for those who cannot' we must not ignore the mass-role of the discretionary **Social Fund** in providing a 'safety net' to millions on low income with additional expenses that are difficult to meet from regular income. The Social Fund was introduced in 1988 and provides budgeting and crisis loans, and community care grants, from a discretionary and cash-limited fund, as well as a number of other payments from a 'regulated' Social Fund. In 2001 alone, 2.3 million people received payments from the discretionary fund.

There is an abundance of literature on the discretionary Social Fund, which has been the cause of considerable controversy since it was introduced, not least because of its discretionary, cash-limited and loan-based nature, but also because of the overwhelming evidence from academic and official reviews, and from many poor people themselves, that it actually *contributes to poverty and hardship* for many people on low incomes, rather than alleviating it (Craig, 1989; Becker and Silburn, 1990; SSRC, 1991; Beresford and Turner, 1997).

The original justification for the introduction of the Social Fund – to target benefits on those most in need through a process of 'considered decision making', and to control expenditure more carefully (Becker and Silburn, 1989) – has spawned a system where many low-income families are forced to live on levels of benefit well below Income Support rates because of the need to repay (interest-free) loans for items and expenditure which they could not afford to meet from their regular income. For example, shortly after Labour came to power, in August 1998, 600,000 Income Support claimants had a deduction in their benefit for a Social Fund repayment. The average deduction was £8.58 per week. Fifty-four per cent of those with deductions were lone parents and 30% were disabled people. Many others were refused a loan in the first place because they were judged as being unable to repay (CPAG, 2002). This is a particularly repugnant part of the Social Fund as the scheme is intended to target money on those in 'most need', many of whom, it seems, are too poor to be able to be helped from it – a Catch-22. In 1998, the budget for community care grants (CCGs) was £98 million, and for loans, £402.7 million. However, within this overall budget there was only £138.2 million 'new money' – the remainder was financed by money recycled from previous applicants and being repaid through loans.

At the time of writing (2002-03), the budget for CCGs stands at £108 million, and for loans, £518 million. In contrast, the money allocated to the old 'single payment' scheme more than a decade earlier (which the Social Fund replaced in 1988) was £334 million – and this was all in the form of grants (Becker and Silburn, 1989). While Labour has increased the grants budget by £11 million (11%) between 1997 and 2002, the budget for grants is still only one third of what was available 14 years earlier under the old system.

The Social Fund exacerbates poverty and fuels *in*security for many people. Applicants to the fund experience uncertainty (as to whether or not an application will be successful – in the absence of clear legal rights); their waiting for a decision – and the terms of any repayments – add to anxiety and apprehension; and many who do get a payment (a loan) have their disposable income reduced below levels which – as we have already seen – are already insufficient to provide a Low Cost but Acceptable standard of living. These outcomes for applicants are the very antipathy of 'security' (see **Box 6.1**).

In 2001, the Social Security Select Committee (now the Committee for Work and Pensions) called for an urgent review of the discretionary Social Fund, and CPAG and others are also now calling on the government to reform the scheme (SSSC, 2001; Howard, 2002). Labour has indicated that the scheme is subject to ongoing review, and despite its own calls (when in opposition) for the discretionary scheme to be abolished, it seems less inclined to do this now that it is in government.

Cash versus care: help available from personal social services

For many vulnerable people who cannot work, their needs are as much for services and support as they are for cash. Labour has recognised that "Services – especially education, health and housing – are at least as important as cash benefits in promoting independence and security; tackling poverty and widening opportunity" (DSS, 1998a, p 4). More recently, the Social Security Advisory Committee has expressed particular concern that there is "so little joint working with health services, and little apparent collaboration between DWP and the Department of Health in addressing the many health-related aspects of economic inactivity" (SSAC, 2002, p 21).

It is estimated that around 20% of the population are pensioners, 16% of all adults have some form of mental illness, 14% of adults have at least one disability and 13% are unpaid family carers. Local authority social services departments exist to keep these and other vulnerable groups – including families with children – safe, and to promote their independence through the provision, primarily, of care-related services. At any one time up to 1.5 million people rely on help from statutory social services.

Statutory social services:

> ... are concerned to protect those unable to participate fully as citizens in an unprotected competitive environment ... [and] the pursuit of fostering greater *social integration* amongst individuals or groups in society who would otherwise be marginalised or socially excluded. More specifically, it is to promote individual personal

> well-being in the face of a disabling condition. (Evandrou and Falkingham, 1998, p 192; emphasis in original)

There is a strong overlap in the care and control functions of social services with the welfare principle of 'work for those who can, security for those who cannot'. The main users of social services are also the most costly (in expenditure terms) clients of social security – older people, sick/disabled people and families (Evandrou and Falkingham, 1998, p 210; Evans, 1998, p 273). Research shows that most users of local authority social services are also in receipt of social security benefits and around half are reliant on means-tested benefits; many social services users come to the attention of social services because of poverty-related circumstances or difficulties in living or maintaining their independence (Becker and MacPherson, 1988; Becker and Silburn, 1990; Becker, 1997).

Most social services provision is provided within a statutory framework. This legal framework is the *service*-based (as opposed to the *cash*-based) side of the 'security for those who cannot' coin, although social services do have some cash-giving powers (**Box 6.3**). This *interrelationship between 'cash' and 'care'* developed in Britain from a concern to manage and regulate poverty and 'difference' (Becker, 1997). Since 1948, cash and care have been provided by separate agencies, unlike most other European countries where the functions are often combined in some way (Hill, 2000, p 119). Today, there are significant overlaps in functions, with social services taking on important income maintenance roles, and social security becoming increasingly concerned with 'the whole person', not just benefits (**Box 6.3**). However, unlike social security, social services have a far more developed programme of research and evaluation focusing on the *quality* and *adequacy* of their services and support to vulnerable children, families and adults – almost all of whom are not in paid work. This programme of local and national inspection and evaluation is conducted through the Social Services Inspectorate, the Care Standards Commission and the General Social Care Council, with the Social Care Institute for Excellence overseeing 'what works' in social care. There is no parallel focus within the Department for Work and Pensions on the adequacy of cash payments to provide security for those who cannot work.

Box 6.3: Overlaps between social security and social services

- Both organisations are concerned *to provide 'security' and promote opportunity, independence, social inclusion (integration) and dignity for vulnerable adults, children and families*. Social security does this primarily by helping people into work and by providing cash benefits; social services do this by providing care-related services or by arranging for others (from the voluntary or private sectors, or from other agencies such as health) to provide services.

- There is a *strong overlap in the client base of both organisations*, with many users of cash and care being older people, disabled people and families who cannot work. Almost all social services clients will be in receipt of benefits, particularly means-tested ones. Many come to social services because of poverty-related problems that have impaired their independence; a common and shared experience of most users of social services, and 'those who cannot work', will be low income, poverty and social exclusion. To a large extent, social security provides a reactive ambulance service to "casualties of social, economic and ideological change" (Evans, 1998, p 303), and the same can be said of social services.

- Because of the overlap in both client base and functions, *changes in the cash system have a knock-on effect on the care system*. So, for example, with the introduction of the Social Fund in 1988, there was an immediate impact on the work of social services, with many poor people seeking additional financial and personal help from social workers and others, including charities. Social services had to develop policies and procedures for containing and managing extra demand, very similar to Social Fund officers. Many aspects of social security policy and delivery frustrate, rather than facilitate, social services responsibilities.

- Many *social security benefits have a care-related component*. Benefits have also been paid for care-related services such as those provided in sheltered accommodation, and social security payments have paid for residential care for older people living in private homes. From 1993 social services took responsibility (and the budget) to finance the care of adults in residential settings. Other payments (such as Social Fund CCGs, Invalid Care Allowance/Carer's Allowance) are provided to groups of people (disabled people, carers, and so on) whose 'care' comes under the auspices of social services departments – which have a statutory duty to provide services and support to these groups under the law.

Box 6.3 continued

- The *social security system has a 'care' or welfare-related function*, to promote well-being. The 1948 National Assistance Act, for example, required income maintenance personnel to promote the welfare of claimants and this was a prominent characteristic of social security delivery up to the late 1970s and into the 1980s, when special case officers continued to advise and help claimants with particular difficulties. Today, this individualised service has resumed through the personal adviser in Jobcentre Plus and the Pension Service. Personal advisers are now the cornerstone of the benefits/work delivery system, providing an individualised service based on individual need.

- *Social services departments have cash-giving and income maintenance functions*; they can make 'direct payments' to some carers and disabled people; they provide Section 17 payments to families with children in need; means tests are commonly applied to older people, disabled and vulnerable adults seeking home care or residential care, using regulations based on Income Support systems; charging for social care takes place; welfare rights workers are employed to maximise the benefits of clients and to help departments maximise their revenue through charges and other means. By charging vulnerable adults (including many on Income Support) for care services, clients often find their disposable income reduced to very low levels, similar to the experience of those repaying Social Fund loans.

Achieving security?

In 1999, Bennett and Walker observed that "the outlines of a complementary Labour strategy to achieve security and dignity for all those not in paid work are as yet confused, contradictory and incomplete" (Bennett and Walker, 1999, p 35). Unfortunately, there has been little if any progress since then. While publicly proclaiming 'work for those who can, security for those who cannot', there is little evidence that Labour in its first term actually considered what 'security' might mean in practice. Labour has no 'standard' or measure from which to judge whether the current benefit system actually provides security to those who cannot work, nor has it commissioned research explicitly designed to find out. We can only hope that this will become more of a priority in Labour's second term of office. The evidence reported here though is irrefutable. To provide 'a decent life' and 'a life of dignity and security' for those who cannot work, people will *need higher disposable incomes*; this will help lift many out of the poverty and hardship that millions experience while living on benefit. For a government concerned to base policy on 'what works', there is little doubt that increasing disposable incomes will work in promoting security and independence.

However, Labour seems more concerned that providing 'adequate' benefit levels and a replacement to the Social Fund 'safety net' may militate against its other principal aim of using the benefit system to promote personal and economic independence through *paid* work. Labour has a deep-rooted belief (and one which has clouded the judgements of policy makers throughout the post-war period, and which has contributed to the worst forms of anti-claimant sentiment) that paying 'adequate' (never mind 'generous') levels of benefits to those who cannot work, and a rights-based and grants-dominated safety net, will reinforce 'dependency' and act as a magnet to attract people into making claims, undermining Labour's other guiding principle, 'work for those who can'. This is why Labour has been so reluctant to engage publicly in a discussion about higher benefit levels and the redistributive function of social security, or the reform of the Social Fund. However, under cover of tax and benefit complexity, and tough talk, Labour has made some improvements to benefit levels that have benefited some groups, particularly children. The 2002 Budget finally made visible Labour's intention to use increased taxation to improve some (universal) public services, notably the NHS, but *not* those services taken up disproportionately by the most disadvantaged, including social security and social care.

To some extent, Labour's difficulties of engaging with what 'real' security might involve for those who cannot work are tied up with its confusion between those who 'cannot' work (because of illness, disability, caring responsibilities, and so on), and its belief that everyone, in theory, *can* and *should* work. There is a sense that Labour equates those who cannot work with another group of workless people – those who *will not* work – or the 'work-shy' or 'scroungers' as they have been referred to in the past (Golding and Middleton, 1982; Becker, 1997). To pay out benefits that provide real security and dignity to a group of people who have refused to engage in their side of the new welfare contract would be anathema to Labour. This group's reluctance or refusal to work – their failure to engage in reciprocity – would in principle cancel out the government's duty to support them. It is the 'will not work' group that poses the most challenges for Labour. There is little evidence about the size or characteristics of this group, although it is often equated in policy discourse with *the underclass* – a "certain type of poor person defined not by his condition, e.g. long-term unemployed, but by his deplorable behaviour in response to that condition, e.g. unwilling to take the jobs that are available to him" (Murray, 1990, p 68). The shadow of this group, and the myths and fears associated with it – including that it epitomises the 'benefit dependency culture' – for itself and its children – has helped fuel Labour's welfare reform project and welfare-to-work programme. But it has also helped to confuse Labour's thinking about security for those who cannot work, and has inhibited it from engaging in a meaningful debate about the adequacy of benefits and the adequacy of the Social Fund in promoting security and dignity.

As we have already identified, Labour has stated that, "Those people for whom work is not an option are entitled to an income which allows for a decent life" (DSS, 1998a, p 63). If Labour truly wants those who cannot work to have an income which allows for 'a decent life' and 'a life of dignity and security' then it has no alternative but to grasp the nettle of **Minimum Income Standards**, and – as the European Commission has suggested – to define a Minimum Income Standard at a level considered "sufficient to cover essential needs with regard to respect for human dignity" (Becker, 1997, p 166; Veit-Wilson, 1998).

Labour will also have to engage in a number of other hard debates. It will need to reconsider the relationship between social insurance, private insurance and means-tested benefits and how each of these relate to issues of personal 'security'. It will also need to recognise that "paid employment is not a viable option for everybody" (Howard et al, 2001, p 205), and that "a substantial proportion of the Department's [DWP's] customers are not in the market for work-focused services. Providing security and support for those whom paid employment may never be a realistic goal, and for people in retirement, will be a major service challenge" (SSAC, 2002, p 3). And Labour will need to engage in a meaningful debate as to the *nature and value of work*. Labour's equating of work as being synonymous with *paid* employment, and its implicit denigration of other forms of unpaid work in the home and community (such as family care-giving, bringing up children, volunteering, and so on), serve to *undervalue those people engaged in unpaid work* and to downgrade their contribution to both society and the economy. The value of unpaid family caring in the UK has been calculated at £57 billion (Carers UK, 2002). If just a small number of Britain's 6 million carers were to give up caring – through ill-health or lack of support – the economic impact would be dramatic, never mind the social and personal costs to individuals, families and communities. Many of the people who provide unpaid work – such as caring and childcare – are women, and many are also clients (or potential clients) of social services and would be priorities for their support services.

It is also important that Labour remembers that 'security' for those who cannot work is not just a function of social security alone (and adequate levels of benefits in particular), but that *security and dignity are best guaranteed through a combination of money and services*. Adequate levels of disposable income and reliable, good quality care and support services, are the necessary foundations for *real* security for those who cannot work, to promote their well-being, independence, dignity and freedom from poverty and exclusion (Becker, 1997). In the future, Labour will need to think about how cash and care policy can become more 'joined-up', and how money and services can be delivered in a seamless manner, to promote security for those both in and out of work.

Overview

- To promote real security for those who cannot work, Labour will need to pay far more attention in its second term to what 'security' and 'dignity' should mean in practice.

- Labour will need to define 'security' and define Minimum Income Standards; it will also need to bring about a closer coordination of the work and functions of social security and social services.

- To have a 'life of dignity and security' people who cannot work will require adequate (which means higher) disposable income, and adequate (which means good quality and reliable) social services. Together, cash and care are the foundations for security, independence and social inclusion.

Questions for discussion

1. Does the British social security system provide security for those who cannot work?

2. What type of evidence is available to help us determine whether or not people who cannot work have achieved a 'life of dignity and security'?

3. What might real 'security' for those who cannot work comprise in practice?

4. What are the key agencies that should provide security and help to those who cannot work?

5. Why do you think Labour has neglected 'security for those who cannot work' and focused far more on 'work for those who can'?

References

ATD Fourth World (2000) *Participation works: Involving people in poverty in policy making*, London: ATD Fourth World.

Becker, S. (1997) *Responding to poverty: The politics of cash and care*, Harlow: Longman.

Becker, S. (2000) 'Carers and indicators of vulnerability to social exclusion', *Benefits*, no 28, pp 1-4.

Becker, S. and MacPherson, S. (eds) (1988) *Public issues private pain: Poverty, social work and social policy*, London: Carematters Books/Insight.

Becker, S. and Silburn, R. (1989) 'Back to the future: the process of considered decision-making', in G. Craig (ed) *Your flexible friend: Voluntary organisations, claimants and the Social Fund*, London: Social Security Consortium/Association of Metropolitan Authorities, pp 24-40.

Becker, S. and Silburn, R. (1990) *The new poor clients: Social work, poverty and the Social Fund*, Sutton: *Community Care*/Reed Business Publishing.

Becker, S. and Silburn, R. (1999) *We're in this together: Conversations with families in caring relationships*, London: Carers National Association.

Bennett, F. and Walker, R. (1999) 'Working with work', *Benefits*, no 25, p 35.

Beresford, P. and Turner, M. (1997) *It's our welfare: Report of the Citizen's Commission on the Future of the Welfare State*, London: National Institute for Social Work.

Beresford, P., Green, D., Lister, R. and Woodard, K. (1999) *Poverty first hand: Poor people speak for themselves*, London: CPAG.

Blair, T. (1998) 'Foreword', in DSS, *A new contract for welfare: Principles into practice,* Cm 4101, London: The Stationery Office, pp iii-iv.

Bradshaw, J. (2001) 'Child poverty under Labour', in G. Fimister (ed) *An end in sight? Tackling child poverty in the UK*, London: CPAG, pp 9-27.

Carers UK (2002) *Without us...? Calculating the value of carers' support*, London: Carers UK.

CPAG (Child Poverty Action Group) (2002) 'Social Fund', www.cpag.org.uk/cro/Briefings/Briefings%201.htm, 30 April.

Craig, G. (ed) (1989) *Your flexible friend: Voluntary organisations, claimants and the Social Fund*, London: Social Security Consortium/Association of Metropolitan Authorities.

Dobson, B. and Middleton, S. (1998) *Paying to care: The cost of childhood disability*, York: York Publishing Services for the Joseph Rowntree Foundation.

DSS (Department of Social Security) (1998a) *New ambitions for our country: A new contract for welfare*, Cm 3805, London: The Stationery Office.

DSS (1998b) *A new contract for welfare: Principles into practice*, London: The Stationery Office.

DSS (1999) *Opportunity for All: Tackling poverty and social exclusion*, Cm 4445, London: The Stationery Office.

DSS (2000) *Opportunity for All, one year on: Making a difference*, Cm 4865, London: The Stationery Office.

DWP (Department for Work and Pensions) (2001a) *Opportunity for All: Making progress*, Cm 5260, London: The Stationery Office.

DWP (2001b) 'Jobcentre Plus – a new agency for people of working age', *Touchbase*, no 24, pp 3-4.

DWP (2002a) *Households Below Average Income 1994/95 to 2000/01*, Leeds: Corporate Document Services.

DWP (2002b) 'Darling announces radical new jobs target', Press release EMP1903-Radical, 19 March, London: DWP press office.

DWP (2002c) 'Budget help for lone parents', Press release EMP1704-BLP, 17 April, London: DWP press office.

Evandrou, M. and Falkingham, J. (1998) 'The personal social services', in H. Glennerster and J. Hills (eds) *The state of welfare: The economics of social spending*, Oxford: Oxford University Press, pp 189-256.

Evans, M. (1998) 'Social security', in H. Glennerster and J. Hills (eds) *The state of welfare: The economics of social spending*, Oxford: Oxford University Press, pp 257-307.

Golding, P. and Middleton, S. (1982) *Images of welfare: Press and public attitudes to poverty*, London: Martin Robertson.

Gordon, D., Adelman, L., Ashworth, K., Bradshaw, J., Levitas, R., Middleton, S., Pantazis, C., Patsios, D., Payne, S., Townsend, P. and Williams, J. (2000) *Poverty and social exclusion in Britain*, York: Joseph Rowntree Foundation.

Hill, M. (2000) *Local authority social services: An introduction*, Oxford: Blackwell Publishers.

Howard, M. (2001) *Paying the price: Carers, poverty and social exclusion*, London: CPAG.

Howard, M. (2002) *Like it or lump it: A role for the Social Fund in ending child poverty*, London: One Parent Families/CPAG/Family Welfare Association.

Howard, M., Garnham, A., Fimister, G. and Veit-Wilson, J. (2001) *Poverty: The facts* (4th edn), London: CPAG.

Kempson, E. (1996) *Life on a low income*, York: York Publishing Services.

Lister, R. (2001a) '"Work for those who can, security for those who cannot": a third way in social security reform or fractured social citizenship?', in R. Edwards and J. Glover (eds) *Risk and citizenship: Key issues in welfare*, London: Routledge, pp 96-110.

Lister, R. (2001b) 'New Labour: a study in ambiguity from a position of ambivalence', *Critical Social Policy*, vol 21, no 4, issue 69, pp 425-47.

Lister, R. (2002) 'A politics of recognition and respect: involving people with experience of poverty in decision-making that affects their lives', *Social Policy and Society*, vol 1, no 1, pp 1-10.

Marsh, A., McKay, S., Smith, A. and Stephenson, A. (2001) *Low-income families in Britain: Work, welfare and social security in 1999*, DSS Research Report No 138, Leeds: Corporate Document Services.

Middleton, S., Ashworth, K. and Braithwaite, I. (1997) *Small fortunes: Spending on children. Childhood poverty and parental sacrifice*, York: Joseph Rowntree Foundation.

Mumford, K. and Power, A. (2003) *East Enders: Family and community in urban neighbourhoods*, Bristol: The Policy Press.

Murray, C. (ed) (1990) *The emerging British underclass*, London: Institute of Economic Affairs.

Oppenheim, C. (1999) 'Welfare reform and the labour market: a "third way"?', *Benefits*, no 25, pp 1-5.

Parker, H. (ed) (1998) *Low Cost but Acceptable: A Minimum Income Standard for the UK: Families with young children*, Bristol: The Policy Press/Zacchaeus 2000 Trust.

Parker, H. (ed) (2000) *Low Cost but Acceptable incomes for older people: A minimum income standard for households aged 65-74 years in the UK*, Bristol: The Policy Press.

Rahman, M., Palmer, G. and Kenway, P. (2001) *Monitoring poverty and social exclusion 2001*, York: York Publishing Services.

SSAC (Social Security Advisory Committee) (2002) 'Promoting social inclusion within the work-focused agenda', Annex C, in SSAC, *Fifteenth report*, London: SSAC, pp 19-25.

SSRC (Social Security Research Consortium) (1991) *Cash limited, limited cash: The impact of the Social Fund on social services and voluntary agencies, and their users*, London: Association of Metropolitan Authorities.

SSSC (Social Security Select Committee) (2001) *A lifeline for the poor – or the fund that likes to say no?*, London: SSSC.

Turner, M. (2000) *Our choice in our future: Benefits*, London: Shaping our Lives/National Institute for Social Work.

UK Coalition Against Poverty (2000) *Listen hear: The right to be heard, Report of the Commission on Poverty, Participation and Power*, Bristol: The Policy Press.

Veit-Wilson, J. (1998) *Setting adequacy standards: How governments define minimum incomes,* Bristol: The Policy Press.

Walker, R. (2000) 'Welfare policy: tendering for evidence', in H.T.O. Davies, S.M. Nutley and P.C. Smith (eds) *What works? Evidence-based policy and practice in public services*, Bristol: The Policy Press, pp 141-66.

Website resources

Child Poverty Action Group	www.cpag.org.uk
Citizen's Income Online	www.citizensincome.org
Department for Work and Pensions	www.dwp.gov.uk
Department of Health	www.doh.gov.uk
Household Below Average Income	www.dwp.gov.uk/asd/hbai.htm
Jobcentre Plus	www.jobcentreplus.gov.uk
National Children's Bureau	www.ncb.org.uk
Rights Net	www.rightsnet.org.uk
Social Fund	www.dwp.gov.uk/lifeevent/benefits the_social_fund.htm
Social Security Advisory Committee	www.ssac.org.uk
Work and Pensions Committee (UK)	www.parliament.uk/commons/ selcom/workpenhome.htm

seven

From wage replacement to wage supplement: benefits and tax credits

Jane Millar

Summary

Paid employment and social security benefits have, until recently, been seen as alternative sources of income. However, as low-paid work has expanded, for some people wages alone are no longer sufficient to provide a household with an adequate standard of living, or with sufficient financial incentive to take up paid work.

Thus employed people have been gradually brought into the social security system, at first through an in-work benefit for low-paid families with children, and now through the introduction of 'tax credits' which, from 2003, will be available to most families with children and all low-paid workers aged 25 and above. This chapter:

- outlines the development of benefits as wage supplements, and explores their impact;

- considers the aims and design of the new system of tax credits.

Introduction: from Family Income Supplement to Family Credit

Beveridge's Plan for social security set out a scheme with three main elements. These were: **national insurance benefits** (funded by contributions from workers, employers and the government; intended as a replacement for earnings loss); **national assistance benefits** (funded from general taxation, means-tested support for people with low incomes); and **family allowances** (funded from general taxation, paid at the same rate for all families, regardless of income level). Thus, with the partial exception of family allowances, the main function of social security benefits was clearly to replace lost earnings, and not to pay benefits to working people.

This wage replacement system operated successfully in the 1950s and into the 1960s, a period characterised by full employment and stable families (see Chapter Two in this volume). Poverty studies at the time suggested that working poverty had been largely eliminated. However, by the mid-1960s the 'rediscovery of poverty' challenged this benign view of welfare state success. In their influential study, Abel-Smith and Townsend (1965) found that poverty was much more widespread than had been thought, and also that it was increasingly a problem for working families, with one in five poor families with children being working families.

Thus by the early 1970s, the gaps and shortfalls of the Beveridge Plan were becoming much more visible and filling some of these gaps became an important part of the policy agenda. The new measures introduced for non-working people in the early to mid-1970s included non-contributory pensions, the extension of widow's benefits, and various benefits for disabled people (see Chapters Eight and Ten in this volume). In relation to poor working families, various alternatives were being debated and considered. One option would have been for stronger measures of wage protection and regulation, including a National Minimum Wage (NMW). But this was not supported either by the governments of the time or by the trades unions, which were committed to free collective bargaining over wages (Brown, 1983; Millar et al, 1997). There was also a proposal for a 'tax credit' scheme, set out by the government (HM Treasury, 1971), and which almost reached the legislative stage before being rejected as too costly. This would have replaced personal tax allowances with a refundable tax credit (see Box 7.1 for definitions), so that people with earnings below the tax threshold would have received cash support instead.

Thus, in the early 1970s, neither wage regulation nor tax reform was seen as able to provide a solution to the problem of poverty among working families. That left the social security system, and the key measure here was the

Box 7.1: Key terms for in-work benefits and taxes

Tax allowances	These exempt a portion of gross income from income tax. They have no value for non-taxpayers or for people earning below the level of the allowance
Tax credits	Tax credits subtract a given sum from the tax bill, with awards assessed and made through the tax system, and can be either non-refundable (they can reduce the tax paid to nil but not involve any further transfer) or refundable (they can reduce tax paid to nil and also pay a refund up to the value of the credit)
National insurance contributions	Deductions from gross wages that are used to fund national insurance benefits (and make a small contribution to NHS funding)
Marginal tax rates	The effective tax rate paid on an additional pound of earnings. This could include income tax, national insurance contributions and the value of any means-tested benefits/tax credits lost
Poverty trap	A situation when an increase in gross wages leads to little or no increase in net income, because of high marginal tax rates
Unemployment trap	A situation when income out of work is as high, or higher, than income in work
Means test	Taking into account income and family circumstances in order to assess benefit entitlement. This might be an income test or an assets test or include both income and assets
Assessment period	The period of time over which income is measured for assessing entitlement to means-tested benefits/tax credits
Award period	The period of time for which entitlement to benefits/tax credits remains the same, regardless of changes in income or circumstances
Unit of assessment	The individual, family, or household unit whose assets are taken into account in assessing entitlement to benefits/tax credits
Disregard	An amount of money, often from a designated source, which is not counted as part of income in the assessment of entitlement to means-tested benefits/tax credits
Taper rate	The rate at which benefits/tax credits are reduced when other income rises

Table 7.1: **Family Income Supplement: receipt and expenditure**

Financial year	Numbers in receipt	Costs (£m) cash	Costs (£m) in 2002/03 real terms
1971/72	71,000	4	32
1972/73	106,000	10	80
1974/75	67,000	12	75
1976/77	97,000	18	78
1978/79	88,000	24	85

Source: Millar et al (1997, Table 1); DWP (2002b, Tables 8, 9)

introduction of **Family Income Supplement** in 1971[1]. This new means-tested benefit was payable to families with dependent children, with an employed parent working at least 30 hours per week, and with wages below a certain level. It was originally introduced as a temporary measure, while the government considered the future of family support more generally (Deacon and Bradshaw, 1983). In the event, although Child Benefit was introduced in 1975 to replace family allowances and child tax allowances, Family Income Supplement continued alongside these. Initially, as Table 7.1 shows, this was a rather small and insignificant benefit, it did not cost very much and not many families received it. **Take-up rates** (the proportion of those eligible who actually received it) started at about 35% in 1971 and had only reached about 50% by 1979 (Brown, 1983).

The **1986 Social Security Act** was an important piece of legislation in this story and one that really established wage supplementation through means-tested benefits as a legitimate, and integral, function of the social security system. Income Support was introduced to replace Supplementary Benefit, and **Family Credit** was introduced to replace Family Income Supplement. Common means tests were established for both, and for Housing Benefit, so that benefits in and out of work were more closely aligned. Family Credit was very much intended to act as a work incentive, as the key objectives show:

> ... to provide extra support to these families in accordance with their needs; to ensure that as far as possible they are better off in work; and to see that they can achieve improvements in family income by greater effort without losing all benefit. (DHSS, 1985, p 29)

---

[1] Family Income Supplement was not the only form of in-work support that became available in the 1970s. Rent and rate rebates were also introduced, and later replaced by Housing Benefit and Council Tax Benefit. Housing Benefit is currently received by just under 4 million households – one in six of all households – at an annual cost of about £11.5 billion. But it is beset with problems – it is complex to administer, with high error rates and long delays, it is open to fraud, and it acts as a financial disincentive to work. The government now proposes to trial the introduction of standard local housing allowances, based on area and family size (DWP, 2002a).

The structure and eligibility conditions for Family Credit were much the same as for Family Income Supplement, although it was a more generous system. It was available for families with children, with earnings below a certain level according to family size, and there was a weekly hours threshold (a minimum of 24 hours per week). Eligibility was assessed with reference to family income over a five-week (or two-month) period, and once awarded the amount paid was fixed for the next six months. It was paid to the main carer, either by an order book (cashable at Post Offices) or directly into bank accounts. This was not what the government originally proposed, which was that it should be paid through the wage packet, and therefore to the wage earner rather than to the main carer. This proposal was strongly resisted by women's groups (including Conservative women) and by employers, who were not very willing to take on the responsibility of administering this. The issues raised are still, as discussed further below, very much part of current debates about the administration of tax credits.

Various rule changes increased the scope of the benefit over the following 10 years, including a reduction in the qualifying hours threshold from 24 to 16 in April 1992, and the introduction of disregards for maintenance and childcare costs. Family Credit receipt started relatively slowly but then started to rise rapidly, as Table 7.2 shows. The number of recipients more than doubled between 1989 and 1996, from almost 300,000 to approximately 700,000. Family Credit was available to lone parents on the same basis as it was to couples, and many employed lone parents were (and are) in low-paid work, and so lone parents made up a significant proportion of those in receipt. Take-up also improved, with the former Department of Social Security estimating take-up rates in the mid-1990s of about 70% by caseload and 82% by expenditure (DSS, 1996)[2]. Research on non-take-up concluded that many

Table 7.2: **Family Credit: receipt and expenditure**

Year	Numbers in receipt	Couples	Lone parents	Costs (£m) cash	Costs (£m) in 2002/03 real terms
1988/89	285,000	177,000	108,000	394	638
1989/90	299,000	180,000	119,000	425	642
1991/92	350,000	213,000	136,000	626	827
1993/94	520,000	293,000	228,000	1,208	1,508
1995/96	693,000	388,000	305,000	1,740	2,084

Source: Millar et al (1997, Table 6); DWP (2002b, Tables 1, 2, 8, 9)

[2] Caseload take-up measures the number of people claiming as a proportion of the number of people eligible. Expenditure take-up estimates the amount of money claimed as a proportion of the total that could be claimed.

of these non-claiming families were probably only eligible for short periods and for relatively small amounts of money (McKay and Marsh, 1995). The Conservative government regarded Family Credit as one of its great successes, and introduced a similar in-work benefit (the Disability Working Allowance) for disabled people in 1992 (see Chapter Eight in this volume). It also piloted a similar 'Earnings Top-Up' for single people and for couples without dependent children (Finlayson et al, 2000).

'Making work pay'

Working Families Tax Credit

By the time the Labour government won the 1997 General Election the principle of supplementing wages through the social security system was thus well established. In the welfare reform Green Paper, *New ambitions for our country: A new contract for welfare* (DSS, 1998, p 1), the second of the three "key problems with our current system" was identified as "people face a series of barriers to paid work, including financial disincentives"[3]. The Paper stressed the importance of work: "Work is at the heart of our welfare reform programme. For those able to undertake it, paid work is the surest route out of poverty" (1998, p 3). Thus, as well as the New Deal programmes to help people find work, there was a commitment to 'ensuring that work pays', to improving the financial returns from working and so increasing the financial incentives to work[4]. These measures included the introduction (for the first time in the UK) of a National Minimum Wage (NMW), reductions in tax and national insurance contributions for low-paid workers, and the introduction of Working Families Tax Credit (WFTC) and Disabled Person's Tax Credit (DPTC).

It was the Treasury in particular that was driving these measures through, and the tax credits story can be traced through a series of Treasury papers called *The modernisation of Britain's tax and benefit system* (HM Treasury, 1997, 1998a, 1998b, 1999, 2000, 2002). The second of these, the report on *work incentives* by Martin Taylor, is a key document in this story (HM Treasury, 1998a). Martin Taylor, Chief Executive of Barclays, was asked to chair a task force set up in May 1997 (immediately after the General Election) with a remit to "examine the interaction of the tax and benefits systems so that they can be streamlined and modernised, so as to fulfil our objectives of promoting work incentives, reducing poverty and welfare dependency, and strengthening

---

[3] The others were rising inequality and the problem of fraud.

[4] See Chapters Three, Five and Eleven in this volume, for further discussion of the range of policies – including the New Deal, and more stringent work requirements applied to more groups of claimants, and the merging of the Benefits Agency and the Employment Service – intended to support paid work.

community and family life" (HM Treasury, 1998a, p 5)[5]. Taylor starts by rejecting a full-scale integration of the tax and benefits systems on the grounds that they have different objectives, do not cover the same people, and have different units of assessment (individual for taxes, family for benefits). He argues that in-work wage supplements are necessary because there are "a large number of people whose labour is not sufficiently well rewarded to allow them to support their families in an acceptable way. It seems to me far better that these people should be working, and receiving in-work benefits to top up their net pay, than that they should be idle" (HM Treasury, 1998a, p 8), and he argues for a tax credit, as opposed to a benefit, because:

> A tax credit will associate the payment in the recipient's mind with the fact of working, a potentially valuable psychological change. I believe that a payment through the tax system, associated with the recipient's work, is likely to prove more acceptable to society at large. And the establishment of a tax credit system is likely to come in useful in future as a broader delivery mechanism, eventually allowing closer integration between the benefits system and conventional income tax. (HM Treasury, 1998a, p 8)

These points were repeated in the next Treasury paper (HM Treasury, 1998b, p 3), which set out the details of the new tax credits:

> As a tax credit rather than a welfare benefit, it will reduce the stigma associated with claiming in-work support, and encourage higher take-up. Its clear link with employment should demonstrate the rewards of work over welfare and help ensure that people move off welfare into work. (HM Treasury, 1998b, p 3)

The key rationale for a tax credit, as opposed to a benefit, is thus that taxes are positively associated with paid work while benefits are negatively associated with dependency. This, it is argued, makes tax credits more acceptable to recipients and to the public in general. The language here is also notable – it clearly reflects the influence of the US, where 'welfare' is a negative term associated with dependency and failure (Walker, 1998; Deacon, 1998, 2002; Hirsch, 2000). Indeed, there has been much policy sharing and policy transfer across countries in respect of tax credit provisions, with the US experience, and values, an important element in this. **Box 7.2** describes the system in the US (see also **Box 7.4** on Australia).

---

[5] The report covered national insurance contributions and benefits for the partners of unemployed claimants as well as tax credits, but we focus on the latter here.

> **Box 7.2: The Earned Income Tax Credit in the US**
>
> The **Earned Income Tax Credit** (EITC) has been in operation in the US since the mid-1970s, but it is only in the past 10 years or so that it has come to play a central role as part of the drive to 'end welfare' and to get people into paid work. It is now a very large programme, costing about $30 billion in 2000 and received by about 19 million people.
>
> The EITC is mainly targeted at families with children, although it is also available, at lower levels of payment, to childless and to single people. It is a refundable credit, which initially rises as earnings rise, then is paid at a maximum rate over a wide range of income, and finally is reduced as earnings increase until it reaches zero. Most families opt to receive their EITC annually, as a lump sum at the end of the year, rather than as an ongoing payment.
>
> The EITC seems to be rather an 'invisible' work incentive in that the payment is not directly related to current work effort and many recipients say they are not sure what the EITC is, or why they receive it. This was one of the reasons it was not more directly copied as a model for the UK. But research evidence does suggest that it has an impact on employment rates. It also has a positive impact on incomes and living standards in work, although not by any means enough to eliminate in-work poverty.
>
> Useful references include: Meyer and Holtz-Eakin (2000); Hotz and Scholz (2002); The *Making Wages Work* website at www.financeprojectinfo.org/mww

However, despite the presentation of these tax credits as something new and different, their structure was in fact very similar to that of Family Credit. As McLaughlin et al (2001, p 164) put it: "WFTC is also a good example of the Labour tendency to re-package 'old' Labour and Tory policies and provision as new and 'modern', despite little substantive change". Like Family Credit, WFTC was available only for families with children, it was paid to those with earnings below a certain level according to family size, and there was still a weekly hours threshold of 16 hours per week. It was assessed over a six-month period and once awarded remained in payment for six months, regardless of changes in income or circumstances. All this mirrored the Family Credit rules, albeit more generously. However there were two differences. The WFTC included a Childcare Tax Credit to replace the disregard of childcare costs, which was intended to offer higher, and more visible, support for meeting costs of childcare. This would meet up to 70% of eligible costs for registered care, subject to a maximum limit, but was only available to couples if both parents were in paid work.

But the most significant difference from Family Credit was in respect of the payment mechanism. Here some of the wallet/purse debates of the mid-1980s were rerun. Again the government proposed that the tax credit should be paid through the wage packet and, given the rationale for having a tax credit rather than a benefit, this was seen by the government as essential: "this mechanism is important in order to reinforce the links between receipt of the credit and rewards of work" (HM Treasury, 1998b, p 7). But again this provoked some strong objections, not least based upon recent research (Goode et al, 1998), which reinforced earlier studies showing that extra money paid through benefits to women was more likely to get directly into the household budget than extra money paid through wages to men. The government, however, were unwilling to back down completely on this and introduced a system in which all lone parents received WFTC through the wage packet, and so did couples *unless* they opted for payment to the non-employed partner through order book or bank transfer.

The impact of Working Families Tax Credit

The WFTC and DPTC were introduced from October 1999. This means that they were hardly in place before plans to abolish them and bring in the 'next generation' of tax credits were being put forward by the Treasury (HM Treasury, 2000)[6]. We look at this in more detail in the next section, but first we should consider the impact of the WFTC, and whether or not it acted as an effective wage supplement. **Table 7.3** gives the basic statistics for receipt[7]. In November 1999, when it was first introduced, there were about 966,000 families in receipt. Lone parents outnumbered couples (as they had done since about November 1998 for Family Credit), and the average payment was about £66 per week. The numbers in receipt rose steadily every year, reaching 1.3 million families with 2.62 million children in May 2002 with an average weekly payment of about £88. Most of the couples, over three quarters, claim on the basis of the man's earnings, but about two thirds elect to receive their payments direct to the main carer, rather than through the pay packet (Bennett, 2002). The number in receipt of the Childcare Tax Credit also rose, from 55,000 to 167,000 (or from about 6 to 12% of all recipients). Lone parents are much more likely to receive this help than couples, not least because both partners in couples must be in paid work to qualify. Even so, only about one fifth of lone parents receiving WFTC also receive the Childcare Tax Credit.

---

[6] Although they had a longer life than the Children's Tax Credit (actually a tax allowance rather than a credit) which was introduced in April 2001 to replace Married Couples Tax Allowance and merged into the Child Tax Credit from April 2003.

[7] The DPTC has much smaller numbers in receipt, with about 34,000 recipients in 2002, of whom about 22,000 were single adults (including lone parents) and about 12,000 were in couples. The average award was £76.55 per week (Inland Revenue, 2002a). See Chapter Eight, this volume.

Table 7.3: Working Families Tax Credit (UK) (number of recipients) (000s)

	Working Families Tax Credit			
Year	Total	Couples	Lone parents	Average weekly amount
1999	966	468	498	£66.20
2000	1,061	513	548	£73.28
2001	1,259	617	642	£79.69
2002	1,320	635	706	£83.74

	Childcare Tax Credit			
Year	Total	Couples	Lone parents	Average weekly amount
1999	55	6	49	£30.98
2000	108	10	98	£32.15
2001	145	15	127	£36.27
2002	162	17	145	£39.46

Note: In May of each year, except 1999 November.

Source: Inland Revenue (2002b)

Overall these are quite substantial numbers and, for many recipients, significant amounts of money. As a result, the costs of tax credits rose from £1,097 million in 1999/00 to £5,525 million in 2001/02 (DWP, 2002b), so these have rapidly become an important element of expenditure[8]. The main aims of WFTC were to improve financial incentives and so help get people into work, to improve take-up ("the onus will be on the government to ensure that as many families as are entitled receive the credit", HM Treasury, 1998b, p 6), and to guarantee a minimum level of income in work and so reduce family poverty.

The Treasury was, perhaps not surprisingly, very upbeat in their assessment of WFTC (HM Treasury, 2000, pp 9-10). It had, they argued, tackled the unemployment trap by ensuring that families were 'generally' better off in work, and tackled the poverty trap by reducing by two thirds the number of families with marginal tax rates of over 70%. Alongside other measures it had also helped to increase the number of people seeking to enter work by about 160,000, and it had helped to increase family incomes, especially for the poorest families, and so contributed to reduced levels of child poverty.

---

[8] The UK accounting system for tax credits is not the same as for social security benefits – benefits are treated as expenditure while tax credits are treated as reductions on tax that would otherwise be received ('tax expenditure'). This means that tax credits are not an item of public expenditure in the same way as benefits, and not such a visible cost – a factor that may also make them more attractive to the government than benefits.

Independent research partly confirmed some of this, but also showed a more complex picture (Blundell and Walker, 2001; Brewer and Gregg, 2001; McLaughlin et al, 2001). The financial gains to work were indeed generally higher, but this applied primarily to full-time work and was much less the case for those receiving Housing Benefit (which is reduced as WFTC is received), and for those with high work costs including childcare costs (which were only partly met by the Childcare Tax Credit). Families in receipt of other means-tested benefits (again, particularly Housing Benefit) still faced high marginal tax rates. The labour supply effect was estimated to be positive for lone parents and for the first earner in a couple. But the incentive for a second earner in a couple to take up work was much reduced[9]. This mainly affects married women, and it was this – along with the decision to pay WFTC through the pay packet – that led some to view the WFTC as "more hostile than helpful to low-income women" (McLaughlin et al, 2001, p 168).

The Inland Revenue estimated that take-up in 2000/01 was in the range of 62-65% by caseload and 73-78% by expenditure (Inland Revenue, 2002c). Lone parents were estimated to have higher take-up rates than couples (77-83% compared with 49-53%) and on average received higher amounts (£79 per week compared with £53). Survey data (McKay, 2002) showed that those receiving WFTC gave it a generally positive assessment – they felt it had helped them more than Family Credit to take, or stay in, employment and they found the claiming process relatively straightforward. However, payment through employers, with wages, was not very popular, with only 11% of people who were, or had ever been, in receipt saying that this was their preferred method of payment. Neither lone parents nor couples preferred payment through employers, mainly for reasons of privacy and for budgeting purposes (being paid at different times could help families to manage their low incomes). Awareness of the WFTC was fairly low among those who were not in receipt. About a third of non-claimants said they had never heard of it, and although many knew the hours rules (that you have to work 16 or more hours a week to receive support), few knew much else about it.

Take-up of Family Credit in 1998/99 was estimated at between 66% and 70% by caseload (excluding self-employed) and between 73% and 79% by expenditure (Inland Revenue, 2002c). Therefore there was, it seems, no substantial increase in take-up rates as the government had hoped and predicted. This reduced the impact on family poverty rates. It had been estimated that child poverty rates would fall by over a million as a result of tax and benefit changes, including the WFTC. But the actual figures for 2000/01 showed that

---

[9] This financial disincentive for a second earner also existed under Family Credit, of course, although less strongly because the level of benefit was lower. This problem is inherent in a family-based means test – when the second earner enters work the amount of benefit received started to reduce. This is one of the arguments used in favour of a more individualised system of benefits (Millar, 1998; McLauglin et al, 2002).

child poverty had only fallen by about 500,000 (DWP, 2002c). Brewer et al (2002) suggest three factors that explain this shortfall: a higher relative poverty line, the full effects of increased benefits and tax credits not yet in place, and the fact that some families were not taking up their full entitlements. Delivering means-tested benefits, even if they are called tax credits, is not as straightforward as governments would like.

Different goals, different instruments: the next generation of tax credits

As of April 2003, two new tax credits came into being: the **Child Tax Credit** and the **Working Tax Credit**. Child Tax Credit will bring all child-related payments, apart from Child Benefit, into one single system. It will thus replace the child components of Income Support and income-related Jobseeker's Allowances, the child components of WFTC and DPTC, and the Children's Tax Credit. It will be paid to the main carer. The main goals for Child Tax Credit are to *support family income* and to *reduce child poverty*. But because it is a single system for both working and non-working families, it should also help to make the transition from unemployment to work easier. (See also Chapter Nine this volume.)

The Working Tax Credit will replace the adult components of WFTC and DPTC, as well as the small employment credit paid to people aged over 50 who are unemployed and enter work[10], and will be available to anyone aged over 25 and working at least 30 hours per week (16 hours for disabled people). It will include a childcare element, which will meet up to 70% of the costs of eligible childcare. The Working Tax Credit will be paid through the pay packet, although the childcare element will be paid alongside Child Tax Credit to the main carer. The goals for Working Tax Credit are to *increase financial incentives to work* and to *reduce in-work poverty* for single people and childless couples.

Introducing these changes, HM Treasury (2000) point to the importance, as they see it, of matching policy goals and policy instruments:

> Using one system to achieve two objectives – in the case of Working Families Tax Credit, better work incentives and increased family support – can give rise to tensions. At the same time, using several different instruments to contribute to a single goal – increased family support in Income Support, the Working Families Tax Credit and the children's tax credit can mean a duplication of effort. (HM Treasury, 2000, p 12)

---

[10] This was originally part of the New Deal 50 Plus, and paid as a flat-rate amount for the first 12 months of employment.

In addition, the tax credits are seen as an opportunity to 'modernise' delivery, and in particular to create a simpler and more effective form of means testing, with administration rationalised into one government department, the Inland Revenue, and assessment based "more closely on the rules and definitions of income on which people's tax bills are paid" (Inland Revenue, 2001, p 10). The new tax credits are intended to be simpler to administer and understand but also well targeted to people's needs:

> ...the income tax system provides a light touch and non-stigmatising way of measuring income.... The advent of the new tax credits offers the opportunity to introduce a new system based on the principle of progressive universalism. This means supporting all families with children, but offering greatest help to those who need it most through a light touch income test. (HM Treasury, 2002, p 4)

Tax credits are set to become a key part of the UK income transfer system. By 2005/06 the planned expenditure on tax credits will have risen to £14.6 billion per year (DWP, 2002b). About £4 billion of this is money that otherwise would have been spent on the children's elements in Income Support/ Jobseeker's Allowance, but much of it is new, reflecting the wider coverage and higher levels of payments. Spending on tax credits for working people is forecast to be almost at the same level as spending on out-of-work benefits for working-age people (about £15.5 billion by 2005/06). Tax credits will thus become an important element of expenditure. They will also be important to the people in receipt. For example, a family with one child and earning under £13,000 per year will receive about £54 per week in Child Benefit and Child Tax Credit (HM Treasury, 2002, p 3).

Tax credits: design and delivery

About 6 million households are expected to come within the range of Child Tax Credit and Working Tax Credit, and making the new system work as intended will be a major administrative challenge. Although these tax credits may be described as separate instruments in formal design terms, they will all be assessed in the same way by the same system, and will be subject to the same withdrawal rates. **Box 7.3** sets out the key features of how the 'light touch' means tests will operate. This is very different from the current system – the use of annual income to assess needs, the annual reconciliation, the less detailed reporting rules in respect of changes in income, and the disregard of £2,500 of income rise in the year in which it happens – are all new.

Box 7.3: Key features of the Child Tax Credit and the Working Tax Credit

The Child Tax Credit is made up of two parts: a family element and a child element. The Working Tax Credit is made up of several parts: an adult element, an element for those working 30 hours or more per week, and a couple/lone parent element. There is also a childcare element. All these elements are added together to calculate a 'maximum amount'. Those with an income below a certain threshold (£5,060 in 2003/04) will receive the maximum amount. Families with children receiving Income Support or income-related Jobseeker's Allowance will automatically receive the maximum amount of Child Tax Credit. Those with an income above that threshold will receive the maximum reduced by 37 pence for each pound of gross income. This reduction will be applied first to the Working Tax Credit, next to the childcare element, and finally to the Child Tax Credit. This means that some Child Tax Credit will continue in payment quite high up the income scale (up to £58,000 in 2003/04), and more if the family includes a baby up to one year of age.

Income is gross income, and tax credits will initially be set on the basis of *previous* tax years' gross annual income (joint income in the case of couples). This award will continue in payment for 12 months, unless families notify changes, with an annual reconciliation to balance payments against actual income. Some changes will end the current award and must therefore be notified – these include changes to the number of adults in the family, ceasing to use childcare or significant reductions in childcare costs, and the birth of a child. Other changes, in particular changes in income, need not be notified unless the recipients choose to do so.

Increases in income of £2,500 will not be taken into account in the year in which the rise is received, so those with increases up to this level will continue to receive the same tax credit award. Whether an income change is reported at the time it happens, or at the end of the year, will make no difference to the tax credit entitlement for that year. At year-end, if there has been an underpayment, this will be covered by a single lump-sum payment. If there has been an overpayment this will be recovered either by adjusting subsequent tax credit awards or (if tax credits are no longer due) by adjustments to Pay-As-You-Earn (PAYE) tax codes.

The Child Tax Credit and the childcare element of the Working Tax Credit will be paid to the 'main carer'. The Working Tax Credit will be paid by the employer through the pay packet.

Table 7.4 gives three examples of how the tax credits are calculated, using rates in 2003/04. The calculation involves adding up all the various elements of the Working Tax Credit and the Child Tax Credit and then comparing these against the first threshold (which is £5,060 in 2003/04 for people working at least 16 hours per week). For the single person, the only possible entitlement is to Working Tax Credit and in this example, with gross income in work of

Table 7.4: The calculation of tax credits, annual rates in payment (2003/04)

	Single person, aged over 25, working over 30 hours per week	Lone parent, one child of school age, works 25 hours per week, childcare costs of £60 per week	Couple, two children of school age, both parents in work one over 30 hours), childcare costs of £50 per week
Working Tax Credit			
Basic element	£1,525	£1,525	£1,525
Couple/lone parent element	–	£1,500	£1,500
30-hour element	£620	–	£620
Childcare element (70% of weekly cost)	–	£2,184	£1,820
Child Tax Credit			
Family element	–	£545	£545
Child element	–	£1,445	£2,890
Maximum entitlement	£2,145	£7,199	£8,900
Gross income	£9,000	£6,500	£18,000
Minus threshold	–£5,060= £3,940	–£5,060= £1,440	–£5,060= £12,940
x 37%	£1,457.80	£532.80	£4,787.80
Total tax credit entitlement[a]	£687.20 (£13.22 per week)	£6,666.20 (£128.20 per week)	£4,112.20 (£79.08 per week)
Total made up of:			
Child Tax Credit	–	£1,990	£3,435
Childcare element	–	£2,184	£677.20
Working Tax Credit	£687.20	£2,492.20	nil
Child Benefit	–	£834	£1,393.60

Note: [a] Maximum entitlement – 37% of excess income.

£9,000 per year, there is a weekly entitlement to Working Tax Credit of almost £690 per year, or about £13 per week. For the lone parent in this example, with a gross income in work of £6,500 per year, there is entitlement to Child Tax Credit, Working Tax Credit and the childcare element. When Child Benefit is added, this gives a total of about £7,500 per year – more than gross earnings. For this couple with gross income in work of £18,000, there is entitlement to Child Tax Credit and a partial payment of the childcare element, but no entitlement to Working Tax Credit (which is withdrawn first). The total tax credit amount would therefore all be paid to the main carer, usually the mother, and so would the Child Benefit.

These next generation tax credits therefore seem to offer a new approach to the delivery of in-work financial support. They are not simply a social security benefit under another name. The objectives for the design of these included creating a system which is "simple for recipients to access and governments to deliver ... simple for people to understand" but which is also "targeted, so families receive the money to which they are entitled, neither being overpaid nor underpaid according to their needs" (HM Treasury, 2000, p 21). Tax credits will be received by people with very different income levels, and so must be responsive to changes in income or circumstances. The Child Tax Credit is intended to be able to "provide continuity of support for those who are not experiencing significant changes in circumstances or income, with the ability to adjust quickly for those who are facing major changes" (HM Treasury, 2002, p 19).

Striking the right balance between simplicity and targeting has long been the aspiration for means-tested benefits. There is also a trade-off to be made between simplicity and responsiveness. The Child Tax Credit and Working Tax Credit means test is simpler in some ways (the tax-based definition of income) but more complex and less transparent in others (some changes have to be reported immediately while others do not). There will no longer be a fixed award period (this was six months for WFTC), as, although awards are initially set for 12 months, this does not remain fixed if certain circumstances change. Families are likely to find it hard to understand what their entitlement is, and why it changes. This lack of transparency and security will particularly affect low-income families, who will be potentially eligible for Child Tax Credit, Working Tax Credit with the childcare element, and possibly Housing Benefit, rather than middle-income families who are just eligible for Child Tax Credit. The responsiveness of the system relies upon the compliance of the recipients – they have to know and understand the rules, to monitor their incomes, and childcare costs, and hours of work, and to inform the Inland Revenue as appropriate. Recipients must meet the working hours conditions for WTC throughout the time of their award, and so need to be aware of the impact of changing hours of work, for both partners in a couple. The treatment of childcare costs seems particularly complex and likely to cause difficulties.

There will be significant challenges for the Inland Revenue in coping with such a large new group of tax credit claimants. There have been some problems in the initial launch of tax credits in April 2003 (*The Guardian*, 28 April 2003). And the rules about reporting changes are complicated. Previous experience with means-tested benefits suggests that families do not necessarily respond to changes in income and circumstances, and there can often be quite significant delays in claiming (Corden, 1995). The number and impact of year-end reconciliation may thus be far larger than the Treasury anticipate. In Australia,

---

Box 7.4: Overpayments of family tax benefits in Australia

There are two main benefits for children delivered through the tax system in Australia: **Family Tax Benefit Part A** is a means-tested payment similar to Child Tax Credit. **Family Tax Benefit Part B** provides extra assistance to single-income families including lone parents, with higher rates for families with children under five years of age. In July 2000, there were two important changes to the delivery. First, there was a shift from assessment on the basis of previous years' earnings to an assessment based on the recipient's estimate of taxable income for the forthcoming tax year. Second, year-end reconciliation was introduced when payments would be assessed against actual income. If actual income were less than estimated income there would be an extra payment. If actual income were more than estimated, overpayments of the family tax benefits would have to be repaid.

When the reconciliation came into effect for the first time at the end of the 200/01 tax year, many families had, in fact, been overpaid and owed a debt to the government. This caused immediate controversy and the government responded by announcing that they would waive the first A$1,000 of all overpayments, at a cost of around A$360 million. Nevertheless problems remained, with objections in particular from families still with debts to pay.

The level of overpayments had increased significantly compared with the previous system. This is partly because many of these overpayments were ignored in the previous system which did not seek to reconcile payments against income. But it seems that families were more likely to underestimate than to overestimate income, perhaps because they were cautious, or because they preferred to receive money now and worry about paying it back later.

The Australian experience was explicitly taken into account in the design of the UK system (HM Treasury, 2002, p 22), in particular in the provision of the £2,500 disregard, which will reduce the level of overpayments in the UK, and in the fact that repayments will take the form of reductions to future tax credit awards (rather than a lump-sum repayment). But the Australian experience also showed that families had far more changes of income and circumstances than had been expected, making it difficult to measure annual income accurately from current income, and this may also be the case for the UK.

Source: Whiteford et al (2003)

as Box 7.4 discusses, the introduction of a system of annual reconciliation for 'family tax' benefits caused significant problems, because many families underestimated their incomes and so received overpayments which then had to be repaid. The UK system is not the same as the Australian system, but it may not entirely avoid some similar problems if, as seems likely, many assessments do change over the course of the year but are not reported.

There are also issues of concern about the wider impact of these tax credits (Bennett and Hirsch, 2001; Brewer et al, 2001; SSSC, 2001; Bennett, 2002). The extension of wage supplements to all low-paid workers aged over 25 may have a significant effect on the low-wage labour market, even with a National Minimum Wage (NMW). The use of a family-based income test means that there will still be financial disincentives for 'second' earners, although these are less than under WFTC. The overall increase in labour supply is therefore likely to be modest. The joint assessment of income for couples arguably compromises the individual base of the tax system. The separation of support for adults from support for children may open the way to greater conditionality and more sanctions to be applied to the payments for adults. The extension of means testing, albeit through the tax rather than the benefit system, to more groups and higher up the income scale takes the UK even further down this road and away from universal or categorical ways of targeting support (see Chapter One in this volume). Tax credits offer substantial increases in income for some individuals and families, but only if they can be delivered to those eligible more effectively than previous means-tested benefits.

Overview

- Benefits to supplement wages have been available in the UK for over 30 years. However, in-work wage supplementation through tax credits is set to become a key part of the UK income transfer system. Within a few years spending on tax credits for working people is forecast to be almost at the same level as spending on out-of-work benefits for non-retired people. Many families and individuals will potentially benefit.

- Eligibility for tax credits will be assessed by the Inland Revenue, through an annual means test, which is intended to be simple, non-intrusive but also responsive to changes in circumstances and needs.

- Getting the tax credits paid to those eligible is a major challenge for the government, or more specifically, for the Inland Revenue. The way in which the means test will operate has many new features but there are question marks over whether or not these will improve take-up rates and provide families with a secure and reliable source of income.

> • The wider impact of wage supplementation – on in-work poverty, on wage levels, and on overall employment levels – also remains to be seen.

Questions for discussion

1. Trace the development of wage supplements in the UK. Why have these become such an important part of the social security system?

2. Are tax credits different from social security benefits?

3. Have the government found the right balance between simplicity, targeting and responsiveness in the design of the Child Tax Credit and the Working Tax Credit?

4. Will tax credits increase financial incentives to work?

References

Abel-Smith, B. and Townsend, P. (1965) *The poor and the poorest,* London: Bell and Sons.

Bennett, F. (2002) 'Gender implications of current social security reforms', *Fiscal Studies,* vol 23, no 4, pp 559-84.

Bennett, F. and Hirsch, D. (2001) *The Employment Tax Credit and issues for the future of in-work support,* York: York Publishing Services for the Joseph Rowntree Foundation.

Blundell, R. and Walker, I. (2001) *Working Families' Tax Credit: A review of the evidence, issues and prospects for further research,* London: Inland Revenue.

Brewer, M. and Gregg, P. (2001) 'Lone parents, the Working Families' Tax Credit and employment in households with children', in R. Dickens, J. Wadsworth and P. Gregg (eds) *The state of working Britain: Update 2001,* London: Centre for Economic Policy.

Brewer, M., Clark, T. and Goodman, A. (2002) *The government's child poverty target: How much progress has been made?,* London: Institute for Fiscal Studies.

Brewer, M., Myck, M. and Reed, H. (2001) *Financial support for families with children: Options for the new integrated child credit,* Commentary No 92, London: Institute for Fiscal Studies.

Brown, J.C. (1983) *Family income supplement: Family income support,* London: Policy Studies Institute.

Corden, A. (1995) *Changing perspectives on benefit take up,* York: Social Policy Research Unit, University of York.

Deacon, A. (1998) 'Learning from the USA? The influence of American ideas on "new" Labour thinking on welfare reform', *Policy & Politics,* vol 28, no 1, pp 5-18.

Deacon, A. (2002) *Perspectives on welfare: Ideas, ideologies and policy debates,* Buckingham: Open University Press.

Deacon, A. and Bradshaw, J. (1983) *Reserved for the poor: The means-test in British social policy*, Oxford: Martin Robertson.

Dean, H. and Shah, A. (2002) 'Insecure families and low-paying labour markets: comments on the British experience', *Journal of Social Policy*, vol 31, no 1, pp 64-80.

DHSS (Department for Health and Social Security) (1985) *The reform of social security*, London: HMSO.

DSS (Department for Social Security) (1996) *Income-related benefits: Estimates of take-up in 1994/95*, London: The Stationery Office.

DSS (1998) *New ambitions for our country: A new contract for welfare*, Cm 3805, London: The Stationery Office.

DWP (Department for Work and Pensions) (2002a) *Building choice and responsibility: A radical agenda for Housing Benefit*, London: The Stationery Office.

DWP (2002b) 'Benefit expenditure tables 2002', www.dwp.gov.uk

DWP (2002c) *Households Below Average Income 1994/95 to 2000/01*, Leeds: Corporate Document Services.

Finlayson, L., Ford, R., Marsh, A., Smith, A. and White, M. (2000) *The first effects of earnings top-up*, DSS Research Report No 112, Leeds: Corporate Document Services.

Goode, J., Callender, C. and Lister, R. (1998) *Purse or wallet: Gender inequalities and income distribution within families on benefits*, London: Policy Studies Institute.

Guardian, The (2003) '300,000 face wait for tax credit cash', 28 April.

Hirsch, D. (2000) *A credit to children: The UK's radical reform of children's benefits in international perspective*, York: York Publishing Services for the Joseph Rowntree Foundation.

HM Treasury (1971) *Reform of personal direct taxation*, Cmnd 4653, London: HMSO.

HM Treasury (1997) *The modernisation of Britain's tax and benefit system number 1: Employment opportunity in a changing labour market*, London: HM Treasury.

HM Treasury (1998a) *The modernisation of Britain's tax and benefit system number 2: Work incentives: A report by Martin Taylor*, London: HM Treasury.

HM Treasury (1998b) *The modernisation of Britain's tax and Benefit system number 3: The Working Families' Tax Credit and work incentives*, London: HM Treasury.

HM Treasury (1999) *The modernisation of Britain's tax and benefit system number 5: Supporting children through the tax and benefit system*, London: HM Treasury.

HM Treasury (2000) *The modernisation of Britain's tax and benefit system number 6: Tackling poverty and making work pay – Tax credits for the 21st century*, London: HM Treasury.

HM Treasury (2002) *The modernisation of Britain's tax and benefit system: The Child and Working Tax Credits*, HM Treasury No 10, London: The Public Enquiry Unit, HM Treasury.

Hotz, V.J. and Scholz, J.K. (2002) 'The Earned Income Tax Credit', in R. Moffitt (ed) *Means-tested transfer programs in the US*, National Bureau for Economic Research, Cambridge, MA (www.nber.org/books/means-tested/index.html).

Inland Revenue (2001) *New tax credits: Supporting families, making work pay and tackling poverty: A consultative document*, London: Inland Revenue.

Inland Revenue (2002a) *Disabled Person's Tax Credit Statistics Quarterly Enquiry: United Kingdom October 2001*, London: Inland Revenue.

Inland Revenue (2002b) *Working Families' Tax Credit Statistics Quarterly Enquiry*, London: Inland Revenue.

Inland Revenue (2002c) *Working Families' Tax Credit: Estimate of take-up rates in 2000-1*, London: Inland Revenue.

McKay, S. (2002) *Low/moderate income families in Britain: Work, Working Families' Tax Credit and childcare in 2000*, DWP Research Report No 161, Leeds: Corporate Document Services.

McKay, S. and Marsh, A. (1995) *Why didn't they claim? A follow-up study of eligible non-claimants of Family Credit*, London: Policy Studies Institute.

McLaughlin, E., Trewsdale, J. and McCay, N. (2001) 'The rise and fall of the UK's first tax credit', *Social Policy and Administration*, vol 35, no 2, pp 163-80.

McLaughlin, E., Yeates, N. and Kelly, G. (2002) *Social protection and units of assessment: Issues and reforms: A comparative study*, TUC Welfare Reform Series No 44, London: TUC.

Meyer, B.D. and Holtz-Eakin, D. (eds) (2000) *Making work pay:The Earned Income Tax Credit and its impact on America's families*, New York, NY: Russell Sage Foundation.

Millar, J. (1998) 'Reforming welfare: the Australian experience', *Benefits*, no 23, pp 32-4.

Millar, J., Webb, S. and Kemp, M. (1997) *Combining work and welfare*, York: Joseph Rowntree Foundation.

SSSC (Social Security Select Committee) (2001) *Integrated child credit*, Second Report, Session 2000-2001, HC 72, London: The Stationery Office.

Walker, R. (1998) 'The Americanisation of British welfare: a case study of policy transfer', *Focus*, vol 19, no 3, pp 32-40.

Whiteford, P., Mendelson, M. and Millar, J. (2003) *Timing it right? Responding to income changes, a comparison of Australia, Canada and the UK*, York: York Publishing Services for the Joseph Rowntree Foundation.

Website resources

HM Treasury	www.hm-treasury.gov.uk
Inland Revenue	www.inlandrevenue.gov.uk
Institute for Fiscal Studies (Pensions and Savings section)	www.ifs.org.uk/pensionsindex.shtml
Low Pay Commission	www.lowpay.gov.uk

eight

Disability, capability and social exclusion

Tania Burchardt

Summary

When Labour came into power in 1997, rates of poverty among disabled people were high, employment rates were low and social exclusion was widespread. The system of support through the benefit system and social services which had been built up over the decades was complex. The government promised to address the needs of disabled people, and to create a more 'joined-up' system of support. This chapter:

- looks at the main developments in policy from 1997 to date for disabled children, disabled people of working age and disabled pensioners;

- considers whether 'welfare-to-work' measures have been enough to make a difference to employment rates among disabled people;

- argues that little has been done to provide security for disabled people who are not in the labour market;

- concludes by examining remaining gaps in provision: at the transition between childhood and adulthood, and the transition between working life and retirement; in the uncertain area between being capable and incapable of work; and on the boundaries of healthcare, social care and social security.

Introduction: welfare policy for disabled people

In Labour's first term in office, welfare policy was clearly divided into 'work' (for those who can) and 'security' (for those who cannot). Disabled people made an appearance on both sides of this divide, and arguably many fell in between. Some disabled people were already in paid employment, and stood to gain from the government's efforts to 'make work pay', through the introduction of the National Minimum Wage (NMW) and enhanced in-work benefits. Other disabled people were actively seeking work, and were eligible for additional assistance through the New Deal for Disabled People. On the other side of the divide, some severely disabled people and disabled children gained from the extension of particular benefits. In between these groups were a large number, with a wide range of impairments and circumstances, who were entitled apparently neither to 'work' nor to 'security'. They might have been able to work had the labour market been differently structured, had employers had less discriminatory attitudes, and had transport been accessible, but in the real world, they were left struggling to make ends meet on means-tested benefits.

Labour's second term signalled a change in the organisation of welfare policy. In the new Department for Work and Pensions, a tripartite distinction was introduced based on age. Benefits for children were rolled up into a tax credit, to be administered by the Inland Revenue. (Although not formally announced, it seems likely that the Child Support Agency will in due course also transfer to Inland Revenue.) A Pension Service was established to deal with state pensions, means-tested benefits for pensioners, and to advise on pension provision more generally. For people of working age, Jobcentre Plus was created to administer benefits, advise on jobs and direct claimants to the most appropriate source of help, whether financial or otherwise. For disabled people of working age, there is a potential advantage to merging the 'work' and 'security' strands in a single organisation, particularly since Jobcentre Plus is committed as an organisation to assessing each person's needs individually rather than on the basis of claimant types. Integrating disability into mainstream programmes could mean, at best, breaking down the barriers for disabled people's entry into employment and moving away from artificial distinctions between work capacity and incapacity. At worst, it could leave disabled people struggling to justify their requirements to generalist staff with little understanding of disability-related issues, and being forced into inappropriate welfare-to-work programmes. Where on the spectrum between best and worst case scenarios we are, is one of the questions this chapter will seek to address.

The Labour government inherited a fragmented system of support for disabled people. Aside from the complex relationship between social services and social security, to which Chapter Six in this volume draws attention, within

> **Box 8.1: Types of benefits for disabled people**
>
> **Extra costs benefits:** designed to help towards additional costs of living incurred by disabled people
>
> for example, *Attendance Allowance, Disability Living Allowance*
>
> **Earnings replacement benefits:** designed to provide an income for people unable to work or carry out household duties due to long-term sickness or disability
>
> for example, *Incapacity Benefit, Severe Disablement Allowance*
>
> **Means-tested benefits:** designed to top up income to a minimum level, often with additional 'premiums' for disabled people
>
> for example, *Income Support, Disabled Person's Tax Credit*
>
> **Compensatory benefits:** designed to compensate people who became disabled as a result of military service or their employment
>
> for example, *Industrial Injuries Disablement Allowance, War Disability Pension*

social security itself there are a multitude of benefits. **Box 8.1** indicates one way in which they can be categorised, according to their underlying purpose.

Eligibility for some of these benefits, such as Incapacity Benefit, depends on having made adequate national insurance contributions; for others, it depends on having family income or earnings below a given level; while yet other benefits are conditional on employment status. This patchwork of provision has developed over the preceding century and, as **Box 8.1** indicates, with a variety of objectives. There was therefore considerable sympathy with the goal which Labour set itself of 'modernising' welfare provision, at least if modernisation was understood to imply simplification and ironing out some of the anachronisms in eligibility. The extent to which this has been achieved is another question to be addressed in this chapter.

In 1997, when Labour came into power, poverty and social exclusion was widespread among disabled people. Two fifths of disabled people of working age had incomes below half the national average and over half of disabled people with children had incomes below this level (Burchardt, 2000)[1]. If incomes are adjusted for the extra costs some disabled people incur as a result of their disability, the figures were even starker, rising to three fifths of disabled people with the most severe impairments[2]. Rates of employment among

---

[1] Income defined as equivalised family net income after housing costs. Based on 1996/97 Family Resources Survey and Disability Follow-Up.

[2] Adjustment based on Berthoud et al (1993) calculations, uprated to 1996/97 prices.

disabled people were low: 31%, according to one definition, compared to 77% of non-disabled people (*Labour Force Survey*, Spring 1997). More broadly, access to services and opportunities for social interaction were limited: fewer than one in five disabled people reported that they went to the cinema, theatre or a concert at least once a month, compared to one in three non-disabled people, and the proportion of disabled people who felt they lacked social support was twice that of non-disabled people (Burchardt, 2000). If the government was to achieve its goal of 'opportunity for all', there was much to be done.

Box 8.2 gives an overview of the main policy developments since 1997. The central question for this chapter is whether the combination of new policies and the reorganisation of delivery have overcome the fragmented nature of support and poor outcomes for disabled people of all ages which Labour inherited. The organisation of the chapter mirrors that of current welfare delivery by being divided into three age groups – children, people of working age, and pensioners – and it concludes by considering the extent to which the twin objectives of joined-up policy making and improved opportunities for disabled people have been achieved.

Box 8.2: Main developments in disability policy (1997-2002)

1997 New Deal for Disabled People pilots of personal adviser service and innovative schemes launched

1999 Welfare Reform Act passed, extending Disability Living Allowance for children, abolishing Severe Disablement Allowance, and altering eligibility for Incapacity Benefit

2000 Disability Rights Commission becomes operational, with responsibility for overseeing implementation of 1995 Disability Discrimination Act and advising government on disability issues

2001 New Deal for Disabled People job brokers service (similar to personal advisers) extended nationally

2001 Special Educational Needs and Disability Act passed, strengthening rights of disabled children to mainstream education, and extending scope of Disability Discrimination Act to education

2001 Learning Disability White Paper published

2002 Jobcentre Plus and Pension Service launched

2002 Working Tax Credit and Child Tax Credit announced, both including additional components for disability

---

Children

Childhood disability is often portrayed as a tragedy or random misfortune, but the marked social class gradient in prevalence rates suggests otherwise (**Figure 8.1**). The proportion of disabled children in the top three socioeconomic groups is lower than the proportion of all children in those groups, while nearly twice the proportion of disabled children are from an unskilled socioeconomic group than the proportion of all children from that group. Factors such as poor maternal health and nutrition, smoking, low birthweight, poor housing conditions and greater risk of accidents combine to produce these differentials.

Disabled children are also correspondingly over-represented among low-income households. One third of children who live in a household which contains a disabled child (whether themselves or a sibling) have incomes below 60% of median income (DWP, 2002, Table 4.5). Surveys in the mid-1980s indicated that while just 6% of all adults said they could not afford new clothes, 33% of adults with disabled children said so. Similarly, 5% of all adults said they could not afford presents for friends and family once a year, compared to 14% of adults with disabled children (Gordon et al, 2000). Part of the reason for these differences is undoubtedly the low incomes of households in which disabled children live. But an additional reason is the costs which families

Figure 8.1: Childhood disability, by social class

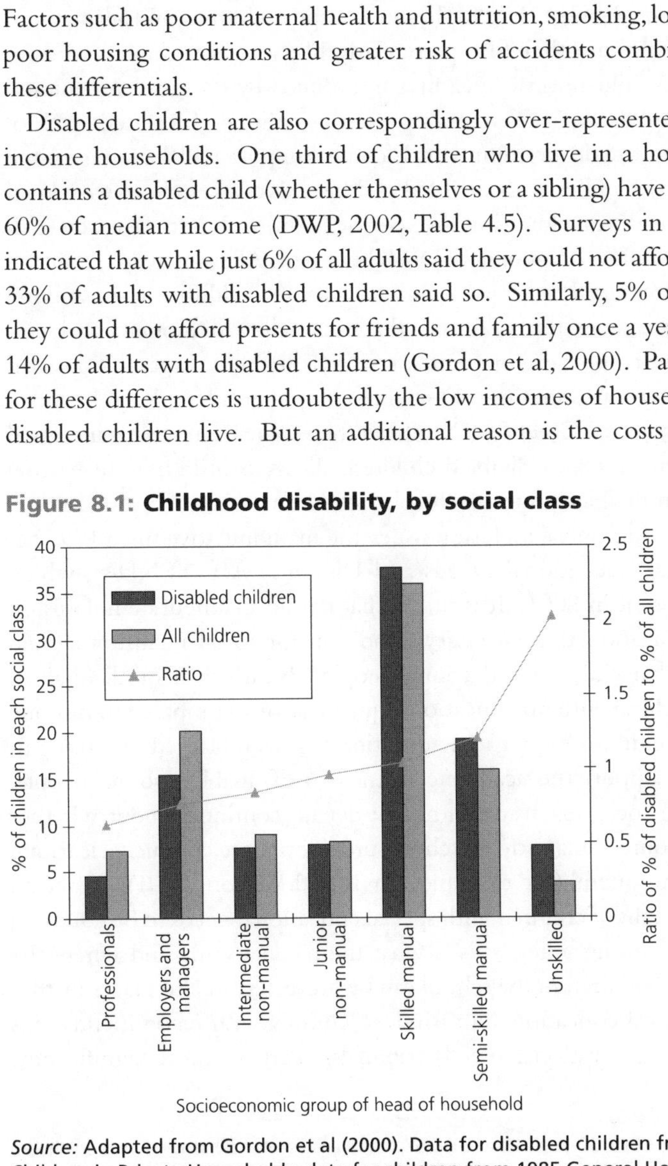

Source: Adapted from Gordon et al (2000). Data for disabled children from 1985 OPCS Survey of Disabled Children in Private Households; data for children from 1985 General Household Survey

incur as a result of the child's disability – costs which parents may well meet before turning to their own needs for clothing or social activities. Estimates based on discussions with parents with and without severely disabled children suggested that the minimum essential costs of bringing up a severely disabled child were around three times as great as for a non-disabled child (Dobson and Middleton, 1998). Parents reported restrictions on their ability to increase their incomes through paid work, due to the lack of suitable childcare, and restrictions on the activities of the family as a whole, through having to prioritise expenditure on the disabled child for health, transport, clothing and adaptations.

Disabled children are therefore particularly likely to have benefited from the general anti-child-poverty measures introduced by the government and discussed in more detail in Chapter Nine of this volume. Increased levels of Child Benefit and child premiums in Income Support will have raised the incomes of many families with disabled children. However, there have been relatively few measures addressing the specific additional costs faced by such families. The mobility component of Disability Living Allowance was extended in 2001 to children aged three and four who have severe difficulty in walking or cannot walk, in recognition of the fact that early help with mobility problems is critical – a welcome development for which disability organisations had been campaigning for some time. Disability components have been included in the design of the new Child Tax Credit, but their value has not been increased relative to benefits for non-disabled children. There is little here to narrow the gap between disabled and non-disabled children.

In terms of broader social inclusion issues, the main initiative since 1997 has been the Special Educational Needs and Disability Act (SENDA), which received royal assent in 2001. It is fitting that the government's emphasis on high-quality education as a necessary condition for social inclusion should extend to disabled children and young people. Nearly half of all disabled children leave school with no educational qualifications, compared to just one in eight of all children[3]. Segregated education has been blamed for failing to encourage and support the academic aspirations of disabled young people, and entrenching social exclusion, although debate continues about whether inadequately resourced mainstream schools provide a more conducive learning and social environment (for example, Davis and Watson, 2001). SENDA strengthens the right of children with special educational needs to be educated in a mainstream setting where this is what the parents want, and where the interests of other children in the school can be protected. It also places further obligations on local education authorities to comply with recommendations made by Special Educational Needs tribunals. Perhaps more significantly,

---

[3] Forty-five per cent of 16- to 29-year-olds in 1996/97, who were disabled at birth or during childhood, had no qualifications. Thirteen per cent of all 16- to 29-year-olds in 1998/99 had no qualifications. *Source*: author's calculations from Family Resources Survey and Disability Follow-Up.

SENDA extends the 1995 Disability Discrimination Act to cover educational establishments; previously state and private schools, and institutions of further and higher education were exempt. This means that it is now illegal for schools and colleges to treat a disabled student less favourably as a result of their disability (without justification), or to fail to make reasonable adjustments to accommodate them. The vague qualifying clauses, 'without justification' and 'reasonable adjustments', continue to cause confusion and permit potential abuse, but at least in the field of non-educational services, case law is beginning to tighten up the definitions (Meager et al, 1999). From 2004, 'reasonable adjustments' will include altering physical features and providing auxiliary aids and services.

Overall, the government's strategy for disabled children has moved towards mainstreaming, both in terms of benefit delivery (incorporating child disability components in the new tax credit), and in terms of education (incorporating children with special educational needs into mainstream provision). But the process is far from complete: Disability Living Allowance for children will not be integrated with other benefits for children, but will be administered by a newly created Disability and Carers Service[4]. Other forms of support will continue to be administered by schools, health authorities, and social services. Moreover, the right to inclusion remains qualified by what is regarded as 'reasonable' by the providers of education and other services and as interpreted by the tribunals. Converting the government's aspiration of equal opportunities for disabled children into a reality will require both increasing the *levels* of financial support available to their families, and dismantling the paradox of 'reasonable discrimination'.

Working-age people

Work for those who can

The government's efforts to enhance employment opportunities for disabled people can be considered under three headings: help with finding a job, ensuring the gap between incomes in and out of work is sufficiently large to provide an incentive to work, and help with job retention.

The first phase of the New Deal for Disabled People (NDDP) was launched in 1997, with a range of projects piloting a personal adviser service and 'innovative schemes' for helping disabled people find work. The pilots were set up as partnerships between the public, private and voluntary sectors with different organisations taking the lead in different parts of the country, and the

---

[4] The exact form of the Disability and Carers Service is yet to be determined at the time of writing, but it is likely to be a national organisation for the administration of benefits such as Disability Living Allowance, Attendance Allowance and Invalid Care Allowance.

emphasis was placed firmly on seeking out what forms of support were most effective. Participation of disabled people in NDDP was voluntary and one of the first findings from the evaluation was a very low take-up rate: just 3% of those who were invited to attend for interview did so (Arthur et al, 1999). Qualitative evidence suggested that fear of losing benefits and being in a poor state of health were contributory factors. The experience of the innovative schemes (Blackburn et al, 1999) and of the personal adviser service was that close contact with employers was crucial to success, so when NDDP was extended nationally in 2001, personal advisers were renamed job brokers and were expected to "work closely with a variety of employers, to identify jobs available, ... promote the advantages of employing disabled people and inform employers of their obligations under Disability Discrimination legislation" (DWP, 2000, p 7). This was an important change in rhetoric from previous 'welfare-to-work' programmes for disabled people, emphasising what the employer might need to do in order to employ a disabled person, not just what a disabled person might need to do in order to be employed. To what extent this is translated into practice remains to be seen.

For most disabled claimants, Jobcentre Plus (formed in 2002 from the reorganisation of the Employment Service and parts of the Benefits Agency) will act as a gateway to other services, such as NDDP. The most significant differences from preceding arrangements will be a work-focused interview for all new claimants of sickness and disability benefits, and the potential for greater integration in the delivery of unemployment and incapacity benefits. As Ashworth et al (2001) and Hedges and Sykes (2001) reveal, the transitions between Jobseeker's Allowance, Income Support and Incapacity Benefit were anything but smooth when the benefits were administered by different agencies. Multiple transitions were not uncommon, sometimes with no change in health status but simply as a result of recategorisation by one or other administrator. Conversely, genuine changes in health status were sometimes treated with suspicion by staff, and claimants experienced delays and hassle in getting the benefits to which they were entitled.

Two initiatives designed to ensure a sufficient income from employment for disabled people can be identified, one general and one specific. The general initiative was the introduction in April 1999 of a National Minimum Wage. Disabled people in work are over-represented in low-skilled and low-pay occupations (Burchardt, 2000), and hence stood to gain from the introduction of a floor under wages. Concerns were expressed by some disability organisations, especially those representing people with learning difficulties and mental health problems, that 'marginal workers' might be laid off or have their hours reduced, if employers believed that their productivity did not warrant an increase in pay (LPC, 2000). However, preliminary evidence indicates that the difference in employment retention rates between disabled and non-disabled people over the period of the introduction of the National

Minimum Wage was slight, and that on average, earnings of low-paid disabled workers increased (Burchardt and McKnight, forthcoming).

The specific initiative designed to 'make work pay' for disabled people was the conversion of Disability Working Allowance into the Disabled Person's Tax Credit (DPTC) in 1999, followed by the proposal to include a disability component in a general Working Tax Credit. Disability Working Allowance, the first in-work benefit for disabled people introduced under the Conservatives in 1992, suffered from obscurity, complex administration and eligibility rules, and comparatively low levels of benefit (Rowlingson and Berthoud, 1996). DPTC remedied some of these flaws and take-up has certainly increased: from 19,445 cases in October 1999 to 32,070 two years later (Inland Revenue, 2002). 'Mainstreaming' the support available to low-paid disabled workers by including it in the Working Tax Credit could help to improve take-up yet further.

Finally, there have been a number of measures designed to help disabled people already in work retain their employment. A spin-off from the main NDDP was a Job Retention and Rehabilitation Pilot, to test different forms of workplace and healthcare interventions which might help people who become sick or disabled while in employment to keep their jobs. The pilots ran into controversy over the use of random assignment as an evaluation methodology, and at the time of writing results are not yet available.

Supported employment was overhauled, with a view to ensuring that as many people as possible move into mainstream employment – as reflected in the new name for the whole supported employment programme, *Workstep*. Critics argued that the targets set by government for progression into unsupported employment were unrealistic and would lead to people being abandoned while still in need of assistance, but the overall direction of the reform was in line with longer-term trends away from segregated employment.

Access to Work is a little-known programme, previously administered by the Department for Education and Employment and now under the aegis of Jobcentre Plus, which helps towards individuals' and employers' costs in employing a disabled person, including, for example, fares to work, personal assistance, or aids and adaptations. The programme is popular with both employers and clients who have used it (although delays in processing payments sometimes cause difficulties); the main complaint has always been that few people know about it (RNIB/RADAR, 1995). In principle Access to Work should help disabled people to secure employment as well as to keep it, but in practice most payments go to those already in work. Funding for Access to Work was increased significantly under Labour from £13.8 million in 1996/97 to £32.4 million in 2000/01 (in 2000/01 prices), but the government still seems reluctant to advertise it. It is possible that bringing it under the Jobcentre Plus umbrella will have the effect of promoting the scheme, but that is dependent on generalist and specialist staff being aware of its existence.

Implementation and enforcement of Disability Discrimination Act employment provisions has continued. Again, although in principle the Disability Discrimination Act covers recruitment, in practice it has been used to a greater extent by individuals challenging dismissal or unfair treatment (Meager et al, 1999). It has been used more intensively in its first years of operation than previous equal opportunity legislation and the existence of the Disability Rights Commission is boosting its public profile.

The government's thinking on promoting employment among disabled people was brought together in a 'green paper' in November 2002 (DWP, 2002a). This provided a good summary of the barriers faced by disabled people, including a lack of educational qualifications and long durations out of work, but was rather short on solutions to tackle these barriers directly. New measures which were proposed included continuing contact between job brokers and claimants after an initial interview, an extension of funds available to advisers to cover jobseeking and back-to-work expenses, and a 'Return to Work' credit, payable for 12 months to those leaving Incapacity Benefit for work. The 'green paper' also announced pilot schemes to 'join up' welfare-to-work efforts with rehabilitiation for back pain, mental health problems and cardio-vascular conditions.

Overall employment rates among disabled people have risen since 1997, for both men and women, and the increases have been faster than for the non-disabled population (**Figures 8.2** and **8.3**). Between autumn 1997 and autumn 2001, disabled men and women's employment rates rose by 32 and 23% respectively, compared to 3 and 4% for non-disabled men and women. Some caution is required in interpreting the figures since the proportion of working-age people reporting disability has also risen over this period, so there may be a compositional effect[5]. It is also not clear how much of the increase in employment rates is due to the specific initiatives discussed above and how much can be put down to the fact that disabled people's employment rates tend to recover more slowly from recession than non-disabled people's (Burchardt, 2000), and hence may still be rising when general employment rates have stabilised. Whatever the combination of causes, there has been a substantial increase in disabled people's employment rates, and in a longer historical perspective this is a significant development: there was little change throughout the 1980s and first half of the 1990s.

---

[5] For example, if people with less severe impairments who previously did not report disability are now reporting themselves to be disabled, one would expect the average employment rate for disabled people to rise, since less severely disabled people are more likely to be employed. However, there is no strong evidence that people now reporting themselves to be disabled *are* less severely impaired than previously.

Figure 8.2: Trends in employment rates, by disability status: men

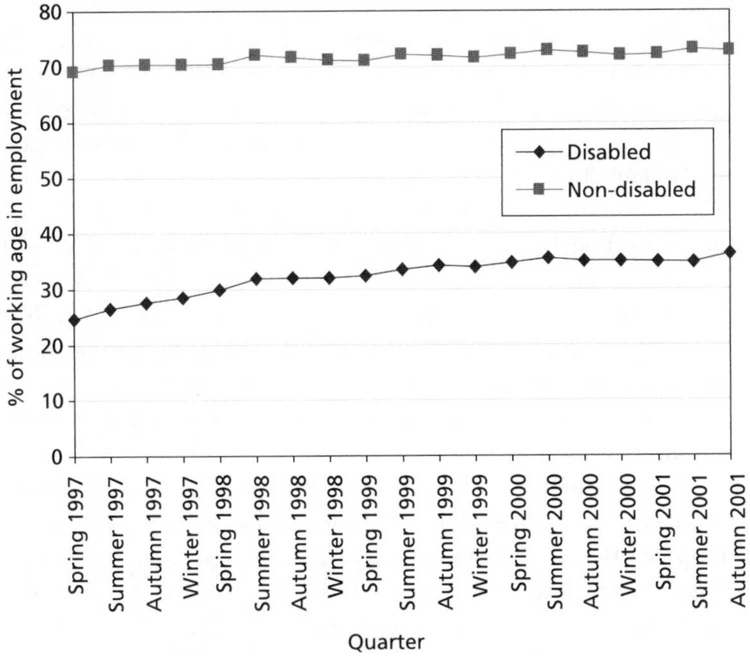

Source: Author's calculations using *Labour Force Survey*

Figure 8.3: Trends in employment rates, by disability status: women

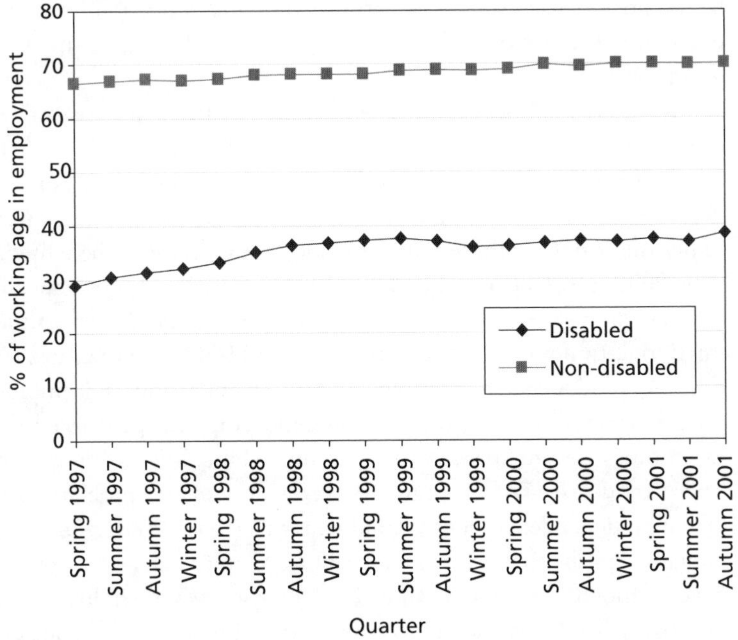

Source: Author's calculations using *Labour Force Survey*

Security for those who cannot

The 1999 Welfare Reform Act was preceded by a period of intense speculation about the future of disability benefits. Some commentators feared that Disability Living Allowance – the main 'extra costs' benefit for people of working age (see **Box 8.1**) – would become means tested. This did not materialise but the Act contained a mixture of cuts and improvements in which it was difficult to detect any coherent programme for people of working age. Entitlement to Incapacity Benefit was withdrawn from people who had been unemployed for three years or more, and means testing against private and occupational pension income was introduced. These measures appeared to be trying to restrict 'hidden unemployment' and early retirement on ill-health grounds, but were oddly targeted: the long-term unemployed *are* at significant risk of developing chronic ill-health, while the number of Incapacity Benefit claimants who have pension income is small.

At the same time, Severe Disablement Allowance was abolished, to be replaced for those who became disabled during childhood with a new entitlement to Incapacity Benefit. Since Incapacity Benefit is paid at a higher rate than Severe Disablement Allowance, this was a net gain for claimants disabled during childhood. Those who become disabled as adults, single claimants or those whose partner is not working may qualify for Income Support, again often paid at a higher rate than Severe Disablement Allowance. The main losers are likely to be spouses, mostly women, who do not work outside the home and hence do not have sufficient national insurance contributions or credits to qualify for Incapacity Benefit. There is now no benefit entitlement for this group.

It is hard to see how the 1999 reforms live up to the promise of 'security for those who cannot'. Long-term unemployed people, those who retired early and 'housewives' were penalised, while individuals who became disabled during childhood – who one might have hoped to have seen being given support under the 'work for those who can' side of the bargain – benefited.

In 2001, the Department of Health published a White Paper on a new strategy for people with learning disabilities (DoH, 2001). Although one might question whether the Department of Health was the most appropriate body to produce such a strategy (why not education and employment, or social security, or the Social Exclusion Unit?), the strategy marked a sea change in attitudes towards people with learning difficulties, from a 'medical' to a 'social' model (see **Box 8.3**), and from containment of a problem to promoting "rights, independence, choice and inclusion" (DoH, 2001). The 11 objectives contained in the strategy include enabling people with learning disabilities to: have as much choice and control as possible over their lives; lead full and purposeful lives and to develop a range of friendships, activities and relationships; undertake paid work; and have access to high quality housing and healthcare.

Box 8.3: Medical and social models of disability

	Medical model	Social model
Cause of disadvantage	Personal tragedy	Discrimination
Resolution	Cure and rehabilitation (changing the person); charity	Changing the physical, social and economic environment
Nature of individual	Passive victim; dependent on others; grateful or heroic	Active agent; can be independent given appropriate support; demanding equal rights
Authority	Professionals	Disabled people

Source: Adapted from Barnes et al (1999)

It is no coincidence that this radical change of direction was produced only after consultation with people with learning disabilities, their organisations, carers and parents, and as a statement of desirable outcomes it is hard to fault. Funding to implement the strategy is, however, limited: £2.3 million per year for three years of 'new' money to expand advocacy services, to set up a helpline and create an information centre; and £50 million per year from existing community care and general health budgets to modernise day centres, close remaining long-stay hospitals, and develop support for independent living.

To summarise, employment opportunities for disabled people have improved over the period Labour has been in office, although whether this is the result of government action or broader trends is unclear. There is still a long way to go: according to recent Labour Force Survey figures, there are 390,000 disabled people in Britain who would like to work and are available to start, but do not have a job (DRC, 2002, Table 7). For those who cannot work or who are not working, improvements have been patchy or non-existent. Attitudes of government departments and service providers have progressed in a helpful direction, partly as a result of the enforcement of the Disability Discrimination Act by the Disability Rights Commission, but exclusion through inaccessibility and old-fashioned poverty remains widespread (Knight and Heaven, 2002). The latest figures on low income show 29% of working-age adults who live in a household containing a disabled adult have incomes below half the national average – even without taking into account extra costs of disability – compared to 19% of all working-age adults (DWP, 2002b, Table 5.5)[6]. The link between disability and poverty has not been broken.

---

[6] Equivalised net household income after housing costs.

Pensioners

People over state pension age make up nearly half of all disabled adults and yet their status as disabled people is often overlooked (Grundy et al, 1999). 'What can you expect at your age?' is a common refrain, and yet even among those aged 70-79, only half report limited functioning in one or more aspects of daily living. Increasing age *is* associated with greater risk of functional limitation, but social exclusion need not be the inevitable result, and the fact that many people of the same age are also experiencing increasing limitation does not imply that the need for physical, emotional and financial support is any the less.

The government's general anti-poverty policies for this age group (discussed in more detail in Chapter Nine in this volume) have benefited disabled pensioners in particular, just as the general anti-child-poverty policies benefited disabled children. In 1996/97, just under one third of disabled single pensioners received Income Support, compared to less than one quarter of all single pensioners: disabled pensioners are over-represented among those with low income (Grundy et al, 1999). Efforts to increase take-up of means-tested benefits and raise the level of means-tested benefits for pensioners through the so-called Minimum Income Guarantee (MIG) will therefore have increased the incomes of many disabled pensioners.

Some disabled pensioners, like people of working age, incur extra costs as a result of their disability. This may be in terms of a need for extra heating, clothing and laundry, or special items such as incontinence aids and adaptations to the accommodation. The UK is unusual in international terms in having an automatic increase in the rate of means-tested benefits payable at the ages of 75 and 80, and an increase in the basic state pension at age 80 (Zaidi and de Vos, 2002). The rationale for these uplifts has not been made explicit, but one interpretation is that they are supposed to reflect increased costs associated with deteriorating health and physical and mental functioning. This is in addition to the disability-specific benefits available to pensioners, namely, Attendance Allowance (for individuals with care needs), and disability premiums added to means-tested benefits. No specific help is available with extra costs arising from mobility difficulties, in contrast to the situation for children and adults below pension age. Again, no official rationale for this discrepancy has been given, but it presumably reflects the assumption that mobility difficulties are part and parcel of the ageing process, and that the costs should be covered from normal pension income. None of these benefits or premiums has been increased above inflation since 1997.

Social services are crucial in facilitating disabled pensioners' daily life, whether that is by helping them to get up and dressed in the morning, meals on wheels, or by giving informal carers and those they look after a break from each other. Along with the huge contribution made by unpaid carers, social services are the backbone of care in the community. Despite this critical role, social services have seen little of the substantial increases in the funding of public services which Labour implemented from 1999 onwards. While planned spending on the NHS rose 43% in cash terms between 1996/97 and 2001/02, the corresponding figure for personal social services was a mere 13% (DoH, 2000). The implications of an ageing society for pension expenditure, and, more recently, health expenditure, have been recognised, but the corresponding impact on social care has yet to be fully acknowledged (see Chapters Six and Nine in this volume).

The response by social services departments to increasing demands on their services with little increase in budget has been twofold: concentrating on the provision of intensive services to the most severely disabled people, and raising the revenue generated by charging clients for services. While prioritisation of this kind is understandable, one result is greater pressure on unpaid carers and voluntary services, and greater social isolation for less severely disabled people who may simply be unable to go out without the kind of support to which they would previously have been entitled. On charging, an Audit Commission report showed that the proportion of local authorities charging for home care services rose from 74% in 1992/93 to 94% in 1998/99, that the proportion of costs covered by charges had increased, and that nearly one in three local authorities applied charges even to clients on Income Support (Audit Commission, 2000). New guidelines were issued following this report to try to ensure that no one was reduced by charges for social services to an income below Income Support levels, but in Scotland, the newly devolved parliament took the more radical step of making all personal care free at the point of use. It will be interesting to see if this is one of the areas in which devolution prompts positive change south of the border.

The values of age- or disability-specific additions and premiums have not been increased relative to the basic rates of benefits during Labour's time in office, while disability-specific costs have risen (at least in England and Wales). In combination with overstretched social services, the likely result is greater difficulty in meeting basic needs and limited opportunities for social and leisure activities: the exact opposite of the goal of social inclusion for all.

Joined-up policy?

In the concluding section to this chapter, the extent to which the aspiration of 'joined-up' policy has been made a reality is considered. A number of different divisions could have been tackled: between disabled people and other client groups, between age groups, between government departments or between 'work' and 'security'. Each of these divisions is considered in turn.

Joining up across disability and other client groups

There is evidence of 'mainstreaming' disability for children and people of working age. The new tax credits include disability as an additional component to the main benefit, rather than creating a separate disability benefit. Disabled claimants of working age initially follow the same route through Jobcentre Plus as any other group. This is a welcome development in terms of breaking down barriers between disabled and non-disabled people, but the quality of the service delivered depends crucially on the degree of awareness on the part of generalist staff on the range of complex issues facing disabled people. Evidence from the prototype for Jobcentre Plus, known as ONE, suggests that disabled claimants in ONE were more likely to report that they had been treated as an individual than claimants in a control group, and had benefited from enhanced access to general support in finding employment. However, very few were referred to specialist schemes or services and the processing of benefit claims took longer (Green et al, 2001).

Joining up across age groups

Organising delivery of welfare by age group seems sensible at first glance: any one person is only part of one age group at any one time, so all their needs can be addressed by a single agency. There are two potential problems with this, however. One is that people live in families which may span two or more age groups, and their circumstances and needs are interrelated. Tackling child poverty requires tackling parental poverty, and tackling parental poverty requires, among other things, ensuring sufficient support for the informal care provided by, and for, grandparents.

The second potential problem arises at the points of transition between age groups. Historically, the transition between childhood and working life has been especially difficult for disabled young people (Hirst and Baldwin, 1994). Lip service is now paid to the importance of formulating 'transition plans' for special educational needs (SEN) pupils but the experience of the process and implementation of the plans is patchy (Polat et al, 2001). The quality of education received by disabled and SEN children has only recently appeared on the agenda but is crucially important in today's economic environment. Without educational qualifications and skills, social inclusion for many disabled young people will not be realised.

The transition from working life to retirement is also far from straightforward for people with health problems or impairments. Early retirement, often on grounds of ill-health, has become something of a trend. A Performance and Innovation Unit report (2000) estimated that two thirds of the early retired had not left employment voluntarily, and that over half did not have any occupational pension income. They were twice as likely as the average person aged 50-64 to be in the bottom fifth of the income distribution. Since late working life is also a time in which people save for retirement, being out of work during this period can have serious consequences for pensioner poverty, especially for men in low-skilled occupational groups (Bardasi and Jenkins, 2002). Prior to 1999, some transitional protection was provided by Incapacity Benefit, which could continue to be claimed past state pension age, but this route was blocked by the Welfare Reform Act. Aside from providing incentives for people aged 50 or over to return to work (through the New Deal for 50 Plus and now the Working Tax Credit), the government has done little to improve the transition to retirement for people with health problems or impairments. The hope seems to be that the problem will disappear of its own accord – that the generation who were especially hard-hit by the decline of manufacturing industry will pass through their fifties and early sixties on a combination of incapacity and unemployment benefits, to be picked up by means-tested benefits in old age.

Joining up across departments

Social security, taxation and employment support are undeniably better integrated in 2002 than they were five years previously. Indeed it will soon be necessary to invent a new term to refer to the combination of tax credits, benefits and programmes which constitute the financial and support in-kind provided through the Inland Revenue, Department for Work and Pensions and their various agencies. However, for disabled people the underlying tension remains unresolved between qualifying for benefits and credits through showing incapacity or reduced capacity to work – and the more significant the incapacity, the greater the entitlement – and then being invited to participate in 'work-focused interviews' and welfare-to-work programmes.

Another departmental boundary of particular significance for disabled people is between financial support on the one hand and health and social care on the other (discussed further in Chapter Six, this volume). This boundary remains rigid in principle but is becoming increasingly blurred in practice. Social services departments have responded to demands from disabled people to provide 'direct payments' in lieu of services, with which they can purchase their own support, and this practice is becoming more widespread. Clients are held to account for the way in which they spend their direct payment, in contrast to any of their benefit income. Given that some benefits are specifically designed to help with costs arising from the need for assistance with care or mobility, this distinction is hard to maintain and is ripe for review.

Joining up across 'work' and 'security'

Considerable effort has been expended by the government to smooth the transition between benefits and work for disabled people. The rules governing the type and amount of work which can be undertaken while in receipt of Incapacity Benefits have been overhauled, to allow claimants to ease themselves gradually into employment. (The main difficulty here seems to be that few claimants know about or understand the rules, so they fail to have the intended effect: see Corden and Sainsbury, 2001.) In-work benefits have been made more generous and less complex, and this has resulted in increased take-up.

Conversely, people making the transition in the opposite direction, from work into benefits, face a potentially large drop in income. National insurance benefits, such as Incapacity Benefit, used to provide a cushion to living standards by including an earnings-related component, but since the removal of these components and new restrictions on eligibility for national insurance benefits generally, this function has lapsed. Greater reliance on means-tested benefits as a mode of out of work support has the additional disadvantage of creating an unemployment trap for the spouse: if one partner has to stop work through ill-health or disability, the other may have to give up his or her job too, in order for the family to qualify for Income Support.

Finally, some people may find themselves falling between the stools of 'work' and 'security'. Those who are deemed capable of work but who are unable to find a job – perhaps because the structural and attitudinal barriers to disabled people's employment are being dismantled only slowly – cannot take advantage of the improved support for severely disabled people on the one hand, nor for disabled people in work on the other. Unemployed, early-retired and home-working disabled people may all find themselves in this position. Combined delivery of benefits and employment support for disabled people through Jobcentre Plus is likely to bring this problem to the fore, but it cannot be addressed by organisational restructuring alone.

Overview

- Tackling the educational deficit of disabled school leavers should be a priority.

- New policies need to be developed to support the transition to retirement of people with health problems and impairments.

- The operation of Jobcentre Plus will need to be monitored carefully from the point of view of disabled claimants, to ensure that they receive the expert assistance that they need.

- Organisational restructuring alone will not be sufficient to address the needs of disabled people who would like to work, but who face a competitive and discriminatory labour market.

Questions for discussion

1. Why might disabled children have benefited particularly from the government's efforts to reduce child poverty?

2. What are the pros and cons of segregated education for disabled children?

3. Should disabled people of working age be required to work?

4. In what ways will Jobcentre Plus be advantageous for disabled people looking for work? What new difficulties might it create?

5. Can pensioners sensibly be considered to be disabled, or is disability just a natural part of ageing?

References

Arthur, S., Corden, A., Green, A., Lewis, J., Loumidis, J., Sainsbury, R., Stafford, B., Thornton, P. and Walker, R. (1999) *New Deal for Disabled People: Early implementation*, DSS Research Report No 106, Leeds: Corporate Document Services.

Ashworth, K., Hartfree, Y. and Stephenson, A. (2001) *Well enough to work?*, DSS Research Report No 145, Leeds: Corporate Document Services.

Audit Commission (2000) *Charging with care: How councils charge for home care*, London: Audit Commission.

Bardasi, E. and Jenkins, S. (2002) *Income in later life: Work history matters*, Bristol/York: The Policy Press/Joseph Rowntree Foundation.

Barnes, C., Mercer, G. and Shakespeare, T. (1999) *Exploring disability: A sociological introduction*, Cambridge: Polity Press.

Berthoud, R., Lakey, J. and McKay, S. (1993) *The economic problems of disabled people*, London: Policy Studies Institute.

Blackburn, V., Child, C. and Hills, D. (1999) *New deal for disabled people: Early findings from the innovative schemes*, In-house report No 61, London: DSS.

Burchardt, T. (2000) *Enduring economic exclusion: Disabled people, income and work*, York: York Publishing Services for the Joseph Rowntree Foundation.

Burchardt, T. and McKnight, A. (forthcoming) *The impact of the national minimum wage on disabled workers*, CASE paper, London: Centre for Analysis of Social Exclusion, London School of Economics and Political Science.

Corden, A. and Sainsbury, R. (2001) *Incapacity Benefits and work incentives*, DSS Research Report No 141, Leeds: Corporate Document Services.

Davis, J. and Watson, N. (2001) 'Where are the children's experiences? Analysing social and cultural exclusion in "special" and "mainstream" schools', *Disability and Society*, vol 16, no 5, pp 671-87.

Dobson, B. and Middleton, S. (1998) *Paying to care: The cost of childhood disability*, York: York Publishing Services for the Joseph Rowntree Foundation.

DoH (Department of Health) (2000) *Departmental Report: The government's expenditure plans 2000-2001*, Cm 4603, London: The Stationery Office.

DoH (2001) *Valuing People: A new strategy for learning disability for the 21st century*, Cm 5086, London: The Stationery Office.

DRC (Disability Rights Commission) (2002) *Disability Briefing: May 2002*, London: DRC.

DWP (Department for Work and Pensions) (2000) *New Deal for Disabled People: Prospectus*, London: DWP.

DWP (2002a) *Pathways to work: Helping people into employment*, Cm 5690, London: The Stationery Office.

DWP (2002b) *Households Below Average Income 1994/95-2000/01*, Leeds: Corporate Document Services.

Gordon, D., Parker, R., Loughran, F. with Heslop, P. (2000) *Disabled children in Britain: A re-analysis of the OPCS Disability Surveys*, London: The Stationery Office.

Green, H., Marsh, A. and Connolly, H. (2001) *The short-term effects of compulsory participation in ONE*, DWP Research Report No 156, Leeds: Corporate Document Services.

Grundy, E., Ahlburg, D., Ali, M., Breeze, E. and Slogett, A. (1999) *Disability in Great Britain: Results from the 1996/97 disability follow-up to the Family Resources Survey*, DSS Research Report No 94, Leeds: Corporate Document Services.

Hedges, A. and Sykes, W. (2001) *Moving between sickness and work*, DWP Research Report No 151, Leeds: Corporate Document Services.

Hirst, M. and Baldwin, S. (1994) *Unequal opportunities: Growing up disabled*, London: HMSO.

Inland Revenue (2002) *Disabled Person's Tax Credit Statistics Quarterly Enquiry: United Kingdom October 2001*, London: Inland Revenue.

Knight, J. and Heaven, C. with Christie, I. (2002) *Inclusive citizenship: The Leonard Cheshire Social Exclusion Report 2002*, London: Leonard Cheshire.

LPC (Low Pay Commission) (2000) *The National Minimum Wage: The story so far*, Second Report of the LPC, Cm 4571, London: The Stationery Office.

Meager, N., Doyle, B., Evans, C., Kersley, B., Williams, M., O'Regan, S. and Tackey, N. (1999) *Monitoring the Disability Discrimination Act (DDA) 1995*, DfEE Research Report No 119, London: DfEE.

PIU (Performance and Innovation Unit) (2000) *Winning the generation game: Improving opportunities for people aged 50-65 in work and community activity*, London: The Stationery Office.

Polat, F., Kalambouka, A., Boyle, W., and Nelson, N. (2001) *Post-16 transitions of pupils with special educational needs*, DfES Research Report No 315, Nottingham: DfES.

Rowlingson, K. and Berthoud, R. (1996) *Disability, benefits and employment*, DSS Research Report No 54, London: The Stationery Office.

RNIB (Royal National Institute for the Blind)/RADAR (Royal Association for Disability and Rehabilitation) (1995) *Access to equality: An analysis of the effectiveness of the Access to Work scheme*, London: RNIB/RADAR.

Zaidi, A. and de Vos, K. (2002) 'Income mobility of the elderly in Britain and the Netherlands', Paper to Welfare Policy and Analysis seminar, London School of Economics and Political Science, June.

Website resources

Department for Work and Pensions	www.dwp.gov.uk
Disability Rights Commission	www.drc.org/drc/default.asp
Inland Revenue	www.inlandrevenue.gov.uk
New Deal for Disabled People	www.newdeal.gov.uk

nine

Benefiting children? The challenge of social security support for children

Tess Ridge

Summary

The Labour government's commitment to eradicating childhood poverty by 2020 has resulted in major welfare reforms, central to which are changes in support for children and their families through the tax and benefit system. This chapter:

- explores how and why the state provides social security support for children and reflects on the challenge of delivering support to children via their families;

- considers the impact of Labour's welfare reforms on children's lives and well-being;

- examines new ways of delivering welfare to children through measures such as the Child Tax Credit, which is intended to create a 'seamless system of support' for children, and the Education Maintenance Allowances, which are targeted directly towards children.

Introduction: state support for children

At the start of the 21st century, the debate about how best to provide state protection and support for children is high on the policy agenda. Labour's pledge to *eradicate child poverty by 2020* has breathed new life into the debate about the type and level of financial support that society and the state should be providing for children and their families. Central to that debate is the issue of where the balance is to be struck between state support for children and state intervention in the private realm of family life. Too much support for children may encourage people to have more children (considered a legitimate use of the social security system in some countries), or might increase the risk of family dissolution; too little support, and children are left to the vagaries of individual family circumstances without any recognition of their social rights and values. Provision of financial support for children and their families is therefore "linked to deep-rooted moral and ideological questions of freedom, dependency, care and mutual responsibility" (Smith, 1998, p 16).

Social security provisions have an impact on many areas of children's lives, and there is a considerable diversity in the type and level of support that is provided. Benefits for children fall into several different categories, and these may have different rules, aims and intentions, and different treatments and equities. **Box 9.1** shows that state involvement in the provision of support for

---

Box 9.1: State provision for children

- **Child Benefit:** universal benefit for all children to acknowledge the costs of raising children
- **Social support and assistance:** means-tested child premiums included in support for low-income families who are not working, for example, Income Support, Jobseeker's Allowance
- **In-work benefits:** means-tested child premiums included in support for low-waged families, for example, Working Families Tax Credit, Disabled Person's Tax Credit
- **Welfare-in-kind:** means-tested provision of non-cash benefits for some low-income children for example, free school meals linked to receipt of Income Support
- **Direct payments:** a relatively new form of means-tested provision where benefits/allowances are paid directly to young people aged 16-18 to encourage them to stay in education, for example, Education Maintenance Allowances
- **Child support:** no cash provision but direct involvement of state in 'private' realm of family relationships. Intended to ensure non-resident parents pay child support for their children. Affects children in lone-parent families receiving means-tested benefits

children can range from Child Benefit, the public acknowledgement of society's interest in sharing the costs of raising all children, to child support, which is concerned with enforcing financial obligations within the family. Children are also supported through child premiums attached to their parents' benefits, which are linked to different rules regarding their parents' marital/employment status and behaviour. For example, in-work benefits such as Working Families Tax Credit (WFTC) are linked to low-wage parental employment of 16 hours or more per week. Children can also receive non-cash benefits such as free school meals if their parents are on the lowest level of means-tested benefits, for example, Income Support.

Benefits for children: numbers in receipt and expenditure

Social security plays a significant role in most children's lives and increased income testing is drawing more children and their families into means-tested state provision (Walker with Howard, 2000). All parents with children under the age of 16 years are entitled to Child Benefit for their children. However, many children's economic security and well-being also depends on other areas of social security provision. Table 9.1 shows the main types of social security support for children and the numbers receiving such support in 2001. The table shows that:

- 12.5 million children living in over 7 million families received a weekly payment of Child Benefit.
- Over 5 million children (40% of all children under the age of 16 in the population) lived in families in receipt of means-tested benefits.
- 2.5 million children lived in families in receipt of WFTC and a further 2.5 million children lived in families that were in receipt of key means-tested benefits.
- Of children living in families in receipt of WFTC, 1.4 million were living in couple families and 1.1 million were living in lone-parent families.
- Of children living in families receiving key means-tested benefits (including Income Support, Jobseeker's Allowance and disability benefits) the majority (over 1.8 million) lived in lone-parent families. Approximately 650,000 children lived in couple families on key benefits and these were mainly living in families receiving sickness and disability benefits (408,000).

Total benefit expenditure on children in the year 2001/02 was £13.7 million (this excludes expenditure on children included in WFTC and Disabled Person's Tax Credit [DPTC] which is administered by the Inland Revenue; DWP, 2002a). Benefit expenditure on children has risen 66% between 1991/92 and 2001/02 (DWP, 2002a), and will continue to rise as the government increasingly

Table 9.1: Social security support for children in 2001

	Number of children[a]	Family type Couple	Family type Lone parent	Number of children under 16	% of all children under 16
Child Benefit	12,520	–	–	11,308	100
Working Families Tax Credit	2,528	1,415	1,113	2,352	20
All children receiving key benefits[b]	2,512	653	1,809	2,343	20
Unemployed	*200*	*184*	*16*	*178*	*2*
Sick/disabled	*659*	*408*	*199*	*588*	*5*
Lone parents	*1,593*	*–*	*1,593*	*1,523*	*13*
Others	*61*	*60*	*1*	*55*	*–*

Notes: [a] Includes children aged under 16 and young adult dependants aged 16-18 in full-time education for whom benefit is being paid.
[b] Key benefits include: Jobseeker's Allowance, Incapacity Benefit, Severe Disablement Allowance, Disability Living Allowance and Income Support (DWP, 2001a).

Source: Inland Revenue (2001); DWP (2001a)

targets benefit increases on children in low-income families to further its pledge to eradicate child poverty. The largest part of the government's expenditure on children comes from Child Benefit which amounted to £8.2 billion in 2001/02 (DSS, 2000a).

Why does the state provide support for children?

Children are beneficiaries of social security benefits that are mainly targeted at their parents and so the nature and level of support is mainly determined by issues that apply to the adults, including labour market concerns (for example, maintaining work incentives and keeping down wage demands), and family and gender issues (such as providing incomes for mothers, or reinforcing parental responsibility). Fiscal, moral and political concerns of the state can also dominate the issue of benefits and support for children. For example, means-tested benefits for families without a wage earner have traditionally been set at a low level to ensure the maintenance of work incentives. This principle of 'less eligibility'[1] has had severe implications for children living in unemployed families who are traditionally some of the poorest (Gregg et al, 1999).

---

[1] The principle of 'less eligibility' stemmed from the Poor Law reforms of 1834 that aimed to ensure that those people receiving poor relief should always be worse off than the lowest paid labourers (Hill, 1994).

Therefore in general, children themselves are rarely the main focus of social security provision. Furthermore, when children are the main focus of social security the underlying aims of that provision may be quite diverse, and informed by very different notions of children and childhood. Box 9.2 shows the possible aims and intentions of social security policies that are directed towards children, and these are then discussed in turn.

Box 9.2: Possible aims of social security support for children

- The relief of poverty
- Investment in children
- Recognition of the costs of children
- Redistribution of resources
- Replacing or enforcing parental support
- Citizenship and children's rights
- Incentive payments

The relief of poverty

The development of benefits for children began in the early 20th century when the extent and severity of child poverty began to emerge as a serious cause for concern, and the welfare of children became an important policy issue (see MacNicol, 1980; and Brown, 1984 for an overview of the development of family allowances and early benefit provision for children). Social security can play a vital role in supporting children when they and their families are at risk of experiencing poverty through low wages, unemployment, sickness, disability and bereavement. Different social, economic and demographic factors affect the likelihood of children experiencing poverty. These include: living in a lone-parent family, living in a minority ethnic household, living in large families, living in families where there is an adult or a child with long-term sickness and/or disability, and living in either a workless household or one dependent on low pay (Gordon et al, 2000; Howard et al, 2001, Millar and Ridge, 2001). These are not discrete factors but elements of disadvantage that can intersect and reinforce each other (Ridge, 2002). However, although these characteristics are important, the extent of child poverty is also dependent on an individual country's labour supply and earnings, and the tax and benefit packages that countries provide to support parents with the costs of raising children (Bradshaw and Barnes, 1999). All economically developed countries provide support for children through the tax and benefit system, and as Bradshaw (1999) argues, "child poverty is not inevitable – countries make more or less explicit choices about how far they employ social and fiscal policies to mitigate the impact of pre-transfer forces" (p 396).

Investment in children

Another reason for which the state might provide fiscal support for children is as a form of investment in the future. The importance of investing in children has been highlighted by the Chancellor of the Exchequer, Gordon Brown, who argues that the complexity of the modern economy requires a future workforce with enhanced knowledge and skills; therefore investment in the children of today will ensure a sound economy in the future. In this instance children are not a private good, relegated to the private realm of the family, but a common interest essential for the future well-being of society (Brown, 2000).

The notion of children as 'investments' is a common and pervasive theme in UK social policy, one that has its origins in times of national renewal and concerns about the future (Daniel and Ivatts, 1998). The appeal of 'investing' in children lies not so much in providing for the best interests of children but in the overriding interests of future economic prosperity and social stability. However, focusing on children as the adult-to-be can lead to policies taking particular forms which focus more on the outcomes of childhood than on addressing the needs and experiences of children during childhood (Ridge, 2002).

Recognition of the costs of children

Social security can also be provided to families in recognition of the costs of having children, and the value that society place on them. However, providing benefits that recognise the costs of raising children again poses questions about the adequacy of current benefits and the appropriate balance between parental support and state support. The costs of raising children are considerable; in 1997, a child reaching his or her 17th birthday may have already cost £50,000 (Middleton et al, 1997). Although state expenditure on children is increasing, the main bulk of the direct costs of children are met by their parents (Smith, 1998). An assessment of children's needs can be obtained from a list of socially perceived necessities (see Middleton et al, 1994, 1997; Gordon et al, 2000), or a 'budget standards' approach that estimates what it costs different types of families to support their children at an acceptable standard of living (Oldfield and Yu, 1993; Parker, 1998). The national Poverty and Social Exclusion Survey (Gordon et al, 2000) lists a diverse range of needs from adequate food and clothing to social participation, developmental stimulation and environmental well-being (Gordon et al, 2000).

This 'consensual' list of necessities has been used to construct an index of childhood deprivation, which classified children as poor if they lacked one or more of the essential items on the list. By this definition 34% of children in 2000 were poor and a further 18% of children lacked two or more essential items (Gordon et al, 2000). Historically, the level of social security support provided for children falls well below the estimated costs of raising children (see Middleton et al, 1997; Dobson and Middleton, 1998; Parker, 1998).

Redistribution of resources

Social security can also be used to redistribute resources between different groups in society. 'Vertical redistribution' between high-income groups to low-income groups plays an important role in supporting children in low-income families. However, children's interests are also served by 'horizontal redistribution', the distribution of resources from those without children to those with them (see Sainsbury, 1999). To ensure that the interests of children are met, it is crucial to find the right mix between vertical and horizontal redistribution, as well as the redistribution of resources on other dimensions.

Replacing or enforcing parental support

There is also an important role for social security to play in family welfare through the provision of support for children when their parents are separated. As the number of lone-parent families has increased (see Chapter Two in this volume) this has become an increasingly significant and sometimes controversial role for social security. Up until the late 1990s, the responsibility for setting and enforcing child maintenance obligations lay with the courts, although there was a requirement to seek support from 'liable relatives' (that is, typically divorced or unmarried fathers) when the lone parent was claiming Income Support.

The 1991 Child Support Act introduced a system whereby levels of child support were determined according to a standard formula, and the new system was administered by a new agency within the (then) Department of Social Security – the Child Support Agency. Lone parents claiming benefits were required to cooperate with the Agency (see Garnham and Knights, 1994 and Barnes et al, 1998 for an overview of the Act). The introduction of this policy was couched in terms of a moral debate about the responsibility of non-resident fathers to pay maintenance for their children (Ford and Millar, 1998) However, underpinning these concerns were also fiscal interests about the high rate of social security expenditure for lone-parent families (Garnham and Knights, 1994).

The measures proved to be very controversial, and were not successful either at increasing compliance with child support obligations or at improving the incomes of children in lone-parent families. Studies of lone-parents both before and after the Child Support Act consistently show only about one in three lone parents receiving regular child support payments (Millar and Ridge, 2001). Families in receipt of Income Support had no financial gain in terms of increased incomes, as the state withdrew any child support payments directly from their families' Income Support payments. Furthermore, in some cases, children experienced the termination of contact with their fathers, who were angered by the imposition of child support (Clarke et al, 1994). In addition to these there was also the potential threat of 'benefit penalties' being applied to mothers who did not cooperate fully with the Child Support Agency, and this could potentially result in children living in families on a reduced benefit income for a period of time. Therefore, although the moral framework for the formulation of the Child Support Act appeared to be the welfare and interests of children in lone-parent families, ultimately the needs and rights of children came very low on the policy agenda.

The Labour government plans to introduce reforms which will include the use of a much simpler formula to calculate liabilities, many separated parents will have lower liabilities than is currently the case, and lone parents on Income Support will be able to keep £10 of any child support received (DSS, 1999a). There are other ways of organising child support payments. The best interests of the child may be better served by a guaranteed payment by the state, which is then claimed back from the non-resident parent. Or the state could assume full support of children by completely replacing the non-resident parent's contribution, thereby ensuring that the well-being of the child is protected during difficult transitional periods of family life.

Citizenship and children's rights

More radical agendas propose that support for children should be based on the principle of equity, the notion of citizenship and children's rights. This is a recognition that society has an obligation towards sharing the costs of children and supporting children as individuals in their own right. To approach social security benefits from a children's rights perspective would again raise the issue of adequacy as children and young people would have a right to social protection and an adequate standard of living regardless of the income and circumstances of their parents (Daniel and Ivatts, 1998). Lister (1990, p 59) has argued that Child Benefit should be seen as the child's 'badge of citizenship'. However, the fortunes of Child Benefit and its predecessor Family Allowances have ebbed and flowed since their inception (see MacNicol, 1980; Brown, 1984). Nonetheless, they have played a vital role for many low-income families, providing support and stability in times of crisis and need (Bradshaw and Stimson, 1997). Yet Child Benefit has rarely been viewed as a benefit for children; it has been bound up with gender and employment issues, the debate about motherhood, and 'purse and wallet' debates about how resources are distributed within the household (Daniel and Ivatts, 1998). Where it has been seen as a benefit for children it has invariably been concerned with children as future investments, rather than as a significant element of children's rights and citizenship during childhood (Daniel and Ivatts, 1998).

Incentive payments

Finally, social security benefits for children might be used as an incentive to encourage or reward particular types of behaviour. This is not uncommon for adult claimants; however, the use of benefit incentives for children and young people is a new policy development. Policies such as the Education Maintenance Allowances (see below for further discussion) and the proposed Child Trust Funds[2] (Treasury, 2001b) are intended to encourage and reward children and young people for particular behaviours. The Child Trust Funds are likely to be linked to financial education in the National Curriculum and used to encourage financial competence and the development of regular savings habits in children. More contentious is the proposed use of benefit sanctions for parents if their child truants from school. Imposing financial penalties on parents of truants has been tried in the US where there is little evidence to show that this measure (known as Learnfare) achieves its objectives. Removing Child Benefit from low-income families who are trying to cope with poverty and disadvantage is unlikely to improve relationships between parents and children (CPAG, 2002).

Labour and support for children

When Labour came to power in 1997 it inherited one of the worst rates of child poverty in the developed world (Bradbury and Jäntti, 2001; Bradshaw, 2001). Following a 20-year period of Conservative free market economic policies, child poverty rates had increased threefold as children disproportionately suffered from changes in economic conditions and demographic structures (Oppenheim and Harker, 1996; Walker and Walker, 1997; Millar, 2001). In 1998/99, when Labour came to power, about 4.5 million children (over one third of all children) were living below 50% of mean household income after housing costs (DSS, 2000a).

Initially Labour's interest in the well-being of children was not apparent, indeed one of their first acts in office was to abolish the One Parent Benefit and One Parent Premium paid to lone parents which undermined the level of support that children in lone-parent families could expect (Millar and Ridge,

---

[2] Child Trust Funds are being proposed by the government as a means to encourage savings and investment by children (and their parents). Children will be endowed with a lump sum at birth, which will be placed in a savings account to which access is restricted, until the child is 18. Children and their parents will be encouraged to add to their savings and develop the habit of saving regularly. For low-income families the state will provide further endowments at key life stages, for example, 5, 11 and 16 years (HM Treasury, 2001a).

2002). However, in 1998, in recognition of spiralling child poverty rates, Prime Minister Blair announced that his government would eradicate child poverty within the next 20 years (Blair, 1999). This was followed by a Public Service Agreement to reduce child poverty by at least a quarter, by 2004 (DSS, 2000b). To monitor the outcomes of its anti-poverty policies Labour committed itself to an annual poverty audit, *Opportunity for All*, which sets out specific and measurable indicators relating to the well-being of children (DSS, 1999b).

Labour's commitment to eradicate child poverty placed children and their families at the centre of the policy process and resulted in a major reconstruction of the welfare system. At the heart of the government's reforming agenda were policy measures to promote paid work (for example, the National Minimum Wage and New Deal programmes), coupled with a radical overhaul of the tax and benefits system to ensure that paid work was rewarded and extra resources were targeted on those who were in the most need (HM Treasury, 1999, 2000). These reforms have fundamentally changed the way in which children are supported by the state. Box 9.3 outlines the main changes to social security and fiscal support for children since 1997[3].

Labour's welfare-to-work policies and children

Central to Labour's policy agenda has been the promotion of paid work to lift children in 'workless' families out of poverty (see Chapter Five in this volume). To support parents in employment, especially lone mothers, the National Childcare Strategy was launched providing a record investment in childcare provision for children aged 0 to 14 (*Meeting the Childcare Challenge*, May 1998). However, the delivery of quality, affordable childcare has proved problematic for Labour, and although provision has increased overall, there is still a considerable shortfall, for example, in 1997, when Labour came to power, there was one place for every nine children under the age of eight, by 2001 there was still only one place for every seven (Daycare Trust, 2001a; Land, 2002). The Childcare Tax Credit for families receiving WFTC is intended to help with the costs of childcare. In 2002 it was worth 70% of childcare costs up to a maximum of £135 for one child and £200 for two or more children. But it is restricted to formal childcare provision and many parents use more informal systems of childcare (see Millar and Ridge, 2001). Furthermore, the cost of formal childcare has escalated (Daycare Trust, 2001b). This means that even with the Childcare Tax Credit meeting some of the costs, childcare is proving too expensive for many families (Daycare Trust, 2001b). The dominance

---

[3] There have also been considerable changes in other areas of support for children that are not our focus here. They include among others; the Sure Start Programme, Education Action Zones, Health Action Zones, the National Childcare Strategy and the National Family and Parenting Institute (DSS, 1999b; Millar and Ridge, 2002).

of paid work to Labour's anti-poverty agenda and the overall lack of support for full-time parental care is also not without its critics (Hirsch, 1999; Lister et al, 1999; Piachaud and Sutherland, 2000). Furthermore, employment does not guarantee that children and their families are lifted out of poverty; in 2000/01 44% of children living in households with one or more workers were below the 60% of median income poverty line (after housing costs) (DWP, 2002b). High levels of parental employment may also not necessarily meet the needs

---

Box 9.3: Changes to social security and fiscal support for children since 1997

- **Removal of One Parent Premium** for lone parents receiving Income Support and of **One Parent Benefit** for working lone parents
- **Increased Child Benefit** (the universal payment for all children). Was worth £11.05 for the first child in 1997, in 2002 worth £15.75 for the eldest child and £10.55 for each following child. Administered by the Department for Work and Pensions
- **Increases in Income Support rates** for children, including removal of age-related differences between under-11s and under-16s. Was worth £16.90 per week for children under-11, and £24.75 for under-16s in 1997. In 2002 worth £33.50 for children under-16 years. Administered by the Department for Work and Pensions
- **Increases in the Maternity Grant** from £100 to £500. Now called the new Sure Start Maternity Grant, this is means tested and in order to receive it the mother, or her partner, must have received information about child healthcare from their doctor, midwife or health visitor. Administered by Department for Work and Pensions
- **The Children's Tax Credit**, which replaced Married Couples Allowance for standard rate taxpayers, worth £20 per week, £1,000 per year, for tax-paying families with children. With an extra £10 per week in the first year of a child's life (HM Treasury, 2001a). Administered by the Inland Revenue
- **Replacement of Family Credit with Working Families Tax Credit**, paid at a higher rate, including a Childcare Tax Credit to offset the costs of childcare. Administered by the Inland Revenue
- **Child Tax Credit** – a single Child Tax Credit to replace Children's Tax Credit, and children's rates of Income Support, Jobseeker's Allowance, Disabled Person's Tax Credit and Working Families' Tax Credit. Administered by the Inland Revenue
- **The Children's Fund** – a Treasury initiative mainly targeted on preventive work with children in the 5 to 13 age group with an initial budget of £450 million over three years. Administered by the Children and Young People's Unit
- **Education Maintenance Allowances** – initially in 15 pilot areas (national roll-out in 2004), means-tested support paid directly to children aged 16-18 years who attend full-time courses at school or college. Administered by local education authorities
- **Reform of Child Support system**, introduction of a simpler formula and giving a disregard of £10 of child support payments for Income Support recipients. Administered by the Child Support Agency

of children; greater involvement of children in institutional care raises concerns about the quality of childcare low-income children will receive and the length of the 'working week' some children will experience with breakfast clubs, after-school clubs and the time costs of travelling to and from childcare (Ridge, 2002). At present there is no strong element of compulsion in New Deal for Lone Parents; however, any future move towards compulsion could result in families receiving 'benefit penalties' for non-compliance, then paradoxically, poor children may find themselves living in families with reduced benefit incomes.

Support for children in 'workless' families

Many parents, particularly lone parents and families where there are disabilities, experience considerable barriers to entering paid employment (Millar and Ridge, 2001). Therefore, the well-being of children in families without paid employment must also be addressed through improved security and support for children. Children living in 'workless' families have received considerable increases in financial support. Research evidence had shown that Income Support rates for children, especially younger children, were inadequate (Middleton et al, 1997), and Labour has uprated the Income Support child premiums in a series of budgets which abolished age-related payments so that all children under the age of 16 years were paid the same (HM Treasury, 2001a). In essence there was an 80% rise in real terms for Income Support rates for young children between 1997 and 2001 (Lister, 2001).

Changes in the tax and benefits system since 1997 have clearly resulted in the redistribution of income towards families with children (Millar, 2001), and increased support for children in the benefit system. The advent of the new Child Tax Credit will signal a further increase in transfer of resources towards children; and Labour's plans to disregard Child Benefit as income from those receiving Income Support and Jobseeker's Allowance will provide a valuable boost to low-income families and right a fundamental inequity in the benefits system[4] (HM Treasury, 2002a).

However, despite the increase in resources towards children there are continuing concerns about the adequacy of adult rates of Income Support/Jobseeker's Allowance (Veit-Wilson, 1998; Land, 1999; Holman, 2000). Income Support rates for adults have not been increased and remain substantially below the 60% of median income poverty line used by the government (Piachaud and Sutherland, 2001). This will necessarily dilute the impact of increases in child premiums, as income provided for children cannot be separated out from

---

[4] Child Benefit is a universal, tax-free benefit paid to all families with children, but it is deducted from families receiving Income Support and Jobseeker's Allowance. This will change when the Child Tax Credits come into effect.

overall family income. Furthermore, many low-income families are heavily burdened by debt and have deductions for utilities and Social Fund loans taken from their benefits, resulting in a reduced income for the household; this means that they will not be able to benefit fully from these changes (see Mannion et al, 1994; Millar and Ridge, 2001). It is still too early to say yet what the impact of these changes will be on the adequacy of means-tested benefits. However, the level by which many of these increases are measured, the 'Low Cost but Acceptable' budget, is not necessarily the level at which society would wish to support children. From a children's rights and a citizenship perspective we might want to go much further towards raising disadvantaged children closer to the average levels enjoyed by other children in society.

New types of financial support for children and young people

Alongside Labour's welfare-to-work reforms and anti-poverty measures for children, two policy changes in particular, the Child Tax Credit and Education Maintenance Allowances, stand out as examples of radical and fundamental reforms in the support of children and young people. Each of these and their implications for children and young people are explored in more detail below.

The Child Tax Credit: a 'seamless system of support for children'

When Labour came to power in 1997 they inherited a complex social security system, and the process of welfare reform has resulted in a fundamental shift in the assessment and delivery of social security benefits involving major restructuring and institutional change. Labour's new Child Tax Credit (which began in April 2003) has taken the process of welfare reform one step further. It is hailed by the Treasury as a "new streamlined system [which] will provide a secure stream of income for children, whether parents are in and out of work, helping people make the move into work and removing stigma from support for children" (Primarolo, 2001).

The key features of the Child Tax Credit are as follows:

- Child Benefit will stay as a 'universal benefit' for all families with children. All other entitlements for children will be combined into one single payment; this will entail rolling up the child components of Jobseeker's Allowance and Income Support, and the child components of WFTC or DPTC plus the Child Tax Credit to create a 'single seamless system of support'. This will become a single payment, administered by the Inland Revenue.
- The Child Tax Credit will be paid to all low-income families regardless of parental work status. This will benefit many families on Income Support/

Jobseeker's Allowance who previously received less support for their children than low-income working families. For example, a family on Income Support with two children under 16 will receive an additional £9 per week when receiving the Child Tax Credit (HM Treasury, 2002a).

• WFTC will cease to exist and a new Working Tax Credit will come in which will be paid to working adults on a low income and will also be available to people without children (unlike WFTC). Low-income 'workless' adults will receive adult-related payment of Income Support or Jobseeker's Allowance. Both will also receive the Child Tax Credit and Child Benefit.

• Entitlement will be determined by a 'light touch' income test, in which information from tax returns will be used to make an annual assessment. The amount awarded will then remain the same for the following 12 months, unless there are significant changes in circumstances (for example, a change in family status) or income (for example, significant falls or rises in family income).

The Child Tax Credit is a radical departure from previous social security support for children. It has a significant role to play in the reduction of child poverty and is set at more generous levels than the benefits it replaces. The method of payment (tax credit) is intended to reduce stigma and improve overall take-up. It will ease the transition into work for low-income parents and potentially improve social inclusion by treating all families alike (Millar, 2001). Payment will be made to the main carer and this addresses 'purse and wallet' concerns that money paid directly to the main carer (usually women) is more likely to be spent on children (Goode et al, 1998). It also acknowledges society's obligations towards children and proposes secure support for children regardless of their parental employment status (for further discussion of Child Tax Credits see Hirsch, 2000; Brewer et al, 2001; Millar, 2001).

However, Child Tax Credit is not a 'universal' benefit for all children but is income-tested. This is intended to be a 'lighter touch' than means testing and introduces a new approach that Labour calls 'progressive universalism'[5] (HM Treasury, 2002a). This will draw in a larger cohort of children than means-tested benefits but will not provide support for all children as a universal citizenship right. Generous income testing means that Child Tax Credit will be available even for those with annual incomes of up to £58,000 (HM Treasury, 2002a). It remains to be seen whether Child Benefit will be sustainable or will lose out in the competition for resources. If it is left to 'wither on the vine', the principle of 'universal' support for all children as a citizenship right, regardless of parental status, will be lost.

---

[5] "This means supporting all families with children, but offering the greatest help to those who need it most through a light touch income test" (HM Treasury, 2002a, p 4).

The administration, assessment and delivery of Child Tax Credits are also potentially problematic and there are concerns about the responsiveness of the Inland Revenue to changing family income and circumstances over the 12-month period (Whiteford et al, 2003; Chapter Seven, this volume). As such, uncertainty about assessments and income testing could lead to greater complexity in the social security system rather than the intended transparency and simplicity.

Education Maintenance Allowances

Education Maintenance Allowances are a new scheme intended to encourage children from low-income families to stay on in further full-time education to improve their skills, qualifications and future employability. Education Maintenance Allowances are paid directly to children, and provide a weekly allowance of up to £40 per week; they therefore represent a radical departure from other support for children, which is paid via their parents. The allowance is paid to young people aged 16-19 from low-income households who attend 'appropriate' full-time courses at school or college. The Education Maintenance Allowance scheme is still being piloted in 56 local education authorities and the pilots explore different variations on the Education Maintenance Allowance theme. In some areas the weekly allowance is paid directly to the young person, in others the payment is made to the parent. Weekly allowances are dependent on parental income, the full allowance is paid for incomes below £13,000, and between £13,000 and £30,000 (£20,000 for the London pilot), the allowance is tapered until a minimum payment of £5 per week is reached. Maximum payments can vary between £20-£40. In some pilots there are also retention bonuses to encourage good attendance and achievement bonuses. Transport costs are met in some pilot areas. Underpinning the measures are also sanctions to encourage compliance. Students must sign a 'learning agreement', which includes agreed learning goals, project deadlines and attendance requirements. A breach of this agreement, for example, poor attendance, may result in payments being stopped or reduced. These diverse schemes give some indication of the potential for benefits and allowances to be used to encourage and control behaviour in a selected group.

Evaluations of the scheme indicate that there has been a positive effect on the participation and retention of young people in post-16 education; it is still too early, however, to assess the impact upon achievement (see Ashworth et al, 2001; Legard et al, 2001; Maguire et al, 2002). The national scheme will be rolled out in September 2004 with £600 million promised in funding (HM Treasury, 2002b). However, funding of Education Maintenance Allowances may be achieved through the abolition of Child Benefit for over-16s in further education whose families are not on a low income (HM Treasury, 1998). This has been hailed by the media as a new stealth tax on middle-income families which is potentially divisive and unfair (Elliott, 2002). Evaluations of Education Maintenance Allowances have indicated that there are already signs that they can cause divisions between groups of young people who are able to claim the Allowance and those who are ineligible (Maguire et al, 2002).

Education Maintenance Allowances highlight the value of independent income for young people's transitions to adulthood. Qualitative evaluations of the scheme show that in families where they are paid to the young person, transitions to independence and financial maturity were enhanced. However, where payments were given to parents, transitions to independence were reduced (Legard et al, 2001). Yet, the financial impact of Education Maintenance Allowances on household finances was greatest in families where the parents received the payment and could be absorbed into the family budget, although when payment was to the young person there was generally a secondary effect as parents could reduce money allocated to that child (Legard et al, 2001). The importance of Education Maintenance Allowances for keeping some families above the 'breadline' was evident and in these cases if young people reneged on their learning agreements then the whole family suffered from the reduction of Education Maintenance Allowance payments (Legard et al, 2001).

At present the final form that Education Maintenance Allowances will take in 2004 is unclear. But they serve to highlight tensions and dilemmas in the provision of benefits for young people. Who should be the prime beneficiaries, should it be parents who are struggling to manage on restricted budgets or should it be young people who are negotiating the difficult transition to adulthood and financial independence? Furthermore, the means testing of family income for Education Maintenance Allowances when payments are intended to be for young people sends "mixed messages about dependence and independence" especially when training allowances for young people are not means tested (Jones and Bell, 2000, p 14).

Benefiting children? The challenge of social security support for children

The concern of the present Labour government to develop support for families and their children has meant that the interests of children have become more central to the policy process (Millar and Ridge, 2002). Labour's focus on child poverty has resulted in increases in tax and benefit provision and greater redistribution of resources to children and their families. However, there are continuing concerns about the dominance of a work-focused policy agenda and the overall adequacy of benefits for children and their parents, particularly those in 'workless' families. Increases in premiums for children have not been matched by increases in premiums for parents.

Labour's most ambitious project for the support of children, the Child Tax

Credit, represents a new commitment to the welfare of children, and seeks to address concerns about take-up, and stigma, in the current system. However, the complexities of assessment and delivery may well determine how successful it is in delivering the promised benefits. At present the principle of universal Child Benefit has been retained but it is challenged by the Child Tax Credit which will be income tested and by the possible future restriction of Child Benefit for over-16-year-olds to low-income young people receiving Education Maintenance Allowances. 'Progressive universalism' is gradually replacing the 'universal principle', and this diminishes the symbolic importance of collective social responsibility for children as individuals in their own right whatever their parents' circumstances.

Education Maintenance Allowances signal support for low-income young people and recognition of the need for incentives to encourage them into further education. However, while the payment of Education Maintenance Allowances directly to young people is an important moral concept that facilitates the transition into adulthood and financial independence, the importance of ensuring an adequate income for families supporting young people through this time must not be overlooked.

The challenge of childhood social security provision for Labour is how to secure the rights of children as individuals to an adequate standard of living suitable for their physical, social and developmental needs. To ensure that social security truly does benefit children, Labour will have to address the less popular issue of support for parents. The needs of children cannot be assumed to be the same as their parents, but equally they cannot be separated out from the overall well-being and security of their families.

Overview

- Social security for children can be informed by very different and sometimes competing discourses of family and childhood, and benefits for children can be underpinned by different aims and intentions.

- There is an ongoing tension between parental responsibility for children and the interests and obligations of society and the state towards ensuring the well-being of children.

- Labour's commitment to eradicating child poverty has resulted in a fundamental change in the way in which children are supported by the state and a redistribution of resources towards children and their families.

- Increased support for children has been provided through WFTC, increased Child Benefit and increases in means-tested child allowances. However, benefit adequacy for parents has not been addressed thereby diluting the impact of these measures.

- The Child Tax Credit and Education Maintenance Allowances represent new ways of delivering benefits to children and young people.

- Benefits for children such as Child Tax Credit are moving away from a 'universal' model of support for all children as a citizenship right, towards a system described by the government as 'progressive universalism'.

- Social security for children needs to respond to the needs and rights of children. However, while children may have different needs to adults they still need to be considered within the context of their households.

Questions for discussion

1. Why and how does the state provide social security for children?

2. Does society have an obligation to provide for the well-being of children?

3. How does the Child Tax Credit differ from previous support for children?

4. Is it right to use Education Maintenance Allowances as incentives for young people and to encourage or control certain behaviours?

References

Ashworth, A., Hardman, J., Woon-Chia, L., Maguire, S., Middleton, S., Dearden, L., Emmerson, C., Frayne, C., Goodman, A., Ichimura, H. and Meghir, C. (2001) *Education maintenance allowance: The first year. A quantitative evaluation*, DfEE Research Report 257, London: DfEE.

Barnes, H., Day, P. and Cronin, N. (1998) *Trial and error: A review of UK child support policy*, London: Family Policy Studies Centre.

Blair, T. (1999) 'Beveridge revisited: a welfare state for the 21st century', reproduced in R. Walker (ed) *Ending child poverty: Popular welfare for the 21st century*, Bristol: The Policy Press, pp 7-20.

Bradbury, B. and Jäntti, M. (2001) 'Child poverty across the industrialised world: evidence from the Luxembourg Income Study', in K. Vleminckx and T.M. Smeeding (eds) *Child wellbeing, child poverty and child policy in modern nations: What do we know?*, Bristol: The Policy Press, pp 11-32.

Bradshaw, J. (1999) 'Child poverty in comparative perspective', *European Journal of Social Security*, vol 1, no 4, pp 383-406.

Bradshaw, J. (2001) 'Child poverty under Labour', in G. Fimister (ed) *An end in sight?: Tackling child poverty in the UK*, London: CPAG, pp 9-27.

Bradshaw, J. and Barnes, H. (1999) 'How do nations monitor the well-being of their children?', Paper to the LIS Child Poverty Conference, York: Social Policy Research Unit, University of York.

Bradshaw, J. and Stimson, C. (1997) *Using Child Benefit in the family budget*, Social Policy Research Centre, London: The Stationery Office.

Brewer, M., Myck, M. and Reed, H. (2001) *Financial support for families with children: Options for the new integrated child credit*, Commentary No 92, London: Institute for Fiscal Studies.

Brown, G. (2000) 'Our children are our future', Speech by the Chancellor of the Exchequer, Gordon Brown MP, to CPAG Conference, London: HM Treasury.

Brown, J.C. (1984) *Children in social security*, London: Policy Studies Institute.

Clarke, K., Glendinning, C. and Craig, G. (1994) *Losing support: Children and the Child Support Act*, London: The Children's Society.

CPAG (Child Poverty Action Group) (June 2002) 'Benefit sanctions for parents: truants' parents to get benefit cut?', *Campaign Newsletter Issue No 22*, London: CPAG.

Daniel, P. and Ivatts, J. (1998) *Children and social policy*, Basingstoke: Macmillan.

Daycare Trust (2001a) 'Making children's places real for all', *Childcare Now*, Issue 15, p 4.

Daycare Trust (2001b) *The price parents pay*, London: Daycare Trust.

Dobson, B. and Middleton, S. (1998) *Paying to care: The cost of childhood disability*, York: York Publishing Services for the Joseph Rowntree Foundation.

DSS (Department of Social Security) (1999a) *Children first: A new approach to child support*, Cm 3992, London: The Stationery Office.

DSS (1999b) *Opportunity for All: Tackling poverty and social exclusion*, Cm 4445, London: The Stationery Office.

DSS (2000a) *Households below Average Income: A statistical analysis 1994/5-1998/9*, Leeds: Corporate Document Services.

DSS (2000b) *Public Service Agreement*, London: The Stationery Office.

DWP (Department for Work and Pensions) (2001) *Client group analysis, Quarterly Bulletin on families with children on key benefits November 2001*, Newcastle upon Tyne: Analytical Services Division.

DWP (2002a) 'Benefit expenditure tables 2002', www.dwp.gov.uk

DWP (2002b) *Households Below Average Income 1994/95 to 2000/01*, Leeds: Corporate Document Services.

Elliott, F. (2002) 'Brown squeezes parents with new £1bn stealth tax', *Sunday Telegraph*, 7 July.

Ford, R. and Millar, J. (1998) *Private lives and public responses: Lone parenthood and future policy in the UK*, London: Policy Studies Institute.

Garnham, A. and Knights, E. (1994) *Putting the Treasury first: The truth about child support*, London: CPAG.

Goode, J., Callender, C. and Lister, R. (1998) *Purse or wallet: Gender inequalities and income distribution within families on benefits*, London: Policy Studies Institute.

Gordon, D., Adelman, L., Ashworth, K., Bradshaw, J., Levitas, J., Middleton, S., Pantazis, C., Patsios, D., Payne, S., Townsend, P. and Williams, J. (2000) *Poverty and social exclusion in Britain*, York: Joseph Rowntree Foundation.

Gregg, P., Harkness, S. and Machin, S. (1999) *Child development and family income*, York: Joseph Rowntree Foundation.

Hill, M. (1994) *Social security policy in Britain*, London: Edward Elgar.

Hirsch, D. (1999) *Welfare beyond work,* York: Joseph Rowntree Foundation.

Hirsch, D. (2000) *A credit to children: The UK's radical reform of children's benefits in international perspective*, York: York Publishing Services for the Joseph Rowntree Foundation.

HM Treasury (1998) *Modern public services for Britain: Investing in reform, Comprehensive Spending Review: New public spending plans 1999-2002*, Cm 4011, London: The Stationery Office.

HM Treasury (1999) *Supporting families through the tax and benefit system*, London: HM Treasury.

HM Treasury (2000) *Budget, March 2000*, London: The Public Enquiry Unit.

HM Treasury (2001a) *Tackling child poverty: Giving every child the best possible start in life*, London: HM Treasury.

HM Treasury (2001b) *The modernisation of Britain's tax and benefit system: Savings and assets for all*, HM Treasury No 8, London: The Public Enquiry Unit, HM Treasury.

HM Treasury (2002a) *The modernisation of Britain's tax and benefit system: The Child and Working Tax Credit*, HM Treasury, No 10, London: The Public Enquiry Unit, HM Treasury.

HM Treasury (2002b) *Opportunity and security for all: Investing in an enterprising, fairer Britain, Spending Review 2002: New public spending plans 2003-2006*, London: The Public Enquiry Unit, HM Treasury.

Holman, B. (2000) 'At the hard end, poverty lives', *New Statesman*, 15 May, pp 23-4.

Howard, M., Garnham, A., Fimister, G. and Veit-Wilson, J. (2001) *Poverty: The facts* (4th edn), London: CPAG.

Inland Revenue (2001) *Working Families' Tax Credit statistics*, Quarterly Enquiry, November, London: ONS.

Jones, G. and Bell, R. (2000) *Balancing acts: Youth parenting and public policy*, York: Joseph Rowntree Foundation.

Land, H. (1999) 'New Labour, new families?', in H. Dean and R. Woods (eds) *Social Policy Review 11*, Luton: University of Luton for the Social Policy Association.

Land, H. (2002) *Meeting the childcare challenge: Why universal childcare is key to ending child poverty*, London: Daycare Trust.

Legard, R., Woodfield, K. and White, C. (2001) *'Staying away or staying on?': A qualitative evaluation of the Education Maintenance Allowance*, DfEE, Research Report 256, London: DfEE.

Lister, R. (1990) *The exclusive society: Citizenship and the poor*, London: CPAG.

Lister, R. (2001) '"Doing good by stealth": the politics of poverty and inequality under New Labour', *New Economy*, July, pp 65-70.

Lister, R., Goode, J. and Callender, C. (1999) 'Income distribution within families and the reform of social security', *Journal of Social Welfare and Family Law*, vol 21, no 3, pp 203-20.

MacNicol, J. (1980) *The movement for family allowances, 1918-1945: A study in social policy development*, London: Heinemann.

Maguire, S., Maguire, M. and Heaver, C. (2002) *Implementation of the Education Maintenance Allowance pilots: The second year*, DfEE, Research Report 333, London: DfEE.

Mannion, R., Hutton, S. and Sainsbury, R. (1994) *Direct payments from Income Support*, DSS Research Report No 33, London: HMSO.

Middleton, S., Ashworth, K. and Walker, R. (1994) *Family fortunes,* London: CPAG.

Middleton, S., Ashworth, K. and Braithwaite, I. (1997) *Small fortunes: Spending on children. Childhood poverty and parental sacrifice*, York: Joseph Rowntree Foundation.

Millar, J. (2001) 'Benefits for children in the UK', in K. Battle and M. Mendelson (eds) *Benefits for children – A four country study*, Ottawa, Canada: The Caledon Institute, pp 187-25.

Millar, J. and Ridge, T. (2001) *Families, poverty, work and care: A review of the literature on lone parents and low-income couple families with children*, DWP Research Report No 153, Leeds: Corporate Document Services.

Millar, J. and Ridge, T. (2002) 'Parents, children, families and New Labour: developing family policy?', in M. Powell *Evaluating New Labour's welfare reforms*, Bristol: The Policy Press, pp 85-106.

Oldfield, N. and Yu, A.C.S. (1993) *The cost of a child: Living standards for the 1990s*, London: CPAG.

Oppenheim, C. and Harker, L. (1996) *Poverty: The facts*, London: CPAG.

Parker, H. (ed) (1998) *Low Cost but Acceptable: A Minimum Income Standard for the UK: Families with young children*, Bristol: The Policy Press/Zacchaeus 2000 Trust.

Piachaud, D. and Sutherland, H. (2000) *How effective is the British government's attempt to reduce child poverty?*, CASE Paper 38, London: Centre for Analysis of Social Exclusion, London School of Economics and Political Science.

Piachaud, D. and Sutherland, H. (2001) 'Child poverty: aims, achievements and prospects for the future', *New Economy* June, pp 71-6.

Primarolo, D. (November 2001) 'Details announced of new tax credits to make work pay, support children and tackle poverty', 29 November, www.hm-treasury.gov.uk/newsroom_and_speeches/press/2001/press_132_01.cfm

Ridge, T. (2002) *Childhood poverty and social exclusion: From a child's perspective*, Bristol: The Policy Press.

Sainsbury, R. (1999) 'The aims of social security', in J. Ditch (ed) *Introduction to social security: Policies, benefits and poverty*, London: Routledge, pp 34-47.

Smith, R. (1998) 'Who pays for children', *Benefits*, no 21.

Veit-Wilson, J. (1998) *Setting adequacy standards: How governments define minimum incomes,* Bristol: The Policy Press.

Walker, R. with Howard, M. (2000) *The making of a welfare class?: Benefit receipt in Britain*, Bristol: The Policy Press.

Walker, A. and Walker, C. (1997) *Britain divided: The growth of social exclusion in the 1980s and 1990s*, London: CPAG.

Whiteford, P., Mandelson, M. and Millar, J. (2003) *Timing it right? Responding to income changes, a comparison of Australia, Canada and the UK*, York: York Publishing Services for the Joseph Rowntree Foundation.

Website resources

Child Benefit	www.dwp.gov.uk/lifeevent/benefits/child_benefit.htm
Education Maintenance Allowance	www.dfes.gov.uk/ema
End Child Poverty	www.ecpc.org.uk
Quids for Kids	www.lga.gov.uk

Reforming pensions: investing in the future

Stephen McKay

Summary

In this chapter we describe issues surrounding recent changes to pensions policy, and the different factors taken into account in pension policy formulation. The chapter investigates:

- the broad detail of different kinds of pensions, and their main features;

- the incomes of today's pensioners;

- changes in population age structure often thought highly relevant for pensions policy;

- changes in labour market behaviour that may affect pensions, and the ability of people to save towards retirement;

- the policy approach of Labour, and the main features of their strategy.

Introduction: providing security in retirement

Many people in Britain want or expect to spend a proportion of their life in 'retirement'. That is, having spent some years working they expect to have a period not in paid work. This feature of the working lifetime is, however, a fairly recent historical development and until the 20th century would have seemed strange. Instead, people worked throughout their lives until forced to stop through death or incapacity. Those unable to work then had to rely on support from their families, or possibly from limited local social support arrangements. The notion that people may actually be retired for a quite substantial number of years is an even more recent phenomenon.

Expressed in such a way, retirement is about the withdrawal from *paid* work. There is no equivalent concept, or possibly even prospect, for those unable to take part in paid employment – those excluded from paid work for reasons of long-term unemployment, disability, or an expectation that they will be engaged in unpaid work (especially mothers). Retirement can, to some extent, be viewed as quite a male concept. You retire from *paid* work – whereas the unpaid work that takes place within the home is, presumably, expected to continue (Walker, 1992). Retirement therefore affects men and women differently, although in future this may change given higher female employment rates among younger population cohorts.

Moreover, retirement can also be viewed less positively as a means of actively excluding older people from the labour market. Between 1931 and 1971 the proportion of men aged 65+ who were retired increased from under one half to more than three quarters. Alan Walker has argued that older people have been used as a reserve army of labour which is tapped into when labour is in short supply, and shed when the demand for labour falls: "The advent of large scale unemployment in the 1930s was crucial in the institutionalisation of retirement, and its return in the early 1980s has resulted in the growth of early retirement" (Walker, 1986, p 210).

Taking this as a starting point, the provision of security in retirement must depend on having some access to financial resources other than earnings from paid work. This package of income will comprise any benefits available from the state (safety net benefits, contributory benefits), and private resources that individuals have managed to save – as cash, as assets of various kinds, or in the form of specific pension products.

For various reasons, the state has a major role in determining the level of people's incomes in retirement across a wide range of countries. This is not just through what the state itself actually provides, but also through how the state regulates the private sector pension market – and indeed often provides financial incentives towards private provision.

In the next section we present an overview of the various sources of income that may be available to pensioners, followed by a discussion of the key factors affecting demand for pensions, and in the final section we look specifically at current government policy in this area.

Sources of income in older age: an overview

There are currently approximately 3.9 million men aged 65+, and 6.9 million women aged 60 or more (the current state pension ages)[1]. That represents around 13% of men in the UK, and 23% of women (GAD, 2000). Figures from the Department for Work and Pensions suggest that almost all receive a key social security benefit (or live in a unit where benefit is being received that includes them as a dependant). Of the 10.4 million people above state pension age receiving a key benefit, some 2.5 million were receiving a disability-related benefit (DWP, 2002a), while close to 700,000 received Minimum Income Guarantee (MIG) (and no disability-related benefits). A total of 7.3 million was covered by the Retirement Pension, without disability-related provision or MIG.

The total cost of pensions includes various forms of tax reliefs and rebates to those of working age who contribute to pensions, as well as direct spending on those in retirement. It is generally easier to find regular figures for spending, rather than for indirect government support, in the form of tax incentives. However, in 1998 the government produced the following figures representing spending on pensions and pensioners (DSS, 1998a, p 21):

- £12.2 billion in tax relief on pension contributions (for those of working age);
- £7 billion on national insurance rebates to people contracted-out of State Earnings-Related Pensions (SERPS) (for those of working age);
- £30 billion on the basic state pension (for current pensioners);
- £17 billion in other social security spending – SERPS, income-related and disability benefits (for current pensioners);
- there was also about £30 billion paid out in private pensions to those of state pension age.

Income sources: pension 'pillars'

There are various sources of income people may receive once they are not working. These may be divided into several different kinds, called 'pillars' or 'tiers'. An influential report by the World Bank (1994) sought to encourage

---

[1] In 1993, the decision was made to equalise state pensions for men and women at 65 (for a discussion see Hutton et al, 1995). This satisfies the needs of formal sex equality, and also helps to keep expenditure lower than alternative equalisation options below the age of 65.

Box 10.1: **Multi-pillar pension arrangements**

The World Bank (1994) has recommended that all countries adopt a 'multi-pillar arrangement' for pensioners' income:

1 A *compulsory publicly managed* pillar, which they propose to be funded from general taxation and to provide a flat-rate benefit (designed to prevent or reduce poverty).
2 A *compulsory privately managed* pillar, funded from people's contributions to either occupational or personal pension plans, and regulated by government (earnings-related pensions, enabling individuals to smooth income over their lifetimes and maintain living standards in retirement comparable or at least proportional to their standard of living while of working age).
3 A *voluntary private pillar* of additional savings vehicles of various kinds, such as personal saving or top-ups to private pensions.

It may be argued that earnings, for those working past 'normal' state pension or retirement age, constitutes a fourth pillar of retirement income.

an approach to state pension reform based on three tiers or pillars (see **Box 10.1**). These three pillars represent different types of public and private forms of pension provision (compulsory publicly managed, compulsory privately managed, and voluntary) which also relate, at least in part, to the different objectives that the World Bank identify for pensions systems – to redistribute incomes towards poor pensioners (who should be provided with a 'safety net'), to provide a savings function for most people to acquire sufficient resources to live off in retirement, and to provide a form of insurance against the different risks to income and health that old people may face. The pensions system in the UK may be described in an analogous manner to the multi-pillar system proposed by the World Bank (1994), although the 'fit' with the World Bank model is far from perfect.

The first pillar comprises the basic pensions provided by government, including:

• The 'basic state pension'[2], which is a contributory benefit for individuals who have made sufficient national insurance contributions over their working lifetime, mostly assuming people have worked for the vast majority of their working-age years.
• A range of income-related benefits that are available for those families whose income falls below a level set by their needs. This includes specific support for pensioners (the MIG, soon to be replaced by the Pension Credit – see

---

[2] In fact there are a number of 'categories' of state retirement pension, depending on the precise circumstances surrounding entitlement. However, for simplicity these may be collectively referred to as the basic state pension.

further discussion below), as well as more general benefits (for example, Housing Benefit and Council Tax Benefit may be paid to those on a low income, to meet the costs of rent or of local taxation).

The second pillar consists of earnings-related compulsory pensions, to which all employees earning more than a low fixed level are required to contribute. This includes:

- *State provision:* SERPS provide an income in retirement based on previous contributions made. Over time SERPS is being replaced by the State Second Pension (S2P), which is expected to move towards a flat rate of payment (see further discussion below).
- *Occupational pensions:* people can choose to opt out of the state earnings-related provision and into an approved occupational or private scheme. Occupational pensions are provided by many companies, and are of two main kinds. 'Defined benefit' schemes are based upon providing a target proportion of final or average earnings when people retire (say, half or two thirds of earnings). 'Defined contribution' schemes provide pension incomes based on the value of a specified level of contributions while working – say 6% of earnings, often enhanced by an employer contribution of similar or greater size – and will depend on the performance of the investments made with those contributions. There are also hybrid arrangements drawing on both principles.
- *Private pensions:* individuals may instead opt for one of a range of personal pensions sold by banks and insurance companies; these are very popular with the self-employed for whom occupational pensions are not available. More recently, 'Stakeholder Pensions' have been introduced with many characteristics of personal pensions, but having to meet particular standards to qualify. They are aimed at 'moderate' earners who do not have access to occupational pensions, and for whom existing personal pension products may provide poor value (see further discussion below).

The third pillar is voluntary provision and can include a number of different financial products which individuals can buy. These include private pension schemes and also other forms of savings, such as in tax-privileged accounts like Individual Savings Accounts (ISAs). Many occupational pensions also allow people to make top-up contributions in the form of Additional Voluntary Contributions (AVCs), or these may be free-standing if provided by a different company. In Britain, the potential of using housing equity to help fund retirement is recognised.

Finally there is, arguably, a fourth pillar consisting of earnings. It used to be common for those of state pension age to continue working, although until 1988 they could not both receive their state pension and continue to work.

The trend is, however, towards people ceasing employment at earlier rather than later ages (see further discussion below, and Smeaton and McKay, 2003).

There are various issues and problems with all these forms of pension provision. The low level of the basic state pension means that many pensioners with little or no other sources of income are eligible for means-tested support. Benefits based on means testing are subject to the criticism that rates of take-up are often low. In 1999-2000 there were around 1.4 million pensioners receiving the MIG but government figures show that several hundred thousand pensioners could be eligible but are not in receipt (DWP, 2001b). The margins of error are wide, with an estimate of 390,000-770,000 who could be receiving MIG but did not (DWP, 2001b, p 15). Means-tested benefits also seem to 'reward' those who have *not* saved for retirement, compared to those who have small private incomes that disqualify them from eligibility. An important question is whether the kinds of criticisms made of means tests are inherent to this method of delivery or instead may be overcome by better design and/or publicity and information.

Earnings-related pensions, public and private, can be criticised on the grounds that they perpetuate inequalities in the labour market into retirement: those with higher earnings will enjoy higher living standards in retirement. Those excluded from the labour market, for long or short periods, will face lower incomes. This has generally not been sufficiently dealt with by 'crediting in' certain groups, such as mothers with young children (who also benefit from 'home responsibilities protection', introduced in 1978).

Occupational pensions may be offering a less secure and lower level of pension. In the past few years there seems to have been a shift towards defined contribution, rather than defined benefit, schemes. Traditionally companies have tended to opt for defined benefit schemes. These are seen as providing a high degree of certainty to employees about the size of their final pension, but they do require companies to take on board issues about how long people are going to live, what level of earnings they will have, and so on, in order to calculate an appropriate level of contributions. By contrast defined contribution schemes involve the company in no such risk, but the level of pension for the employee is rather uncertain. Balanced against this, defined contribution schemes have generally been more portable when people move jobs. Defined contribution schemes have become more common in recent years and some employers do not allow new recruits to join existing defined benefit schemes, and in extreme cases they are even closing down such schemes.

Various governments have sought to increase the use of private pensions. In the late 1980s, it became possible for people to contract out of SERPS into a personal pension. At the same time, the right of employers to make membership of occupational schemes compulsory was abolished, in favour of giving people a freer choice of pension product. However, aggressive sales tactics created a rush towards personal pensions, which provide a worse deal for many people.

Government intervention forced the payment of compensation in what became a large misselling scandal.

In fact the issue of trust, or rather lack of trust, in pension provisions is a major overarching issue for both state and private sectors. It seems that the level of trust and faith in pensions of all kinds is at a low ebb. A number of controversies have afflicted both the state and non-state sectors, as briefly outlined in **Box 10.2**. The need to find a secure and stable system of support is thus very central to current policy objectives (discussed in more detail below).

Box 10.2: Failure of trust in pensions?

I State pensions

SERPS is paid to widow(er)s on the death of their spouse. The 1986 Social Security Act halved the amount that could be inherited by the surviving spouse, from all to 50% of the SERPS additional pension. The Department of Social Security did not update the information available to the public, and staff gave wrong information when people asked about SERPS, despite the 14-year lead time for the legislation to take effect. A redress package has been put in place. Two official reports, published in 2000, investigated what had happened.

> ... the Parliamentary Ombudsman finds the Department guilty of maladministration.... I strongly criticise the DSS for failing to make their leaflets on retirement pensions and surviving spouses' benefits sufficiently comprehensive and up to date in this important respect following the enactment of the 1986 Act, and for their repeated failure to do so until spring 1996. (Parliamentary Ombudsman, 2000, para 34)

> The full cost of resolving this problem will be at least £2.5 billion and probably considerably more. (NAO, 2000, p 6)

II Private pensions
Occupational: The Maxwell scandal (1991)

20,000 people lost £480 million in pension funds which were used by Robert Maxwell to (temporarily) prop up ailing companies in his group (the missing money was mostly made good by £100 million from government and a settlement for £276 million from financial institutions).

We might also add problems occurring at the Equitable Life company (issues about guaranteed levels of pension income given to some, but not all policy holders).

Personal: the misselling of pension products
During 1988-94, many people who would have been better off in employer pension schemes were wrongly sold personal pensions. A total exceeding £13 billion is expected to be paid out in recompense by the financial services industry (FSA, 2000).

The distribution of pensioner incomes

There are thus a range of different sources of pension income, but which are more important? In the overall composition of pensioner income in 1999–2000 (DWP/ASD, 2001):

- 52% was benefit income;
- 26% was from occupational pensions;
- 14% was from investment income;
- 8% was from earnings;
- 1% was from other sources.

However, this income was very unequally distributed between pensioners. As **Figure 10.1** shows, for pensioner couples, state benefits provided most pensioner income among the poorest two fifths of couples. Among the richest fifth, private sources of income were about double the size of income from state sources. For pensioner couples, the richest fifth had incomes over four times as large as the poorest fifth. In recent times the clear trend has been towards growing inequality, as state benefits have struggled to keep pace with the increases found among private sources of income (DWP, 2002b).

First-tier pensions (the basic state pension, MIG) are relatively redistributive towards groups experiencing lower earnings during their working-age life, and also 'credit in' those out of the labour market for reasons of unemployment, or raising children. However, second-tier pensions (both privately provided and through SERPS) are linked to the size of contributions while in work. As such, these additional pensions tend to be higher among those who had higher

Figure 10.1: Income distribution of couple pensioners in 1999/2000

earnings during their working lifetimes. Those more likely to be out of the labour market, or on lower earnings, will generally accumulate smaller additional pensions – or none at all.

Ginn and Arber (2001) have looked at the working-age population, and rates of contributing to private pensions. These tend to be lower among women than men, and among minority ethnic groups compared to whites – leading to lower incomes in retirement. The Pension Provision Group (1998) examined the concentration of pensioners on low incomes, finding in particular that:

- incomes were lower for women than for men (although comparisons were not always straightforward); on individual-level incomes the Women and Equality Unit (2002) found that incomes for women were:
  - lower than for men, but also more variable; and that
  - differences in the level of income between women and men were smaller for single persons than for those living as a couple (see also EOC, 1997);
- incomes were lower among those older than younger (reflecting the effects of unindexed non-state pensions, and different working life experience), above age 80, women outnumber men by two to one; and
- incomes were lower among tenants than owner-occupiers.

Panel data has shown that the risk of having a low income in older age is related to work history – men were least likely to be poor if they worked in professional and clerical occupations; for women, those working in professional, clerical and managerial occupations were most likely to avoid low incomes post 60 years of age (Bardasi and Jenkins, 2002). This research study also found that divorced women, in particular, had substantially high rates of poverty, particularly compared with women living with a partner.

The self-employed are not included in the S2P, and so have entitlement only to the basic state pension unless they make separate private provision of their own.

Factors affecting the demand for pensions

Population ageing

Much of the debate about the future of pensions takes place somewhat under a cloud of demographic developments. It is well known that the population of the UK, like that of most richer countries, is 'ageing'. A greater proportion of people are in older years, associated with retirement, and a lower proportion is of working age, or are young. This trend may best be depicted in the form of 'population pyramids'. These graphs show the number of men and women at different ages in the population, at a given date. The population of the UK in 2001 is shown in **Figure 10.2**.

Figure 10.2: Population of the UK: 2001 (thousand people per five-year age group)

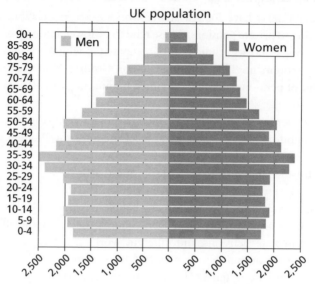

In 2001, there is a large 'bulge' in the age range of 30-34 and 35-39. These represent people born in the 1960s 'baby boom'. The smaller bulge for those in their early fifties are the children of a post-war boom in birth rates. Above 65, each age group is successively smaller as a result of mortality. From ages 80+, women strongly outnumber men, reflecting their higher life expectancy. The number of children (in each five-year age group) is less than the number of those aged 30-34, or 35-39. This represents a relatively small family size among today's people of family-bearing age: rather than having two children per mother in order to 'replace' each generation, average family sizes are more in the region of 1.5 children per woman. This leads to population ageing, and in time (other things being equal) to population decline.

In developing countries, these graphs resemble Egyptian-style pyramids, with many young people and few old – mostly reflecting high birth rates, and to a lesser extent, higher mortality. The reduction in family sizes is mostly responsible for the overall ageing of populations, as recent generations do not have enough children to 'replace' themselves. The effect of lower mortality is less critical, but does contribute to overall ageing.

By 2031 in the UK, the bulge of the baby boom people (shown above) is reaching retirement and pensionable ages (**Figure 10.3**), and so the age groups 60-64 and 65-69 are the largest age groups. As birth rates are projected to have remained relatively low, the numbers of children continue to fall behind the numbers of those at slightly older ages. In this way, the population as a whole may be said to be ageing.

Figure 10.3: Projected population of the UK: 2031

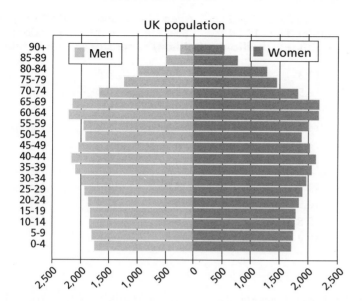

It is possible to summarise the ageing of this population in **Table 10.1**, which indicates the number of people of working age, compared to those who are expected (generally) not to be working. The ratio of workers to pensioners is sometimes known as the 'dependency ratio' (or 'support ratio').

As shown in **Table 10.1**, in 1971 there were around 4.6 people of working age for every person aged 65 or more. By 2001 this will have changed to 4.1, and by 2041 onwards will have changed to 2.4. A slightly different picture emerges if we look at the ratio of workers to those at either end of the age distribution. This shows an apparent 'improvement' in the dependency ratio until 2001, and only then a decline after 2021. The overall size of the change is, however, less than for pensioners only – as a result of the projected reductions in the number of children in the population.

It should be remembered, of course, that figures far into the future are projections, based on current assumptions about life expectancy, migration and, in particular, birth rates. We can have a fairly good idea of how many 60-year-olds there will be in 20 years' time – as many 40-year-olds as there are now, less an allowance for deaths, plus a number based on expected net in-migration. But to know how many children under five there will be in 20 years introduces a range of assumptions about family formation patterns in the future. Some of the parents who might have children in 20 years' time are not yet born themselves. Even so, despite the range of uncertainty about future population, a good deal of 'momentum' is built into population trend

Table 10.1: The 'dependency ratio' (1971-2061)

	Year	Aged under 16 (million)	Aged 16-64 (million)	Aged 65+ (million)	Workers per pensioner	Workers per pensioner plus child
Estimates	1971	14.3	34.3	7.4	4.6	1.6
	1981	12.5	35.3	8.5	4.2	1.7
	1991	11.7	37.0	9.1	4.1	1.8
Projections	2001	12.1	38.5	9.3	4.1	1.8
	2011	11.3	40.2	10.2	3.9	1.9
	2021	11.3	40.1	12.2	3.3	1.7
Longer-term projections	2031	11.3	38.7	14.8	2.6	1.5
	2041	10.9	38.0	15.9	2.4	1.4
	2051	10.8	37.7	15.5	2.4	1.4
	2061	10.7	36.8	15.5	2.4	1.4

Source: GAD (2000)

figures by the characteristics of today's population – future fertility and mortality can alter the extent of ageing, but rapid population ageing over the next few decades will occur under any plausible scenario (Shaw, 2001).

The effects of population ageing on constraining policy choices has sometimes been dubbed the 'demographic time-bomb'. The analogy is far from perfect, since clearly the consequences of demographic change are likely to be felt gradually (rather than abruptly as with a 'bomb' analogy), plus many of the effects are exaggerated. In particular, there is scope for policies that change the real factors – numbers in work, numbers supported by them. For instance, as people live longer the retirement age could be altered – a policy that has attracted much recent attention (O'Connell, 2002). This has already been announced for women, whose state pension age is rising from 60 to 65 between 2010 and 2020. Plus, the number of people in work is rather different from the number of people of working age. Policy has not really tried, as yet, to reverse a situation where the state pension age has ceased to be a very significant threshold in affecting rates of leaving the labour market. The most recent Green Paper (DWP, 2002c) seeks to encourage longer working lives, through incentives to delay pension receipt and an employment focus for the 50+ group. However, it does not suggest any change to the state pension age at 65 years.

These trends are repeated across many countries. The cost to public pensions in terms of extra payments does, however, vary depending with the degree of ageing expected, and the relative generosity of state pensions. As shown in **Table 10.2**, the proportion of national income going to public pensions is quite low in the UK at present. And, because many elements of pension

Table 10.2: Comparative picture of public pension costs: projected spending on public pensions as % of GDP

	2000	2030
UK	5.1	4.7
Germany	10.3	13.2
Spain	9.4	12.9
France	12.1	16.0
Italy	14.2	15.9

Source: European Commission (2001)

benefits are uprated only by prices and not by total growth in the economy (such as in line with earnings). However, when expressed as an amount of money (tens of billions of pounds), even this kind of downward trend can be made to appear as a quite alarming increase! The difference reflects differences in price growth compared to overall income growth.

One of the main reasons expressed for concern about population ageing is that state pensions are mostly based on a 'Pay-As-You-Go' (PAYG) basis. This means that the pensions of today are paid for by taxing the workers of today. In the future, there will be fewer workers to tax for each pensioner, and hence potentially, concerns about affordability. This is then said to contrast with private sector pensions, which are based on paying pensions out of contributions that people make during their working lifetime.

As we have seen, there is little reason for the UK to be unduly concerned by the affordability of its public sector pensions. State retirement pensions are rising in line with prices, not earnings, and thus projected to decline as a proportion of national income. In any case, this kind of argument is somewhat flawed. The needs and wants of older groups must be met from what the workforce is able to produce. In a PAYG system, this is operationalised by levying taxes on workers. In a funded system, assets are mostly invested in companies, meaning that pensions are met from company profits – which might otherwise have gone to workers. Barr (2000) also provides refutations of similar myths about pension funding choices – what might appear sensible for an individual acting alone might not be feasible when applied across a whole society.

There is no 'planet pension fund' where resources may be discretely stored and then retrieved when people retire. There are, however, important choices about how production may be allocated between workers and non-workers, and the ages at which people cease working. Other things being equal, higher incomes for pensioners mean lower incomes for workers (or vice versa), unless the numbers of workers or pensioners may be altered through labour market policies.

Employment trends

Simple demographic statistics are often based on numbers of people of working age, compared to those older than state retirement age. However, in practice the number of people of working age is rather different from the number of those working. The number of workers is by no means fixed. For instance, the number of women, and particularly mothers in paid work, has risen in recent decades.

At the same time, it is increasingly common for people to leave work many years before state pension age. Sometimes this is by choice, among those with generous financial resources, but more often this is triggered by unemployment (perhaps disguised as early retirement) and ill-health. Overall one third of men and women aged between 50 and state pension age are not in paid work (some 2.8 million people). Campbell (1999) has figured this decline over time – two fifths of men aged between 55 and 65 were without work by the late 1990s, compared with one fifth in 1979. It is now a policy priority to try to reverse this trend of early retirement.

Rates of employment among people *above* state pension age are even lower and have been falling for some time, now standing at around 14% for men aged 65-69, 6% for men aged 70-74; and 27% for women aged 60-64, 8% for women aged 65-69. These figures are, however, above the European average for this age group (Vlasblom and Nekkers, 2001, Tables 3.1 and 3.2).

Government policy since 1997

In 1998, a Green Paper set out the main proposed direction of government reforms to pensions (DSS, 1998a). This suggested that there were two main objectives of pensions policy. The first, aimed at lower-income groups, was to ensure that everyone enjoyed a decent income in retirement. The second, addressing a wider group, was to rebuild trust in the overall pensions system, which they believed had been eroded, perhaps particularly in non-state pensions. The government identified a number of key problems with the system they inherited (see also DWP, 2001a, 2002c):

- growing inequality of incomes among pensioners;
- large numbers of pensioners living in poverty;
- too many people of working age failing to make sufficient provision for retirement;
- inadequate provision through SERPS for people with low earnings or interrupted employment histories;
- a lack of confidence in the pensions system.

For current pensioners, the main aim of the proposed reforms was therefore to tackle pensioner poverty. For future pensioners, there were a number of key aims: to help people to save for retirement; to offer better support to those who cannot save; to regulate the pension system effectively; and to enable the private sector to provide affordable and secure second pensions (DSS, 1998a).

The Green Paper and subsequent reforms amounted to a wide-ranging series of reforms. A number of the key reforms are shown in **Box 10.3**. In the first pillar, the role of the basic state pension is becoming less important, despite some increases above the rate of inflation. Prior to 1980 the state Retirement Pension was increased in line with rises in earnings, or in line with price changes if they were higher. However, in 1980 the break with earnings was made. From that point pensions have only been increased in line with price changes. In 1977, the state Retirement Pension was worth 20% of average male earnings, but 20 years later was worth nearer to 15%. In the longer term the value compared to earnings will continue to decline to well below 10%.

Thus the most significant change to state provision has been the replacement of Income Support for pensions with MIG. This is a means-tested (or income-related) system that provides an income top-up to pensioners whose income falls below the level of guarantee. This element of reform has proved to be one of the most controversial areas of change. Government has argued that this represents the best means of channelling additional funds to poorer groups. Some poorer pensioners do not receive the full basic pension or, if they do, they receive income-related benefits on top (such as MIG or Housing Benefit) which are reduced when pensions rise. So, they argue, increases in the basic pension are not well targeted towards the poorest pensioners. The response from critics has been twofold, in replies that emphasise the disadvantages long associated with a means-tested approach (McKay and Rowlingson, 1999). First, that many people do not claim the benefits to which they are entitled. As noted above, in 1999-2000, only around two thirds of those entitled to MIG received it. For reasons of lack of knowledge, or perhaps the stigma of having to claim an income top-up, many of those entitled to MIG do not receive it. The second set of criticisms are based on the incentive effects of means testing. The presence of MIG means that those who have saved towards retirement may be no better off than those who did not – because the MIG is reduced for those with savings, or small amounts of personal income. This undermines the incentive to make such self-provision, and may be regarded as itself somewhat unjust.

The response to both criticisms is the Pension Credit, introduced in April 2003. The Pension Credit combines the MIG, with (from age 65 for both sexes) a savings credit that aims to reward small additional incomes. One of the main innovations is that the assessment of resources ('means test') is designed to only take place every five years. The assessment of Pension Credit is designed

---

Box 10.3: Major pension reforms since 1997

1 The first pillar: state pensions
- The basic state pension was increased in 2001 and 2002 by more than inflation, but in the previous year by only 75 pence (which was in line with inflation).
- Introduction of MIG, replacing/renaming Income Support for pensioners, linked to earnings growth and increased significantly in 2001/02.
- Introduction of Pension Credit (2003) subsuming MIG and paying a credit for people having savings or earnings.

2 The second pillar: earnings-related provision
- Reformed SERPS, to be replaced by the S2P, benefiting lower earners (from 2002).
- Changes to the regulation of occupational pensions, their investment strategies and governance.

3 The third pillar: private (personal) pensions
- Introduction of Stakeholder Pensions for moderate earners (starting April 2001).
- Formation of the Financial Services Authority (FSA), becoming the single regulator for financial services in the UK (from 2001).

4 Other
- Introduction of Winter Fuel Payments (now at £200), and free TV licences for families with someone aged 75+.
- Introduction of 'pension sharing' for divorced couples.
- Introduction of the 'Pension Service' as a separate agency dealing with people of pensionable age (from 2002).

---

to be conducted at (or just prior to) the point of receiving the basic state pension, and any award of Pension Credit would then continue for five years without change (DWP, 2001b). Telephone applications are permitted.

Reassessment of Pension Credit is voluntary if a person's income drops over that time (when they might therefore receive a higher level of Pension Credit). Otherwise, only major life changes need be reported. These steps are part of the attempt to overcome problems of take-up. This reform also aims to provide small rewards for those with savings income (or income from earnings, or any second pension *including* SERPS/S2P). It is too early to say what effect this may have on stigma and rates of take-up – in other words, whether the long-running problems associated with means testing may be overcome by changes to benefit design.

In the second pillar, the most important reform has been the introduction of a new Second State Pension, replacing SERPS. The plan is that over time S2P will become a flat-rate benefit, similar to the basic state pension, rather than being related proportionately to previous contributions (like SERPS, and non-state pensions in general). This means it will become more redistributional, since those on lower earnings will receive the same S2P, when the scheme matures, than those on higher earnings (non contracted-out). Moreover, those earnings less than £10,800 will be treated as if they earned £10,800 a year, in calculating benefits. Again, advantaging lower earners. Critics allege that S2P is "best seen as a measure to compensate for the low level of the basic pension rather than as a replacement for SERPS" (Blackburn, 2002, p 305).

In the third pillar, the key reform has been the introduction of the Stakeholder Pension, following the 1999 Welfare Reform and Pensions Act. They are designed to be low-cost personal pensions for people who cannot join an occupational pension scheme and who earn over £10,000 a year. Employees with earnings less than this may be better off remaining in SERPS/S2P. Stakeholder Pensions schemes cannot make charges of more than 1% per year on the value of each member's funds, and members must be able to transfer in and out of the scheme without any extra charges. They should accept small levels of contributions (at least £20). Employers with more than five staff must designate a stakeholder scheme, unless they have approved alternative provision in place.

Stakeholder Pensions remain voluntary, and dependent on the marketing activity of providers. Their low charges imply that advice is unlikely to be part of the deal, and it remains unclear how portable they will prove among those changing employers. There must also be an open question about how far lower-income earners will genuinely benefit from them, while means-tested provision remains an important part of pensioner income. And, whether they are able to afford even the modest contributions they are permitted to make. For those with varying incomes, in particular, the choice between remaining in the S2P or instead taking out a Stakeholder Pension must be finely balanced.

The regulatory framework for pensions has been somewhat rationalised, with the formation of the Financial Services Authority (FSA) from 2001, bringing together a number of different regulators. However, the legislation governing pensions is still covered both by the Department for Work and Pensions and Inland Revenue, and there are other bodies with a regulatory function such as OPRA (Occupational Pensions Regulatory Authority), which covers some aspects of Stakeholder Pensions.

A Green Paper (DWP, 2002c) has proposed considerable simplification, not just of regulatory requirements on schemes but also in the tax treatment of pensions. Finally, we list other changes that have taken place. There have been some extra resources put in to help in paying for winter fuel and television licences for the poorest pensioners. The Welfare Reform and Pensions Act introduced 'pension sharing' for divorcing couples from December 2000 (see DSS, 1998b; Joshi and Davies, 1998). This permits (although does not compel) the division of occupational pension rights between husbands and wives, in a way that treats pensions rights as another asset to be taken into account. It allows the option for couples to completely separate their financial affairs at that point rather than later. Previously it was only possible to 'offset' the value of pension rights, or (since 1995) 'earmark' the final pension benefits for the partner when the pension matures. There has also been a significant administrative change with the introduction of the 'Pension Service' within the Department for Work and Pensions. The Pension Service is responsible for the delivery of state pensions and for providing information and advice on pensions in general[3] (see also Chapter Eleven in this volume).

Issues, gaps and problems

Thus there have been two main planks to government reform. First, a renewed emphasis on means testing within the state sector, which may alternatively be described as targeting those in greatest need, and which is evolving into the complex new Pension Credit. Critics allege that means testing will never eliminate poverty, because of incomplete take-up, and may damage incentives in other ways. Second, encouragement to greater private sector provision, through the new Stakeholder Pensions in particular. However, so far, Stakeholder Pensions have not been a visible success. There were no specific targets announced for Stakeholder Pensions, and the rate of take-up hoped for. After their first year, just over 750,000 people had bought a Stakeholder Pension; 69% of these were purchased by men (ABI, 2002).

One of the aims of policy, as set out in the 1998 Green Paper, was that the split private and public forms of pensioner support should move from a ratio of 40:60 private to public to a ratio of 60:40 private to public. That is, that 60% of pensioner incomes should come from private sources (occupational and personal pensions, in the main), rather than state support. This looks difficult to achieve because of the considerable loss of confidence in savings products in the light of stockmarket downturns, the general move away from more generous occupational pensions schemes, and the introduction of the state Pension Credit extending benefits to a wider group.

The government's overall strategy for pensions has been criticised by the Institute for Public Policy Research (IPPR, 2001, p 3): "There is, however, concern from a number of quarters – the public, the financial services industry, health and social care workers – that the government's strategy is unravelling".

---

[3] See the Customer Charter at www.thepensionservice.gov.uk/pdf/cust.pdf

IPPR (2002) suggest that a more coherent approach would involve building on the basic state pension, increasing it to the level of current means-tested benefits, and uprating it in line with earnings, while abolishing SERPS/S2P and increasing the retirement age to 67 (over time). These proposals are interesting, in that they take a holistic approach to the pensions arena, rather than debating the merits of the individual components.

A remaining issue is that of inequality. Most pensions are based on contributions made during the working lifetime. As a result, the kinds of incomes people have in retirement are roughly proportional to the kinds of *earnings* they had during their pre-retirement lifetime. Those excluded from the labour market, or on low earnings, will have low pensions. This includes, most notably, women, people from minority ethnic groups, the self-employed – although of course there is considerable diversity within each group. Any move away from universalistic state pensions towards earnings-related second-tier pensions, will increase inequalities of these kinds.

Overview

- State pensions are among the oldest features of social security systems, and often account for a high proportion of total spending. In the UK, there is also an active private sector for pensions.

- Over the next 30 years, UK governments face the prospect of rapid population ageing. Even more rapid than population change in recent times has been the fast rate of exit from the labour market, prior to state pension age. The relatively low levels of state support for pensioners (compared to other countries) mean there is still room for policy manoeuvre.

- Recent policy has focused attention (and additional spending) on the poorest pensioners, while encouraging employees on moderate earnings to save more towards their retirement.

Questions for discussion

1. Is the role of the private sector in pension provision now too great, or still too small?

2. What should the role of the state be in respect of pensions, both in making provision and in regulation? Should the state do more than alleviate poverty? Should individuals be allowed to save for retirement as much as they choose to?

3. How far will demographic changes force government to reduce pension levels in the future?

References

ABI (Association of British Insurers) (2002) *One year on – Stakeholders revealed*, London: ABI.

Bardasi, E. and Jenkins, S. (2002) *Income in later life: Work history matters*, Bristol/York: The Policy Press/Joseph Rowntree Foundation.

Barr, N. (2000) *Reforming pensions: Myths, truths and policy choices*, IMF Working Paper WP/00/139, Washington DC: IMF Fiscal Affairs Department.

Blackburn, R. (2002) *Banking on death*, London: Verso.

Campbell, N. (1999) *The decline of employment among older people in Britain*, CASE Paper 19, London: Centre for Analysis of Social Exclusion, London School of Economics and Political Science.

DSS (Department of Social Security) (1998a) *A new contract for welfare: Partnership in pensions*, London: The Stationery Office.

DSS (1998b) *Pensions sharing on divorce: Reforming pensions for a fairer future*, London: DSS Consultation Paper (part 1 consultation, part 2 draft legislation).

DWP (Department for Work and Pensions) (2001a) *The pension credit: The government's proposals*, London: DWP.

DWP (2001b) *Income related benefits estimates of take-up in 1999/2000*, London: DWP.

DWP (2002a) *Client group analysis: Quarterly bulletin on the population over state pension age November 2001*, National Statistics, London: DWP.

DWP (2002b) *The pensioners' incomes series 2000/1*, London: DWP Pensions Analysts Division.

DWP (2002c) *Simplicity, security and choice: Working and saving for retirement*, Cm 5677, London: The Stationery Office.

DWP/ASD (Analytical Services Division) (2001) *The pensioners' income series 1999/00*, London: DWP/ASD.

EOC (Equal Opportunities Commission) (1997) *Analysis of incomes received by men and women pensioners 1975 and 1994/95*, Manchester: EOC.

European Commission (2001) *Public finances in EMU 2001*, Luxembourg: Office for Official Publications of the European Commission.

FSA (Financial Services Authority) (2000) 'FSA announces progress and updated redress costs of the pensions review', Press release FSA/PN/147/2000,1 December.

GAD (Government Actuary's Department) (2000) *National population projections 1998-based*, London: The Stationery Office.

Ginn, J. and Arber, S. (2001) 'Pension prospects of minority ethnic groups: inequalities by gender and ethnicity', *British Journal of Sociology*, September, pp 519-39.

Hutton, S., Kennedy, S. and Whiteford, P. (1995) *Equalisation of state pension ages: The gender impact*, Manchester: EOC.

IPPR (Institute for Public Policy Research) (2001) *A new contract for retirement: Interim report*, London: IPPR.

IPPR (2002) *A new contract for retirement*, London: IPPR.

Joshi, H. and Davies, H. (1998) *Pension sharing on divorce: Comments on consultation document and draft bill*, Discussion Paper PI-9812, London: The Pensions Institute (Birkbeck College).

McKay, S. and Rowlingson, K. (1999) *Social security in Britain*, Basingstoke: Macmillan.

NAO (National Audit Office) (2000) *State Earnings-Related Pension scheme: The failure to inform the public of reduced pension rights for widows and widowers*, London: The Stationery Office.

O'Connell, A. (2002) *Raising state pension age: Are we ready?*, London: Pensions Policy Institute.

Parliamentary Ombudsman (2000) *State earnings-related pension scheme (SERPS) inheritance provisions*, 3rd Report for Session 1999-2000, London: The Stationery Office.

Pension Provision Group (1998) *We all need pensions – The prospects for pension provision*, London: The Stationery Office.

Shaw, C. (2001) 'United Kingdom population trends in the 21st century', *Population Trends 103*, London: The Stationery Office, pp 37-46.

Smeaton, D. and McKay, S. (2003) *Working after state pension age*, DWP Research Report No 182, Leeds: Corporate Document Services.

Vlasblom, J. and Nekkers, G. (2001) 'Regional differences in labour force activity rates of persons aged 55+ in the European Union', Eurostat Working Paper 3/2001/E/no, Luxembourg: Office for Official Publications of the European Commission.

Walker, A. (1986) 'Pensions and the production of poverty in old age', in C. Philipson and A. Walker (eds) *Ageing and social policy*, Aldershot: Gower, pp 184-216.

Walker, A. (1992) 'The poor relation: poverty among older women', in C. Glendinning and J. Millar (eds) *Women and poverty in Britain in the 1990s*, London: Harvester Wheatsheaf, pp 178-98.

Women and Equality Unit (2002) *Individual incomes of men and women 1996/97 to 2000/01*, London: Cabinet Office.

World Bank (1994) *Averting the old age crisis: Policies to protect the old and promote growth*, New York, NY: Oxford University Press.

Website resources

Cabinet Office	www.cabinet-office.gov.uk
Centre for Pensions and Social Insurance	www.bbk.ac.uk/res/cpsi
Department for Work and Pensions	www.dwp.gov.uk
DWP statistics on pensioners	www.dwp.gov.uk/asdpensioners.html
Financial Services Authority	www.fsa.gov.uk
HM Treasury	www.hm-treasury.gov.uk
Institute for Fiscal Studies (Pensions and Savings section)	www.ifs.org.uk/pensionsindex.shtml
International Labour Organization	www.ilo.org/public/english
International Monetary Fund	www.imf.org/external
Minimum Income Guarantee	www.thepensionservice.gov.uk/mig/mig.asp
Occupational Pensions Regulatory Authority	www.opra.gov.uk
Pension Service	www.thepensionservice.gov.uk
Pensions News Focus, from Watson Wyatt	www.watsonwyatt.com/europe/pubs/pensionfocus/default.asp
Pensions Policy Institute	www.pensionspolicyinstitute.org.uk
Price Waterhouse Coppers: pensions	www.pricewaterhousecoopers.co.uk/uk/eng/ins-sol/publ/pensions/pensions.html
Work and Pensions Committee (UK)	www.parliament.uk/commons/selcom/workpenhome.htm
World Bank	www.worldbank.org

Part 3: Changing delivery

eleven

Service delivery and the user

Bruce Stafford

Summary

This chapter focuses on users' experiences of social security and how it is delivered. It:

- looks at recent development in service delivery;

- identifies the main characteristics of the user base that have an affect on delivery;

- explores the non-take-up of benefits;

- considers ministerial criticisms of pre-1997 service delivery, the evidence supporting their claims and the key themes that characterise recent policy initiatives;

- examines how Housing Benefit and Council Tax Benefit is administered by local authorities;

- concludes by discussing the arguments for and against users having a greater say in decisions affecting service delivery.

Introduction: delivering social security

Delivery is at the heart of the Labour government's reform of social security, because it recognises that the effectiveness of policies is influenced by how they are implemented and delivered. Under Labour there has been a period of piloting, experimentation, and restructuring of the organisations responsible for delivering benefits and support services (see **Box 11.1**). Initiatives of particular significance are the use of personal advisers (or caseworkers) in the New Deal, the increased use of telephony, and the ONE pilot. The introduction of personal advisers has transformed the delivery of benefits and support services to users of working age. They provide a more personalised service than hitherto, while the ONE pilot brought together the Benefits Agency, Employment Service and local authorities in a 'one-stop shop' for people of working age.

At the time of writing (spring, 2002), there are six main organisational forms emerging for the delivery of social security in the UK:

- The centralised delivery of Child Benefit and tax credits and the collection of national insurance contributions by the Inland Revenue. Applications for Child Benefit and tax credits tend to be dealt with by post. For most people in work their employer deducts national insurance contributions.
- Jobcentre Plus, formed from the merger of the Benefits Agency and Employment Service, delivers at local level several out-of-work benefits (principally, Jobseeker's Allowance, Incapacity Benefit and Income Support) and employment services to people of working age. New claimants are encouraged to make their first contact by telephone. An adviser asks about their personal circumstances, assesses their job readiness, if appropriate searches for vacancies, and books an appointment with a personal adviser. Claim forms are posted to the claimant. At the Jobcentre, the interview with the personal adviser should be work-focused and a financial adviser checks the completed claim forms. Follow-up meetings with the personal adviser are also arranged (although jobseekers continue to have to sign on fortnightly).
- The Pension Service replaces the pension services delivered by the Benefits Agency. The service, which is mainly telephone-based, is delivered through a national network of 26 pension centres. Also planned are locally based services to run in partnership with local authorities and voluntary organisations.
- A Disability and Carers Service is to be established for the delivery of disability and carer benefits.
- The Child Support Agency administers child support services through six regional centres and a National Enquiry telephone line.
- Local authorities have responsibility for the administration of Housing Benefit and Council Tax Benefit.

Box 11.1: Recent key milestones for users of social security since 1990

1990 • Employment Service gains executive agency status

1991 • Benefits Agency established as an executive agency to administer over 20 benefits
  • Launch of the Citizens' Charter

1993 • Child Support Agency established

1994 • Benefits Agency introduces One Stop – a 'one-stop shop' approach to service delivery
  • War Pensions Agency established

1996 • Change Programme (replaces One Stop)
  • Green Paper *Improving decision making and appeals in social security* published (DSS, 1996)

1997 • Evidence requirement regulations – claimants have a set time period within which to complete claim forms and supply any supporting information
  • Active Modern Service launched – a customer focused and active service

1998 • Social Security Act reforms social security decision making and appeal procedures
  • Green Paper *New ambitions for our country* published (DSS, 1998a)
  • Green Paper *The gateway to work* published (DSS, 1998b)
  • Lewisham Integrated Service Prototype launched – joint working between Benefits Agency and Lewisham Borough Council
  • Lone Parent Prototype launched – joint working between the Benefits Agency, Child Support Agency and London Borough of Camden
  • Service First Unit launched (formerly Citizen's Charter Unit)

1999 • White Paper *Modernising government* published (Cabinet Office, 1999)
  • Contributions Agency transferred from Department of Social Security to Inland Revenue
  • ONE pilot launched (voluntary phase)
  • Inland Revenue administers tax credits

2000 • The Appeals Service became operational (replacing the Independent Tribunal Service)
  • Teleclaim service for Retirement Pension and Minimum Income Guarantee Claim launched

2001 • Department for Work and Pensions formed from Department of Social Security and part of Department for Education and Employment
  • War Pensions Agency transferred from Department of Social Security to Ministry of Defence
  • 56 pathfinder Jobcentre Plus offices operational
  • Care Direct pilots launched (brings together range of government services, including benefits, at local level for pensioners)

2002 • The Pension Service operational
  • Jobcentre Plus replaces Employment Service and Benefits Agency for people of working age (national roll out to be completed 2006)

2003 • Administration of Child Benefit transfers to Inland Revenue

In addition, the Appeals Service administers appeals for benefit, tax credit and child support services; and the Home Office and the Ministry of Defence have responsibility for benefits for asylum seekers and war pensions respectively. So, despite recent institutional reforms, the delivery of social security – defined in its broad terms – remains organisationally disparate in the UK.

Throughout this chapter the term 'user' is used in preference to 'customer' or 'client'. A characteristic of the labels used by the system, such as client, is that they are not empowering terms. A user, by contrast, is often taken to imply a 'citizen', someone with social rights that extend to having a say in how services are delivered. While people currently consuming social security are not 'users' in this sense, the arguments for and against user involvement in the delivery of social security are presented later in this chapter.

The next section outlines the size of the user 'base' and the key characteristics that affect the delivery of social security; the issue of the non-take-up of benefits is also briefly discussed. The 1997 Labour government's concerns about the delivery of social security, the supporting evidence and the key policy themes underpinning their policy response is then outlined. The administration of Housing Benefit and Council Tax Benefit is outlined, because, exceptionally, in Britain it is undertaken by local authorities. The final section discusses user involvement and consumerism in social security.

Users

Who are they?

Arguably, in the UK, everyone is at some point in his or her life a user of the social security system. Parents or guardians may receive Child Benefit for their children, many people of working age pay national insurance contributions and claim out-of-work and/or in-work benefits or tax credits, and older people receive benefits and/or the state pension. Two key features follow from this: first, the user base for social security is very large (see **Box 11.2**); and second, there is a great deal of variation within and between groups of users.

In addition, employers are a major 'user' group. They have a key role in the collecting of national insurance contributions, paying tax credits to low-income employees, providing second-tier pensions, supplying placements for the New Deals and other work programmes and offering job vacancies. However, the following sections concentrate on individuals, not firms, as users.

Some people's contacts with the social security system are non-problematic and routine. For others, however, dealings with the social security system occur at key transitional points in their lives, for example, when a partner has left them, or when they have lost a job. Many users come into direct contact with the system when they are at their most vulnerable, suffering a loss of self-esteem and unsure of what the future may hold. This is a situation that may be

---

Box 11.2: Size of the social security user base

The users of the social security system can included at a given point in time:

Children and families
- 2.6 million children (20%) living in 1.4 million families claiming Jobseeker's Allowance, Incapacity Benefit, Severe Disablement Allowance, Disability Living Allowance and/or Income Support (May 2001)
- 2.3 million children living in 1.2 million families with a parent in work claiming a tax credit (May 2001)
- 12.7 million children in 7.1 million families receiving Child Benefit (May 2001)
- 1 million 'live' Child Support cases with full maintenance assessments (August 2001)

Working-age population
- 5 million people of working age (14%) claiming Jobseeker's Allowance, Incapacity Benefit, Severe Disablement Allowance, Disability Living Allowance and/or Income Support (August 2001)

Population over state pension age
- 10.3 million people over state pension age and living in Britain (98%) claiming Attendance Allowance, Incapacity Benefit, Severe Disablement Allowance, Disability Living Allowance, Minimum Income Guarantee[a] and/or Retirement Pension (May 2001)

Other key benefits
- 3.9 million people receiving Housing Benefit (May 2001)
- 4.7 million people receiving Council Tax Benefit (May 2001)
- 1.2 million people awarded a Social Fund budgeting loan and 0.9 million a crisis loan (2000/01)

Contributors
- 65 million national insurance accounts

Notes: All figures relate to Britain. The tax credits are Working Families' Tax Credit and Disabled Person's Tax Credit.

[a] From 2003 the Minimum Income Guarantee became part of the Pension Credit.

Sources: DWP (2001, 2002a, 2002b, 2002c, 2002e); Inland Revenue (2002)

compounded by a reluctance to deal with the service and a concern about being stigmatised through having to use it.

Contacts with the social security system are further complicated when users have problems with literacy and numeracy. Indeed, the benefit population has a greater proportion of people with poor basic skills than the non-benefit population. Dominy and Harrop (1998) report on findings from the 1996

British Adult Literacy Survey, which shows that 31% of recipients[1] required help with reading government information, 18% help with writing notes or letters and 28% needed assistance filling out forms (compared to 23%, 8% and 16% respectively of non-benefit recipients).

Users have a range of requirements of the social security system. Bailey and Pryes (1996), based on a qualitative study of 24 Income Support claimants, proposed a threefold typology of benefit users in terms of users' levels of confidence and competence:

High confidence and competence: place few demands on the service – need little personal contact; complete forms and supply evidence required themselves; able to establish their benefit entitlement themselves.

Medium confidence and competence: moderate requirements – need personal contact with staff to reassure themselves they are doing things correctly; want someone to check forms and associated documentation before submitting it; require information and help on benefit entitlements.

Low confidence and competence: major need for personal contact with service; need advice on benefit entitlement; help with completing forms and instructions on what documentation to provide.

This typology could, arguably, be extended to other types of benefit claimant and suggests that a variety of pathways to the social security system are required to meet the varied needs of users.

Take-up of benefits and in-work support

However, some people do not take up their entitlement to benefit or in-work support. To claim benefits or in-work support (such as tax credits) it is the responsibility of the potential recipient to make the claim. Inevitably, not all eligible users claim their benefits and in-work support. Non-take-up of benefits and in-work support not only means lower incomes for recipients (Craig, 1991), but also undermines the effective implementation of policies, such as reducing child poverty.

Take-up rates vary by benefit; some like Retirement Pension and Child Benefit are near universal, and insurance-based benefits tend to have higher take-up rates than income-related benefits. Official estimates of non-take-up suggest that pensioners have lower take-up rates of income-related benefits

---

[1] Defined as people in receipt of one of the following: Unemployment Benefit, One Parent Benefit, Disability Living Allowance, Attendance Allowance, Family Credit, Invalid Care Allowance, Income Support, Social Fund, Incapacity Benefit and Severe Disablement Allowance.

than other client groups. Take-up is also often lower among people from minority ethnic groups (Amin and Oppenheim, 1992; and see Chapter Thirteen in this volume), and among those with impairments and owner-occupiers claiming Council Tax Benefit.

There is extensive literature on the take-up of benefits, which will not be reviewed here (see Craig, 1991; Oorschot, 1995; Corden, 1999), but the key factors affecting take-up include:

- *Structure of the benefit/in-work support system:* take-up will be lower when people have to make a claim, eligibility rules are complex, criteria of entitlement are vague, benefits are means tested, the benefit interacts with other support measures, and benefit is targeted at social groups having negative connotations.
- *Administrative arrangements:* take-up will be lower when: application forms are long and difficult to complete, information on benefits is not accessible and/or provided in a concise and clear format, and there are known to be errors and/or delays in processing claims.
- *Client characteristics:* take-up will be higher when potential recipients perceive a need for the benefit/in-work support, they know it exists, they believe they are eligible, they feel that the benefits exceed the costs (or inconveniences) of claiming, there is little or no stigma attached to receipt, and their current adverse financial situation is perceived as likely to continue (Kerr, 1983).
- *Dynamics of benefits:* different benefits may have dissimilar 'attainable take-up rates' that reflect the dynamics of the receipt of benefits and in-work support (Walker, 1996). A benefit targeted at a population that frequently moves in and out of eligibility is likely to have a low take-up if it is awarded for a short duration than if paid for a longer spell.

The case for modernisation

The 1997 Labour government was initially highly critical of the way in which benefits were being delivered. For instance, the then Secretary of State for Social Security, Harriet Harman, commented:

> The way that social security is delivered at the moment is resented by the public who pay for it, the clients who use it, and the staff who run it. For many people, the current system is fragmented, reactive, inflexible and confusing.... I am determined to overhaul the service that we have inherited I want to develop a modern integrated system that is simpler, streamlined and more efficient. (DSS, 1997, p 1)

Research tends to support ministers' critical comments of the then practices for delivering social security:

- There was evidence that the complexity of the benefits system could be a 'big hassle' for many claimants (Shaw et al, 1996; Stafford et al, 1996).
- People had to deal with more than one organisation and provide the same item of information more than once (Vincent et al, 1995; Kellard and Stafford, 1997; Ritchie and Chetwynd, 1997).
- Claim forms were lengthy and complicated and contained poorly worded questions (Corden and Craig, 1991; Hedges and Thomas, 1994; Cummins, 1996; Kellard and Stafford, 1997; Ritchie and Chetwynd, 1997; Stafford et al, 1997).
- Clients might lack knowledge about what information (either on the form and/or as supporting evidence) was required (Stafford et al, 1996; Vincent and Dobson, 1997). This could be compounded by some clients having a haphazard rather than systematic approach to form filling (Bailey and Pryes, 1996; Ritchie and Chetwynd, 1997), being unable to recall certain details and/or the required documents were difficult to obtain (Ritchie and Chetwynd, 1997).
- Unsurprisingly there was an 'us-and-them' culture in claimants' dealings with the Benefits Agency (Walker et al, 1994; Vincent et al, 1995).

The policy response

Labour's policy response has been to 'modernise' service delivery. The incoming administration inherited the *Change Programme* and an associated Green Paper (DSS, 1996) from the Conservative government outlining proposals to simplify decision making and appeal procedures. The Labour government implemented these in the 1998 Social Security Act. The Change Programme sought to re-engineer business processes in order to reduce complexity and the potential for errors, to increase the use of Information and Communication Technologies (ICTs) in benefit processing and to introduce the 'purchaser–provider split', allowing the private and voluntary sectors to be involved in benefit delivery. It entailed increases in productivity in the then Department of Social Security and its agencies by 25% over a three-year period, but was widely seen as an administrative cost-cutting exercise. Some commentators were highly critical of these measures (see, for example, NACAB, 1997; and Adler and Sainsbury, 1998). The reforms were seen as undermining claimants' ability to challenge decision makers' decisions on benefit entitlement, and leading to the withdrawal of benefit outreach and advice services. For users the reforms led to some improvements in the design of claim forms, but also stricter requirements on providing supporting documentation so that claims without all the relevant evidence would not be processed until it was supplied (see Hedges and Sykes, 1999), a greater emphasis on combating fraud, and the introduction of the Appeals Service to handle appeals.

In addition, Labour has made a number of delivery related initiatives (see Box 11.1) that are, to varying degrees, underpinned by five key themes/ changes: the use of 'caseworking', the single gateway, integrated service delivery, e-government, and the increased use of compulsion. We now consider each in turn.

Caseworking: use of personal advisers

The welfare reform Green Paper, *New ambitions for our country: A new contract for welfare*, proposed a *"flexible, professional, personalised service"* (DSS, 1998a, p 28; bold in original) to help people meet the obligations that accompany benefit receipt and to assist people into work. The then current personal adviser service available to lone parents under the New Deal for Lone Parents was extended to other client groups of working age. Although a caseworker approach had been piloted by the Conservative government (Vincent et al, 1998), Labour has developed and extended the concept within social security. The aim is to provide a personalised service with the potential for tailoring advice and support to users. Personal advisers meet with users to discuss work aspirations and options, to assist with job search, to explore training needs and provision, to produce indicative calculations of whether a client is better off in work or remaining on benefit, and to advise (as appropriate) on childcare provision and the availability of specialist referral services (for example, to deal with drug or alcohol abuse).

Generally, both staff and users have positive views about the personal adviser model (Legard et al, 1998; Arthur et al, 1999; Atkinson, 1999; Finch et al, 1999; Legard and Ritchie, 1999; Woodfield et al, 1999; Lewis et al, 2000; Kelleher et al, 2002; Osgood et al, 2002). The personal adviser service is seen as being more effective, friendlier, and relaxed than past provision. The personal adviser–client relationship is seen as central to the success of the government's welfare-to-work policy. Nevertheless, there is a degree of ambiguity about the scope and nature of the personal adviser's role and some users have mixed views about the service received. Personal advisers adopt a variety of roles and approaches when dealing with users, giving rise to the concern that the system might be too discretionary.

One of the main tasks of personal advisers is to identify clients' needs and any barriers to labour market participation (DSS, 1998a). However, the scope of this could range from a narrow focus on work-related issues to a more 'holistic' approach that examined the wider social and economic needs of the individual (Lewis et al, 2000). Although some users can be expected to have no desire to involve personal advisers in non-work aspects of their lives, for others a more comprehensive service might be welcome. Findings from the New Deals for Lone Parents (Finch et al, 1999; Lewis et al, 2000) and Young People (Legard and Ritchie, 1999) show that clients valued the interest some personal advisers showed in them as individuals. However, within the New Deals there is also evidence that personal advisers were generally providing a service more narrowly focused on work outcomes. Furthermore, personal advisers in the ONE pilot could only provide limited support to (non-Jobseeker's Allowance) users with complex needs (Kelleher et al, 2002). Lewis et al (2000) also show that personal advisers in the New Deal for Lone Parents did not always provide clients with adequate information, which in turn made it difficult for users to articulate their needs of the programme.

Notwithstanding this emphasis on employment in the New Deals, the evaluation of the ONE pilot shows that delivering a work-focused interview (that is, when a user met with a personal adviser to explore work aspirations, and the barriers to and opportunities for employment) can be problematic (Kelleher et al, 2002; Osgood et al, 2002). The early meetings with users tended to concentrate on their claim for benefit, and work-related issues were generally neglected. The work-focused element tended to be limited to collating basic details and undertaking a job search for clients, and there was no systematic assessment of users' employability. This was because of time pressures and, as might be expected, sorting out the claim was the primary focus of users[2]. Nevertheless, some users were disappointed because there could be no discussion of training opportunities.

Personal advisers have a caseload that they manage[3]. However, the extent to which users are caseloaded varies, and cases are not always actively prioritised. In both the New Deal for Disabled People (Arthur et al, 1999; Loumidis et al, 2001) and ONE (Kelleher et al, 2002) pilots, the most job-ready users were caseloaded. This was partly a response to a lack of resources: increasing numbers of clients and limited staff made it difficult to schedule follow-up meetings, particularly for users with complex or long-term employment issues. In addition, personal advisers could lack the skills and experience to deal with some sensitive cases and placement targets encouraged staff to focus on those most job ready. Managerially, the response can be referral of more difficult cases to internal or external specialists (such as lone-parent advisers or disability employment advisers), deselecting cases and/or teamworking. This makes service delivery more disjointed, but Osgood et al (2002) report that users in the ONE pilot were indifferent to this lack of continuity.

---

[2] See Chapter Twelve in this volume for a discussion of the way the implementation of policy is affected by the constraints on, and approach of, 'street-level' workers.

[3] The Child Support Agency also uses a caseworker model (CSA, 2002). Users are allocated to a team of caseworkers who deal with and process the case until a regular pattern of payments has been established. Within these teams the Agency tries to ensure caseworker continuity, but this is not always possible.

As caseworkers, personal advisers have an advocacy role – championing their clients' needs and abilities both within their own organisation and with others, including service providers and employers. On the other hand, personal advisers have a resource/service allocation function, effectively acting as a 'gatekeeper' and, if necessary, referring cases for decisions on benefit sanctions. The degree to which personal advisers are gatekeepers may limit the rapport they are able to develop with their clients, and there are also implications for confidentiality.

The Gateway

Gateways provide single routes of entry to the social security system that are client-focused. The gateway concept was central to the ONE pilot (DSS, 1998b), where users, such as lone parents, people with disabilities and jobseekers, received a similar service, although their claims were still subject to different benefit regulations. For the working-age population the gateway has a work focus – that is, there should be an early emphasis on (re-)entry to the labour market – and it provides a mechanism for progressing an individual through the benefit and employment maze. To achieve this, users have to be referred to specialist help and support services. However, the number of referrals by personal advisers may be relatively low because advisers may:

- be reluctant to give up exclusive 'ownership' of a client;
- not want their clients to undergo another familiarisation and orientation process with someone else;
- be unaware of the full range of services available locally;
- be unable to caseload users (see above);
- lack the assessment skills to identify the need for a referral;
- believe that a provider will impose a course of action that does not address the client's needs; and
- know that some providers have a reputation for delivering a poor quality service (Arthur et al, 1999; Tavistock Institute, 1999; Kelleher et al, 2002).

Osgood et al (2002) report that in the ONE pilot some clients considered that the pathways they were directed towards were unsuitable. Training provision could be poorly received and the job search undertaken perceived as producing low-paid, unskilled and unsustainable employment. However, other clients appreciated referrals to specialist personal advisers and to disability specialists (disability employment advisers).

Integrated service delivery

Users are often confused about which organisations administer which benefits and services (Dibden, 1994; Kellard and Stafford, 1997; Stafford et al, 1997, 1998). Various initiatives have been taken since the 1990s to improve joint working across the system, especially between the Benefits Agency, Child Support Agency, Employment Service and local authorities (see Dibden, 1994; Kellard and Stafford, 1997; Stafford et al, 1998; Rose, 1999; Thomas et al, 1999; Chang et al, 2001; Kelleher et al, 2002). In terms of joint working, distinctions can be made between:

- *closer working*, whereby staff from one organisation provide an advice and information service about the services of another agency (including referrals);
- *co-located services*, when staff from different organisations offer the services of their respective organisations from the same location; and
- *integrated services*, when staff provide services from across a range of formally different organisations.

Neither closer working nor co-location provide a comprehensive service as users continue to be passed between agencies. In addition, they do not address differences in organisational cultures nor conflicting benefit and organisational rules (Chang et al, 2001). Although integrated working provides a more 'customer-friendly' service and is a step towards caseworking, it does not mean frontline staff are 'all knowing' generalists as they have to refer people to others on occasions. The policy emphasis since 1998 has been on integrated service delivery.

Joint working is liked by users, and is often seen as a logical extension of previous multi-agency provision (Rose, 1999; Thomas et al, 1999). In particular, users only have to give information once and the claiming process can be simpler and quicker, and consequently less stressful. However, users are less satisfied if joint working leads to delays in the processing and payment of benefit (Thomas et al, 1999). There is also a risk of users being misinformed by inexperienced staff.

Various studies have demonstrated that it was easier to get joint working between the Benefits Agency, Child Support Agency and the Employment Service than between the Benefits Agency and local authorities (Stafford et al, 1998; Thomas et al, 1999; Kelleher et al, 2002). Links with local authorities seemed to be marred by poor communications and a reluctance for local managers to take ownership of initiatives. More generally joint working seems to be constrained by insufficient investment in information technology and staff training.

e-government

The White Paper *Modernising government* (Cabinet Office, 1999) aims for the joined-up delivery of public services that are responsive to customers' needs and of a high quality, and made the commitment that all dealings with government will be deliverable electronically by 2008. While there is some use of the Internet, email and kiosks by users of Department for Work and Pensions services, the Department's principal development of electronic methods has been telephony[4]. Call centres and helplines have been established for a wide range of services, notably child support and pension services. For example, the Minimum Income Guarantee Claim Line was launched in May 2000, whereby call-handlers complete electronic claim forms that are posted to pensioners for checking, completing and signing.

Conducting business with social security agencies by telephone has been associated with users having high assessments of the quality of service and high satisfaction levels compared to other modes of contact[5] (Stafford et al, 1997; Rose, 1999; Thomas et al, 1999; Bunt et al, 2001; Osgood et al, 2002). However, there are also disadvantages to telephone contacts. For example, users can have insufficient time to reflect before having to answer questions, and users whose first language is not English can experience difficulty in understanding some questions (Stafford et al, 1997; Rose, 1999; Thomas et al, 1999; Bunt et al, 2001).

Increased use of compulsion

For the working-age population there has been an increase in the use of compulsion, with new and renewal claimants required to attend a work-focused interview at the beginning of their claim for out-of-work benefits. This does not mean that non-Jobseeker's Allowance recipients have to seek work, merely that they are required to discuss work-related matters with a personal adviser. (Jobseeker's Allowance recipients continue to have to be available for work and actively seeking work.) A mandatory work-focused interview will become commonplace under Jobcentre Plus. Compulsory early interviews are seen as providing immediate help and support to those who would otherwise become dependent on benefits. However, mandatory interviews may overemphasise attitudinal and motivational barriers to work at the expense of other more 'real' obstacles (Bennett and Walker, 1998). Some users are concerned that mandatory interviews are too demanding for non-Jobseeker's Allowance

---

[4] The use of ICT in social security and the delivery of services is not considered in detail in this chapter; instead see Chapter Thirteen in this volume.

[5] Although a survey of users of the Child Support Agency conducted in 2000 showed that they had no clear preference for either telephone or written communications with the Agency (Wikeley et al, 2001).

claimants, and that personal advisers should have more discretion about the need for and timing of interviews (Osgood et al, 2002). There is also the risk of the interview being counterproductive and demotivating if the personal adviser fails to manage it sensitively and/or the claimant feels that the adviser lacked sufficient knowledge about relevant issues, such as benefits or the local labour market.

Development of a 'welfare mix' in service delivery

Benefit, in-work support and employment services are overwhelmingly delivered by the public sector. However, there has been an increase in the delivery of services by private and voluntary organisations, which are seen by government to offer innovation and efficiency in delivery. For example, four of the twelve ONE pilot sites were run by private/voluntary sector bodies and several New Deals include an element of non-public sector provision. The risk is that a welfare 'mix' will undermine attempts to provide a more integrated service. Managing a network of providers may be more problematic than coordinating governmental agencies and local authorities.

Delivery by local authorities

The administration of benefit, child support and in-work support services is (to varying degrees) centralised in the UK. Claims are processed centrally (for example, tax credits) and/or the procedures and methods to be followed are determined nationally. The administration of Housing Benefit and Council Tax Benefit is an exception. Local authorities administer Housing Benefit and Council Tax Benefit on behalf of the Department for Work and Pensions. Although legislation details national entitlement and benefit rates and there are national performance standards, local authorities have a relatively high degree of discretion in administering the benefits. They can, for instance, design their own claim forms and procure computer systems from different suppliers. As a consequence local authorities do differ in the way in which they deliver Housing Benefit and Council Tax Benefit (Stafford et al, 1999).

Critics have highlighted the wide variation in local authorities' performance in delivering Housing Benefit and Council Tax Benefit. For instance, the speed with which claims are processed varies considerably; in 1997/98 approximately 80% of authorities determined claims within a nationally set target of 14 days (Stafford et al, 2000). The Audit Commission (1999) claimed that the administration of Housing Benefit was poor in 44% of local authorities. This means that users receive a different quality of service depending upon where they live. The government appears to be trying to simplify Housing Benefit administration and to make standards of service delivery more uniform. However, it can be argued that benefit delivery by local authority offers:

- increased democracy and local accountability, although benefit administration is rarely an election issue; and
- the opportunity for local politicians and managers to adapt delivery to the local social and economic environment and to the size and composition of the caseload.

With calls for further devolution and decentralisation in the UK there may be a case for more, not less, involvement by local authorities or regional assemblies in the delivery of social security.

Consumers or users?

From one perspective recent changes in the delivery of social security can be seen as radical: new organisations, such as Jobcentre Plus and the Pension Service, have been created to deliver social security, the introduction of personal advisers, the increased use of telephony, and so on. However, from a 'user' perspective the delivery of social security remains inherently 'consumerist'; the individual is not treated as a citizen but as a customer (Ling, 1994). New public sector management has had a 'customer-focus' since the mid-1980s (Clarke and Newman, 1997), and being 'customer-friendly' underpins the policy themes outlined above. Consumerism in social security (and elsewhere in the public sector) aims to make those delivering services more responsive to the needs of their 'customers', in effect, to mimic consumer sovereignty in the competitive market. While user involvement implies some form of participation by customers in the provision and delivery of services, it is a participatory form of democracy. The objectives are to give individuals and the wider community a 'voice' and some control over the decisions being made. The arguments for and against user involvement in social security are summarised in **Box 11.3**.

Hirschman (1970) points out that individuals dissatisfied with the provision of a good or service can either remain *loyal* to the provider organisation, *voice* their dissatisfaction or exit and transfer their custom elsewhere. In social security a voluntary *exit* and private insurance is possible, but this may entail financial and other hardships, so that for most there is no real alternative except 'voice' and 'loyalty'. Consumerism as it has developed in the public sector is an attempt to redress the imbalance of power between providers and receivers of services through giving customers a voice in service provision and delivery. It has found expression in the UK through the Citizens' Charter and Charter Mark awards. Charters have been produced for the Benefits Agency, Child Support Agency, jobseekers, and the Contributions Agency. Such approaches are helpful, as they focus attention on the delivery of services. However, managers determine delivery priorities and service standards, and there is no engagement with users on defining service quality. In other areas of social

Box 11.3: Summary of arguments for and against user involvement in social security

The case for user involvement in social security

- User involvement gives customers and staff a Hirschman-type 'voice' to air their dissatisfaction with services, and so helps ensure their needs and expectations are met in ways that they consider to be appropriate and accessible (Deakin and Wright, 1990).
- User involvement allows both community and individual needs to be articulated (Sanderson, 1992; Potter, 1994). As a public good, the welfare a person derives from the consumption of social security partly depends on the knowledge that others are also benefiting from the service. These are community needs which consumerism, with its emphasis on individualised consumption, does not articulate.
- User involvement helps stakeholders better understand one another's concerns and views.
- User involvement engenders better communications between a provider organisation and its users.
- User involvement redresses the balance of power between users and providers (Barnes and Walker, 1996) and so improves the quality of decision making for both organisations and individuals.
- User involvement combats the stigma associated with receipt of welfare benefits (Spicker, 1995).
- User involvement promotes personal growth and development (Barnes and Walker, 1996). Empowerment can develop a person's confidence, and social and interpersonal skills, and lead to people having more control over their own lives.
- User involvement promotes citizenship and democracy in civil society (Plant, 1990).

Possible obstacles to user involvement in social security

- Those participating may be unrepresentative of the user base.
- Who determines the agenda? If officials do, there is the danger that items important to users will be excluded. Conversely, if customers formulate the agenda, there is the concern that they may, for instance, raise substantive policy issues which managers feel should be discussed elsewhere and are beyond the terms of reference of the group.
- Ensuring that individual cases are not discussed may be difficult to enforce.
- Possible staff opposition, because they stand to lose some of their power in decision making (Plant, 1990), may result in tokenistic participation by users.
- Social security in the UK is administered both centrally and locally and ensuring user access to, for example, meetings, for the centrally administered benefits could be problematic.
- User involvement lengthens the decision-making process.
- Possible imbalance in the communication skills and levels of confidence of officials and users.
- Sufficient resources to support user involvement may not be available.

policy, for example, social housing and personal social services, users can be more actively involved in decision making.

There are various consultative arrangements between the Department for Work and Pensions and users, for example, the Annual Benefits Forum where Department for Work and Pensions ministers and senior staff meet user representatives and hold regular liaison and consultation meetings with groups such as Age Concern and the National Association of Citizens' Advice Bureaux. While these links are to be welcomed, they constitute a limited form of user engagement. There have been some attempts to secure greater involvement by users (see, for example, Swift et al, 1994; and NCC et al, 1999). However, there are a number of 'challenges' to introducing greater user involvement in the social security system (see **Box 11.3**), and a degree of creativity and experimentation to produce workable forms of user involvement would be required.

Overview

In summary, the individual users of the social security system are a large and very diverse population. A significant proportion have problems with literacy and numeracy; consequently some are more confident and competent than others when dealing with the system, and, arguably, too many (for structural, administrative and personal reasons) fail to claim their entitlement.

It is this user base that largely explains the different models of service delivery utilised and the present government's willingness to experiment with alternative delivery methods and to restructure the agencies involved. The key themes that underpin recent policy initiatives to modernise service delivery are:

- the extensive use of caseworking through personal advisers for users of working age;

- the development of a service gateway for the working-age population, to speed up individuals' passage through the system;

- attempts to integrate service delivery;

- the development of e-government, notably of telephony;

- the introduction of the requirement that most people of working age making new or renewed claims for out-of-work benefits must attend a work-focused interview as a condition of benefit entitlement;

- the involvement of for-profit and not-for-profit organisations in service delivery.

Other than local authority involvement in initiatives to promote integrated service delivery, the administration of Housing Benefit and Council Tax Benefit has been largely unreformed, despite criticisms by some of their performance.

From one perspective the government's agenda has been radical, especially the institutional changes commencing in 2002. However, their approach to reform remains 'consumerist' and there are persuasive arguments for greater user involvement in social security policy making. There are also formidable obstacles, but other public services have successfully addressed these and found ways of ensuring that users participate in decision making on service delivery issues.

Questions for discussion

1. Is the introduction of Jobcentre Plus and the Pension Service, in the words of the Secretary of State, "... the most comprehensive shake-up of welfare delivery for a generation with a clear focus on individual needs" (DWP, 2002d, p 1)?

2. Should the delivery of social security be primarily concerned with ensuring 'the right amount of benefit, first time, every time', or are there other objectives in the delivery of welfare services?

3. What factors do policy makers need to consider when designing systems to deliver social security?

References

Adler, M. and Sainsbury, R. (eds) (1998) *Adjudication matters: Reforming decision making and appeals in social security*, Edinburgh: Department of Social Policy, University of Edinburgh.

Amin, K. and Oppenheim, C. (1992) *Poverty in black and white: Deprivation and ethnic communities*, London: CPAG.

Arthur, S., Corden, A., Green, A., Lewis, J., Loumidis, J., Sainsbury, R., Stafford, B., Thornton, P. and Walker, R. (1999) *New Deal for Disabled People: Early implementation*, DSS Research Report No 106, Leeds: Corporate Document Services.

Atkinson, J. (1999) *New Deal for Young Unemployed People: A summary of progress*, Research and Development Report ESR13, Sheffield: Employment Service.

Audit Commission (1999) *Fraud and lodging: Progress in tackling fraud and error in Housing Benefit*, London: Audit Commission.

Bailey, L. and Pryes, J. (1996) *Communications with the Benefits Agency*, DSS In-house Report 20, London: DSS.

Barnes, M. and Walker, G. (1996) 'Consumerism v. empowerment', *Policy & Politics*, vol 24, no 4, pp 375-93.

Bennett, F. and Walker, R. (1998) *Working with work: An initial assessment of welfare to work*, York: York Publishing Services for the Joseph Rowntree Foundation.

Bunt, K., Adams, L. and Jones, A.-M. (2001) *Evaluation of the Minimum Income Guarantee Claim Line*, DWP Research Report No 147, Leeds: Corporate Document Services.

Cabinet Office (1999) *Modernising government*, Cm 4310, London: The Stationery Office.

Chang, D., Spicer, N., Irving, A., Sparham, I. and Neeve, L. (2001) *Modernising service delivery: The Better Government for Older People prototypes*, DSS Research Report No 136, Leeds: Corporate Document Services.

Clarke, J. and Newman, J. (1997) *The managerial state: Power, politics and ideology in the re-making of social welfare*, London: Sage Publications.

Corden, A. (1999) 'Claiming entitlements', in J. Ditch (ed) *Introduction to social security*, London: Routledge, pp 134-55.

Corden, A. and Craig, P. (1991) *Perceptions of Family Credit*, London: HMSO.

Craig, P. (1991) 'Cash and benefits: a review of research on take-up of income-related benefits', *Journal of Social Policy*, vol 20, no 4, pp 537-66.

CSA (Child Support Agency) (2002) 'Child support reform operational vision', DWP, www.csa.gov.UK/op_vis.htm, downloaded 5 April.

Cummins, J. (1996) *Benefits Agency national customer survey 1995*, Leeds: Benefits Agency.

Deakin, N. and Wright, A. (1990) *Consuming public services*, London: Routledge.

Dibden, J. (1994) *Employment Service evaluation of the Remote Access Terminal (RAT) pilots*, Employment Service REB Report No 90, Sheffield: Employment Service.

Dominy, N. and Harrop, A. (1998) 'Literacy amongst benefit recipients in Britain', *Research Yearbook 1997/98*, Leeds: Corporate Document Services.

DSS (Department of Social Security) (1996) *Improving decision making and appeals in social security*, Cm 3328, London: The Stationery Office.

DSS (1997) 'Harriet Harman sets out plans to transform delivery of social security', DSS press release, 22 July.

DSS (1998a) *New ambitions for our country: A new contract for welfare*, Cm 3805, London: The Stationery Office.

DSS (1998b) *A new contract for welfare: The gateway to work*, Cm 4102, London: The Stationery Office.

DWP (Department for Work and Pensions) (2001) *Work and pension statistics 2001*, National Statistics, London: DWP.

DWP (2002a) *Client group analysis: Quarterly bulletin on families with children on key benefits May 2001*, National Statistics, London: DWP.

DWP (2002b) *Client group analysis: Quarterly bulletin on the population of working age on key benefits August 2001*, National Statistics, London: DWP.

DWP (2002c) *Client group analysis: Quarterly bulletin on the population over state pension age claiming key benefits May 2001*, National Statistics, London: DWP.

DWP (2002d) 'Darling announces radical new jobs target', Press release EMP 1903-Radical, 19 March, London: DWP press office.

DWP (2002e) 'Statistical summary – December 2001, Client group analysis', Press release, National Statistics, 10 January.

Finch, H., O'Connor, W. with Millar, J., Hales, J., Shaw, A. and Roth, W. (1999) *The New Deal for Lone Parents: Learning from the prototype areas*, DSS Research Report No 92, Leeds: Corporate Document Services.

Hedges, A. and Sykes, W. (1999) *Behavioural response to evidence requirements*, DSS In-house Report No 54, London: DSS.

Hedges, A. and Thomas, A. (1994) *Making a claim for disability benefits*, London: HMSO.

Hirschman, A. (1970) *Exit, voice and loyalty: Responses to decline in firms, organisations and states*, London: Harvard University Press.

Inland Revenue (2002) 'National Insurance Contributions Office – About us', www.inlandrevenue.gov.uk/nic/nicwho.htm, download date 25 March.

Kellard, K. and Stafford, B. (1997) *Delivering benefits to unemployed people*, DSS Research Report No 69, London: The Stationery Office.

Kelleher, J., Youll, P., Nelson, A., Hadjivassiliou, K., Lyons, C. and Hills, J. (2002) *Delivering a work-focused service: Final findings from ONE case studies and staff research*, DWP Research Report No 166, Leeds: Corporate Document Services.

Kerr, S. (1983) *Making ends meet: An investigation into the non-claiming of Supplementary Pensions*, London: Bedford Square Press.

Legard, R. and Ritchie, J. (1999) *New Deal for Young Unemployed People: National gateway*, Research and Development Report ESR16, Sheffield: Employment Service.

Legard, R., Ritchie, J., Keegan, J. and Turner, R. (1998) *New Deal for Young Unemployed People: The gateway*, Research and Development Report ESR8, Sheffield: Employment Service.

Lewis, J., Mitchell, L., Sanderson, T., O'Connor, W. and Clayden, M. (2000) *Lone parents and personal advisers: Roles and relationships*, DSS Research Report No 122, Leeds: Corporate Document Services.

Ling, T. (1994) 'Case study: the Benefits Agency – claimants as customers', in H. Tam (ed) *Marketing, competition and the public sector: Key trends and issues*, Harlow: Longman, pp 38-60.

Loumidis, J., Stafford, B., Youngs, R., Green, A., Arthur, S., Legard, R., Lessof, C., Lewis, J., Walker, R., Corden, A., Thornton, P. and Sainsbury, R. (2001) *Evaluation of New Deal for Disabled People personal adviser service pilot*, DSS Research Report No 144, Leeds: Corporate Document Services.

NACAB (National Association of Citizens' Advice Bureaux) (1997) *Short changed: A briefing on cuts in social security running costs*, London: NACAB.

NCC (National Consumer Council), Consumer Congress and Cabinet Office (1999) *Involving users: Improving the delivery of benefits*, London: Cabinet Office.

Oorschot, W. van (1995) *Realizing rights*, Aldershot: Avebury.

Osgood, J., Stone, V. and Thomas, A. (2002) *Delivering a work-focused service: Views and experience of clients*, DWP Research Report No 167, Leeds: Corporate Document Services.

Plant, R. (1990) 'Citizenship and rights', in R. Plant and N. Barry (eds) *Citizenship and rights in Thatcher's Britain: Two views*, London: Institute of Economic Affairs.

Potter, J. (1994) 'Consumerism and the public sector, "How well does the coat fit?"', in D. McKevitt and A. Lawson (eds) *Public sector management: Theory, critique, and practice*, London: Sage Publications, pp 250-64.

Ritchie, J. and Chetwynd, M. (1997) *Claimants' perceptions of the claim process*, London: The Stationery Office.

Rose, T. (1999) *Modernising service delivery: The integrated services prototype*, DSS Research Report No 104, Leeds: Corporate Document Services.

Sanderson, I. (1992) *Management of quality in local government*, Harlow: Longman.

Shaw, A., Walker, R., Ashworth, K., Jenkins, S. and Middleton, S. (1996) *Moving off Income Support*, DSS Research Report No 53, London: The Stationery Office.

Spicker, P. (1995) *Social policy: Themes and approaches*, London: Prentice Hall.

Stafford, B., Kellard, K. and Horsley, E. (1997) *Customer contact with the Benefits Agency*, DSS Research Report No 65, London: The Stationery Office.

Stafford, B., Adelman, L., Trickey, H. and Ashworth, K. (2000) *Housing Benefit administration and the speed of claims processing*, DSS In-house Report No 69, London: DSS.

Stafford, B., Heaver, C., Croden, N., Smith, A., Maguire, S. and Vincent, J. (1998) *Moving into work: Bridging housing costs*, DSS Research Report No 79, London: The Stationery Office.

Stafford, B., Walker, R., Hull, L. and Horsley, E. (1996) *Customer contact and communication with the Benefits Agency: Literature review*, DSS In-house Report No 17, London: DSS.

Stafford, B., Vincent, J., Walker, R. and Beach, J. (1999) *The Beacon Council scheme: Modern service delivery – Improving Housing Benefit and Council Tax Benefit administration – Output 2*, DETR, DSS, IDA websites, CRSP Working Paper 373, Loughborough: Centre for Research in Social Policy, Loughborough University.

Swift, P., Grant, G. and McGrath, M. (1994) *Participation in the social security system*, Aldershot: Avebury.

Tavistock Institute (1999) *New Deal for Young Unemployed People: Case studies of delivery and impact in pathfinder areas*, Research and Development Report ESR7, Sheffield: Employment Service.

Thomas, A., Stone, V. and Cotton, D. (1999) *Modernising service delivery: The lone parent prototype*, DSS Research Report No 90, Leeds: Corporate Document Services.

Vincent, J. and Dobson, B. (1997) *Jobseeker's Allowance evaluation: Qualitative research on disallowed and disqualified claimants*, Research Report No 15, London: DfEE.

Vincent, J., Leeming, A., Peaker, A. and Walker, R. (1995) *Choosing advice on benefits*, London: HMSO.

Vincent, J., Walker, R., Dobson, B., Stafford, B., Barnes, M. and Bottomley, D. (1998) *Lone parent caseworker pilots evaluation final report*, Working Paper 263, Loughborough: Centre for Research in Social Policy, Loughborough University.

Walker, R. (1996) 'Benefit dynamics, targeting and take-up', in W. van Oorschot (ed) *New perspectives on the non-take-up of social security benefits*, Netherlands: Tilbury University Press, pp 98-127.

Walker, R., Shaw, A. and Kellard, K. (1994) 'Trapped on benefit? Barriers to movement off IS', Unpublished CRSP Working Paper 229, Loughborough: Centre for Research in Social Policy, Loughborough University.

Wikeley, N., Barnett, S., Brown, J., Davis, B., Diamond, I., Draper, T. and Smith, P. (2001) *National survey of Child Support Agency clients*, DWP Research Report No 152, Leeds: Corporate Document Services.

Woodfield, K., Turner, R. and Ritchie, J. (1999) *New Deal for Young People: The pathfinder options*, ES Research and Development Report ES25, Sheffield: Employment Service.

Website resources

Cabinet Office	www.cabinet-office.gov.uk
Child Support Agency	www.csa.gov.uk
Department for Work and Pensions	www.dwp.gov.uk
Jobcentre Plus	www.jobcentreplus.gov.uk
Pension Service	www.thepensionservice.gov.uk
Service First	www.servicefirst.gov.uk

twelve

The street-level implementation of unemployment policy

Sharon Wright

Summary

Policy does not fully exist until it is brought into being by social actors through interaction. Lipsky's theory of street-level bureaucracy has been particularly influential in setting out a framework for understanding the role that those responsible for policy implementation play in interpreting and, to some extent, recreating policy. This chapter:

- explores the delivery of policy to unemployed people;

- discusses policy implementation as a social process;

- explains Lipsky's theory of street-level bureaucracy in more detail;

- highlights variations in the way in which clients are processed and treated.

Introduction: street-level bureaucracy

In the UK a network of local Jobcentre offices exists to administer benefits to unemployed people and to provide access to job vacancies. The workers in these offices conduct face-to-face interviews with individuals in order to process their benefit claims, to assist them in finding work and to ensure that they are fulfilling the work requirements placed upon them. This means that the Jobcentre staff are required to police clients as well as to help them (Fletcher, 1997), and there is a potential tension in the dual role that the staff must manage on a day-to-day level in their interactions with individual clients (see also Finn et al, 1998; Finn and Taylor, 1990; Blackmore, 2001). The limited resources available to them, particularly of time, may further exacerbate this tension. This chapter explores some of the ways in which Jobcentre staff deal with this in practice, and considers in particular how their role as 'street-level bureaucrats' can lead to policy in practice being rather different from policy as intended.

The chapter starts by discussing the concept of *street-level bureaucracy* and then describes how Jobcentre staff categorise unemployed clients. These categorisations – administrative and moral – are important because they explain variation in the application of policy to different clients, resulting in different opportunities and different outcomes for individuals. The analysis is based on an ethnographic study of a Jobcentre office, carried out over six months in 1998[1]. The study thus predated the merger of the Employment Service and the Benefits Agency into Jobcentre Plus.

Street-level implementation and the accomplishment of policy

Traditional understandings of policy implementation have been based on an ideal type, with perfect implementation as the goal, presenting implementation as a problem (Hogwood and Gunn, 1984) rather than an area of study or a source of understanding (Hill, 1997). Within this conceptualisation, implementation is seen as occurring in a distinct place and time outside of the inner decision-making sanctum that is inhabited by elite politicians and civil servants of the central state. Policy implementation is presented as happening after policies have been 'made' (Easton, 1965) and consists of processes that involve 'low-level' local officials who put the written words into action.

---

[1] The fieldwork consisted of direct observation during 74 visits to one office, including interviews between staff and clients, informal interviews with 48 members of staff and semi-structured interviews with 35 unemployed people. Information was also collected about the vacancies advertised in the office and documentary analysis was conducted on staff guidance materials. All of the interviewees were white, in a region where people from minority ethnic groups comprised less than 0.03% of the population in the 1991 population Census.

However, a body of literature has emerged to challenge this account of the policy process (Pressman and Wildavsky, 1973; Elmore, 1978; Bowe et al, 1992) arguing instead that it is necessary to understand implementation as a form of policy making. Barrett and Fudge (1981) argue:

> Rather than treating implementation as the transmission of policy into a series of consequential actions, the policy–action relationship needs to be regarded as a process of interaction and negotiation, taking place over time, between those seeking to put policy into effect and those upon whom action depends. (1981, p 25)

Lipsky's (1980) theory of street-level bureaucracy (see also Weatherley and Lipsky, 1977; Prottas, 1979; Weatherley, 1979) has been particularly influential in setting out a framework for understanding the role that those responsible for policy implementation play in interpreting and, to some extent, recreating policy. Lipsky defines street-level bureaucrats as "public service workers who interact directly with citizens in the course of their jobs, and who have substantial discretion in the execution of their work" (1980, p 3). This includes a wide range of public sector workers such as doctors, police officers, social workers and benefit officials. Lipsky sees these actors as policy makers within an environment that they do not control. The legal framework, policy context and organisational apparatus structure the work of street-level bureaucrats and limit the scope of their actions. However, despite these constraints and also because of them, street-level bureaucrats make policy in two senses: in their discretionary decision making and through the collective effects of their individual actions.

According to Lipsky these officials experience dilemmas that are centred around conflicts in their goals. The core tension is between serving client-centred goals and organisation-centred goals. Street-level bureaucrats are required to provide a flexible, responsive and caring service to meet individual needs, but at the same time they are bound by the impersonal and detached rules of the organisational bureaucracy within which they work. The site of this dilemma is in their interaction with, and decisions about, clients. They are also constrained by the lack of resources for the extremely high demand for the services they provide. Street-level bureaucrats therefore organise their work in response to these pressures in three ways: by limiting demand for services; by maximising the use of available resources; and by ensuring client compliance. They develop their own "routines and simplifications" (1980, p 83) as practical solutions to make their jobs manageable. In essence, "the decisions of street-level bureaucrats, the routines they establish and the devices they invent to cope with uncertainties and work pressures, effectively become the public policies they carry out" (1980, p xii).

Applying this neglected approach (Hudson, 1993) to the work of Jobcentre staff, it has been argued that frontline practices do have the effect of recreating policy on the ground (Blackmore, 2001; Wright, 2001). Here, the focus is on the way in which Jobcentre frontline staff cope with the demands of their work by the 'categorisation' of clients into various 'types'. Lipsky argues that the use of stereotypes is one of the main 'psychological coping mechanisms' used by street-level bureaucrats. These client types provide staff with a way of distinguishing between the many different clients that they see every day, and a way of controlling their demands. Previous literature has highlighted a binary division between 'deserving' and 'undeserving' clients and this discourse has dominated British accounts of client categorisation (Cooper, 1985; Howe, 1990; Dean, 1991; Handler and Hasenfeld, 1991). The social problems literature provides an alternative typification of clients, dividing service users into 'regular clients' and 'difficult clients' (Anderson, 1999, p 229; also see Miller, 1991; Miller and Holstein, 1995). Two types of client categorisation could be distinguished from the way that Jobcentre staff talked about clients. The first, *administrative categorisation*, was a necessary part of how the Jobcentre operated, which governed entitlement to benefits and influenced how clients would be processed. The second type, *moral categorisation*, was based on staff beliefs and moral judgements about clients (see Giller and Morris, 1981). Both forms of categorisation affected the way in which clients were treated and the type of outcomes that were possible for them. However, clients are not simply passive recipients of this process, but are sometimes able to negotiate actively to influence the policy they receive.

Administrative categorisation: the process of constructing clients

Box 12.1 sets out the eligibility conditions for claiming Jobseeker's Allowance, and the procedures involved in making a claim (see Barnes et al, 1998; Bivand, 1999, for regulations at the time when the research was conducted).

The first step in making a claim involves attending the Jobcentre, and the way in which clients are categorised at initial and later interviews determines how they are subsequently processed. There are clear rules for this administrative categorisation but in practice the interactions between staff and clients are important in determining how clients are classified and consequently what else is required of them, or offered to them.

Becoming a client

The initial interview was very important in determining the category in which clients were placed. It was the receptionists who acted as the first gatekeepers, being in a position to either grant or deny access to the services on offer (Rees, 1978, p 10; see also Hall, 1974). It was possible for the receptionist to give an indication of whether someone was likely to receive Jobseeker's

Box 12.1: 'Active' social security for registered unemployed people

1996 Jobseeker's Allowance
Has two forms:
- Contributions-based Jobseeker's Allowance (insurance-based, available for a maximum of six months, conditional on being able to work, available and actively seeking work)
- Income-based Jobseeker's Allowance (means-tested, available for an unlimited period but now conditional on participation in compulsory welfare-to-work programmes).

Features:
- tighter actively seeking work conditions, including the introduction of a Jobseeker's Agreement contract stating specific job-seeking activities and the requirement to log job search activities;
- harsher sanctions;
- greater discretionary powers for employment officers (for example, to issue Jobseeker Directions (for example, dictating that a client should change their appearance).

The process of making a claim involves a series of interviews with intake staff at reception and an adviser at Fresh Claims stage. Clients must 'sign-on' fortnightly to re-register their claim. Compulsory review interviews are triggered at different stages (for example, 13 weeks) and clients might be referred to a range of courses (for example, the Programme Centre for job search advice).

1998 New Deal for Young People

A compulsory welfare-to-work programme for 18- to 24-year-olds who have been unemployed for six months or more (see Employment Service, 1997). After a 'gateway' period of intensive interviews, clients must accept one of four options:

- job (possibly subsidised)
- training
- voluntary sector placement
- Environmental Task Force.

This was followed by several other New Deal programmes, each with different arrangements, options and levels of compulsion, for long-term unemployed people (aged 25 and over), lone parents, disabled people, people aged over 50 and partners of unemployed people (see Millar, 2000 for details).

Box 12.1 continued

Features:

- even tighter actively seeking work conditions, particularly for young people and long-term unemployed people, with the introduction of Action Plans for finding work and more frequent interviews with employment officers;
- even harsher sanctions;
- greater emphasis on in-depth one-to-one interviews with personal advisers who have increased discretion.

2001 Jobcentre Plus

Following the creation of the Department for Work and Pensions, the Benefits Agency and Employment Service merged to form Jobcentre Plus. New offices (currently only in Pathfinder areas but soon to be introduced nationwide) are to provide an integrated service, based on work-focused interviews to clients receiving or applying for a wide range of benefits (including those with full-time caring responsibilities and people who are sick or disabled).

Features:

- wider client group required to consider actively seeking work;
- new sanctions for failure to attend a work-focused interview;
- even greater emphasis on the personal adviser model.

Allowance, which might cause a potential client not to pursue a claim because they may have thought that they might not be eligible. Receptionists therefore held the key to the first administrative category – that of becoming a Jobseeker's Allowance client (see Kingfisher, 1998, for further insight into how people are reconstituted as clients). This task was entrusted to workers who were of the lowest administrative grade, often on short-term contracts (only one of the receptionists had been employed for more than a few months), who had not received in-depth training and therefore did not have the detailed knowledge of the complex benefits system that would enable them to make an accurate decision about whether someone would or would not be eligible for payment. The receptionists were aware of the importance of their role as gatekeepers:

> "First of all we assess the person and decide if they should sign on. We decide which type of benefit they would qualify for. We issue them with forms. We basically assess everyone. We decide what's happening for each client." (receptionist)

What the receptionists did in this initial part of the claiming process was not confined to collecting information. Workers could 'coach' clients on how to fill in the claims forms. In this way the receptionists influenced how clients were categorised and therefore the way that they would be treated later on in the process. Receptionists were also required to check the information provided by clients. This involved querying the type of work sought and hours of availability, during which clients could be persuaded to amend their forms to what the receptionist regarded as 'reasonable' hours of availability, usually persuading clients to comply with maximum availability for work. Miller (1991) and Anderson (1999) describe such persuasion strategies as 'witcraft', emphasising the ways in which state employment agencies led clients to fulfil particular goals. Jobcentre advisers also used 'witcraft' to persuade clients to take certain courses of action during other types of interviews, for instance to convince clients to participate in training courses.

Occupational classification

Following reception, the next stage of the process was a 'Fresh Claim' interview, in which the advisers converted the information provided by the client on the application form (and vetted by the receptionists) into a series of entries in the Labour Market System (LMS) computer system. An important part of this was to enter Standard Occupational Classification (SOC) codes for each client. Staff used a smaller sub-section of SOC codes in their everyday use than the full range available to them, which is an example of one of the simplifications adopted to make the job manageable (Lipsky, 1980, p 83). The interviews provided only a limited opportunity for clients to negotiate their administrative categorisation.

These codes were used to establish the level of work requirements that would be imposed, with clients required to make different types of effort to find work according to how they had been classified. The codes were also used to search the computer system for job vacancies that would suit the client. Thus the categorisations could mean the difference between a client having an opportunity to apply for a job and not having that opportunity. Despite job matching being an officially dictated part of every signing-on interview, staff were more likely to carry out job searches for some clients than others, according to the type of work they were looking for. If frontline staff considered there to be very few vacancies in certain occupations (for example, teaching) they developed a habit of not conducting vacancy searches for clients seeking those types of work unless specifically requested by the client. Similarly, occupational categories such as SOC code 990, 'Other elementary occupations', for which there was a large proportion of vacancies, also signalled non-action for staff. This time staff were unlikely to check for vacancies because there were almost twice as many unemployed people seeking this type of work than there were notified vacancies (statistics from the Office for National Statistics, 2000).

Frontline staff also played an important role in controlling access to the vacancies advertised in the Jobcentre. Staff rationed vacancies by being selective about which clients they would allow to apply for vacancies and again this varied according to administrative categorisation. But there were also examples of access being denied to certain vacancies on the grounds of age and sex, and previous experience of a particular type of work was often viewed by staff as a prerequisite for applying for positions, whether the employer had specified this or not:

> "This is the people we're getting in this afternoon [pointed at files]. The first one there is a labourer so there was nothing for him. The second one's a waiter, but he hasn't done any waiting so there's no point putting him forward for anything because an employer wouldn't want him." (employment officer)

Although vacancies were usually advertised on the self-service boards in the office, a client might assume that if the worker did not mention a suitable vacancy then nothing was available. So although there was another way of finding out about vacancies, staff did limit access to information based on an assumption about what employers would want in relation to an administrative category. They did not view this as discrimination against long-term unemployed people, but as a rational decision that an employer would have made anyway. A similar tendency was identified by Anderson (1999), who demonstrated the ways in which US employment agency staff used a variety of strategies to influence clients' decisions about whether to apply for jobs or not, persuading some to apply for jobs they did not want and deflecting others from opportunities that they were keen to pursue.

Moral categorisations: constructing 'good' and 'bad' clients

Moral categorisations differed from administrative categorisations in that they were less precise and were characterised by some degree of ambiguity. These constructions of clients were made subjectively, based on judgements about clients' attributes, behaviour or attitudes. The initial moral distinction made by staff was between 'good' and 'bad' clients, which was similar to the constructions of clients found by Kingfisher (1996), and the importance of 'moral character' identified by Giller and Morris (1981) and Hasenfeld (1987). The type of treatment that clients received depended upon the moral judgements made by frontline staff.

'Good' clients

Many of the people who used the services of the Jobcentre were thought to be 'good' clients, the great majority having been deemed indifferently as 'all right'. Staff demonstrated a preference for compliant clients and praised those who made their jobs easier because processing became a quick and uneventful matter of routine. Being "keen", "smart and presentable", well-humoured, vulnerable and even "nice looking" counted in a client's favour. Clients who were deemed to be worthy or deserving of the service offered by staff were thought of as 'good' clients and "decent people". Employment officers identified genuine cases as those who were willing to work. The "really nice ones" might secure a better standard of service in terms of more staff time and effort. Staff were more sympathetic towards certain types of clients and they would make concessions or bend the rules for them. For instance, older clients were often seen as more deserving, particularly since they had "paid in all of their life", pointing to the prevailing recognition of earned entitlement to benefit:

> "You know the genuine ones. There are some men in their late forties or early fifties who've been employed for years. Then they get made redundant. That's very difficult. You really feel for them. They're just not going to get work again." (personal adviser)

The most likely reason for clients to be constructed as deserving was if they showed a willingness to work. 'Good' clients were thought to be unemployed through no fault of their own, their lack of employment being explained in terms of external circumstances rather then individual failings. Commitment to the work ethic was demonstrated by those who worked hard at finding work. In fact, being "keen" to find work was the one characteristic that could override other negative attributes. In the following quote the adviser praised her long-term unemployed client for his willingness to work:

> "One thing that I'm sure of is that he does want to work. He's got a criminal record and he's a bit simple so it makes it hard." (personal adviser)

'Bad' clients

There was greater variation in the range of 'bad' client types constructed by staff, although they were usually non-compliant in some sense. 'Bad' clients were often thought to be undeserving of the service provided by staff. Moral constructions of clients could be fluid and overlapping, with individuals often fitted into more than one category. This section outlines some examples of client types that were constructed in negative terms.

"Wasters"

Constructing 'bad' clients was similar to constructing 'good' clients in that willingness to work was one of the key defining moral criteria. There was criticism of clients who were thought to be unwilling to work or not actively seeking work. These clients were sometimes referred to as "wasters". Being a "waster" was related to various individual failings of behaviour and attitude. For instance, one New Deal personal adviser referred to one of his clients as a "lazy big shite" and another senior employment officer remarked that "if they're any good they should have a job". "Wasters" were those who appeared to want something for nothing:

> "I think there is 1% that you get in all walks of life that are not wanting to work and are just wanting to sponge the system." (employment officer)

One personal adviser described how she reacted to clients who were not well motivated and expressed a preference to work with keener clients who she admitted she would help more:

> "You're supposed to spend more time on them than I do. That's terrible isn't it? If they sit down and they're like [made fed-up face and shrugged], I'm like 'why should I bother then?' It's a terrible attitude. One guy wanted to do construction. I arranged a job for him and he got work boots and everything. It was meant to start on Monday. Did he turn up? No he did not. I was fizzing. Fizzing. I said 'You've not seen my anger yet, but you will'. He's not been in yet. He was meant to come in but he didn't show. He's got another appointment for next week. He's probably too scared. It was only for six to eight weeks right enough, but it's a foot in the door. That was £25 for nothing. If they're keen I help them more." (personal adviser)

The level of motivation displayed by a client was therefore a key factor in determining the level of help they would receive from staff. Those who were disadvantaged most were likely to have least motivation and were therefore likely to receive less help from staff. This means that staff behaviour could compound the difficulties already faced by some clients (Handler, 1992).

Although failing to actively seek work was a breach of the conditions for claiming benefit, clients were often able to avoid penalties for various reasons.

Staff were reluctant to take action to stop a client's benefit because it required a lot of effort on their part to complete the paperwork. Thus clients who were labelled as "wasters" were nevertheless able to continue claiming Jobseeker's Allowance because they paid lip service to the labour market conditions they were required to meet:

> "I hate it when you get the guys that come in and they're stinking of cigarette smoke and it's obvious that they've just come down from the pub. They think that you're not going to realise that they're going straight back up there again as soon as they've signed on. 'Are you looking for work?' 'Aye' [indignant tone]." (employment officer)

Young men were often felt to be "wasters" since "a lot of them can't be bothered working" or they "don't know how to work". Staff expected these clients to be less compliant, and particularly unlikely to attend appointments, especially early morning appointments.

The unemployables: "They're useless some of them"

"Wasters" were a closely related category to "unemployables". "Wasters" would not work, whereas "unemployables" could not work. Staff made critical assessments of clients' employability according to a range of criteria including appearance (for example, "she's a bit fat and she's got a ring in her nose"), mental and physical health, personal hygiene and habits such as time-keeping, alongside evaluations about work experience, qualifications and relevant skills for the job. Unemployable clients were almost always categorised as long-term unemployed for administrative purposes. The category of long-term unemployed could also be understood in moral terms:

> "With the long-term some of them are unemployable, not that the Department will admit to it, but they are. If we sent all the riff-raff we would lose the employers. They're useless some of them. Because of their lack of qualifications, or lack of skills, their background, their age even, they're unemployable." (employment officer)

Staff therefore accepted that there were clients who would never work again. Long-term unemployment was more readily linked with blame than sympathy as an emotional response. Long-term unemployed people were also seen to have "got into a bad habit". From the staff perspective there were only a limited number of logical explanations for long-term unemployment (barring fraud):

> "They're either not looking for work or they can't work." (fresh claims officer)

Despite most "unemployable" clients being pressured to find work, a small minority of clients had their unemployable status legitimated by staff who took no further action when they were officially meant to do so. Part of the reason for allowing this to pass was that workers knew there was no other benefit option for clients in this position:

> "I've got one long-term I passed over because I saw him twice and realised I was wasting my time. He was a 58-year-old alcoholic. I wasn't going to get anywhere with him." (personal adviser)

Some of the long-term unemployed clients had been unemployed for a number of years and these clients were often referred to as the "hard core", who were "not a choice group". In some cases there were extra years which had not been officially calculated as unemployment if, for instance, they were claiming Incapacity Benefit, had been in prison, or had been full-time carers. These clients were difficult to process because staff had "no idea what to say to them" and it was thought to be impossible to 'market' this type of client to an employer. Some officials felt that clients had needs that were beyond the scope of the help available:

> "You don't know what you're going to be dealing with when they sit down. I had one the other day that was a murderer. He said to me 'No one will ever employ me'. I said 'I'm sure we'll be able to get you something'. He said 'I've served a life sentence for murdering the wife'. Just like that, matter of fact." (personal adviser)

This meant that even measures that had been specifically designed to target long-term unemployed clients could be viewed by advisers as "just going through the motions". Staff viewed their work with these clients as futile, their time being better spent on those with a keener attitude or a greater probability of finding work. This meant that even the most active labour market policy could become an empty bureaucratic process if it was divorced from the realities of clients' circumstances or the structure and workings of the local labour market.

"Nutters" and "numpties": the benefits and costs of non-compliance

Staff were agreed that "the odd one or two" of their clients were "nutters" and "numpties". At the extreme end of this category were alcoholics, drug addicts and those known or thought to be violent. "Nutters" were also likely to be long-term unemployed. These were the clients who were "really abusive" or "always in causing hassle". "Numpties" were a milder version of "nutters", constituting a nuisance to staff rather than a distinct danger. These labels were applied to clients who challenged the workings of the Jobcentre bureaucracy or displayed discontent, anger or a reluctance to comply. "Nutters" and "numpties" were often, but not always, male. Behind the scenes, they were in turn likely to be referred to derogatorily by staff using such terms as "wee bastard", "pain in the arse", "cunt" or "arsehole". The dynamics of the staff–client relationship were therefore very different for these clients than for the compliant, keen, "nice ones" (see also Hasenfeld and Weaver, 1996).

"Nutters" and "numpties" varied in their attitudes towards paid employment. It was not necessarily the case that they did not want to work, but they were unlikely to be considered as employable. In fact, one reason for this classification could be because the client was making excessive demands for staff assistance in finding work. Being keen to work therefore appeared to have an optimum level.

"Nutters" could represent a danger to staff, particularly because the Jobcentre office was open plan and unscreened, which while conducive to a more friendly environment, also meant that staff had to take greater risks with clients who could be violent. A small number of clients had their files marked 'PV' for 'potentially violent' as a warning that they could be dangerous. However, some employment officers felt that this labelling might have a detrimental effect on staff–client relations. A criminal record made it more difficult for clients to get a job.

It was possible for "nutters" and "numpties" to exercise some control over their interaction with staff by being intimidating. This could help them to get what they wanted, which might be a quick and painless processing of their claim, or alternatively to command a greater amount of time and effort from staff. When clients asserted themselves in this way it was possible for parts of policy to be negotiated. In the following example the young administrative grade worker described how he adapted his practice as a response to the demands of a "nutter":

> "He's mental like. He comes in here and he's sitting tapping his fingers while you're getting the vacancy up on the screen for him. Sometimes you're not supposed to give out the employer's details and that, their address and telephone number. But he's like 'And just give me their number as well.' And you're like 'Okay there you are'. He can be really scary!" (employment officer)

To say that policy is accomplished, and even jointly negotiated in some instances, is therefore not to imply that staff and clients are engaged in a harmonious joint venture; indeed conflict was frequently a feature of interactions between staff and clients. There were instances of trouble when clients were not compliant with the rules of the bureaucracy (cf Lipsky, 1980). This is an example of the ways in which social policy is contested. Trouble was usually caused by those labelled as "nutters" or "numpties", which was part of the reason for that label being applied to them. Trouble was also caused by clients who had not demonstrated any other problematic behaviour but who had become agitated or irate because of the particular circumstances in which they found themselves. One of the primary reasons for conflict was if a client had been denied access to the benefit that they needed.

The "hoity-toity" "snooty" ones

Some of the clients that staff found difficult to deal with were those who were better qualified, middle-class or professional. Employment officers often got the impression that the "snooty ones" felt that visiting the Jobcentre and being processed as a client was "a bit beneath them". The "professional people" were contrasted with "normal folk". These "hoity-toity people" could make staff feel intimidated or "a bit out of your depth" because they had attributes that shifted the balance of power in the staff–client relationship. One adviser said they made her feel like "a silly little girl". It was these "posh" or "well-to-do" clients who were most likely to be described as arrogant or snobby. One particular client who fell into this category was referred to as "an arrogant shite".

One implication of these feelings that staff had about more qualified clients was that "hoity-toity ones" could evade close scrutiny of their job search, especially since the Jobcentre was unlikely to advertise vacancies for professional positions. The following quote was taken from an informal interview with a fresh claims adviser directly after his interview with a professional client. During the interview the adviser had been less probing with a company secretary than he would have been with someone of a more usual occupation because he was afraid that his lack of specialist knowledge would be revealed:

> "Sometimes you get different ones, like that guy [previous client] who was a company secretary. Once I had a minister in and I didn't know what to say to him. We're not like the careers service. We don't know about jobs and we don't know about pay either. One time I had a GP in who put her minimum expected salary down as £60,000. And I mean I don't know if that's reasonable or not. Because I don't know what GPs get paid. And so when that guy was in, the company secretary, I wanted to ask him what a secretary did. I didn't want to ask him cause I didn't want to feel daft." (fresh claims adviser)

There was, therefore, a shift in the balance of power in the staff–client relationship. Unlike "nutters" or "numpties", these clients could be intimidating even without being consciously aware of it, by virtue of their apparent more privileged socioeconomic position.

The *"at it"* label

Some clients were labelled as being "at it", meaning that they were involved in some aspect of benefit fraud (although the actual term "fraudster" was very rarely used by staff). "Wasters" were usually thought of as lazy or passive, whereas those who were "at it" were actively abusing the system. Being "at it" was a source of criticism but did not necessarily cause staff to take the officially warranted action for reasons outlined earlier in this chapter. Making a moral judgement was therefore not necessarily linked to taking action on that categorisation. Certain client types, such as those who lived in rural areas and signed on by post, were thought to be more likely to be "at it". Those signing on by post were suspected of fraud because their infrequent visits to the office meant they could not be the subject of close surveillance. In this case an administrative category coincided with a moral one.

Client rule-breaking was usually a source of irritation or inconvenience. But in certain circumstances rule-breaking was condoned by staff, who conspired with clients to outwit the system:

> "There was another guy that I had one time years ago and he was signing on but I'd had an employer on the 'phone down at a building site saying that he just needed somebody for the day. It was £50. So I said to the guy. I told him where it was and said 'Just go up and you'll get your money and that. But if anybody finds out, I knew nothing about it.' So he went and did the job and I signed him as usual and overlooked the whole thing." (supervisor)

Clients who were able to elicit sympathy from staff could therefore have an impact on outcomes, as could those clients who did this through intimidation.

Policy accomplishment and client categorisation

Unemployment policy is accomplished at street level through the face-to-face interaction between staff and clients. The main focus for this chapter was the categorisation process that staff imposed on clients. Administrative categorisations were made as a necessary part of the 'people-processing' (Prottas, 1979) function of the Jobcentre as a welfare bureaucracy. Even these seemingly bland classifications of occupations and previous experience influenced how clients were treated differentially by staff and could determine the opportunities available to clients. Moral categorisations were made subjectively by staff according to their own value judgements about the attributes, behaviour and attitudes of clients. The main distinction was between 'good' and 'bad' clients, who could secure different levels and types of service according to the way they interacted with staff. The 'bad' client type provided an example of the ambiguous and contested nature of policy accomplishment and also demonstrated some cases in which clients were able to assert their agency in such a way as to influence the outcomes they received. This is significant because staff mediate between citizen and the state. They do so not as empty vessels of policy delivery, but as social actors who have their own deep-seated understandings and belief systems. In Weber's ideal type, bureaucracies are said to operate "without regard for persons" (1991, p 215). It has been demonstrated that in practice the Jobcentre bureaucracy operated 'with regard for persons'.

The importance of these processes of categorisation, particularly the disinclination of staff to assist those who are categorised as 'bad', is brought into sharper focus when recent policy developments are considered. The active labour market policies of Jobseeker's Allowance, the New Deal programmes and the work-focused interviews for almost all benefit claimants under Jobcentre Plus, have increased attention on the role of frontline staff. Each of these changes has afforded staff greater discretion, made sanctions tougher and increased the emphasis on one-to-one interaction. These developments can be interpreted as positive for clients in as much as they formally represent a greater dedication of staff time and effort and increased opportunities to discuss job vacancies and prospects. However, this chapter has demonstrated the limitations of time, the lack of job search activity and the subjective basis on which decisions about clients can be based. It is possible to predict a situation in which 'good' clients fare well in the developing system of work-based social security, while those deemed as 'bad' are, at least, ignored and, at worst, have their disadvantage punished and compounded.

Overview

- Policy implementation has been identified as a two-way process of interaction between staff and clients of welfare services.

- Lipsky provided an explanation for the constraints that street-level bureaucrats work under and showed how staff developed their own 'routines and simplifications' to make their work manageable.

- Dealing with people according to categorisations was one such simplification.

- People 'become' clients through an official process of administrative classification, but this could have important consequences for the opportunities and outcomes that are later available to them.

- Staff made moral categorisations according to subjective criteria and gave preference to clients who they deemed to be more 'worthy' or 'deserving' over those who were labelled as 'bad' for a variety of reasons.

Questions for discussion

1. What aspect of policy in practice does Lipsky point our attention to?

2. Which processes of categorisation were identified and on what basis were they made?

3. What are the possible consequences of categorisation for unemployed clients?

4. Give examples of policy as 'accomplished', 'negotiated' and 'contested'?

References

Anderson, L. (1999) 'Witcraft in a state employment office: rhetorical strategies for managing difficult clients', *Perspectives on Social Problems*, vol 11, pp 219-38.

Barnes, M., Ravell, M. and Lakhani, B. (1998) *Jobseeker's Allowance handbook* (3rd edn, 1998/99), London: CPAG.

Barrett, S. and Fudge, C. (eds) (1981) *Policy and action*, London: Methuen.

Bivand, P. (1999) 'Policy analysis: Employment Service annual report', *Working Brief*, Issue 109, November, pp 19-20.

Blackmore, M. (2001) 'Mind the gap: exploring the implementation deficit in the administration of stricter benefits regime', *Social Policy and Administration*, vol 23, no 2, pp 145-62.

Bowe, R., Ball, S.J. and Gold, A. (1992) *Reforming education and changing schools*, London: Routledge.

Cooper, S. (1985) *Observations in Supplementary Benefit Offices, The Reform of Supplementary Benefit Working Paper C*, London: Policy Studies Institute.

Dean, H. (1991) *Social security and social control*, London: Routledge.

Easton, D. (1965) *A systems analysis of political life*, New York, NY: Wiley.

Elmore, R. (1978) 'Organisational models of social program implementation', *Public Policy*, vol 26, pp 185-228, reprinted in M. Hill (1993) *The policy process: A reader*, London: Harvester Wheatsheaf.

Employment Service (1997) *Design of the New Deal for 18-24 year olds*, London: DfEE/ Welsh Office/Scottish Office.

Finn, D. and Taylor, D. (1990) *The future of Jobcentres: Labour market policy and the Employment Service*, Employment Chapter No 1, London: IPPR.

Finn, D., Blackmore, M. and Nimmo, M. (1998) *Welfare-to-work and the long-term unemployed*, London: Unemployment Unit and Youthaid.

Fletcher, D.R. (1997) 'Evaluating special measures for the unemployed: some reflections on the UK experience', *Policy & Politics*, vol 25, no 2, pp 173-84.

Giller, H. and Morris, A. (1981) '"What type of case is this?" Social workers' decisions about children who offend', in M. Adler and S. Asquith (eds) *Discretion and welfare*, London: Heinemann Educational, pp 69-81.

Hall, A. (1974) *The point of entry: A study of client reception in the social services*, London: George Allen and Unwin.

Handler, J. (1992) 'Power, quiescence, and trust', in K. Hawkins (ed) *The uses of discretion*, Oxford: Clarendon Press, pp 331-60.

Handler, J. and Hasenfeld, Y. (1991) *The moral contstruction of poverty: Welfare reform in America*, London: Newbury Park.

Hasenfeld, Y. (1987) 'Power and social work practice', *Social Service Review*, September, pp 469-83.

Hasenfeld, Y. and Weaver, D. (1996) 'Enforcement, compliance, and disputes in welfare-to-work programs', *Social Science Review*, vol 70, no 2, pp 235-56.

Hill, M. (1997) *The policy process in the modern state* (3rd edn), London: Prentice Hall.

Hogwood, B.W. and Gunn, L. (1984) *Policy analysis for the real world*, London: Oxford University Press.

Howe, L. (1990) *Being unemployed in Northern Ireland: An ethnographic study*, Cambridge: Cambridge University Press.

Hudson, B. (1993) 'Michael Lipsky and street-level bureaucracy in neglected perspective', in M. Hill (ed) *The policy process: A reader*, London: Harvester Wheatsheaf.

Kingfisher, C. (1996) *Women in the American welfare trap*, Philadelphia, PA: University of Pennsylvania Press.

Kingfisher, C. (1998) 'How providers make policy: an analysis of everyday conversation in a welfare office', *Journal of Community and Applied Social Psychology*, vol 8, pp 119-36.

Lipsky, M. (1980) *Street-level bureaucracy: Dilemmas of the individual in public services*, London: Harvester Wheatsheaf.

Millar, J. (2000) *Keeping track of welfare reform: The New Deal Programmes*, York: Joseph Rowntree Foundation/York Publishing Services.

Miller, G. (1991) *Enforcing the work ethic: Rhetoric and everyday life in a work incentive program*, Albany, NY: SUNY Press.

Miller, G. and Holstein, J.A. (1995) 'Dispute domains: organisational contexts and dispute processing', *The Sociological Quarterly*, vol 36, no 1, pp 37-59.

Office for National Statistics (2000) *NOMIS claimant count by occupation*, London: The Stationery Office (data available from www.nomisweb.co.uk).

Pressman, J. and Wildavsky, A. (1973) *Implementation*, Berkeley, CA: University of California Press.

Prottas, J.M. (1979) *People-processing: The street-level bureaucrat in public service bureaucracies*, Massachusetts, MA: Lexington Books.

Rees, S. (1978) *Social work face to face*, London: Edward Arnold.

Weatherley, R. (1979) *Reforming special education: Policy implementation from state level to street level*, Cambridge, MA: MIT Press.

Weatherley, R. and Lipsky, M. (1977) 'Street-level bureaucrats and institutional innovation: implementing special-education reform', *Harvard Educational Review*, vol 47, no 2, May, pp 171-97.

Weber, M. (1991) 'Bureaucracy', in H.H. Gerth and C.W. Mills (eds) *From Max Weber: Essays in sociology*, London: Routledge, pp 196-244.

Wright, S. (2001) 'Activating the unemployed: the street-level implementation of UK policy', in J. Clasen (ed) *What future for social security? Debates and reforms in national and cross-national perspective*, The Hague: Kluwer Law International, pp 235-50.

Website resources

Jobcentre Plus	www.jobcentreplus.gov.uk
Jobseeker's Allowance	www.dwp.gov.uk/lifeevent/ jobseeker's_allowance.htm
New Deal for Young People	www.dwp.gov.uk/lifeevent/benefits/ new_deal_for_young_people.htm
Unemployment Unit and Youthaid (now the Centre for Economic and Social Inclusion)	www.cesi.org.uk

thirteen

Social security in a multi-ethnic society

Lucinda Platt

Summary

The measured minority group population of England and Wales stands at at around 9% of the total population, and people from minority ethnic groups are more likely to receive means-tested benefits than the white population. This chapter:

- describes the principal minority ethnic groups in Britain and the features of immigration history, immigration policy, employment experience and family structure that have shaped and continue to shape their relationship with social security;

- examines the extent to which some minority ethnic groups are greater users of social security or certain types of social security;

- explores the extent to which social security law, rates and regulation impact differentially on different ethnic groups;

- concludes by examining the extent to which delivery is differently experienced by different ethnic groups.

Introduction: population and immigration policy

Britain has a heterogeneous population made up of a wide range of ethnic groups. Table 13.1 indicates the numbers in the different minority groups according to the 2001 Census (see Box 13.1 for a discussion of the categories used).

As Table 13.1 shows, no single minority group accounts for more than 2% of the population, with the Indian group being the largest single group at 2%. However, the minority group populations are not evenly spread but show substantial geographical concentration. A majority of all the black groups as well as of Bangladeshis and of other Asians reside in London, a city which accounts for nearly half of all the minority group population in aggregate; and over a quarter of London's population comes from a minority group. Forty per cent of Indians also live in London – although predominantly the outer rather than the inner areas – and Indians also have concentrations in the East and West Midlands; there are substantial Pakistani communities in Yorkshire, the West Midlands and the North West (ONS, 2001a). Nor do minority groups reflect the demographic profile of the overall population, all groups having distinct age and sex profiles. The differential distributions and demographic profiles of minority groups represent their histories and patterns of immigration and settlement alongside the skills, traditions and experience they brought with them. These differences have implications for the use and experience of social security by different groups.

Table 13.1: **The ethnic group populations of England and Wales (2001)**

	Number	%
Total	52,041,916	100
White groups	47,520,866	91.3
Black Caribbean	563,843	1.1
Black African	479,665	0.9
Black Other (non-mixed)	96,069	0.2
Black Mixed	316,331	0.6
Indian	1,036,807	2.0
Pakistani	714,826	1.4
Bangladeshi	280,830	0.5
Chinese	226,948	0.4
Other Asian (non-mixed)	241,274	0.5
Other-Other (non-mixed)	219,754	0.4
Other-Mixed	344,703	0.7
All Minorities	6,508,175	8.7

Source: National Statistics website (www.statistics.gov.uk); Crown Copyright material is reproduced with the permission of the Controller of HMSO.

> **Box 13.1: Ethnic group categories**
>
> The 2001 Census ethnic group classification differed from the 1991 Census classification and those schemes based on the 1991 groups by introducing a number of 'mixed' groups: White and Black Caribbean; White and Black African; White and Asian; Other Mixed. These were offered as options in addition to the 1991 minority group categories of Black African, Black Caribbean, Black Other, Indian, Pakistani, Bangladeshi, Chinese, Other Asian and Other. It also offered three 'white' categories: British, Irish and Other White. Most surveys and other administrative sources have moved (or are moving) over to the 2001 system. Nevertheless, much existing information, including most of the evidence given here, employs the 1991 categories. The two systems are not directly comparable as those who now select one of the mixed categories may have previously included themselves in either White or in one of the 'Other' groups or in one of the specific minority groups depending on their identification. In addition, some whose parentage may be 'mixed' may nevertheless identify with a particular group and continue to associate themselves with a 'non-mixed' classification.

Britain has always been a diverse nation, with a population stemming from multiple roots and complex patterns of inward, outward and return migration through processes of conquest, union, colonisation and decolonisation[1]. It was the post–war period that saw a sustained level of inward migration from commonwealth or former commonwealth countries to supply labour. This migration did not occur all at the same time; rather, migration from the Caribbean was followed by that from India and Pakistan and subsequently Bangladesh. Although much primary migration was male, with family reunification (that is, applying for dependants from abroad to join them here), being a subsequent step, this was not the case for Caribbean immigration where there were large numbers of women among primary migrants who came, for example, to take up work in the health service. Expulsion also resulted in settlement by numbers of Vietnamese and East African Asian families around 1970. Since 1970, most primary immigration for employment has been at a standstill, with family reunification and fertility being the routes through which minority groups have expanded. Refugees have also contributed to a diverse minority group population, a recent phenomenon being the arrival of asylum-seekers from within Europe as well as from further afield[2].

---

[1] See, for example, the broad overview of this history in Parekh (2000).
[2] In 2000 28% of asylum applications were from European nationals, although the number of applications from nationals of the Federal Republic of Yugoslavia seem to be declining (Matz et al, 2001).

As well as reason for arrival, timing of arrival has implications for employment and employment history, with the earlier migrants being concentrated in manufacturing, and in areas and industries, for example, the textile industry, which subsequently suffered from processes of deindustrialisation. Later migrants were concentrated less in northern industrial towns and more in the midlands and, particularly, London. While London offers many opportunities, it also suffers high unemployment and extreme housing pressure. Forced settlement in poorer areas can also result in more limited educational opportunities which continue to restrict the options for future, non-migrant, generations. The very high concentration of Bangladeshis in Tower Hamlets is evidence of both migration history, limited occupational opportunities, and the way that multiple disadvantage can reproduce itself. Employment in vulnerable sectors, alongside discrimination, concentration in poorer areas which offer fewer opportunities and for some groups, notably Pakistanis, Bangladeshis and Black Caribbeans, greater difficulty in obtaining high levels of qualifications, have resulted in both high unemployment for many minority groups, especially Caribbeans, Pakistanis and, particularly, Bangladeshis, and much higher rates of self-employment among certain groups, in particular Indians, Chinese and Pakistanis. The role of ethnicity in determining differential labour market outcomes for minority groups has been described as an ethnic penalty (see **Box 13.2**). These two features of employment experience – greater vulnerability to unemployment and higher rates of self-employment among certain groups – have implications for groups' relationship with social security, as is explored below.

Immigration history thus has implications for the profile of groups, and is therefore relevant to their experience of social security, as is amplified below. However, there are also ways in which immigration law has interacted directly with social security that has limited the possibilities for claiming for those in a transitional status or for those seeking family reunification. The two main points of interaction have been the rules around recourse to public funds and the provisions for those seeking refugee status. The 1971 Immigration Act introduced the requirement that those seeking family reunification – that is, applying for dependants from abroad to join them – should have no 'recourse to public funds' at the time of the application until the dependants should be

---

Box 13.2: Ethnic penalty

Heath and McMahon (1997) "use the expression 'ethnic penalty' to refer to all the sources of disadvantage that might lead an ethnic group to fare less well in the labour market than do similarly qualified Whites. In other words, it is a broader concept than that of discrimination, although discrimination is likely to be a major component of the ethnic penalty" (p 91).

granted residence. This usually occurs a year after arrival, although the new immigration and asylum White Paper that preceded the 2002 Nationality, Immigration and Asylum Act proposed that the probationary period for spouses should be extended to two years (Home Office, 2002). 'Public funds' for these purposes include the means-tested benefits – Housing Benefit, Council Tax Benefit and Income Support/income-based Jobseeker's Allowance as well as the Disabled Person's and the Working Families' Tax Credits – and the non-contributory benefits – Child Benefit, Attendance Allowance, Disability Living Allowance, Invalid Care Allowance and Severe Disablement Allowance[3]. Thus applicants have to demonstrate that they can support their dependants; and should they make a claim following their arrival they risk their dependants' status.

Those seeking asylum have also been constrained in terms of their ability to work and to claim benefits. The 1999 Immigration Act established the National Asylum Support Service (NASS) apart from the Department of Social Security provision to arrange accommodation and provide vouchers at 70% of Income Support rates for adults (although 100% for child dependants). Although the voucher system was phased out in autumn 2002, the provision of funds for basic support has remained with NASS and is distinct from social security although tied into Income Support rates.

Immigration law has also inhibited family reunification through visa requirements, which mean that applications have to be made before departure. The geographical distance of immigration officers making visa decisions from the British legal process can limit their accountability (Bevan, 1986). A further obstacle was supplied by the former, notorious, 'primary purpose' rule, which required that a spouse's primary reason for immigration should not be to live in Britain. The delays caused by such inhibitions have implications for settlement and integration of family members. For example, more recent arrivals including those, particularly women, who come to join spouses in Britain, are less likely to have acquired English language skills. This may be exacerbated where language communities are highly socially or economically concentrated or segregated (Cantle, 2001). Language fluency can have implications for access to claiming and appropriate information, as well as to take-up of the kinds of additional support offered with the New Deals.

In sum, then, aspects of the different minority groups' history, settlement and reasons for settlement will have a bearing on their relationship with social security provision, which needs to be borne in mind when such relationships are considered.

When the Labour government came to power in 1997, its focus was on an inclusive society, suggesting a more proactive approach to race equality issues. The challenge to achieve this in social security is enhanced by the presence of

---

[3] See CPAG (2000) for a more comprehensive and detailed discussion of the law in this area.

> **Box 13.3: Significant moments in immigration policy relevant to social security**
>
> *1948 British Nationality Act:* enshrined the right of all commonwealth citizens to reside in the UK.
>
> *1962 Commonwealth Immigrants Act:* first legislation to restrict right of commonwealth citizens to reside in the UK, it introduced a voucher system for primary immigration.
>
> *1971 Immigration Act:* introduced recourse to public funds provisions; and notion of patriality, which favoured immigration by those from 'White' commonwealth countries (for example, Australia, South Africa, Canada) above that from other commonwealth countries.
>
> *1993 Asylum and Immigration Appeals Act:* introduced fingerprinting and removed rights to public sector housing.
>
> *1996 Asylum and Immigration Act:* penalised employers who employed those without the appropriate documentation.
>
> *1999 Immigration and Asylum Act:* introduced vouchers for support and the dispersal and accommodation system devolved to NASS.
>
> 2002 White Paper *Secure borders, safe haven* announced phasing out of vouchers, but support and accommodation to remain with NASS.

the potentially conflicting policy objectives of moving claimants of means-tested benefits into work and continuing to restrict immigration. In the next three sections I consider these challenges alongside policy and the extent to which it tends to increase equality.

Minority ethnic groups and use of social security

Patterns of use of social security vary widely by ethnic group, as do the reasons for their variation. All minority groups show a greater use of means-tested benefits than the white population, as Table 13.2 illustrates. According to the table, which shows 'benefit units'[4] where a means-tested benefit is in payment,

---

[4] 'Benefit unit' refers to the immediate family unit of individual, partner if any and dependent children if any. It is such units which are used as the basis of assessment for entitlement to means-tested benefits and for the calculation of the amount of benefit payable.

Table 13.2: Proportion of benefit units in receipt of selected means-tested benefits, by ethnic group (1999-2000) (%)

	All groups	Black groups	Indian	Pakistani and Bangladeshi	Other	White
Income Support	11	19	14	22	16	10
Jobseeker's Allowance[a]	3	8	4	9	4	3
Housing Benefit	14	28	9	19	19	14
Council Tax Benefit	18	29	15	29	20	18
Any income-related benefit	23	37	24	44	27	23

Note: [a] This includes the contributory as well as the means-tested elements; however, the contributory element accounts for a relatively small proportion of benefit recipients (around 20% at February 2002 figures).

Source: Adapted from DSS (2001, Table 3.17, p 56)

by ethnic group, 44% of Pakistani and Bangladeshi benefit units are in this position compared to only 23% of units overall. Looking just at Income Support and Jobseeker's Allowance shows that 27% of Black benefit units are in receipt of one of these benefits and nearly a third of Pakistani and Bangladeshi benefit units are; while 18% of Indian benefit units are supported by one of these benefits, compared to 14% in the population as a whole.

By contrast, **Table 13.3** illustrates receipt of non–means-tested benefits by ethnic group and shows that all minority groups make lower use of non–income-related benefits than the population as a whole, and than the white population in particular. This is despite the fact that receipt of Child Benefit is substantially higher among minority groups, especially among Pakistanis and Bangladeshis. The reasons for differential reliance on means-tested and non–means-tested benefits are various. Greater dependence on means-tested elements is due to:

- Excess unemployment, which leads to higher claiming of Income Support and income-based Jobseeker's Allowance[5]. This is evidenced among all minority groups, but particularly among Pakistanis and Bangladeshis, and Black Caribbeans (ONS, 2000; DSS, 2001). Bangladeshis and Pakistanis experience exceptionally high rates of unemployment despite also having

---

[5] For an overview of the different minority ethnic groups' relationship to the labour market and the different factors involved see Platt (2002).

Table 13.3: Proportion of benefit units in receipt of selected contributory and categorical benefits, by ethnic group (1999-2000) (%)

	All groups	Black groups	Indian	Pakistani and Bangladeshi	Other	White
Retirement Pension	24	13	8	6	6	25
Child Benefit	23	30	34	42	27	22
Incapacity Benefit	5	2	4	3	2	5
Any non-income-related benefit	55	47	47	52	39	55

Source: Adapted from DSS (2001, Table 3.17, p 56)

high rates of economic inactivity, both of which factors make them more likely to depend on means-tested support. Young Caribbeans also experience disproportionately high unemployment, even when compared with white men of a similar age (Berthoud, 1999). Even highly qualified Indian families experience an 'ethnic penalty' in employment (Heath and McMahon, 1997; Modood et al, 1997); and the mismatch between qualifications and employment prospects is even more evident for Black Africans (Modood, 1997).

- Different patterns of family structure. For example, Black Caribbean families show a much greater prevalence of lone mothers than the population as a whole; and lone mothers have a very high probability of claiming means-tested assistance. In fact Black Caribbean lone mothers are rather less likely to claim means-tested benefits than other lone mothers, but they are still more likely to do so than not. Bangladeshis, and to a lesser extent Pakistanis, have large families compared to the national average. Large families are more likely to be in poverty and are harder to support on the relatively low earnings that apply to the sectors in which these families are most likely to be concentrated (Platt and Noble, 1999; Berthoud, 2000; Platt, 2003: forthcoming).

- Long-term poverty among pensioners or unemployed people. Some minority groups are less likely to have accrued assets and are thus more likely to need to claim Income Support or the Minimum Income Guarantee (MIG). Throughout their lives some minority groups would appear to acquire fewer assets or savings which will give them less of a cushion during any periods of unemployment and translate into greater hardship in old age.

According to *Social trends*, nearly 60% of Pakistanis and Bangladeshis had no savings compared to 28% of the population as a whole, while over 80% had savings below £1,500 (ONS, 2001b). This compared with a similar proportion of black groups, but under half of Indian and white people. Ability to build up assets is itself affected not only by higher risk of unemployment, discussed above, but also with minority group earnings differentials for those who are in work (Modood et al, 1997; Berthoud, 1998; Blackaby et al, 2002). According to a recent analysis of pensioners' incomes, those from minority ethnic groups appeared to be disadvantaged relative to all pensioners (DSS, 2000).

On the other hand, ethnic minority groups have a lower reliance on contributory benefits, but a greater use of the categorical benefit, Child Benefit. The reasons for this include the following:

- Different age profiles. The main contributory benefit, the basic state pension, is obviously going to be claimed only by those aged 60/65 and over. Where this older group forms a higher proportion of the population, the benefit is more likely to be in receipt. All minority groups have a younger population profile than the population as a whole, but this pattern is enhanced for the Pakistani and more so the Bangladeshi groups, as well as for the Black Other group. The median age among all minority groups is 10 years below that of the whole population (26 compared with 36); this varies with the particular group, though, such that the median age for Indians and Chinese is 31, while for Bangladeshis and Black Others it is only 18 (ONS, 2001a)[6]. On the other hand, the proportion of the White population aged 65 and over is 21%, while this age range makes up 15% of the Black Caribbean group, 10% of the Indian group and 6% of the Bangladeshi group.
- Differential fertility. The age profiles account, in part, for the higher rates of Child Benefit receipt among minority groups. However, this pattern is also due to the fact that certain groups, notably Pakistanis and Bangladeshis, also have higher female fertility with families started at a younger age (Peach, 1996).
- Unemployment. For some minority groups unemployment is both more prevalent (as discussed above), and more likely to be long term, particularly for Caribbeans (Berthoud, 1999). Thus, entitlement to contributions-based Jobseeker's Allowance is less likely to be accrued; and, in addition, even where it is accrued, it is more likely to be exhausted before re-employment is gained.

---

[6] In the case of the Black Other group, the demographic profile is largely an artefact of the classification, as respondents in this category tended to be the children of parents who would classify themselves as Black Caribbean (Peach, 1996).

- Insufficient residence to build up contributions records. For those who migrated in adulthood the opportunity to build up a contributions record, sufficient to claim the basic state pension, may not have been available; while for those who migrated recently, such as refugees, a contributions record may not have been acquired.
- Interrupted contributions records. For those with attachments to the country of origin, contributions records may have been interrupted due to extended visits.

The implications of these patterns of claiming are that minority groups, or at least some minority groups, may develop a less rights-based relationship with social security than that which holds for the population as a whole. The relative concentration of certain minority groups on means-tested benefits, which of necessity require greater evidence to be provided to support a claim, may also impact on the experience of claiming and the relationship between the Department for Work and Pensions and the group member. The inherent requirement in traditional means-tested benefits for greater scrutiny and evidence may be reinforced by citizenship and immigration status interactions with means-tested benefits, discussed above. This may lead to the use of passport and status checking which will impact more on means-tested benefit recipients, but may additionally be targeted by officers on particular groups (Gordon and Newnham, 1985). Law et al (1994b) found that the Chinese claimants in their study were particularly likely to be asked for passports. This in turn may have implications for the relationship of minority groups to benefit claiming and receipt. It may problematise perceived legitimacy of claims on both sides of the relationship. This is an issue explored further below.

The greater use of means-tested benefits among certain minority groups also leads to the danger of great stigma being attached to them, and exacerbates the danger of social exclusion, often associated with Income Support receipt. On the other hand, they are likely to have less investment in adjustments to the basic state pension, often argued by campaigners to be non-problematically a benefit of desert and entitlement.

So how has recent policy impacted upon these differences in experience of type of benefit receipt? There are two types of policy which are pertinent here: those which are focused on the underlying problems (unemployment, low earnings) and those which focus on the institutional and discriminatory ways in which minority groups are over-represented in disadvantaged groups. Thus the 'welfare-to-work' policies (discussed in Chapter Five in this volume), which aim to find the means to move people into work, begin to address some of the issues of those who have had limited options of employment. These could be expected to have a greater impact on members of certain minority ethnic groups, given higher unemployment rates among Caribbean males, and among Pakistanis and Bangladeshis, and, to a lesser extent, Indians.

Caribbean lone mothers might also be anticipated to benefit from the options offered through welfare-to-work given their existing greater propensity to take employment. The New Deals are notable in having been subject to ethnic monitoring of both participation and outcomes. Despite non-comprehensive coverage of ethnicity, indications are, however, that different groups experience different pathways through and out of provision (DWP, 2002a; see also DfEE, 1999, Chapter 4). Indians, according to figures to the end of 2001, are over-represented in moves into employment and Bangladeshis are most likely to take up the voluntary sector option, with Black Africans more likely to take up further education and training[7]. Thus, as *Jobs for all* (DfEE, 1999) indicates, there may be particular issues in the operation and effectiveness of welfare-to-work for different ethnic groups. There is additionally evidence that the access to New Deals may be limited by the greater tendency to enable minority groups to remain on Income Support rather than income-based Jobseeker's Allowance. While this may protect minority group members to a certain extent from the coercive aspects of welfare-to-work (see Chapter Five in this volume), it may also reduce their opportunities.

The introduction of the National Minimum Wage (NMW) in April 1999 is also likely to have an impact on the particular patterns of social security claiming. Given the earnings disadvantage discussed above, the NMW may well have a differential impact on those minority group members who low pay has kept locked in the poverty trap. The original report on the NMW, prepared by the Low Pay Commission (1998), identified that minority group members already in employment were likely to be particular beneficiaries. However, their subsequent reports (LPC, 2000, 2001) identified minority ethnic group workers as being more likely to be unaware of and not receiving the NMW. It is clearly plausible that minority groups who have been stuck in a benefit poverty trap will also benefit from the NMW, especially given the introduction of in-work tax credits that have taken place at the same time.

The greater generosity of Working Families Tax Credit (WFTC) over Family Credit and of Disabled Person's Tax Credit (DPTC) over Disability Working Allowance may have positive impacts on the possibilities of moving into work for those groups with a greater tendency towards both larger families and low wages (Bangladeshis and Pakistanis), and those groups with higher rates of disability (Bangladeshis and Pakistanis, again). The childcare element of WFTC is likely to be relatively enabling for lone parents and thus could be expected to be constructive in reducing Caribbean lone parents' use of Income Support. The current evidence suggests that Black and especially Pakistani and Bangladeshi families are over-represented in the WFTC caseload (PIU, 2002,

---

[7] Although the Performance and Innovation Unit summary of the evidence paints a rather different picture of the patterns of outcomes (PIU, 2002, p 133).

p 139). On the other hand, changes to Income Support, in particular the increases to the child payments and the equalising of the rates for younger and older children, can be predicted to make Income Support a more attractive option than it has been for larger families, and families with young children in particular (Platt, 2003: forthcoming). While positive for the overall welfare of those on benefit, these latter changes may also tend to reinforce some of the existing patterns in claiming.

The impacts of these policies and developments on particular minority groups is only likely to become evident over a longer stretch of time.

As for changing the factors which keep people from minority ethnic groups in a disadvantaged position, and which lead in part to their high use of means-tested and low use of contributory benefits, it is those policies which focus on the wider race relations agenda that are most relevant. Thus the requirements of race relations legislation from 1976, recently reinforced in the 2000 Race Relations Amendment Act, outlaws discrimination on the grounds of 'race' and places positive duties on public authorities to demonstrate that the way they work does not have unequal impact. The long-standing economic disadvantage of certain minority groups despite over a quarter of a century of race relations legislation indicates that the confrontation of individual acts of discrimination is not sufficient to achieve fundamental changes in the position of minority groups, although it clearly has a role. The provisions in the Race Relations Amendment Act are more far-reaching and should make institutional factors in minority group disadvantage both more visible and more open to correction – at least those which operate in the public sector[8]. They have led to the active pursuit of strategies for achieving greater equality within government and its departments, for example the Home Office's *Race equality in public services* reports (Home Office, 2000, 2001).

Social security rules and regulations and minority ethnic groups

There are a number of ways in which benefit rules can disadvantage certain minority group members. Residence requirements, through the 'habitual residence test', can impact on those who have spent or spend substantial periods of time abroad, or who have interests or partners abroad. Where people have geographically distant ties, they may choose, or be obliged, to spend substantial periods away from Britain, a pattern that has been particularly noted for South Asian groups. This may mean that they lose certain social security entitlements. The habitual residence test does not refer to a specific duration of residence prior to claiming, which is required for it to be fulfilled. Partly as a result of its

---

[8] For an overview of British 'race' relations legislation and guidance on the Race Relations Amendment Act see the Commission for Racial Equality, www.cre.gov.uk

imprecision it has been variously and often restrictively interpreted. Among those operating it there has been a tendency to target particular groups, especially those from minority ethnic groups, as being subject to the test (Bloch, 1997; CPAG, 2000, p 826). It applies only to a certain group of benefits: Income Support, income-based Jobseeker's Allowance, and Council Tax Benefit. Nevertheless, it tends to reinforce a perceived relationship between means-tested benefits, minority ethnic groups and particular scrutiny, or consideration, of claims. As the National Association of Citizens' Advice Bureaux put it in 1996, the "habitual residence test has created a space where prejudices and unexamined assumptions concerning race and culture can appear legitimate" (NACAB, 1996, p 20).

In addition, where benefits have been in payment but the claimant is absent for a period, the family may not claim the support due (Bloch, 1997). And it has already been noted, above, how social security and immigration law have increasingly been linked. Those 'subject to immigration control' are not able to claim a range of means-tested and non-contributory benefits. Thus an individual's options for claiming social security may be limited by their immigration status, by that of their dependants or by concerns about status and the connections between the Home Office and benefit provision. On the other hand, responsibility for support to family members is not taken account of when assessing circumstances if those members are in another country. The sending of remittances may place impossible demands on limited benefit income (Law, 1996).

The implications of the operation of social security law in relation to minority ethnic groups is that it introduces assumptions about the need for greater scrutiny of minority groups, particularly for those who 'appear foreign' through, for example, limited English language fluency. It links complex gradations of citizenship status with the provision of welfare; and can lead to questioning the legitimacy of benefit claims by those who are regarded as not belonging, at the same time as their options for support from employment are curtailed (Bloch, 1999), thus increasing their exclusion. There are also implications for delivery which are discussed in the next section.

So how has Labour's policy responded to the negative impact of certain regulations on minority groups and of the interaction of social security and immigration law? Aside from the removal of the punitive and arbitrary 'primary purpose rule' on coming to power in 1997, Labour policy has, in fact, shown a continuing emphasis on restricting the citizenship rights of those who are in intermediate status. Given that almost the only route for primary immigration is through making a claim for asylum, it is in this area that policy has tended to focus. The 1999 Immigration and Asylum Act saw the separation of provisions for asylum-seekers (that is, those awaiting the outcome of a claim for refugee status) from mainstream provision under the (then) Department of Social Security. Instead, as discussed above, NASS was established to arrange the dispersal and accommodation of asylum-seekers who were not being detained and provide them with support in the form of vouchers. This will have served to have marked a dividing line between those with more assured status and the vilified asylum-seekers. But it has also marked out a separate tier of basic support outside the main safety net system, which carries an inherent stigma. The separation of treatment of asylum-seekers from social security provision is set to continue, according to the provisions in the 2002 White Paper *Secure borders, safe haven*, although the "humiliating and stigmatising" (Patel, 2002, p 42) voucher scheme has been phased out. Other problematic aspects of the rules governing social security provision have not been addressed by the current administration. Instead, the focus has been on delivery issues, which are considered next.

Delivery of social security in a multi-ethnic society

There are many issues that raise particular problems for, or obstacles to, the equitable delivery of social security across all ethnic groups. This section outlines these and also relates them to the issues that have been raised in the preceding two sections.

The main issue for delivery is finding ways to ensure that those who are entitled to benefit claim their due: the issue of take-up. Inhibiting full take-up by minority group members are a number of perceived obstacles and attitudes, which hinder the most effective claiming process (see **Box 13.4**). A number of these have been indicated in the discussion above; in this section they are expanded upon and the attempts that have been made to correct them are outlined.

There is currently little conclusive evidence on the extent of under-claiming by different minority groups and whether it shows substantial differences by group. The lack of evidence in this area and the need for research was highlighted by Craig in 1991; succeeding evidence has been predominantly anecdotal, inferential, or inconclusive. Law, who earlier conducted a qualitative

> **Box 13.4: Possible reasons for non-take-up by members of certain minority ethnic groups**
>
> - Language problems and lack of information
> - Excessive demands for evidence
> - Difficulty of claiming when self-employed
> - Discriminatory attitudes of staff
> - Culturally based attitudes to claiming
> - The operation of discretion

study of attitudes to take-up (Law et al, 1994a), was still identifying in 2002 that the understanding of attitudes to claiming and claiming behaviour is an area in which there "is still very little empirical research" (Law, 2002, p 30). Nevertheless, what evidence we have points to the fact that incomplete take-up may be an issue for minority groups, and one which could clearly be critical for their welfare. Fry and Stark (1993) identified the role that stigma and (lack of) information could play in non-take-up. These are both likely to be greater for minority groups for the reasons discussed above. In addition, local studies have indicated differences in claiming patterns according to ethnicity (Bloch, 1993). Law et al (1994a, 1994b), in their Leeds study, found clear evidence of delayed claiming and non-claiming, particularly among Chinese and Bangladeshi respondents; while the National Association of Citizens' Advice Bureaux (1991) identified the possibility of eligible non-claiming through officer error. There is also internal evidence from poverty rates themselves, which indicate a possible failure in getting the social security system to work for some minority groups. Adelman and Bradshaw (1999) have pointed out how Income Support is relatively protective against poverty for some minority groups, in that a number are worse off if they are not on Income Support. On similar lines, Berthoud's analysis of income in the Policy Studies Institute study (Modood et al, 1997) illustrated the strikingly low incomes of Bangladeshis and Pakistanis *in work*. Both these sources indicate that social security is not providing an adequate safety net for those from the most disadvantaged minority groups. This may be for reasons of demographics and family structure or as a result of structural factors within benefits themselves. A further possibility is that minority groups are hindered or inhibited from claiming even where there is entitlement.

One area that has been highlighted in past research and more recently in good practice recommendations is that of *comprehension*. For those whose first language is not English, the availability of documents in appropriate languages and interpreters for personal interviews can be critical. In addition, there may be those who are not literate in their first language for whom it is important to find alternative ways to disseminate relevant information. The information needs of members of different minority groups as well as the diverse routes by which people access or fail to access information were explored by Bloch (1993; see also NACAB, 1991). Language and accessibility are recognised foci for ensuring adequate understanding and take-up of eligible benefits. The Department for Work and Pensions provides information on its website in nine minority languages in addition to English (www.dwp.gov.uk), and has emphasised this aspect of its provision in its Race Equality Scheme (DWP, 2002b). Local benefits offices in England and Wales has also responded to language issues by both community liaison work and provision of materials in a range of languages (Home Office, 2001). Nevertheless, officers' assumptions about 'foreigners' may continue to impinge on those making use of translation and second language provision as long as the regulations contain within them implicit or explicit distinctions around entitlement and belonging, as discussed in the previous section. Appropriate language provision is also unlikely to be able to counteract the atmosphere created by a persistent media message that asserts "immigrants are a welfare burden" and "minorities are frequently constructed as a social problem" (Law, 2002, p 30). Nor is appropriate language provision on its own able to counter other reasons for non-claiming such as those associated with perceived stigma.

Discriminatory treatment may also be an issue in the way benefit entitlement is established, for example, in the use of the habitual residence test or in the extent to which requests for passports or other "excessive demands for evidence" (Simpson, 1991, p 14) are made when claims are being conducted. As indicated above, the probability of discriminatory treatment may itself be enhanced by, for example, the greater relative dependence on means-tested support among some groups and the higher prevalence of lone parents (already a relatively stigmatised group) among Caribbeans (Law et al, 1994a; Law, 1996). Studies have revealed that discriminatory treatment can be an issue in the provision or refusal of benefits: the National Association of Citizens' Advice Bureaux highlighted a number of concerns and complaints and examples of benefit wrongly refused which they summarised in their report on the 'barriers to benefit' in the early 1990s (NACAB, 1991). The 2000 Race Relations Amendment Act requires public authorities to give more detailed consideration to their practices and to place responsibility for discriminatory behaviours with the management of the authorities. The requirements of the Act came into force in April 2002 and business areas that come under the Department for Work and Pensions have produced statements of commitment to equitable services and how they intend to monitor their success[9]. The overarching principles on which these statements have been made were supplied in the Department's Race Equality strategy document, *Equality, opportunity and independence for all* (2002b). This document commits itself to assessing the possible differential impact of its services and policies and prioritising monitoring and evaluation in relation to the possible scale of the impact. It also commits the Department to effective ethnic monitoring in all areas of delivery and among its employees, and to evaluations of future policy impact. It may be that the areas of possible differential impact outlined below will, in time, be both confirmed and addressed by such monitoring and evaluation, but it remains to be seen how effectively and how swiftly the commitments translate into change.

---

[9] The nine Department for Work and Pensions business areas which have produced their own Race Equality Schemes are: Children and Housing Group, Child Support Agency, Disability and Carers Directorate, Human Resources, Jobcentre Plus, Law and Special Policy Group, Pensions Group, the Appeals Service Agency, and Work and Welfare Strategy and Fraud, Planning and Presentation Strategy.

The existence of discretion in certain areas of social security provision, such as the Social Fund, may increase the likelihood of discriminatory action. The New Deals themselves have aspects of discretion in the form that personal advice can take and in the ways that opportunities and skills are developed. In addition, access to the New Deal itself can be impeded, as mentioned above, by identifying claimants as eligible for Income Support rather than Jobseeker's Allowance. Here again, the provision of the Race Relations Amendment Act will require the demonstration that unequal impact is being both assessed and addressed.

Claiming in-work benefits (such as Family Credit) while self-employed has been identified as more difficult than claiming as an employee (Corden and Craig, 1991). The higher rates of self-employment among certain minority groups (Indians, Chinese, Pakistanis and Bangladeshis) may therefore result in disproportionately high rates of rejected or unsuccessful claims for in-work benefits.

Finally, Law et al's (1994a) detailed study of attitudes to rights and benefits in Leeds indicates that claimant attitudes may themselves inhibit claiming in certain cultural or religious contexts. The qualitative evidence presented did not indicate that adherence to particular religious views or cultural affiliations would *necessarily* lead to predictable attitudes to benefit claiming. Rather, the study stressed the importance of considering the cultural dimension in the wider context of approaches to claiming (and appealing against decisions); and the ways in which experience and behaviour is both vindicated and resisted, as well as being caused by, attitudes and beliefs. These belief systems based on wider attitudes about rights and entitlement and justice will necessarily interact, in the context of benefit claiming or non-claiming, with the costs of claiming in terms of stigma (Falkingham, 1986), information costs, probability (or perceived probability) of rejection and alternatives or perceived alternatives. As the literature on take-up has identified, eligible non-claiming is not necessarily an irrational behaviour (Craig, 1991), and can be expected to persist in an atmosphere which gives high costs to claiming.

Box 13.5 summarises the key post-1997 policies and guidance relevant to considering social security provision in a multi-ethnic society.

This chapter has shown that the provision of social security in a fashion which is equitable and which enhances the inclusion of disadvantaged, marginalised or discriminated groups has to engage with both the dangers of ignoring difference and of assuming it.

Ignoring difference may lead to:

- the underprovision or inaccessibility of information;
- ineffectiveness of welfare-to-work strategies;
- penalising those who do not work in conventional forms of employment (for example, the self-employed);

Box 13.5: Policies and guidance post-1997 relevant to the provision of social security in a multi-ethnic context

1997	'Primary purpose rule' rescinded
from 1997	New Deals, which monitor ethnicity and which try to find ways to move those particularly likely to have difficulty engaging in the labour market into work
1999	Immigration and Asylum Act (see above)
April 1999	Introduction of the NMW
October 1999	Introduction of WFTC
1999	Macpherson Report on the death of Stephen Lawrence identified the pervasive problem of institutional racism in public services
April, October 2000	Equalisation of Income Support dependent child rates across ages; and substantial increase of these rates to £30.95
2000	Home Office's *Race equality in public services* annual reports (starting in 2000), which describe and monitor the activity of the government and its departments in ensuring and enhancing racial equality
2000	The Macpherson Report led to the Race Relations Amendment Act, which placed a positive duty on public authorities to scrutinise their practices and demonstrate how they were ensuring non-discriminatory provision
2001, 2002	Policy and Innovation Unit project looking at improving the labour market achievements of minority ethnic groups in British society, and thus examining related issues of benefit use and transitions, established 2001, interim report 2002
2002	Publication of the Department for Work and Pensions' Race equality consultation document, *Equality, opportunity and independence for all*, on the provisions of the Race Relations Amendment Act coming into force

- failing to take account of contexts which produce greater poverty and greater reliance on particular benefits and benefit types.

On the other hand, making too many, or *inappropriate assumptions* about difference may lead to:

- obstructing access to welfare-to-work strategies;
- operating rules in a discriminatory fashion;
- making claims harder to undertake, by asking for additional 'proof';

- making assumptions about individuals' engagement or potential engagement with the labour market, and acting accordingly.

Policies need to find the balance between the fairness implied by rigidity and the flexibility to take account of extreme or untypical circumstances. The Macpherson report and the ensuing Race Relations Amendment Act drew attention to the processes by which discriminatory practices within institutions could develop and be sustained. They also indicated ways in which public bodies could both question the equity of their own systems and practices and reform them. However, it is not simply the case that individual agencies reforming their practices will transform the delivery of social security to minority ethnic groups; rather that has to be part of a process which also looks more fundamentally at the context of, and restrictions on, people's lives (as, for example, the Social Exclusion Unit is doing; see SEU, 2000), and also considers the way policy regulations themselves are created and maintained.

Overview

Although there is significant diversity of circumstances and experiences among and within different minority ethnic groups, there is often a high risk of unemployment, poverty and reliance on means-tested benefits. Social security law, rates and regulations impact differentially on different ethnic groups. Benefit delivery, including issues of take-up, are also experienced differently by different ethnic groups.

These issues are closely interconnected. The socioeconomic context and the structure of the benefits system both have an impact upon how delivery is perceived and experienced. Past immigration policy has also structured the settlement patterns and current opportunities of many minority groups and thus their relative dependence on social security. And there have been explicit links between immigration rules and social security entitlements. Thus, while some issues – for example, that of language (interpretation, translation and so on) – can be considered as primarily issues of delivery, few aspects of the delivery and take-up of benefits can be divorced from questions about the wider experience and history of the different minority groups, and the particular relevance of certain social security provisions for them.

Questions for discussion

1. What is the relationship between social security policy and immigration policy?

2. Why do patterns of social security receipt vary between ethnic groups?

3. What factors need to be taken into account when considering appropriate delivery of social security in a multi-cultural context?

4. What are the key ways in which government has attempted to improve delivery of social security to minority ethnic groups?

References

Adelman, L. and Bradshaw, J. (1999) *Children in poverty in Britain: Analysis of the Family Resources Survey 1994/95*, York: Social Policy Research Unit, University of York.

Berthoud, R. (1998) *The incomes of ethnic minorities*, Colchester: Institute for Economic and Social Research, University of Essex.

Berthoud, R. (1999) *Young Caribbean men and the labour market: A comparison with other ethnic groups*, York: York Publishing Services for the Joseph Rowntree Foundation.

Berthoud, R. (2000) *Family formation in multi-cultural Britain: Three patterns of diversity*, Colchester: Institute for Social and Economic Research, University of Essex.

Bevan, V. (1986) *The development of British immigration law*, London: Croom Helm.

Blackaby, D.H., Leslie, D.G., Murphy, P.D. and O'Leary, N.C. (2002) 'White/ethnic minority earnings and employment differentials in Britain: evidence from the LFS', *Oxford Economic Papers*, vol 54, pp 270-97.

Bloch, A. (1993) *Access to benefits: The information needs of minority ethnic groups*, London: Policy Studies Institute.

Bloch, A. (1997) 'Ethnic inequality and social security', in A. Walker and C. Walker (eds) *Britain divided: The growth of social exclusion in the 1980s and 1990s*, London: CPAG, pp 111-22.

Bloch, A. (1999) 'As if being a refugee isn't hard enough: the policy of exclusion', in P. Cohen (ed) *New ethnicities, old racisms*, London: Zed Books, pp 111-30.

Cantle, T. (2001) *Community cohesion: A report of the Independent Review Team chaired by Ted Cantle*, London: Home Office.

Corden, A. and Craig, P. (1991) *Perceptions of Family Credit*, London: HMSO.

CPAG (Child Poverty Action Group) (2000) *Welfare benefits handbook 2000/2001*, London: CPAG.

Craig, P. (1991) 'Cash and benefits: a review of research on take-up of income related benefits', *Journal of Social Policy*, vol 10, no 4, pp 537-66.

DfEE (Department for Education and Employment) (1999) *Jobs for all*, London: DfEE.

DSS (Department of Social Security) (2000) *The changing welfare state: Pensioner incomes*, DSS Paper No 2, London: DSS.

DSS (2001) *Family Resources Survey: Great Britain 1999-2000*, Leeds: Corporate Document Services.

DWP (Department for Work and Pensions) (2002a) 'New Deal for Young People and Long-Term Unemployed People aged 25+: Statistics to December 2001', *Statistics First Release*, February.

DWP (2002b) *Equality, opportunity and independence for all*, Race Equality Consultation Document, London: DWP.

Falkingham, F. (1986) *Take up of benefits: A literature review*, Nottingham: Benefits Research Unit, Nottingham University.

Fry, V. and Stark, G. (1993) *The take-up of means-tested benefits 1984-90*, London: Institute for Fiscal Studies.

Gordon, P. and Newnham, A. (1985) *Passport to benefits? Racism in social security*, London: CPAG/Runnymede Trust.

Heath, A. and McMahon, D. (1997) 'Education and occupational attainments: the impact of ethnic origins', in V. Karn (ed) *Ethnicity in the 1991 Census. Volume Four: Employment, education and housing among the ethnic minority populations of Britain*, London: The Stationery Office, pp 91-113.

Home Office (2000) *Race equality in public services*, London: Home Office Communications Directorate.

Home Office (2001) *Race equality in public services*, London: Home Office Communications Directorate.

Home Office (2002) *Secure borders, safe haven*, Immigration and Asylum White Paper, Cm 5387, London: The Stationery Office.

Law, I. (1996) *Racism, ethnicity and social policy*, Hemel Hempstead: Prentice Hall.

Law, I. (2002) 'Racism, ethnicity and benefits', *Benefits*, vol 10 issue 1, pp 30-1.

Law, I., Hylton, C., Karmani, A. and Deacon, A. (1994a) *Racial equality and social security sevice delivery: A study of the perceptions and experiences of Black minority ethnic people eligible for benefit in Leeds*, Leeds: University of Leeds.

Law, I., Hylton, C., Karmani, A. and Deacon, A. (1994b) 'The effect of ethnicity on claiming benefits: evidence from Chinese and Bangladeshi communities', *Benefits*, January, pp 7-11.

LPC (Low Pay Commission) (1998) *The National Minimum Wage*, First Report, Cm 3976, London: The Stationery Office.

LPC (2000) *The National Minimum Wage: The story so far*, Second Report, Cm 4571, London: The Stationery Office.

LPC (2001) *The National Minimum Wage: Making a difference*, Third Report, Cm 5075, London: The Stationery Office.

Matz, D., Hill, R. and Heath, T. (2001) *Asylum statistics, United Kingdom 2000*, London: Home Office Statistical Bulletin.

Modood, T. (1997) 'Qualifications and English language', in T. Modood, R. Berthoud et al *Ethnic minorities in Britain: Diversity and disadvantage*, London: Policy Studies Institute, pp 60-82.

Modood, T., Berthoud, R. et al (1997) *Ethnic minorities in Britain: Diversity and disadvantage*, London: Policy Studies Institute.

NACAB (National Association of Citizens' Advice Bureaux) (1991) *Barriers to benefit: Black claimants and social security*, London: NACAB.

NACAB (1996) 'Failing the test', *Benefits*, April/May, pp 19-20.

ONS (Office for National Statistics) (2000) *Labour market trends*, March, London: The Stationery Office.

ONS (2001a) *Population Trends*, vol 105, autumn, London: The Stationery Office.

ONS (2001b) *Social Trends*, vol 31, London: The Stationery Office.

Parekh, B. (2000) *The future of multi-ethnic Britain: The Parekh report*, London: Profile Books.

Patel, B. (2002) 'All change for asylum support policy, but will it be any more humane and fair?', *Benefits*, vol 10, issue 1, pp 41-4.

Peach, C. (ed) (1996) *Ethnicity in the 1991 Census. Volume Two: The ethnic minority populations of Great Britain*, London: The Stationery Office.

PIU (Performance and Innovation Unit) (2002) *Ethnic minorities and the labour market: Interim analytical report*, London: Cabinet Office.

Platt, L. (2002) *Parallel lives? Poverty among ethnic minority groups*, London: CPAG.

Platt, L. (2003: forthcoming) 'Ethnicity and inequality: British children's experience of means-tested benefits', *Journal of Comparative Family Studies*, Special Issue on Families' and Children's Inequalities, vol 34, no 3.

Platt, L. and Noble, M. (1999) *Race, place and poverty*, York: York Publishing Services for the Joseph Rowntree Foundation.

Simpson, N. (1991) 'Equal treatment? – Black claimants and social security', *Benefits*, September/October, pp 14-17.

SEU (Social Exclusion Unit) (2000) *Minority ethnic issues in social exclusion and neighbourhood renewal*, London: Cabinet Office.

Website resources

Commission for Racial Equality	www.cre.gov.uk
Department for Education and Skills	www.dfes.gov.uk
Department for Work and Pensions	www.dwp.gov.uk
Home Office	www.homeoffice.gov.uk
Low Pay Commission	www.lowpay.gov.uk
Refugee Council	www.refugeecouncil.org.uk
Runnymede Trust	www.runnymedetrust.org
Social Exclusion Unit	www.socialexclusionunit.gov.uk

fourteen

Understanding social security fraud

Roy Sainsbury

Summary

Social security fraud is a serious issue for governments for a number of reasons: it is a drain on public finances, it undermines support for social security, and it is antithetical to the government's welfare reform agenda. This chapter:

- increases understanding of social security fraud, its complexity and diversity;

- enables readers to interpret official statistics on fraud and puts the rhetoric of fraud (from politicians and the media) into perspective;

- examines the question of why people commit fraud and explores what policy makers have attempted to do in response to the 'problem'.

Introduction: understanding fraud

For anyone taking an interest in social security over the last 10-15 years references to benefit fraud will be only too familiar. Successive governments have sought to present fraud as a serious issue, not just for themselves as policy makers and custodians of the public purse, but also for every one of us as citizens whose welfare system is under attack. The message has been consistent: fraud is widespread, fraud is depriving the nation of resources badly needed elsewhere, fraud deserves a tough and uncompromising response.

In this chapter we will be looking at the phenomenon of social security fraud. To begin we will pose some simple questions: what is 'fraud'? Why is it seemingly such an important issue? It will soon become apparent that fraud is complex and diverse. We will then critically examine official sources of data about fraud to assess what they do, and do not, tell us about fraud. We then go on to explore why people commit fraud; policy responses to fraud; and public attitudes and political and media representations of fraud.

What is fraud?

Fraud can be defined as *the deliberate misrepresentation of circumstances with the intent of gaining some advantage*. This is a definition of fraud at the conceptual level. It applies equally to the public sphere (including the social security system, and the tax and tax credits systems) and the private sphere (including, for example, insurance). For the purposes of this chapter we will concentrate on *benefit* fraud, by which we mean obtaining money through the benefit system by fraudulent means. Misrepresenting circumstances with the intention of avoiding making payments of national insurance contributions or through the child maintenance system is also fraud, but as yet too little is known from official or research sources to make an informed analysis.

The *deliberate misrepresentation of circumstances* in the definition can be either by *commission*, actively giving false information on a claim form or in an interview, or by *omission*, knowingly withholding information that might affect a claim. The possibilities for misrepresenting personal circumstances are enormous, but it is also possible to do this unintentionally. Given the complexities of the benefit system and the large amount of personal information needed on claim forms, it is not surprising that people make mistakes, miss things out or misunderstand what is required. Genuine mistakes may lead to an overpayment of benefit, but because there has been no *intent* to defraud then by definition no fraud has been committed. In principle, any of the rules contained in the various Acts of Parliament or statutory instruments for determining entitlement to a benefit can be defrauded. Some common examples are set out in Box 14.1.

Defining fraud and giving hypothetical examples of how fraud can be

> **Box 14.1: Some common benefit frauds**
>
> - Not declaring earnings from work
> - Not declaring other income, such as an occupational pension
> - Claiming as a single person while living with someone else
> - Creating a false identity and claiming benefit
> - Not declaring savings
> - Feigning or exaggerating illness or disability
> - Claiming Child Benefit for non-existent children
> - Creating a false tenancy and claiming Housing Benefit

committed is, as mentioned above, easy. Identifying a case of fraud in practice is less straightforward. Yet it is important to be able to distinguish fraudulent from non-fraudulent cases if we are to attempt to measure the amount of fraud in the social security system, a measure policy makers need to know in order to devise appropriate policy responses and to make decisions about the deployment of resources. We will return to the problems of measuring fraud below, but before then it is worth considering the question of why fraud is perceived (at least by politicians and policy makers) to be such a problem.

Why is fraud an important issue?

Fraud can be considered an issue for governments on a number of different levels. First, it is an *economic issue*. Social security spending in the UK is around £110 billion a year. It accounts for about 30% of all public expenditure. Thus even when a small percentage of expenditure is the result of fraud, large amounts of money are involved. Losses to fraud are often presented in terms of opportunities lost. In its 1998 Green Paper, *Beating fraud is everyone's business* (DSS, 1998b, p 2), the government claimed that the £2 billion that it estimated was lost to fraud each year "could be used to meet the cost of income support for one million pensioners who do not currently take up their entitlement *and* to pay £2 a week in child benefit for 12 million children". More recently, Malcolm Wicks, in his capacity as Minister of State responsible for fraud policy, was quoted as saying that the money saved from reducing fraud between 1998 and 2001 "would pay for an extra 2,500 doctors or nearly 6,000 nurses" (DWP, 2002b).

Fraud can also be construed as an *issue for society* in a number of other ways. Fraud is often characterised as theft, as stealing from law-abiding citizens who either pay their taxes or who receive benefits legitimately. Theft, as crime, is unacceptable and therefore, the argument continues, cannot be condoned. Fraudsters are characterised as criminals and therefore no tolerance should be shown in dealing with them. Furthermore, it is also sometimes argued that if fraud is not detected and stopped it may become an established pattern of behaviour that can spread to others, creating a subculture of criminal activity that may be passed from generation to generation.

Fraud, and particularly people getting away with fraud, is also perceived by politicians as undermining public support for the social security system:

> Fraud undermines the integrity and purpose of the social security system. Taxpayers and genuine claimants support the system on the basis that resources go to those who are entitled, not to those who are dishonest. (DSS, 1998a, p 67)

Overall, therefore, fraud is an important *political issue*. The contours of the issue have changed over time. At one time in the early 1990s, it appeared that getting tough on fraud was perceived as a vote winner by the then Secretary of State for Social Security, Peter Lilley, who carved out a reputation at successive Conservative party conferences as a hard-line adversary of fraudsters. For the Labour government of 2002 fraud is presented as a challenge to the type of society that it is attempting to create, a society where earned income through work is a central element of social inclusion. It is an issue, therefore, because of its connections to the major project of the Blair government, the reform of the welfare system away from being a passive supplier of income to people disconnected from the world of work to being an active instrument of policy designed to help people join the labour market.

Examining the evidence base

Since the beginning of the 1990s governments have been seemingly mesmerised by measuring the amount of fraud in the social security system and assessing the impact of their counter-fraud operations.

Early attempts at measuring fraud

The first systematic attempts to measure fraud were made in the mid-1990s in a series of what were called *national benefit reviews*. These were one-off exercises in which a large sample of cases was scrutinised to identify incorrect payments that were then categorised as either cases of fraud or error. Between 1995 and 1998 benefit reviews were carried out on Income Support (twice, in 1995 and 1997), Housing Benefit (twice, in 1996 and 1998), Unemployment Benefit (1995), Retirement Pension (1996), Invalid Care Allowance (1996), Disability Living Allowance (1997) and Child Benefit (1998). The methodology represented an important step forward but there were a number of criticisms and problems with the national benefit reviews that cast doubt on their reliability and accuracy (Sainsbury, 1996). Despite the technical difficulties with the national reviews, it is probable that the unhelpful results they produced contributed to their demise. For example, it was with some embarrassment that the Labour government announced in 1997 that the second Income Support review revealed an *increase* in the amount of fraud (from £1,400 million to £1,800 million) despite record levels of resources being ploughed into counter-fraud work. Also, the review of Disability Living Allowance apparently showed that there was a greater proportion of fraud (12.2% of claims) on this benefit by disabled people than any of the other benefits investigated – for example, the rate for Income Support was 11.1% in 1997, and 7.8% for Unemployment Benefit in 1995 (DSS, 1998b, p 56)[1].

Before this programme of reviews was completed, work was already underway to develop the next generation measurement system that would deliver a continuous measure of the amount of fraud and error rather than snapshot measures.

Next generation measurement: the big picture

The new system, called *area benefit reviews* (ABRs), is based on a rolling monthly sample of a number of cases from each of the 13 'area directorates' of the Department for Work and Pensions[2] (for a more detailed, and critical, assessment of ABR methodology, see Sainsbury, 2001). This was a big and costly operation and introduced initially for only two benefits, Income Support and Jobseeker's Allowance. A one-off ABR report for Incapacity Benefit appeared in 2001, and the system is being extended to Housing Benefit with the first report expected later in 2003.

Before looking at some results for Income Support and Jobseeker's Allowance, we should be clear that the ABR methodology excludes two important types of fraud. First, because only individual claims are checked, the reviews do not identify large frauds involving networks or gangs of individuals, usually referred to as *organised fraud*. (We shall return to the problem of organised fraud in the next section.) Also, they do not identify frauds that are based on the theft or counterfeiting of benefit order books, known in the jargon of the Department as *instrument of payment* (IOP) *frauds*. The figures presented in ABR reports are therefore underestimates of the extent of fraud in the social security system. The headline figure produced in the ABR reports, cited by politicians in speeches and press releases, refers to the total amount of *fraud and error* (that is, not fraud alone) in Income Support and Jobseeker's Allowance combined. The reports also contain data on the amount of money underpaid to claimants

---

[1] The subsequent special programme (called the 'Benefit Integrity Project') targeting people with high rates of Disability Living Allowance awards was a policy and public relations disaster for the new government (Allirajah, 1997; Sainsbury, 1998).

[2] Following the merger of the Benefits Agency and the Employment Service in 2001 to form 'Jobcentre Plus' the 13 area directorates were amalgamated into seven Government Office Regions.

due to errors made by themselves or by social security officials, although these do not receive the same publicity as the amounts of money lost. The latest figures (DWP, 2002a) show:

- a headline figure of about £1.2 billion was estimated to have been overpaid due to fraud and error in Income Support and Jobseeker's Allowance in 2000/01;
- of the total lost, about £774 million was due to fraud, the remaining £426 million was due to error;
- 5.4% of Income Support cases (204,000) and 8.6% of Jobseeker's Allowance cases (86,000) were found to be fraudulent. In contrast, claimant error was found in 7.8% (296,000) of Income Support cases, and 2.0% (20,000) of Jobseeker's Allowance cases;
- the most common types of fraud were failing to declare earnings (over 30% of the total overpayments) and failure to declare a partner (nearly 25% of the total);
- in addition, about £189 million was estimated to have been lost to individuals as a result of underpayments in Income Support and Jobseeker's Allowance caused by errors by claimants and officials;
- most (almost 70%) of the underpayments of Income Support and Jobseeker's Allowance was a result of official error; the rest was as a result of claimant error. The largest proportion of these underpayments (40% of the total amount lost to individual claimants) was in relation to payments to pensioners.

Trends over time

Figure 14.1 shows the trends since 1997/98 in fraud and error for Income Support and Jobseeker's Allowance separately, and combined (the headline figure). The 1997/98 figures provide the baseline from which targets for fraud reductions have been set (see further discussion below). At that time it was estimated that about 9% of the money paid out in Income Support and Jobseeker's Allowance was the result of fraud and error. This has fallen steadily since then. Jobseeker's Allowance fraud and error rose to 14% in 1998/99 but has since fallen quite sharply to about 10%. Income Support fraud and error was already lower and has fallen steadily.

The ABR reports also allow us to distinguish between fraud and error. This is important since, although both fraud and error represent money leaking from the social security system, they present different policy challenges. **Table 14.1** shows trends since 1997/98 in the amounts of money lost in fraud compared with the losses to fraud and error combined.

Table 14.1 clearly shows how efforts to reduce fraud and error have had differential impacts. The smooth decline in the headline figure masks some

Figure 14.1: Trends in Income Support and Jobseeker's Allowance fraud and error (1997-2001)

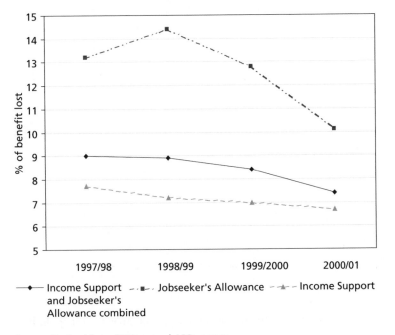

Source: Derived from DWP annual ABR reports

interesting variations. For example, in 1999-2000, the amount of fraud actually rose, and the overall reduction in fraud and error was due entirely to reductions in error. The overall reduction in Income Support and Jobseeker's Allowance over the four years since 1997-98 was 13% (from £1.38 billion to £1.2 billion). However, the reduction in the amount lost to Income Support fraud fell by only 4% during this period and has been rising for the past two years. In contrast, Jobseeker's Allowance fraud fell dramatically by 33% in the four-year period.

Table 14.1: Amount of money lost to fraud and error in Income Support and Jobseeker's Allowance (1997-2001) (£)

	1997-98	1998-99	1999-2000	2000-01
All error	482 m	565 m	495 m	426 m
All fraud	898 m	805 m	825 m	774 m
Income Support fraud only	*596 m*	*549 m*	*559 m*	*573 m*
Jobseeker's Allowance fraud only	*302 m*	*256 m*	*266 m*	*201 m*
Income Support and Jobseeker's Allowance (fraud + all error)	1.38 bn	1.37 bn	1.32 bn	1.20 bn

Source: Derived from DWP annual ABR reports

Figure 14.2: Trends in benefit lost to Income Support/Jobseeker's Allowance fraud, by claimant group (1997/98 to 2000/01)

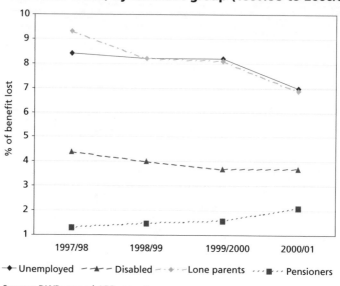

Source: DWP annual ABR reports

Figure 14.2 presents trends in the amount of fraud (that is, not including errors) for each of the four main claimant groups receiving Income Support or Jobseeker's Allowance. It is interesting to note that unemployed people and lone parents are responsible for the highest levels of fraud compared with disabled people and pensioners, but that these levels are declining in line with the decline in the headline figures (as shown in **Figure 14.1**). In fact the only group who appear to be bucking this trend are pensioners whose level of fraud (although still small) has risen year on year since measurements began (from 1.3% in 1997/98 to 2.1% in 2000/01).

To sum up, the evidence base from the ABRs for the amount of fraud in the social security system is better now than at any time in the past. Evidence from the earlier series of national benefit reviews must now be regarded with a great deal of caution, and old statistics on the amounts of savings made from counter-fraud activity must be considered seriously flawed. However, we now have an official source of statistics that provides not only a headline figure on which performance targets have been based, but also data at a disaggregated level (for example, claimant type, type of fraud, geographical area) which is useful for informing policy thinking. Nevertheless, what we have at present is only partial information. The new measurement system has provided figures only for Income Support and Jobseeker's Allowance since 1998, and organised fraud, and IOP frauds, are not captured in the official statistics. Interpreting fraud statistics, therefore, should always be done with a healthy degree of caution, and for data before 1998 with some scepticism.

Understanding fraudulent behaviour

There is a growing evidence base on the reasons why people commit social security fraud. Some evidence has come from studies that have deliberately set out to investigate fraud or aspects of the informal economy (MacDonald, 1994; Evason and Woods, 1995; Dean and Melrose, 1996; Rowlingson et al, 1997). Other evidence has emerged in the course of work investigating the experiences and aspirations of people living on low incomes (Bradshaw and Holmes, 1989; Cook, 1989; Jordan et al, 1992). Interestingly, only one of these sources (Rowlingson et al, 1997) is a government-funded piece of work.

The research cited above is mainly concerned with fraud committed by individual claimants, rather than organised gangs, and cover a variety of frauds, although the dominant example is people working while still claiming. There are some examples of lone parents living with a partner but claiming as a single person, or failing to declare sources of income, but few instances of other types of fraud. The frauds are also mainly committed while claiming means-tested benefits such as Income Support and Housing Benefit, rather than other benefits such as Incapacity Benefit or Disability Living Allowance. The research evidence is therefore limited to a degree but nonetheless useful.

People tend to offer different types of explanation for their fraudulent behaviour. The most common explanation is couched in terms of economic necessity. People say that they cannot manage on the low level of income provided by the social security system to meet the needs of themselves and their families, what Dean and Melrose (1996) call a discourse of 'deprivation and hardship'. This is sometimes accompanied by arguments around economic rationality (Rowlingson et al, 1997) or justified disobedience (Dean and Melrose, 1996). People say that if they did declare income from a one-off or short-term piece of work then they would either be worse off (because they would lose more benefit than they gained in wages) or risk a cash crisis while their benefit was being reassessed. It is therefore rational for them *not* to declare earnings. Claimants who deploy arguments around justified disobedience direct the responsibility for their fraud on to the benefit system itself, arguing that the low level of benefits and the cumbersome and unreliable processes of administration (what Jordan et al, 1992, call 'administrative traps') effectively force them into some form of fraudulent activity to survive.

In their study of fraudulent claimants in the mid-1990s, Dean and Melrose (1996, 1997) analysed people's accounts and explanations for their behaviour in terms of two dimensions: what they called the *reflexivity* and the *anxiety* contained within them. By reflexivity, they are referring to the extent to which people reflect or think about their actions while engaged in fraudulent activity, and by anxiety the extent to which they harbour feelings of conflict or insecurity and concerns about the possible consequences of their actions. Dean and Melrose argue that it is possible to categorise each of their respondents as having relatively high or low levels of reflexivity and anxiety, and that by combining the dimensions a fourfold typology of fraudsters emerges, as shown in Box 14.2.

Subversive claimants often used a discourse of justified disobedience, and were able to offer quite complex explanations for their behaviour, without being troubled by conflicts or worries about the consequences of their actions. They thought about what they did but were confident and comfortable with their actions in the context of a mean and punitive social security system. *Desperate* claimants could also explain their actions but were more likely to refer to economic necessity and to display feelings of doubt and insecurity. They too knew what they were doing but did not feel comfortable and they worried about being found out. The *fatalistic* claimants, in contrast, only had weakly argued justifications for their frauds, which were often impulsive and opportunistic, and about which they worried afterwards. The final group is perhaps the most challenging in policy terms. *Unprincipled* claimants tended not to justify their actions at all, or feel the need to, and seemed insulated from feelings of conflict or anxiety. They lived on (or beyond) the fringes of legal economic activity and the social security system to them was just one of possibly several sources of (illicit) income. This analysis suggests that distinctive policy responses might be needed for each of the four ideal types of fraudster, for example, policies aimed at desperate claimants should look different to those aimed at curbing the unprincipled group of fraudsters.

As yet we lack comparable research evidence on the motivations of people who defraud the social security system in other ways (such as failing to declare income or savings, or who feign or exaggerate illness or disability). Similarly, we know little about the people who perpetrate large, organised frauds. However, in designing measures to counter organised fraud, there is perhaps less need to understand motivations than to understand how such frauds are committed.

Box 14.2: The Dean–Melrose typology of fraudulent claimants

		Anxiety	
		Low	High
Reflexivity	High	'Subversive' claimants (self-confident philosophers)	'Desperate' claimants (calculative worriers)
	Low	'Unprincipled' claimants (macho survivors)	'Fatalistic' claimants (unreflexive opportunists)

Source: Derived from Dean and Melrose (1996, 1997)

Fraud cultures and careers

Studies of individual fraudsters also reveal the extent to which they are connected to networks that either facilitate fraudulent behaviour or provide opportunities for collusion with the intent of committing fraud (Jordan et al, 1992; MacDonald, 1994). In an interesting, unpublished study to investigate fraud within a small seaside town, Haines (1999) found that a small fraudulent 'community' had developed based around a number of pubs in the town centre, in which tips and advice were exchanged, opportunities for work passed on, and 'new' fraudsters initiated into social security fraud (by, for example, passing on knowledge about benefits and administrative processes, and providing help with completing claim forms). Haines also suggests that, while it was possible to identify people in her sample who conformed to the Dean and Melrose ideal types, it was apparent that the typology was not static, but dynamic, in that people could move between types. For example an opportunistic fraudster in the fatalistic category could become a subversive or an unprincipled fraudster after committing a series of unconnected, but undetected, frauds. Similarly, an initial desperate claimant might become subversive if they changed their justification for their fraud away from inward-looking reflections about their own need and towards an external focus on the unfairness or meanness of the benefit system.

An important and consistent finding of these studies is that while fraudulent cultures might develop, these do not, for many of the individuals involved, conflict with or undermine a more dominant culture based on an acceptance of the moral value of paid work (Jordan et al, 1992; MacDonald, 1994; Evason and Woods, 1995; Dean and Melrose, 1996; Rowlingson et al, 1997). There is, in other words, little evidence for the existence of a persistent and distinct class of people who reject, and choose to live outside, the mainstream values of society.

It also appears that the rules and regulations of the social security system are ill-suited to the lives of many people whom it is meant to serve. Modern patterns of household formation and of economic activity (driven partly by new forms of work and remuneration) are not reflected in benefit rules with their roots in a post-war period typified by full employment, the two-parent family, and the dominant role of the male breadwinner. Many people are therefore faced with hard choices between acting legally, and suffering hardship, or acting illegally, and making ends meet.

It appears clear that lessons learned from more exploration of the nature and causes of fraud could usefully be turned into ideas for reforming the benefit system, which in turn might redefine the 'problem' of fraud.

Counter-fraud policies

In its welfare reform Green Paper, the Labour government set out the broad parameters of its 'campaign against fraud', which were "more effective deterrence; better prevention; and improved detection" (DSS, 1998a, p 67). These three elements of counter-fraud policy have been features of successive governments' approaches to fraud, but, as we shall see, the balance between them has shifted from an emphasis on detection towards a greater prominence for prevention and deterrence.

This change in balance is particularly marked after 1997. Before then, under the stewardship of Peter Lilley as Conservative Secretary of State for Social Security, thinking about fraud was dominated by the implicit understanding (that is, in the absence of any systematic knowledge about its extent and nature) that fraud in the social security system was widespread and had to be stopped by identifying and dealing with existing cases of fraud. This approach was perhaps inadvertently reinforced by the long-standing administrative practice of calculating the *benefit savings* that accrued from stopping fraud. At the beginning of the 1990s, benefit savings were the only measure of the effect of counter-fraud activity. It is not surprising therefore that Lilley adopted savings as the basis of performance targets for the then Benefits Agency and for local authorities. What resulted was a counter-fraud culture in both policy and delivery that emphasised the *detection* of fraud. If performance was measured and, importantly, staff were rewarded by the amount of savings generated by catching fraudsters, then it is little wonder that less attention was paid to preventing or deterring fraud.

The clearest manifestation of the policy interest in detection was the release of resources to recruit more fraud officers in the Benefits Agency and local authorities. By the mid-1990s around 5,000 staff of the then Department of Social Security were engaged in counter-fraud work (of a total staff of around 80,000). Despite this preoccupation with detecting fraud there was also a growing realisation within policy-making circles that prevention and deterrence could perhaps play an increased role in tackling fraud. Under the Lilley administration, therefore, we saw the introduction of highly publicised local counter-fraud campaigns aimed at deterring potential fraudsters. Special teams of investigators were assigned to a local area for a short time during which they actively sought out cases of fraud (rather than passively waiting for referrals and tip-offs), which would then be the basis for an aggressive assault on the media. During this time, the Department of Social Security were also developing administrative systems aimed at increasing the verification of information provided by social security claimants when making initial claims for benefit, in an attempt to prevent fraud entering the system. Underpinning all this activity, as outlined above, was the first systematic (although flawed) attempt at measuring the amount of fraud.

In the year or so leading up to the 1997 General Election, the Conservative government had been working on another wave of counter-fraud measures that needed primary legislation. In fact, the last piece of legislation passed by the outgoing government was the 1997 Social Security Administration (Fraud) Act (see McKeever, 1999). The Bill was largely unchallenged by the Labour opposition as it was pushed hurriedly through the parliamentary process. The Act contained a variety of measures aimed at increasing the powers of detection, prevention and deterrence of fraud, including:

- new powers to share information between government departments (including tax records held by the Inland Revenue);
- the introduction of 'administrative penalties' which benefit authorities could use in place of the sanction of prosecution;
- powers to recover benefit payments from landlords;
- powers to prevent the redirecting of mail (to prevent the use of false addresses in the commission of fraud);
- the establishment of a new inspectorate, the Benefit Fraud Inspectorate, charged with investigating the quality of counter-fraud working in the Benefits Agency and local authorities.

Despite inheriting a piece of legislation aimed specifically at tackling fraud, the Labour government maintained, and possibly increased, its policy interest in fraud. Fraud was the subject of a whole chapter of the government's welfare reform Green Paper in 1998 (DSS, 1998a). A review of fraud begun by John Denham, a junior minister in the Department of Social Security was completed by Frank Field when he assumed ministerial responsibility for fraud in 1998, and resulted in a separate Green Paper, *Beating fraud is everyone's business* (DSS, 1998b). After a period of consultation, the government's blueprint for action was set out by the Secretary of State, Alistair Darling, in a strategy document *Safeguarding social security* (DSS, 1999). This unprecedented level of policy activity reflects the seriousness with which the Labour government viewed fraud. As explained earlier, fraud and error were recognised as significant drains on public finances, as well as being seen as dangerous threats to the integrity of a social security system whose reform stood at the heart of the government's major social policy project.

Many of the changes outlined in *Safeguarding social security* could be implemented administratively, but some needed further legislation. The administrative changes included:

- the introduction of targets for the reduction of fraud and error;
- moving away from payments by order book towards payment by automatic transfers to bank accounts for the majority of benefit recipients;
- the introduction of professional training and qualifications for fraud officers;

- measures to increase cooperation between benefit authorities and the police;
- tighter verification procedures of information provided by claimants;
- tightening procedures for people applying for national insurance numbers.

In addition, Alistair Darling set in train reviews of organised fraud and of the range of penalties for fraudsters. The review of organised fraud was completed in 2000 (Scampion, 2000) and led to a reorganisation of the counter-fraud branches of the Department of Social Security (now the Department for Work and Pensions). The review of penalties fed into the provisions of a new Bill aimed at fraud, which became the 2001 Social Security Fraud Act.

The 2001 Act is therefore the latest in a long line of policy change and innovation stretching back over 10-12 years. Its main provisions are:

- new powers for fraud officers to access information from a variety of organisations, such as banks, building societies, insurance companies and utility companies, where a case of fraud is suspected;
- tougher penalties for employers who collude in frauds;
- new laws ('two strikes and you're out') to punish persistent offenders.

Taking stock in 2002, the changes in *Safeguarding social security* and in the 2001 Social Security Fraud Act were at various stages of implementation and further ideas are under consideration (such as the introduction of a credit card style 'entitlement card'). Overall, the policy and administrative environment of counter-fraud activity is a very different one from that of the late 1980s and early 1990s. Every aspect of counter-fraud work – deterrence, prevention and detection – has been expanded and strengthened, and in theory it should be harder than ever for people to carry out successful frauds or to remain undetected if they do.

However, other policy developments are likely to bring new fraud issues to the fore. The introduction of tax credits to replace old social security benefits brings with it new opportunities for the potential fraudulent claimant and fraudulent employer, which must be addressed not by the fraud-experienced Department for Work and Pensions but by the comparative newcomers, the Inland Revenue. New joined-up benefit and employment policies, with new sources of funding (for example, for training) available to eligible claimants, will also present new opportunities for fraud. And the policy decision to replace order books with automatic bank transfer payments brings with it the risk of new, high-tech assaults on the social security budget.

Fraud in the public domain

Ministers have always sought opportunities to make political capital from social security fraud. The tone of their public presentations of fraud has changed over the past 10-15 years but the type of content has remained largely consistent. Speeches and press releases have usually contained either an announcement of the latest policy initiative taken against fraudsters, or the latest figures demonstrating successes in dealing with the problem. The tone has always been tough and robust, sometimes theatrical (bordering on the distasteful when groups of the claiming population such as lone mothers have been singled out for particular opprobrium; see Golding, 1999), but more recently comparatively low key. The rhetoric of the policy analysis of, and policy responses to, fraud, has frequently adopted the vocabulary of battle. In the 'war', 'battle' or 'fight' against fraud the latest 'weapons' and 'campaigns' are launched against fraudsters who constantly 'attack' the social security system. The last Conservative governments up to 1997 tended to favour a rather bombastic style combining searing condemnation of fraudsters and grand claims for their own achievements in combating them, combining huge sums of money and lurid accounts of the exploits of fraudsters (see Golding, 1999). The Labour government continued in similar vein when it took office in 1997. In 2000, for example, the then Secretary of State for Social Security, Alistair Darling, was claiming that "... we are winning the fight against fraud" (DSS, 2000) in a press release announcing that the amount of fraud and error in Income Support and Jobseeker's Allowance had fallen from 9 to 8.9%. In recent years, however, the government has stepped back from grand claims for its successes and has adopted an unfamiliar downbeat approach. When the level of fraud fell to 7.4% in the year 2000-01, thus reaching the government's own target over a year ahead of schedule, the accompanying press release (DWP, 2001) used language devoid of any rhetoric whatsoever: "Secretary of State for Work and Pensions, Alistair Darling today welcomed figures showing that the Government has achieved an 18 per cent reduction in the amount of fraud and error in Income Support and Jobseeker's Allowance".

This unemotional and accurate style of reporting is not in use consistently, however. In 2002, a government press release (DWP, 2002b) claimed that "Since 1998 we have saved £180 million by cracking down on fraud in income support and jobseeker's allowance". If we look at the government's own figures, however (see **Table 14.1** above), we see that the £180 million refers to *both* fraud and error, not just fraud (where the reduction is 50% less at £124 million). Also, this way of presenting a reduction in the stock of fraud as 'savings' might be considered a little misrepresentative in itself.

It is interesting to contrast the fluctuating style of ministerial pronouncements about fraud with the consistently sensationalist tone adopted by the popular press in Britain. Golding and Middleton (1982) and Golding (1999) chronicle the tabloid press' fascination and indignation over the past 25 years or so with people who defraud social security. (This preoccupation is nothing new. Deacon [1976, 1978] has analysed how unemployed claimants in the 1920s and 1930s were at the time similarly vilified as 'scroungers'.) Examples from recent years include: "Benefit cheat trapped by his wife's Mercedes" (*Daily Telegraph*, 7 April 2001); "£1.2m benefit fraud: we can't stop the benefit fraudsters. Five favourite scams of the handout thieves" (*Daily Mail*, 12 January 2000); "Benefit cheat claimed for 43 children" (*Daily Mail*, 25 January 2000).

The consistent picture painted by the tabloids (and sometimes the so-called quality press) over the years may help to explain public perceptions of social security fraud. For over 15 years the British Social Attitudes survey has asked respondents to agree or disagree with the following two statements:

• 'large numbers of people these days falsely claim benefits';
• 'most people on the dole are fiddling in one way or another'.

The trends in the responses to these questions are interesting but not necessarily easy to interpret. Levels of agreement with the first question have been consistently high. In 1994, 72% of respondents believed that large numbers of people falsely claimed benefits, rising to 83% in 1998 before falling back to 77% in 2000 (Hills, 2001). In 1987, 32% of respondents agreed that 'most people on the dole are fiddling'. This figure rose only marginally to 34% in 1994, but reached a 15-year high in 2000 at 40% (Hills and Lelkes, 1999; Hills, 2001). It is possible that people might understand the rather old-fashioned language of 'the dole' to mean all social security benefits or, more narrowly, Unemployment Benefits. Notwithstanding this possible ambiguity, official statistics show clearly that *most* claimants do not fiddle their social security. As we have seen above, only 5.4% of Income Support cases and 8.6% of Jobseeker's Allowance cases were deemed to be fraudulent in 2000-01 (DWP, 2002a).

It appears therefore that the public have an exaggerated view of the extent of social security fraud. Despite the improvements in official statistics that show otherwise, public perceptions, as reflected in successive Social Attitudes Surveys, appear to have changed little away from the notion that fraud is widespread. Whether the explanation for this mismatch between perceptions and evidence is largely accounted for by the presentation of fraud and social security claimants in the popular press is unclear. Personal experience, the pronouncements of public figures such as government ministers, and ignorance and prejudice will also inform opinions. Nevertheless, if large sections of the public think fraud is rife, it is a fact that politicians would be ill-advised to ignore. High levels of public concern are not necessarily a bad thing for the Department for Work and Pensions, they can be mobilised in the fight for resources within government and for getting public support for counter-fraud policies that might be construed as increasing the barriers people face in claiming benefits.

Overview

Social security fraud has exerted a powerful grip on the imaginations of politicians, policy makers, the media and the public for many years. However, it is only recently that any reliable estimates of the extent of fraud have been produced, and these are still partial and incomplete. The data suggest that the overall levels of fraud and error have been falling since 1997.

We know comparatively little about why people commit fraud. Different motivations for different types of fraudulent behaviour have been explored in research, including the idea of 'fraudulent cultures', but this issue is largely ignored in government analyses and policy documents. Fraud is also a construct of the rules, but there is little evidence that lessons about fraud have been translated into ideas for changing the benefit system.

There has been a significant amount of counter-fraud policy activity in recent years, including Green Papers, strategy documents and two Acts of Parliament. In particular, fraud officers have new powers to access information from a variety of sources, public and private, in cases where fraud is suspected. Detection of fraud remains central to counter-fraud activity, but in recent years prevention and deterrence have begun to play a more prominent role.

The challenge for policy makers is always to keep one step ahead of the hardened fraudster in the context of both social security benefits and the new tax credits; to ensure that counter-fraud activity and publicity does not discourage genuine claimants from claiming benefits to which they are entitled; and to make more creative and imaginative use of lessons derived from tackling fraud in thinking about reforms to the social security system.

Questions for discussion

1. Who, or what, do you think is most to blame for social security fraud? What is your evidence, and how robust is it?

2. What are the principal influences on the development of counter-fraud policy?

3. What challenges face the government in combating fraud in the social security, tax and employment budgets in the next 10 years?

References

Allirajah, D. (1997) 'Disability Living Allowance "Benefits Integrity Project"', *Welfare Rights Bulletin*, vol 139, August, p 7.

Bradshaw, J. and Holmes, H. (1989) *Living on the edge*, London: CPAG.

Cook, D. (1989) *Rich law, poor law*, Milton Keynes: Open University Press.

Deacon, A. (1976) *In search of the scrounger: The administration of Unemployment Insurance 1920-31*, Occasional Papers in Social Administration No 60, London: G. Bell & Sons Ltd.

Deacon, A. (1978) 'The scrounging controversy: public attitudes towards the unemployed in contemporary Britain', *Social and Economic Administration*, vol 12, no 2, pp 120-35.

Dean, H. and Melrose, M. (1996) 'Unravelling citizenship: the significance of social security fraud', *Critical Social Policy*, 48, vol 16, no 3, pp 3-31.

Dean, H. and Melrose, M. (1997) 'Manageable discord: fraud and resistance in the social security system', *Social Policy and Administration*, vol 31, no 2, pp 103-18.

DSS (Department of Social Security) (1998a) *New ambitions for our country: A new contract for welfare*, Cm 3805, London: The Stationery Office.

DSS (1998b) *Beating fraud is everyone's business: Securing the future*, Cm 4012, London: The Stationery Office.

DSS (1999) *A new contract for welfare: Safeguarding social security*, Cm 4276, London: The Stationery Office.

DSS (2000) 'Darling welcomes successes in fighting benefit fraud', Press release, 28 January.

DWP (Department for Work and Pensions) (2001) '2002 benefit fraud target met almost twice over – Darling', Press release, 29 November.

DWP (2002a) *The results of the area benefit review and the quality support team from April 2000 to March 2001: Fraud and error for Income Support and Jobseeker's Allowance*, London: DWP.

DWP (2002b) 'Wicks – £180 million saved in benefit fraud', Press release, 22 February.

Evason, E. and Woods, R. (1995) 'Poverty, deregulation of the labour market and benefit fraud', *Social Policy and Administration*, vol 29, no 1, pp 40-54.

Golding, P. (1999) 'Thinking the unthinkable: welfare reform and the media', in B. Franklin (ed) *Social policy, the media and misrepresentation*, London: Routledge, pp 145-56.

Golding, P. and Middleton, S. (1982) *Images of welfare*, Oxford: Basil Blackwell and Martin Robertson.

Haines, F. (1999) 'A few white lies', Unpublished MA dissertation, University of York.

Hills, J. (2001) 'Poverty and social security: what rights? Whose responsibilities?', in A. Park, J. Curtice, K. Thompson, L. Jarvis and C. Bromley, *British social attitudes: The 18th Report*, London: Sage Publications.

Hills, J. and Lelkes, O. (1999) 'Social security, selective universalism and patchwork redistribution', in R. Jowell, J. Curtice, A. Park and K. Thompson, *British social attitudes: The 16th Report*, London: Sage Publications.

Jordan, B., James, S., Kay, H. and Redley, M. (1992) *Trapped in poverty*, London: Routledge.

MacDonald, R. (1994) 'Fiddly jobs, undeclared working and the something for nothing society', *Work, Employment and Society*, vol 8, no 4, pp 507-30.

McKeever, G. (1999) 'Detecting, prosecuting and punishing benefit fraud: the Social Security Administration (Fraud) Act 1997', *Modern Law Review*, vol 62, no 2, pp 261-70.

Rowlingson, K., Whyley, C., Newburn, T. and Berthoud, R. (1997) *Social security fraud: The role of penalties*, DSS Research Report No 64, London: The Stationery Office.

Sainsbury, R. (1996) 'Rooting out fraud – innocent until proven fraudulent', *Poverty*, April, pp 17-20.

Sainsbury, R. (1998) 'The missing half billion – getting the real measure of fraud', *Disability Rights Bulletin*, Summer, pp 4-6.

Sainsbury, R. (2001) 'Getting the measure of fraud', *Poverty*, issue 108, winter, pp 10-14.

Scampion, J. (2000) *Organised benefit fraud*, London: DSS.

Website resources

Benefit Fraud Inspectorate   www.bfi.gov.uk

Targeting Fraud   www.targetingfraud.gov.uk

fifteen

Wired-up welfare: the impact of information and communication technology on social security

Karen Kellard

Summary

This final chapter examines the modernisation of welfare services through the development of information and communication technology (ICT). It covers three main areas:

- What is the government's vision for the use of information technology? How is this being applied to social security systems?

- What are the barriers to, or challenges involved in, the implementation of this?

- What impact will this have upon those using and those delivering benefits, tax credits and related services? Can ICT provide a modernised welfare system with improved accessibility, accuracy and efficiency, both for the users of services as well as for those who are responsible for delivering the services?

Introduction: wired-up welfare

The modernisation of the organisation and delivery of social security and welfare services is at the heart of the government's welfare reform agenda. Developments in information and communication technology (ICT) are bringing about significant changes in how benefit-related services are administered and delivered. The government committed itself to having a quarter of its services accessible electronically by 2002, with all government services being deliverable electronically by 2005. By 2005 people should be able to access electronically a claim form for whichever benefit or tax credit they want to claim, complete it online, return it electronically to the relevant department, receive notification in the same way, and have the money paid directly into their bank account – which, of course, they can also access online.

But how realistic a vision is this? In this chapter we first summarise the government's vision for the use of information technology (IT). The next section focuses upon the use of ICT in the social security system and discusses some of the barriers to, or challenges involved in, the implementation of this. And finally we discuss the likely impact on those using, and delivering, social security benefits, tax credits and services. Will greater use of ICT open up services to more people or, as some have suggested, will it lead to new forms of exclusion because of difficulty accessing ICTs, or the inability to use them to their full potential (Selwyn, 2002)? These concerns have particular implications for users of social security services, who are often those most needy, with many already facing significant disadvantage.

Modernising government: Labour's electronic vision

Shortly after their election in 1997, Labour laid the foundations for their welfare modernisation strategy through their consultation paper *New ambitions for our country: A new contract for welfare* (DSS, 1998), which outlined improvements to the way in which benefits and related services were organised and delivered. Improving service delivery electronically was a key theme of the White Paper *Modernising government*, published in March of the following year (DSS, 1999). In the following year, the 'UK online' campaign was launched, to meet the challenges presented through the modernisation programme, including universal access to the Internet, and ensuring that all government services are available online, via the Internet. The campaign is led by the Office for the e-Envoy and its minister for e-government. The *Modernising government* agenda is also supported by the Prime Minister's Delivery Unit, as the Office of Public Services Reform. The modernisation agenda has attracted significant investment. In the latest Comprehensive Spending Review (2002), over

£2.4 billion was earmarked to improve electronic service delivery, although notably a relatively small proportion was allocated to improvements to social security systems.

Box 15.1 summaries the specific goals for the modernisation of government. The scale of change required to achieve these goals is immense. For example, huge investment is required in joining up government IT systems between different departments[1] to ensure that they are able to provide a 'seamless' service. Furthermore, it requires universal knowledge, ability and inclination of the public to use such services.

Broadly speaking, ICT can be used by governments in three main ways. First, it can be used for the delivery of *information* about government activities, benefits and services. The main route for this is the UK online website (ukonline.gov.uk) which provides a citizen gateway, organised into key life events (such as having a baby, death and bereavement and moving home), as well as providing information about standard search and query facilities. The driver behind the website is that the user will not need to know or understand how government services are organised and delivered, or how functions are divided among different agencies and central and local government. Further plans for ukonline.gov.uk include the facility to personalise the site to enable relevant updates on government information and services to be delivered directly to the individual.

Second, ICT can be used as a way of *accessing* benefits and services. The government gateway (www.gateway.gov.uk) is the cornerstone of this, providing a single route of access to electronic transactions. At the time of writing, however, only a limited number of services are available through the website, each requiring registration to obtain a digital authentication certificate. The services currently available include certain Inland Revenue transactions (for

---

Box 15.1: Key goals for the modernisation of public services

- Modernised public services – joined-up and focused on the citizen
- Accessible information and services – 24 hours a day, 7 days a week, with citizens being able to interact with government from home, at work or on the move
- Ensuring that the government electronic service delivery is driven by the use that citizens make of it
- Citizen driven electronic government – government services organised and delivered in the way the citizen wants
- Multi-channel access – including new electronic channels which will enhance existing traditional channels

Source: ukonline.gov.uk overview report (2001)

---

[1] The programme of investment in government IT is one of the biggest in Europe.

example, VAT returns, Corporation Tax, Pay-As-You-Earn [PAYE] services and self-assessment tax returns), as well as export licence applications (Department for Trade and Industry) and Area Aid Applications for farmers (Department for Environment, Food and Rural Affairs).

Third, ICT could also be used as a vehicle for *public participation*. It could be used to *consult* people about proposed policy changes, as a way of getting people involved in *policy making*. There are some initiatives, such as the Ukonline website 'citizen space', which encourages citizens to present and share their views on government issues and policies. However, they are still relatively few in number. What exists tends to be targeted towards already e-literate or vocal populations. Recent examples include encouraging citizens to submit e-petitions, which requires them to set up a website – a skill which most citizens are unlikely to have (see www.number-10.gov.uk/output/page297.asp); and encouraging knowledgeable public organisations and pressure groups to respond to policy consultations using electronic means. If technology is to be used to encourage participation from those who ordinarily do not have a voice, public knowledge of, and access to, the mechanisms for doing so must be raised. In the summer of 2002, the government launched a public consultation – In the Service of Democracy – on a possible policy on e-democracy, to give people more opportunity to participate in the democratic process by finding new ways for government to seek the views, knowledge and experiences of citizens.

As the following sections show, significant progress has been made in the electronic delivery of *information* about social security services. Rather less progress has been made with regard to accessing *transactional* facilities, and although a few opportunities do exist to enable *consultation* of citizens over key policy issues, this has yet to translate into real opportunity for the involvement of citizens in developing policies that affect their everyday lives.

Current developments in the use of ICT in social security

We now consider the main developments in ICT within the administration and delivery of social security benefits and tax credits. Such developments fall into two broad categories: access to information about benefits and tax credits, including how to apply; and the receipt of benefits or tax credits by electronic means.

Using ICT to obtain information and claim benefits/tax credits

There are a number of ways in which technology can be used to access benefit and tax credit information. The most commonplace of these is the telephone. However, the Internet is also rapidly developing to become perhaps one of the most effective mechanisms for communicating information. ICT is also being used to modernise the services in the 'frontline' Jobcentre public offices.

Telephone-based services and call centres

Developments in technology enable many telephone-based services to operate through centralised call centres. Call 'handlers' are able to work remotely with customers, using networked computers which contain details of the customer, and enable the call 'handler' to be guided through a tailored script appropriate to the caller. This means that, in theory, callers receive a personalised service from the comfort of their own home. Furthermore, operating a telephone-based service brings significant resource savings compared to delivering a face-to-face service.

Call centres are increasingly operated within social security services. Probably the first large-scale call centre was established for Family Credit (the predecessor to Working Families' Tax Credit) in Blackpool. More recently, telephone claims lines ('tele-claiming') have been set up, for example, for the Minimum Income Guarantee (MIG – income support for pensioners). Research to evaluate the MIG Claim Line found that the majority were satisfied with the service, and would be likely to use a similar telephone-based service to claim other benefits (Bunt et al, 2001). Call centres have also been developed for the new Jobcentre Plus service, which was rolled out nationally in October 2001. Under the new service, all new claimants of working age are required to make initial contact by telephone to a 'contact centre'. During the telephone conversation, first contact officers should take basic information, provide a limited 'work readiness' assessment, and conduct job searches for the caller (if appropriate), and arrange an appointment for a 'work-focused interview', all of which is done using a scripted computer programme ('Vantive'). However, the service appears to be hindered by difficulties with the IT system, including whether and how it is able to communicate with other computer systems (such as the personal adviser appointment bookings system) and the availability of IT support for staff.

In April 2002 a new Pension Service was introduced, to provide a call centre-based service for benefits and other services for current (and future) pensioners. The service operates through a network of Pension Centres, with links to local services and outreach facilities for those customers who require it. It is planned that, by 2006, Pension Service customers will also be able to access services through electronic means.

Also from April 2002, the delivery of some disability benefits (including Disability Living Allowance, Attendance Allowance and Incapacity Benefit) is through the Disability and Carers Service, which also provides a predominantly telephone-based service. Other social security related developments which utilise the opportunities brought by ICT include Employer Direct, a telephone-based job vacancy notification system for employers, a new computer system for the Child Support Agency, and the transactional facility available online to claim the new tax credits through the Inland Revenue website.

Mobile phone technology, and ownership, has also developed rapidly. Although, there are no concrete plans for public services to use mobile phone technology to communicate with their customers, anecdotal[2], pilot[3] and unpublished[4] information does suggest that it may be an effective medium for communication, in that people may be more likely to respond to a text message than to, say, an e-mail or telephone message. There may be scope, therefore, for further development of these opportunities.

However, telephone-based services will not suit all customers. Those with particularly complex circumstances, or those who find it difficult to communicate over the telephone, are likely to continue to prefer a face-to-face service. When the national rollout of the new Jobcentre Plus service is complete, the majority of its more personalised services (such as those delivered through a personal adviser) will be through face-to-face contact for people of working age. Developments are underway to ensure that one-stop face-to-face services will also be available for other groups such as older people, which will include a wide range of services in addition to those relating to benefits. These may be delivered through public locations such as a local library, or council offices, or through the network of Pension Centres mentioned above.

The Internet: online social security and welfare information

Research conducted with customers of welfare and social security services has consistently highlighted difficulties in accessing information (see, for example, Shaw et al, 1996; Kellard and Stafford, 1997). Ultimately, this also means that customers do not always receive the services they are entitled to, often because of confusion over which government agency to contact as well as being deterred due to complex procedures. Developments in initiatives such as ukonline.gov.uk are being designed around life events (including moving house, leaving work, or a new family member) rather than organisational functions, aiming to increase accessibility to citizens. Nevertheless, this still requires all citizens to be able, and willing, to access the Internet.

To facilitate this, the UK government is investing considerable effort (and resources) in establishing a network of 6,000 UK online centres throughout England, in publicly accessible locations including the high street, libraries

---

[2] The NHS provide a free text messaging service to people wanting to give up smoking, to provide information and offer encouragement to the recipient.

[3] In the 2001 Election, the Labour Party did trial sending text messages to young voters, in the hope of encouraging higher voting turnout, although the impact of the exercise is unknown.

[4] An Employment Service district did some preliminary testing of notifying of job vacancies via text messaging to their customers.

(supported by the Lottery-funded People's Network Scheme) as well as in schools and colleges. Internet access was also piloted in some Post Offices but the evaluation of the pilot concluded that while usage was relatively high, it did not generate sufficient new business for the service to be cost-effective. This suggests that those who are being targeted are already existing users of services. The initiative will not, therefore, be extended nationally (*Loughborough Echo*, 24 October 2002).

Accessing online information using touchscreen technology is now fairly commonplace in the UK. The benefit of such technology is that it enables the unskilled user to access information easily, without the need for keyboard skills. Within a welfare context, it has been used in a number of trials designed to improve access to services, for example through the Better Government for Older People Initiative (www.bettergovernmentforolderpeople.gov.uk) as well as through a number of locally developed initiatives such as Sheffield Public DataWeb (www.sheffield.gov.uk). Within the public services arena, touch screen technology is now being used in all Jobcentre public offices, through 'job points' containing national job vacancies (see below). Job point kiosks are also being installed on a trial basis in supermarkets and other public areas.

The modernised Jobcentre Plus public office

Jobcentres have been undergoing a significant modernisation programme in recent years, at both central organisational and local delivery levels. At a local level, touchscreen job points have replaced the traditional job vacancy display boards across all Jobcentres. The job points contain details of all vacancies notified to Jobcentre Plus, which can be accessed via user-friendly touchscreen technology. One of the advantages of this system is that it now enables the viewer to search for jobs nationally (and overseas) as well as locally. In general, job points have been well received by staff and customers alike (GHK, 2002). Customers have generally found it easy to use and more private. Staff are more confident that the vacancies are up-to-date, and the new system has reduced some of the more mundane tasks (such as changing the job vacancy cards). However, some disadvantages have been highlighted by customers, including not being able to browse vacancies (as was possible with the previous vacancy display boards), and the need to specify detailed search criteria such as required hours of work, and specific job title (GHK, 2002; unpublished Jobcentre Plus evaluation).

With the national rollout of the new Jobcentre Plus service, there are now also Internet points within the new 'pathfinder' offices. This allows searching and viewing of job vacancies via the Internet Job Bank. In addition, customers can access Jobseeker Direct, a telephone-based service, through 'warm phones' located in the Jobcentre Plus public office. Technological changes are also apparent for staff. Most Jobcentre offices now have at least one computer that provides Internet access, although usage is limited due to other work pressures, as well as the need to share access with other members of staff (GHK, 2002). The introduction of Employer Direct has also impacted on their work practices. Employer Direct is a telephone-based service for employers to notify their vacancies to the Jobcentre, and operates on a similar model to the Contact Centre (see earlier). The service provides a single telephone number for employers shared across a number of Jobcentres, and ensures that the information is collected in a systematic manner.

Transactional services: electronic claims

As illustrated above, significant steps have been taken to provide access to public service information for citizens through ICTs, but there has been less progress in providing transactional or interactive services such as claiming (and receiving) a benefit online. However, recent research has indicated that although just under a third (29%) of citizens are interested in receiving government information electronically, almost two thirds (62%) expressed a desire for online transactions (KPMG, 2001). Clearly, therefore, there is a demand for more transactional services. This section outlines the main developments in this area relevant to social security, notably the electronic payment of benefits, and moves towards claiming benefits online.

The electronic payment of benefits

At present, there are three main methods of paying benefits:

- by giro, which is effectively a cheque that can be cashed at designated Post Offices (typically fortnightly) or deposited into a bank account;
- by order book, which contains a series of dated payment slips to take to a designated Post Office for encashment on the date the payment is due (typically fortnightly);
- Automated Credit Transfer (ACT), whereby payments are authorised through a computerised system and paid directly into a recipient's bank account at specified frequencies (typically every four weeks).

Although about three fifths of benefit recipients receive their payment through either an order book or giro (Kempson and Whyley, 2001), processing order books and giro payments are administratively burdensome, and are considered as a relatively risky instrument of payment, through loss or theft. So from 2005, the Department for Work and Pensions aims to have 85% of its customers paid directly into their bank account, usually on a four-week cycle using ACT, and new applicants are encouraged to choose to receive their benefit through this method. For the new tax credits which were introduced from

April 2003, the only method of payment is through a bank or building society account (via an employer for Working Tax Credit), although recipients are able to choose a weekly or four-weekly payment cycle. Research has indicated that those on a low income typically prefer to receive their benefit payments weekly via an order book or giro, which makes it easier to manage their often very restricted budget (Snape and Molloy, 1999; Thomas and Pettigrew, 1999; ESRC, 2002).

A small but significant proportion of the population does not have access to a bank or building society account. Depending on the source used, this is estimated at between 6 and 9% (FSA, 2000; Kempson and Whyley, 2001). This is related to income, with those in the lowest income brackets being the least likely to have any kind of account. In particular, unemployed people, lone parents, those out of employment because of a long-term sickness or disability and retired people living on low incomes are the most likely to be without accounts. In addition, some minority ethnic groups are disproportionately more likely not to have an account. For example, taking into account other factors such as personal and social circumstances, Pakistani and Bangladeshi women are far less likely to have an account than other groups (FSA, 2000).

There are also geographical differences in bank account ownership, particularly in areas of recent bank closures, which are more likely to occur in low-income neighbourhoods. Although approximately 85% of the urban population lives within a mile of a bank (or within four miles for those living in rural areas), some groups such as older people and disabled people are likely to face difficulties in getting to a branch, or using cashpoint facilities (FSA, 2000). Post Offices are more accessible, with only 3% of the population reporting difficulties in access (ONS, 2002), and thus are providing an appropriate outlet for the location of the new universal bank facility. For some, however, having physical access to banking facilities is perhaps less of a barrier for some than psychological concerns about having a bank account. A main concern appears to be related to fears of going into debt and incurring banking charges (Kempson and Whyley, 2001). Others may be unable to access mainstream banking facilities due to poor (or non-existent) credit ratings.

Families and individuals within families, particularly those living with limited resources, often have sophisticated mechanisms to manage and control their income. For those in receipt of benefit, different benefits may have different payment dates and frequencies and so can be used for different purposes (Snape and Molloy, 1999; Thomas and Pettigrew, 1999; ESRC, 2002). Furthermore, some benefits may be paid to or collected by the main carer, who may not themselves have access to or use a bank account. The move to automating the payment of benefits and tax credits into bank accounts may thus change the way in which households and individuals access, control and use their finances (Goode et al, 1998; Pahl, 1999).

The Department for Work and Pensions has a clear responsibility to ensure that the universal payment of benefits through bank accounts does not exacerbate financial exclusion and that the social security payments continue to reach those that they were intended for. To this end, the Department has been working to ensure that appropriate banking facilities become available to those who do not currently have access to them. After several years' negotiation, the main high street banks have now agreed to provide basic bank accounts or 'universal banking' through the Post Office. This will enable customers to continue to withdraw their benefits in cash at local Post Office branches, which are seen by customers as accessible, trustworthy and reliable, and can provide a valued link with the community.

Claiming benefits and tax credits online

At present, there is currently no provision to claim benefits online because of difficulties in providing electronic identity verification (although online applications for tax credits are possible, through the Inland Revenue site – see further discussion below – and claims for Child Benefit can be submitted electronically, although birth verification is still required via post). One anticipated method of providing identity authenticity is through a secure 'smart' card that can be used to provide an electronic signature. Many other countries have tested the use of 'smart' identity cards that use digital technology and biometric identifiers (such as fingerprints). The proposed introduction of these 'smart cards' has, however, raised some public concern both here and abroad, particularly regarding privacy and the misuse of data, as well as inaccurate storing of information. Countries that have been most successful in the introduction of 'smart' identity cards appear to be those where take-up and usage of the card is voluntary (for example, Sweden and Finland), and where the benefits to the citizen are presented in an open and transparent fashion. Closer to home, Ireland has also successfully introduced a smart card for all citizens, which is used to authenticate benefit payments through networks of local Post Offices (see www.reach.ie.gov).

However, in the UK, the development of a 'smart card' has had limited success to date. In the 1990s, a benefit payment card project was developed in conjunction with the Post Office, but faced significant technological difficulties, and notable project overspend, which eventually led to the project being terminated amidst some controversy (see below). More recently, the Connexions card has been introduced on a voluntary basis for young adults. The card can be used to record, among other things, attendance at college, as well as providing identification to access certain services. Although still in its infancy, the scheme has also faced criticism with regard to how the information is to be used, and by whom. Nevertheless, the government remains committed to the development of smart card technology for verification or authenticity purposes, and a government framework has now been developed for smart card policy by the Office of the e-envoy. From 1 April 2003 a new card account system was launched by the government and the Post Office to enable citizens to access benefit and pensions payments at any Post Office. Should the challenge of providing identification electronically be overcome, the demand from many citizens to be able to carry out transactions online from the comfort of one's own home may well be realised.

Challenges in securing the vision of e-government

The previous section provided an outline of current developments relevant to the organisation and delivery of social security services, raising some of the inherent challenges in implementing these changes. This section expands on those challenges, which include issues relating to government capacity, data privacy and data sharing, achieving universal access and take-up of services, the impact on staff responsible for delivering such services, and the role of the public and private sector.

The government's capacity to implement and manage change

Historically, one of the main challenges to the introduction and improvement to the Department for Work and Pensions' modernisation programme has been the capability of the technology itself. In particular, the Department and its agencies are host to numerous computer systems developed piecemeal over the years, and few of them are able to communicate with each other. For Department staff operating at a local level, this results in the need to double or sometimes triple 'key' information into different computer programmes, which increases the risk of data entry error as well as significantly increasing administrative costs. Furthermore, cases deemed as 'complex' have to be maintained clerically, because the IT systems are unable to administer them.

In recognition of the need for specialist IT support, the government has enlisted the help of private IT experts to assist them in the design and implementation of streamlined and seamless programmes. Significant progress has been made in some areas, such as the matching of benefit and local authority data to identify error and fraud. However, in other areas it seems that both government and its private partners have underestimated the extent of the transformation required. This has resulted in several failed IT initiatives, as well as vast project overspend. The most notable of these was the cancellation of the benefits payment card project. The project was designed to link benefit transactions at Post Offices to the IT systems within the Benefits Agency, and to replace the existing paper-based method of paying benefits with a magnetic stripe payment card. Post Office Counters and the Benefits Agency awarded the contract to develop the actual card to a private company (Pathways). It was one of the first projects to be awarded under the Private Finance Initiative, supposedly to transfer most of the 'risks' of the project to the private sector. The project began in 1996, but three years later was terminated because it was unable to deliver within the specified time period, and within the resources agreed between the partners. The reasons for the failure, according to the National Audit Office, were primarily related to divided control, unrealistic timescales, and insufficient risk management (NAO, 2000).

Although lessons have been learnt from the much-publicised failure of the benefit payment card project, the Department still experiences difficulties in implementing large-scale IT changes. The most recent of these difficulties relates to the introduction of a new computer system for the already much criticised Child Support Agency, as part of its overall reform. The new system aims to improve efficiency and accuracy, as well as making administrative savings by increased use of automation in issuing leaflets, notifications and forms. However, the system is already an estimated £50 million over its £200 million budget, and the introduction was delayed by nearly 12 months (BBC website http://news.bbc.co.uk). Because the contract to provide the new technology was awarded under the Private Finance Initiative (to Electronic Data Systems Ltd: EDS), there are already debates about who should pay for the budget overspend (KableNET, 2002).

The IT required to fully support the new Jobcentre Plus service also appears to require some 'behind the scenes' improvement in the pathfinder offices (unpublished research) to ensure smooth national rollout of the service. However, the development of the online service to apply for tax credits appears to be more promising. Although the Inland Revenue has experienced difficulties in integrating with other computer systems to process tax credit applications (such as local authorities), it is currently possible to calculate a family's tax credit entitlement online, as well as complete and send an online application (although at the time of writing responses are posted using the more traditional 'snail mail').

Data sharing and protecting the rights of citizens

The information collected by government through statutory bodies forms a huge, possibly the largest, information resource on individuals including information relating to, for example, household and family composition, income and savings, and health. Advances in IT mean that it is increasingly easy to collect and share such personal information. At present in the UK, there is no coherent legal statement of rights with regard to privacy, and the disclosure of personal data within the public sector, although both the 1998 Human Rights Act and the 1998 Data Protection Act provide a legal framework to protect citizens' rights to privacy. Within the Data Protection Act in particular, personal data must be used 'lawfully and fairly' (PIU, 2002).

The 1992 Social Security Administration Act and 1996 Social Security Administration Bill enables information from the Inland Revenue and Customs and Excise to supply the Department for Work and Pensions with data in connection with the prevention of social security fraud, as well as for checking the accuracy of social security information and cutting down on 'red tape'. This may, for example, include matching of Working Families Tax Credit data with national insurance data. The Department may also supply data to local authorities, which are responsible for administering Housing Benefit and Council Tax Benefit, for purposes of efficiency and error. In 1998/99 the (then) Department of Social Security estimated that £150 million was saved through data sharing (PIU, www.cabinet-office.gov.uk/innovation/2000/privacy/datascope.htm). Certainly considerable improvements in the reduction of fraud and error have been made. By March 2001, fraud and error in Income Support and Jobseeker's Allowance claims was reduced by 18%, some of which may be attributed to improved IT (DWP, 2001).

Data sharing and data matching can also provide useful policy-making information. For example, it can identify areas of severe need by geo-demographical profiling, using combined data from social security administrative records, health records and education information systems. This can ensure that resources are allocated where they are most needed, thus tackling social exclusion more effectively at a local level. This method has been used to identify areas of deprivation for programmes such as Sure Start and various Action Zones and regeneration programmes. It can also be used to increase benefit take-up among eligible populations. For example, the London Borough of Newham has used IT innovatively to generate over £2 million in unclaimed means-tested benefits, by data matching using Housing Benefit and Council Tax Benefit records, as well as to improve planning and services (Davies, 2002).

A central concern with regard to the sharing of personal data is the issue of privacy. This is covered by the 1998 Data Protection Act, and the 1998 Human Rights Act, as well as by European Union legal boundaries. Government has the responsibility of balancing the benefits offered by data sharing and ensuring that sufficient safeguards are in place so that personal information is used appropriately. The government's role is therefore twofold: to ensure that legal requirements are adhered to, and to ensure public confidence in the way that personal information about them is used responsibly and securely. Government (and other) bodies responsible for the collection and collation of personal data need to ensure that it is protected from misuse.

Evidence suggests that the public generally are unclear about how personal data collected and stored by government departments is used (ONS, 2002). One of the risks central to the public concern is (mis)identification of individuals. This risk is exacerbated by the absence of a single identifier – at present individuals have numerous identifiers from government bodies, including national health numbers, national insurance numbers and tax identifiers. A combination of confusion and mistrust may make it difficult for citizens to see any benefits of data sharing. This suggests that public awareness needs to be raised of the potential benefits of data sharing between public organisations, such as increasing the take-up of benefits or increasing the efficiency of processing combined benefit claims.

Achieving universal access and take-up

As highlighted earlier in this chapter, one of the government's key goals is to ensure universal access to electronic services to 'everyone who wants it'. While many citizens will want and use electronic services, there remains a significant proportion who appear to show a lack of interest. These are disproportionately represented among groups already at a greater risk of social exclusion, including those on low incomes, older people, households without children, disabled people and women (Coleman et al, 2002). Considerable effort has been made to improve access to ICT, for example through the establishment of (to date) over 2,000 UK online centres, through internet access at Jobcentre Plus offices, and, for the future, through digital television. However, there remains an as yet unresolved challenge in changing perceptions of, and attitudes towards ICT. In other words, even if all services are deliverable electronically by 2005, there is no guarantee that they will be used. How can more citizens be encouraged to *want* to access social security services through ICT means?

Although the government's online strategy is to expand multi-channel access to government services, rather than replace the traditional service delivery channels (such as face-to-face and telephone contact) (ukonline.gov.uk, 2002), more resources are directed towards electronic means of communication. This may result in a two-tier service emerging, whereby those who continue to use the more traditional (and more costly) forms of contact, such as face-to-face communication, receive a less efficient service than those using new IT-driven service delivery channels.

In order for customers to change the way that they interact with organisations such as the Department for Work and Pensions, the advantages need to be made clear. Research evidence suggests that the main concerns customers of the Department have in using electronic forms of communication are that it is impersonal, there will be no one to help, it is less confidential, difficult to use and might break down (Cabinet Office, 1998a). Over a quarter of all benefit claimants (27%) can see no advantages in using electronic methods to deal with benefits. Where advantages were cited, they were mostly relating to being quicker and saving time (Cabinet Office, 1998a).

Impact on staff and local level delivery

Modernising social security and welfare services places considerable demands on those who are responsible for the delivery of such services, not least in terms of fostering new ways of working and acquiring knowledge about, and new skills to implement, the new technology. Within the new Jobcentre Plus service, for example, the co-location of services for the working-age population means that staff from the Benefits Agency and the Employment Service were 'integrated' into one organisation, and one office. This represented the convergence of two very different organisations both operationally and culturally, and was not without some difficulties, particularly relating to staff grades and pay, working practices and different IT systems.

Furthermore, as more relatively routine procedures become automated through advances in ICT, the skill levels of staff are changing. In the new Jobcentre Plus service, staff are becoming increasingly 'tiered' with the separation of functions within the service into initial contact, making a claim, and having a work-focused discussion, each of which is carried out by a different staff role. Some staff are performing relatively routine depersonalised functions through a call centre, and others are increasingly required to deliver a personalised, tailor-made face-to-face service.

This presents a significant challenge for the Department, not least in ensuring job satisfaction, job retention and opportunities for career development and progression. In a recent examination of departments' e-strategies, 19 out of 20 departments identified the need for significant development in civil servants' ability and aptitude to use IT, in order to successfully implement e-government strategies (NAO, 2002).

Modernisation: the role of the private sector

The government has made it clear that it intends to develop the UK's online strategy in conjunction with both the private and voluntary sectors (ukonline.gov.uk, 2001). Most IT is outsourced, through the government's Modernisation Fund, which is managed by the e-envoy. This may be through the Private Finance Initiative, through a public–private partnership, or through some other framework agreement. Most of the Department for Work and Pensions' partners work through a framework agreement – ACCORD – which names a preferred supplier (EDS) as well as several other service providers. However, the involvement of external organisations has, to date, been less than smooth, and certainly costly. Reference has already been made in this chapter to the difficulties in implementing the new Child Support Agency IT programme, which is being developed by EDS through the Private Finance Initiative. Private finance was also used to support the development of the doomed benefits payment card.

Overview

- This chapter has looked forward to the developments that are taking place within social security, brought about through technological advances. Many of these developments are ambitious, requiring significant resources and large-scale change.

- Such developments may not see immediate fruition but if the benefits are improved efficiency, better customer services and improved access to services for those who are most in need of them, then the long-term gain will pay off.

- Over time, many people will gain the skills and access required to take on board the opportunities presented through e-government. For children and young people still in education, ICT is a core part of the curriculum, with virtually all schools wired up. Over 95% of businesses are online, meaning that many of those in work are exposed, to a greater or lesser degree, to ICT

- However, for those not in economic activity, whether it is because of unemployment, ill-health or disability, or caring responsibilities, the opportunity to take-up and benefit from e-services is far less. For e-government services to be successful, then the benefits must be for *all* citizens.

- This means that the opportunities presented to users of new ICTs must be sufficiently attractive for continued and enhanced usage. This is particularly important in the development of ICT-driven social security services. What is offered to the customer needs to be *at least* as good as existing services. Telephone services need to be *as good* as face-to-face services. Automated benefit payments need to be as *reliable and accurate* as current benefit payment systems. Information about benefits and tax credits needs to be *more accessible, and understandable*, than currently presented.

- At the same time, people who are unable to make use of ICT developments, for whatever reason, should not receive a lesser service than those who do. This in itself presents an inherent tension in the development of ICT policies.

Questions for discussion

1. What are the main ways in which the government is seeking to introduce ICTs into the social security system?

2. Will the use of IT help to reduce, or to increase, social exclusion?

3. What will the government need to do in order to meet the target of payment of benefits/tax credits through automated bank transfer?

References

Bunt, K., Adams, L. and Jones, A.-M. (2001) *Evaluation of the Minimum Income Guarantee Claim Line*, DWP Research Report No147, Leeds: Corporate Document Services.

Cabinet Office (1998a) 'Electronic government: the view from the queue', www.e-envoy.gov.uk

Cabinet Office (1998b) *New ambitions for our country: A new contract for welfare*, Cm 3805, London: The Stationery Office.

Coleman, N., Jeeawody, F. and Wapshott, J. (2002) *Electronic government at the Department for Work and Pensions*, DWP Research Report No 176, Leeds: Corporate Document Services.

Davies, R. (2002) 'Making the most of IT: the role of local government in benefits take-up', *Benefits*, vol 34, vol 10, issue 2, pp 135-9.

DWP (Department for Work and Pensions) (1999) *Modernising government*, Cm 4310, London: The Stationery Office.

DWP (2001) *Departmental report: The government's expenditure plans 2001-2 and 2003-4*, London: DWP.

ESRC (Economic and Social Research Council) (2002) 'How people on low incomes manage their finances', Seminar proceedings, 13 December, Westminster.

FSA (Financial Services Authority) (2000) *In or out? Financial exclusion: A literature and research review*, London: FSA.

GHK (2002) *Modernising the Employment Service summary report year 1*, London: DWP.

Goode, J., Lister, R. and Callender, C. (1998) *Purse or wallet?: Gender inequalities and income distribution within families on benefits*, London: Policy Studies Institute.

KableNET (2002) 'No sign of child support computer', Press release, 13 August, Kablenet.com

Kellard, K. and Stafford, B. (1997) *Delivering benefits to unemployed people*, DSS Research Report No 69, London: The Stationery Office.

Kempson, E. and Whyley, C. (2001) *Payment of pensions and benefits: A survey of social security recipients paid by order book or girocheck*, DWP Research Report No 146, London: The Stationery Office.

KPMG (2001) *E-government for all: Second e-government survey*, London: KPMG.

NAO (National Audit Office) (2000) *The cancellation of the benefits payment card project*, HC 857, Parliamentary Session 1999-00, London: NAO.

NAO (2002) *Government on the web II*, HC 764, London: The Stationery Office.

ONS (Office for National Statistics) (2002) 'Results from the July National Statistics Omnibus Survey', www.statistics.gov.uk/pdfdir/inter0900.pdf

Pahl, J. (1999) *Invisible money: Family finances in the electronic economy*, Bristol/York: The Policy Press/Joseph Rowntree Foundation.

PIU (Performance and Innovation Unit) (2002) 'Data privacy and sharing', Cabinet Office, www.cabinet-office.gov.uk

Selwyn, N. (2002) 'E-stablishing an inclusive society? Technology, social exclusion and UK government policy making', *Journal of Social Policy*, vol 31, no 1, pp 1-20.

Shaw, A., Walker, R., Ashworth, K., Jenkins, S. and Middleton, S. (1996) *Moving off Income Support*, DSS Research Report No 53, London: The Stationery Office.

Snape, D. and Molloy, D. with Kumar, M. (1999) *Relying on the state, relying on each other*, DSS Research Report No 103, London: The Stationery Office.

Thomas, A. and Pettigrew, N. (1999) *Attitudes towards methods of paying benefits*, DSS In-house Report No 51, London: DSS.

Website resources

Cabinet Office	www.cabinet-office.gov.uk
Department for Work and Pensions	www.dwp.gov.uk
Jobcentre Plus	www.jobcentreplus.gov.uk
KableNet	www.kablenet.com
Service First	www.cabinet-office.servicefirst
UK Government Gateway	www.gateway.gov.uk
UK Government Online	www.ukonline.gov.uk

Appendix: Website addresses

Name of Organisation	Website address
Benefit Fraud Inspectorate	www.bfi.gov.uk
Benefits Now: provides independent advice on Disability Living Allowance, Attendance Allowance and a self-assessment guide	www.benefitsnow.co.uk
Better Government for Older People programme	www.cabinet-office.gov.uk/ servicefirst/index/opmenu.htm
British Library: social policy information service	www.bl.uk/services/information/ welfare/issue1/sswelfare.html
Cabinet Office	www.cabinet-office.gov.uk
Cabinet Office Performance and Innovation Unit	www.cabinet-office.gov.uk/ innovation/
Centre for Europe's Children	http://eurochild.gla.ac.uk
Centre for Pensions and Social Insurance: based at Birkbeck College, University of London, contains a variety of resources	www.bbk.ac.uk/res/cpsi
Child Benefit	www.dwp.gov.uk/lifeevent/benefits/ child_benefit.htm
Child Poverty Action Group: provides information to help people campaign against poverty	www.cpag.org.uk
Child Support Agency	www.csa.gov.uk
Citizen's Income Online: overseen by the Citizen's Income Trust, formerly the Basic Income Research Group	www.citizensincome.org
Commission for Racial Equality	www.cre.gov.uk
Connexions guidance and support for 13- to 19-year-olds	www.connexions.gov.uk
Council for Employment, Income and Social Cohesion	www.cerc.gouv.fr

Council of Europe	www.coe.int
Department for Education and Skills	www.dfes.gov.uk
Department for Work and Pensions	www.dwp.gov.uk
DWP families with children page	www.dwp.gov.uk/lifeevent/famchild
DWP publications	www.corpdocs.co.uk
DWP statistics on pensioners	www.dwp.gov.uk/asd/pensioners.html
Department of Health (DoH)	www.doh.gov.uk
Disability Rights Commission	www.drc.org/drc/default.asp
Education Maintenance Allowance	www.dfes.gov.uk/ema
End Child Poverty	www.ecpc.org.uk
Entitled to: web-based means of assessing eligibility for benefits and tax credits	www.entitledto.co.uk
European Union	www.eu.int
EURONET: European Children's Network	http://europeanchildrensnetwork.org
Financial Services Authority	www.fsa.gov.uk
Gingerbread: support organisation for lone-parent families in England and Wales	www.gingerbread.org.uk
HM Treasury	www.hm-treasury.gov.uk
Home Office	www.homeoffice.gov.uk
House of Commons library	www.parliament.uk/commons/lib/research
Households Below Average Income data	www.dwp.gov.uk/asd/hbai.htm
Inland Revenue	www.inlandrevenue.gov.uk
Institute for Fiscal Studies (Pensions and Savings section)	www.ifs.org.uk/pensionsindex.shtml
International Council on Social Welfare	www.icsw.org
International Labour Organization	www.ilo.org/public/english
International Monetary Fund	www.imf.org/external
International Social Security Association (ISSA): set up in 1927 to promote social security as a basic human right and as an issue that affects everyone, globally	www.issa.int/engl.homef.htm

Jobcentre Plus	www.jobcentreplus.gov.uk
Jobseeker's Allowance	www.dwp.gov.uk/lifeevent/ jobseeker's_allowance.htm
KableNet: independent authority on e-government	www.kablenet.com
Low Pay Commission	www.lowpay.gov.uk
Minimum Income Guarantee	www.thepensionservice.gov.uk/mig/ mig.asp
National Association of Citizens' Advice Bureaux: provides free independent advice on matters including benefits, pensions and child support	www.nacab.org.uk
National Children's Bureau	www.ncb.org.uk
National Council for One Parent Families	www.ncopf.org.uk
National Statistics	www.statistics.gov.uk
New Deal for Disabled People	www.newdeal.gov.uk
New Deal for Young People	www.newdeal.gov.uk
Occupational Pensions Regulatory Authority	www.opra.gov.uk
Organisation for Economic Co-operation and Development	www.oecd.org
Pension Service	www.thepensionservice.gov.uk
Pensions News Focus, from Watson Wyatt	www.watsonwyatt.com/europe/pubs/ pensionfocus/default.asp
Pensions Policy Institute	www.pensionspolicyinstitute.org.uk
Policy Studies Institute	www.psi.org.uk
Price Waterhouse Coppers: pensions	www.pricewaterhousecoopers.co.uk/ uk/eng/ins-sol/publ/pensions/ pensions.html
Public Service target	www.hm-treasury.gov.uk/ performance
Quids for Kids	www.lga.gov.uk
Refugee Council	www.refugeecouncil.org.uk

Rights Net: provides up-to-date social security information and news for advice workers	www.rightsnet.org.uk
Runnymede Trust	www.runnymedetrust.org
Service First	www.servicefirst.gov.uk
Social Exclusion Unit	www.socialexclusionunit.gov.uk
Social Fund	www.dwp.gov.uk/lifeevent/benefits/ the_social_fund.htm
Social Policy Virtual Library	www.social-policy.org
New Deal for Young People	www.dwp.gov.uk/lifeevent/benefits/ new_deal_for_young_people.htm
Social Protection Advisory Service, World Bank: contains documents on disability, labour markets, pensions, safety nets and social funds	www.worldbank.org/sp
Social Security Advisory Committee	www.ssac.org.uk
Striving for Better Services	www.servicefirst.gov.uk
Support 4 Learning (Education Maintenance Allowances)	www.support4learning.org.uk/ money/ funds_ema.htm
Targeting Fraud	www.targetingfraud.gov.uk
Trade Unions Council: welfare-to-work, and so on	www.tuc.org.uk/welfare
Unemployment Unit and Youthaid (now the Centre for Economic and Social Inclusion)	www.cesi.org.uk
UK Government Gateway	www.gateway.gov.uk
UK Government Online	www.ukonline.gov.uk
UK Government Office of the e-envoy	www.e-envoy.gov.uk
Work and Pensions Committee (UK)	www.parliament.uk/commons/ selcom/workpenhome.htm
Worktrain (the national jobs and learning site)	www.worktrain.gov.uk
World Bank	www.worldbank.org
World Trade Organization	www.wto.org

Index

Page references for tables, figures and boxes are in *italics*; those for notes are followed by n

Benefits

A Journal of Social Security Research, Policy and Practice

(3 issues) February, June and October
ISSN 0962 7898

"Benefits *provides an authoritative, up-to-date and lively insight into an important and fast-moving policy area. It is essential reading for anyone with an interest in social security policy, practice and research.*" **Jane Millar, Department of Social and Policy Sciences, University of Bath**

"*... essential reading for all service providers. We ensure that it is available to all our team as it covers both policy and practice issues in a stimulating way.*"
John Hannam, Head of Welfare Rights, Nottinghamshire County Council

FREE sample issue online at
www.policypress.org.uk/benefits.htm

FREE online access to subscribers

Benefits is the only journal focusing specifically on social security, social inclusion and anti-poverty policies in the UK. Established over ten years ago, the journal has a well-earned reputation for up-to-date information and analysis of development in policy and practice. Edited and written by both academics and practitioners, the journal is essential reading for anyone studying, researching or practising in the social security and welfare rights fields. It is highly accessible and each issue provides a wide range of articles around a theme alongside popular regular features, such as Research Round-up and Policy Review.

Who should read *Benefits*?

- Welfare rights workers in both the statutory and voluntary sectors
- Frontline and managerial staff working in the Pensions Service, Department for Work and Pensions and Jobcentre Plus
- Policy makers
- Academics, researchers and teachers in the field of social policy and related disciplines
- Students of social policy and related disciplines

To subscribe, please contact:

The Policy Press
c/o Portland Press Ltd
Commerce Way
Whitehall Industrial Estate
Colchester CO2 8HP
UK
Tel: +44 (0)1206 796351
Fax: +44 (0)1206 799331
E-mail: sales@portlandpress.co.uk